COLLINS
NEW ENCYCLOPEDIA OF
FISHING
in Britain and Ireland

MOUNTAIN TARN OR CORRIE LAKE

Always cold, vegetation and animal life is very poor. Small trout and charr may be present if the water is deep enough to withstand freezing to base.

A

B

C

Some of the aquatic creatures that form part of the fishes' food chain.

A The water louse, *Asellus aquaticus*, related to marine crustaceans. It is found in most slow-running and stillwaters. Feeds on decaying matter on the bottom of streams and ponds. *B* A water-beetle larva, one of the many species of carnivorous beetles found during the warmer months in freshwater. *C* Snails and their eggs are a source of food for many species of fish. The great pond snail, *Limnaea* (or *Lymnaea*) *stagnalis*, and ramshorn snail, *Planorbis planorbis*, with their spawn.

LOWLAND LAKE

Vegetation marginal and rich.

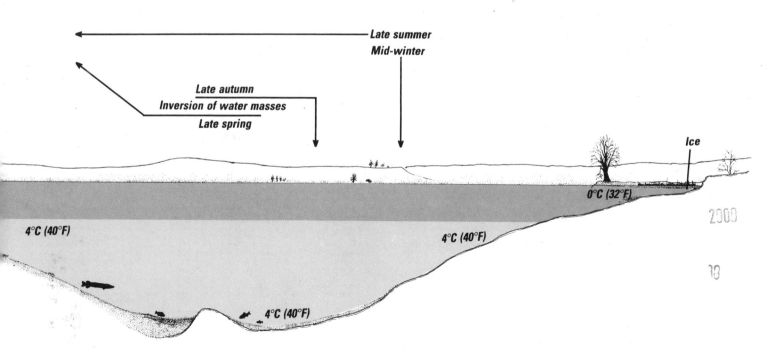

Late summer
Mid-winter

Late autumn
Inversion of water masses
Late spring

Ice

0°C (32°F)

4°C (40°F)   *4°C (40°F)*

4°C (40°F)

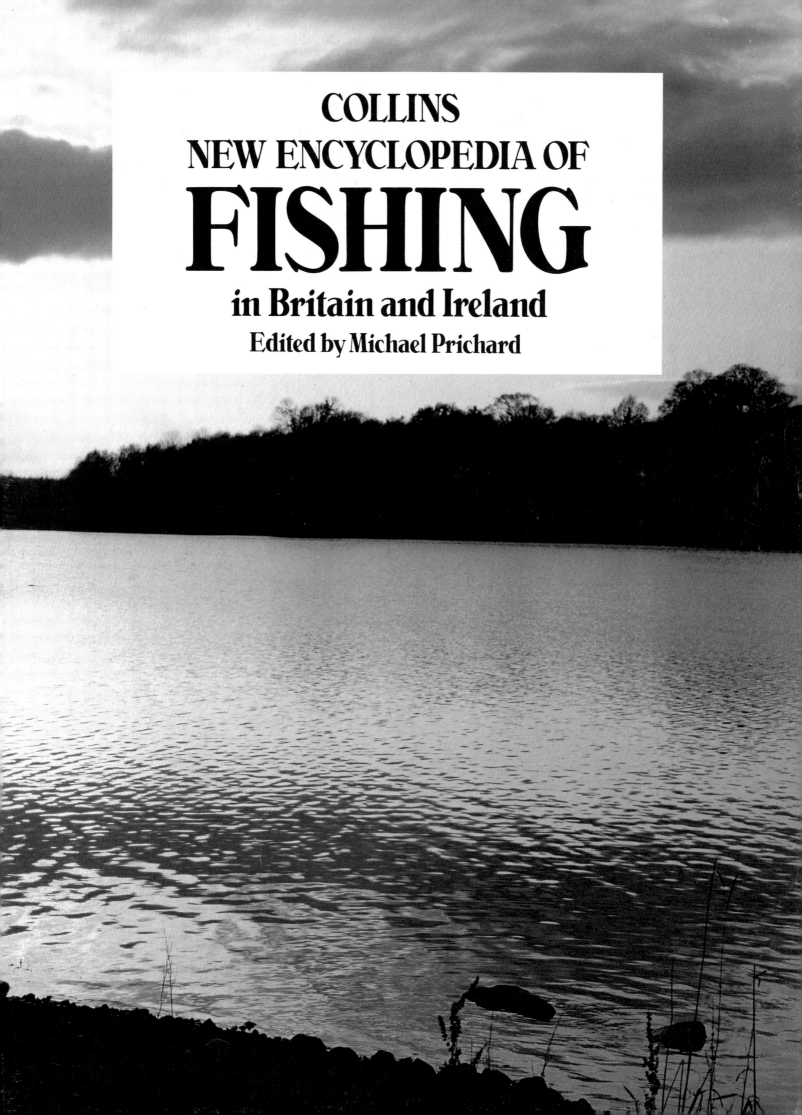

COLLINS
NEW ENCYCLOPEDIA OF
FISHING
in Britain and Ireland
Edited by Michael Prichard

Credits

Photographs (other than those listed below) *by Michael Prichard ARPS*
Design and Illustration *by Peter Burt and Rod Sutterby*
Fish Species Illustrations *by Dietrich Burkel*

Page 5. photograph *by Malcolm Greenhalgh*
Page 8. photograph *by Roy Stevenson*
Page 49. Pic. A *by Bob Baldock*
Page 173. Pic. B *by Bob Carnill*
Page 187. Pic. B *by Simon Farrell*
Page 190. Pic. A *by Malcolm Greenhalgh*
Page 191. Pic. C *by Malcolm Greenhalgh*
Page 196. Pic. A *by Malcolm Greenhalgh*
Page 197. Pic. B *by David Winterbottom*
Page 198. Pic. A *by David Winterbottom*
Page 199. Pic. B *by Simon Farrell*
Page 203. Pic. A *by Rod Sutterby*
Page 205. Pic. D *by Malcolm Greenhalgh*
Page 206. Pic. B *by Malcolm Greenhalgh*
Page 207. Pic. C *by David Winterbottom*

First published in 1990 by
William Collins Sons & Co. Ltd
London · Glasgow · Sydney · Auckland ·
Toronto · Johannesburg

© **William Collins Sons & Co. Ltd 1977, 1990**

The fish illustrations by Dr. Dietrich Burkel and
some of the diagrams and photographs ap-
peared in the Encyclopedia of Fishing in the
British Isles, first published in 1977 and re-
printed, with revisions in 1982, eleven times. All
other illustrations and photographs and all text
are new to this book.

A CIP catalogue record for this book is available
from the British Library

ISBN 0 00 218354 4

Photoset by Rowland Phototypesetting Ltd,
Bury St Edmunds, Suffolk
Colour reproduction by Bright Arts, Hong Kong
Printed and bound by
William Collins Sons & Co. Ltd, Glasgow

Introduction

The real angler is one for whom the state of perfect happiness is achieved only when he (or she, some of the best anglers are women) holds a fishing rod in the hands or is sorting out fishing tackle and planning the next trip to the water. If you are thinking of taking up the sport of angling, beware! Angling is a wonderful disease that creeps on slowly and usually lasts for life.

Compared with almost every other sport, angling offers the greatest diversity of action. In cricket it is simply a matter of which side gets the most runs and loses fewest wickets; in soccer how many times 22 players knock a spherical object into a big landing-net using only their toes or heads. In angling the result might be a big thornback ray caught on a wrecking trip, a mixed bag of codling and dabs from the end of the pier, a super bass from an estuary, a brace of fine tench caught at dawn from a reed-fringed mere, a catch of big winter roach from a clearing river, some lurking chub taken on free-lined floating crust from a sun-drenched stream, a beautifully speckled wild trout caught on the most delicate of dry flies, a brace of silver sea trout taken on a big fly in the dead of night, a salmon fresh from the sea, *ad infinitum*.

There is also something unpredictable about angling, for no one can be sure what will take the bait, spinner or fly. The whole mackerel bait might be taken by a tiny jack or a 20 lb-plus pike. A Size 16 grayling wet fly might at any time be grabbed by a huge salmon. Two maggots on a Size 16 hook meant for a 1 lb roach could easily be sucked down by a 10 lb carp. This sort of thing happens – often, judging by reports in the angling press.

Of course, most anglers become specialists in just one or two aspects of the sport. This is usually a consequence of where they live as well as personal preferences. It is not surprising, for example, that only a tiny proportion (indeed if any!) of anglers in the Outer Hebrides go match fishing or that few anglers from London fish frequently for salmon. However, I would advise any who do not fish at present and are thinking seriously of taking up the sport to sample as wide a range of fishing that they can. Go wreck-fishing and beachcasting. Try fly fishing. Go piking in the winter. Try to catch some specimen coarse fish. Enter a couple of coarse fishing matches. When you have sampled, you will find that you are quickly drawn to the kind of fishing that suits you best.

Most of my time is spent fishing with a fly rod for salmon, trout, sea trout and grayling. But I have many happy memories of sea fishing, specimen hunting for coarse fish and match angling. And I still enjoy these kinds of fishing a few days every year. In my opinion this is important, for some anglers can get quite snobbish about their chosen branch of fishing. There is no need to adopt this attitude. We are all brothers and sisters of the angle. As Martin James, that great specimen hunter of coarse

fishes and good all-round angler, put it: 'Provided it bends the stick and pulls the string, I am happy!'

This book provides a thorough description of all the kinds of angling that are available in and around the British Isles, written by a team of enthusiastic well-known specialists. Follow their advice and you will not go far wrong.

However, one point must be made at the start. In angling the fish should always come first. If you want to kill a fish to eat then kill it as soon as you have landed it. Never let a fish die slowly. Never kill more than you can eat. Remember that every thornback, cod, trout, roach or salmon that you return unharmed to the water alive might provide sport for you in the future.

Handle carefully all fish that you are going to put back. Unhook them in the landing net and release them immediately. The heat of the hand can damage the slime that covers and protects the fish's skin and let in fatal infection. If you have to handle a fish, cool and wet your hands in the water first.

Each year thousands of innocent waterside creatures die because careless anglers discard hooks, shot, monofilament fishing line and litter. Always take everything home with you. Leave only your footprints.

All anglers should be members of the Anglers' Co-operative Association. The ACA is the organisation that fights for anglers against the government, water industry and polluters to try to keep our lakes, rivers and seas clean and pure so that we have more fish and fishing. Join the ACA. Their address is: 3, Castlegate, Grantham, Lincolnshire, NG31 6SW. You owe it to your sport.

MALCOLM GREENHALGH | 5

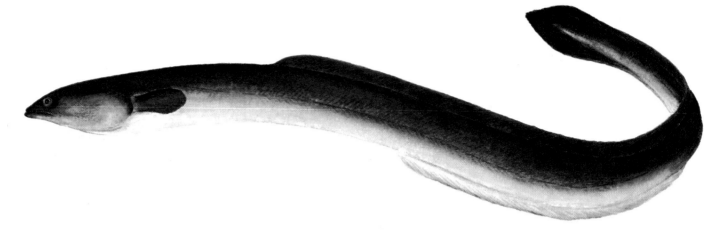

Index to Fish Illustrations

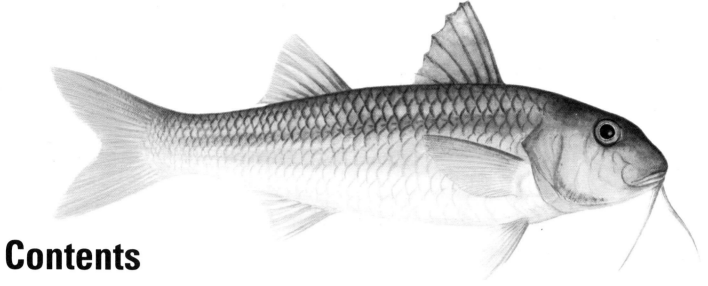

Contents

Contributors

Dietrich Burkel
The Artist

Born in 1936 in Wildau, Germany, Dr Dietrich Burkel studied natural history, especially fish. In 1948 the family went to Scotland where he gained a PhD in palaeontology at Glasgow University. Burkel fished for pike on Loch Lomond and tope in Luce Bay. In the early 1970s he caught the first rod-caught Scottish porbeagle, 81.6 kg (179 lb), from a dinghy near the Mull lighthouse. He went to Hamburg University in 1975, joining German ichthyologists on a research voyage to the West Coast of Britain. Once fish recorder for the Scottish Federation of Sea Anglers, he drew accurate identification lecture aids as well as collecting museum specimens. Dr Burkel is now Keeper of the Public Exhibition of the Zoological Museum of the University of Hamburg. The illustrations in this book show him to be a gifted artist.

Allen Edwards
Coarse Fishing for Pleasure

Born on the opening day of the coarse fishing season in 1930, Allen Edwards took his first roach under the tuition of 'Ginger' Brain from Cannon Hill Park pool and has been fishing for this classic coarse species ever since. Edwards has written for many angling magazines and a newspaper. He is also well known to Nottinghamshire radio listeners as the BBC's angling correspondent. As Director of the Anglers' Cooperative Association, Allen Edwards is angling's fighter against pollution. He is carefully monitoring water privatisation and all that that implies. Describing himself as a 'family-man angler' Allen Edwards dedicates his contribution to this volume to his wife Helen and grandson Ian.

Tom Pickering
Matchfishing to Win

Tom Pickering is deadly with every matchfishing method. His greatest gift, apart from the sheer mastery of methods, is to know exactly what to do in every given situation. While in England's World Championship side he has fished eight times for his country and helped England to their first and long-awaited team title in 1986. He was there when they won for the second time in 1987 and won the World Individual title in Bulgaria in 1989; was Macpherson UK champion in the same year and won the prestigious Swan Vesta crown just before his World Championship triumph. In his early 30s, Tom Pickering is regarded as one of the outstanding talents in British matchfishing. Not a full-time professional, Tom Pickering runs a tackle business in Doncaster and the National Angling Exhibition.

Michael Prichard
Boat Fishing

Well-known photographer-journalist, author of six Collins fishing books and General Editor of this encylopedia, Michael Prichard will fish for almost any fresh or saltwater species, but prefers porbeagle and reef pollack fishing. He has taken halibut off Japan, sea trout in Norway, swordfish in Portugal, sharks in the Arabian Gulf and charr and trout in Greenland. Prichard insists that some of the world's finest fishing is still to be had off the British Isles. Mike's local fishing changed when he left England to live in Holland, so his sea angling involves lengthy journeys to Ireland and mainland Britain. Prichard believes that the true angler and sportsman understands both the need to conserve creature habitat and ensure species preservation.

Alan Yates
Sea Angling from the Shore

At 14, Alan Yates caught his first 4.5 kg (10 lb) shore bass. Winner of over 1,000 Open competitions at home and abroad, he has captained the English shore team since 1978, winning seven Home Championships. Qualifying for the British Open Casting Championships in 1961 he cast over 183 m (200 yards). Shore catches include a 15.8 kg (35 lb) conger, 2.7 kg (6 lb) plaice, 2.7 kg (6 lb) mullet, 5.5 kg (12 lb) bass, 13.6 kg (30 lb) stingray, 2 kg (4 lb 8 oz) black bream, 12.8 kg (28 lb) cod and his biggest fish, a 76.2 kg (167 lb) bronze whaler shark. In 1980 Yates helped to form the National Sea League and the Sea Anglers' Match Federation. He is Secretary of SAMF and Vice-Chairman of the NFSA South East Division.

Bob Carnill
Fly Fishing for Trout

Nottingham-born Bob Carnill began fishing the Trent and local gravel-pit at the age of four and became a dedicated coarse angler for the next 18 years. At 24, Bob began fly fishing for trout, learning from books, tips given by other fly fishermen, and experience. In the following 26 years he designed new ranges of flies; ran courses in fly fishing and fly tying; contributed to a best-selling book on the same subject; made two videos on fly fishing and fly tying, and wrote over 100 magazine articles. He organises and judges the Benson & Hedges Fly Tying Competition. He has achieved one of two ambitions: on August 29 1980 at Rutland Water, landing a 3.8 kg (8 lb 1 oz) rainbow from the bank. His next target is a brown trout of 4.5 kg (10 lb) or more either on a fly or lure.

Crawford Little
Salmon: Amazing and Marvellous

Crawford Little, one of the modern generation of thinking salmon fishermen, is also a champion of traditional techniques and values. He caught his first fish, a roach, at the age of three and the following year was learning to fish for salmon on the River Spey. Little trained in Estate Management, subsequently working for an earl, a duke and a prince, later starting a publishing company and sporting magazine. He now divides his time between writing, casting demonstrations, instructing, and running his own agency for sportsmen seeking shooting or fishing in Scotland. With his wife and sons he lives close to a salmon river in Dumfriesshire. He travels widely in his study and pursuit of the silver leaper.

Len Cacutt
Associate Editor

For over 25 years Len Cacutt has been engaged in every form of angling journalism. He was Founder-Editor of a National fishing newspaper, then Editor and compiler of angling books, partworks and magazines, at the same time writing books and articles. He has fished for almost every salt and freshwater species both in home waters and abroad but the competitive side of the sport has never appealed to him. For years he was Chairman, Sea Commodore and finally President of the City of London Piscatorial Society and holds membership of a number of other angling societies. Over the years Len Cacutt has developed a great interest in fish evolution and ichthyology which, added to fishing, keeps him closely in touch with the all-important matter of conservation.

ALLEN EDWARDS

COARSE FISHING FOR PLEASURE

Fishing is a pleasure. The satisfaction which the sport engenders is a compound of a love of nature, excitement, competition with the elements and friendly rivalry with angling companions. This recipe is an intensely personal thing. I am among those for whom the pleasure comes with the quiet seeking of each species in turn as the seasons pass. And so for me, late winter is the time to be fishing for pike.

It is a human nature to boast. Some do it so quietly and skilfully that they become known for their modesty. For these piscatorial paragons the pike will furnish ample raw material for their 'one which did *not* get away' story, for the following reasons. In the winter, pike, which gather in loose packs to follow their fodder fish, begin to respond to the urge to reproduce. If water conditions are satisfactory, pike spawn from late February until May or even later at the northern edge of their distribution. Year after year, the species tends to return to the same spawning areas and these gathering points become the angler's 'hot spots' – the places from which big pike may be caught, but locating them can be the pleasure angler's biggest problem.

WINTER PIKE

The most important factor governing the situation of holding points of big pike is the closeness of cover. This may be in the form of relatively deep water or, in late spawning situations, among weedbeds which are easily visible. For instance, pike spawn on readily recognisable

Fishing is a pleasure . . . even when the angler is alone. Only the wind hissing through the reeds and the occasional curlew fluting over the wetlands breaks his concentration.

The scientific (Latin) descriptions of freshwater fishes follow Greenwood, Rosen, Weitzman and Myers, Bull. Am. Mus. Nat. Hist 131(4) 339–457. The general classification follows the European Fisheries Advisory Commission publication EIFAC.

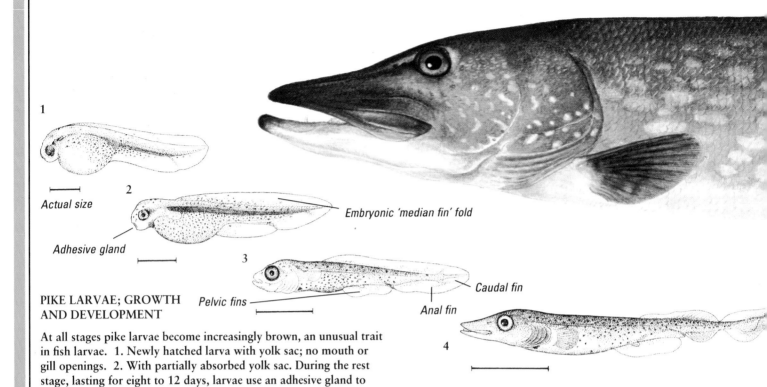

1

Actual size

2

Adhesive gland

Embryonic 'median fin' fold

3

Pelvic fins

Caudal fin

Anal fin

4

PIKE LARVAE; GROWTH AND DEVELOPMENT

At all stages pike larvae become increasingly brown, an unusual trait in fish larvae. 1. Newly hatched larva with yolk sac; no mouth or gill openings. 2. With partially absorbed yolk sac. During the rest stage, lasting for eight to 12 days, larvae use an adhesive gland to hang from underwater objects while the body absorbs the yolk sac; the body elongates and mouth and gill openings form. 3. Caudal and anal fins develop from median fin fold. Larvae begin feeding on plankton. 4. Fins are now well differentiated, but the tail is still heterocercal, reflecting the ancestral form where the vertebrae run up into the upper lobe of the caudal fin. Although still but a few inches long, the pike is now a fully developed predator and also cannibalistic if there is no other food source. Growth from stages 3 to 4 takes only a few days.

flooded and marshy meadow land or in shallow drains and ditches.

Of course, the pike *will* spawn, and if all other factors are borne in mind an intelligent assessment can be made as to where this is likely to be. It is not necessary, nor is it even desirable, that such prospecting should be carried out solely with the eyes. It makes much more sense to use the sporting method of fishing to locate the ideal, but possibly unrecognisable, spawning points, but when found these areas will hold the larger female fish.

Spinning in all its forms must rank as the most attractive method of taking pike and as a tool for pin-pointing concentrations of *Esox* it has no rivals. On most waters a good tackle combination is a 2.4 m (8 ft) medium spinning-rod of carbon, used with a fixed-spool reel holding 3.6 kg (8 lb) breaking strain (b.s.) line. The rig is completed by tying a swivel to the reel line and then attaching a 0.3 m (12 in) wire trace with a link swivel at the end. On to this, a wobbling or a spinning lure is mounted. Some lures are prone to cause kinking of the line unless an anti-kink vane or weight is used, which should be placed on the reel line just above the top swivel.

In all but the strongest of waters a lure of 21–28 g (¾– 1 oz) will give a positive fall through the water once a cast has been made. It is possible to find the deeper, holding waters by casting, engaging the pick-up and counting the seconds until the bait reaches the bottom. As soon as the lure touches the lake or river-bed, the rod-top should be lifted and the bait retrieved in as slow and erratic a manner as possible. Three casts into each area are enough, including one to get the depth and to create an interest in the pike. The lure should not be allowed to hit the bottom on casts two or three. Start the retrieve just a second or so before the spoon is due to touch. After the third cast the angler should move to another spot. These actions should be made in a series of fan-shaped casts. (Fig. 3, p. 14)

It is not always necessary to catch a pike to recognise that a holding area has been discovered. A close watch should be kept behind the bait at the moment it is being lifted from the water. Quite often pike will follow the retrieve of a spoon or wobbling bait in an interested but wary manner and the first sign the angler has is the fish's two baleful, forward-looking eyes close behind the lure. For this reason the angler must stand back from the bank so that a carelessly cast shadow does not spook the fish.

Once a gathering point has been located, the angler's problems become much more simple. It comes down to a question of choice: Which method will prove to be the most effective in the prevailing conditions? Which method gives the angler the most pleasure? Some will prefer to carry on using spinning lures; others will decide that a static or moving dead-bait is the way to take their fish. Others will use their spinning gear allied with plugs.

Spinning will account for big pike and it is an active

PIKE
Esox lucius

The pike, widely distributed throughout the British Isles and Republic of Ireland, is found in rivers, lakes, canals, gravel-pits and the smallest of farm ponds. Its principal requirement is a good supply of fodder fish which might be perch in a Scottish loch, bream in a Midland reservoir or trout in a neglected stretch of a Southern chalkstream. In British waters the maximum weight is probably about 22.8 kg (50 lb), but any double-figure pike is considered a good fish on most waters.

Bait: Most freshwater fish are acceptable livebaits; herring, sprat and mackerel are deadbaits, with all spinning lures being very effective.

5

5. The fully formed pike, still brown and with an elongated body. Growth now depends on availability of suitable food, including plankton and larvae of fish including its own species.

way in which to fish. But the technique has a disadvantage which is not always apparent. It is repetitive and reduces many anglers to the level of an automaton: the lure is cast, the reel handle turned and the pick-up engaged, the lure retrieved. The movements become automatic and the angler ceases to think. Sheer boredom can impel the angler to move – often away from where the pike are concentrated. Apart from this danger, spinning will take pike of all sizes although many anglers believe that it accounts for mainly smaller fish. Spinners work because they induce a feeding response from the pike by triggering unpremeditated and reflex actions.

Spinning should begin in earnest once pike have been

located but a heavy spoon, used to pin-point the fish, may not be the ideal weapon with which to catch them. A lighter lure can often be retrieved more slowly, thus creating more opportunities for the pike to attack on every cast. Spin as close to the bottom as conditions will allow.

Pike need a reasonably steady target on which to focus their binocular vision. Ideal retrieves are those which retrieve the bait through 0.9 m (3 ft) long, level or slightly rising movements. This is because throughout its life a pike instinctively drives into shoals of fodder fish. The natural response of these small fish is to panic and escape as quickly as possible, the action resulting in an upwards and curving movement, a glitter of silver and red and this

FIG 1 **SPINNING FOR PIKE**

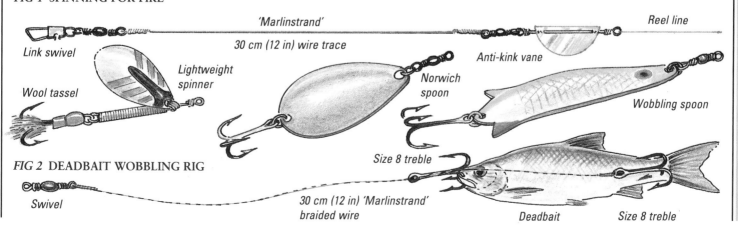

Link swivel

Wool tassel

Lightweight spinner

'Marlinstrand'

30 cm (12 in) wire trace

Norwich spoon

Anti-kink vane

Reel line

Wobbling spoon

Size 8 treble

FIG 2 **DEADBAIT WOBBLING RIG**

Swivel

30 cm (12 in) 'Marlinstrand' braided wire

Deadbait

Size 8 treble

13

A

B

C

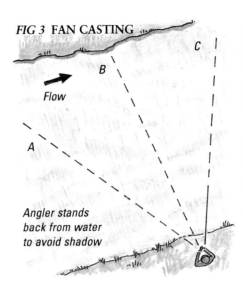

Flow

Angler stands
back from water
to avoid shadow

flash is the final trigger for the pike's attack. It makes sense for the angler to try to imitate this escaping-prey effect to induce a take from the pike.

To catch pike in any way is a pleasure but I get the most satisfaction from taking them with spinning tackle using deadbaits to imitate that escaping-prey movement. The rod and reel are the same as those used for ordinary spinning but the terminal rig is different. I make a trace of braided wire (Marlin Strand) and find that 6.4 kg (14 lb) b.s. is fine and flexible enough both in knot and twist to enable a swivel to be fixed at one end and a pair of Size 8 treble hooks in tandem at the other. The upper treble is used to close the mouth of the deadbait, the other is nicked through the wrist of the tail of the bait. The little fish, a smelt or sprat, or any freshwater fish, should be kept as straight as possible and wobble *but not spin*. (Figs 1, 2, p. 13)

This rig, which permits an instant strike by the angler, is used to tempt the pike into reacting at once: here is a meal and it must be grabbed quickly before it escapes. If larger baits are used it is important to take into account the pike's method of attack, which is usually a short, savage lunge from ambush. The prey is seized crosswise and gripped in the large canine-like teeth while the pike returns to its holt. There, the baitfish will be turned and swallowed head-first. This attack-and-swallow pattern will appear to be a continuous movement and in clear water I have watched a pike strike, then settle on the bottom to digest its meal and the only visible sign of any action has been a water-borne settling and twinkling of scales dislodged in the first moments of the pike's attack and a hovering cloud of mud disturbed by the powerful sweep of its tail-fin. The holding and pressure work from the pike's powerful jaws is often longer for a large baitfish.

If fish baits heavier than 57–85 g (2–3 oz) are used it is sensible to step up the scale of the tackle. A 3.6 m (12 ft) carbon rod which has a test curve of 1.14 kg (2½ lb) will cast baits of around 142 g (5 oz) well and is an ideal weapon to beat the largest pike. Not that the weight of the bait to be used is the only consideration, it is not, for the greatest problem in pike fishing is that of setting the hooks. Pike have strong, bony jaws and the rod must be capable of transmitting sufficient power to pull the hook-point through the bait and into those jaws.

A Making a Marlin Strand pike trace. Pass the wire twice through the eye of the swivel, then clip surgical forceps to the short, loose end. **B** Hold the swivel in one hand and the wire in the other, then spin the forceps round the wire to bind the short wire end tightly.

C The trace wire joined securely to the swivel, the knot tight. Clip off the short wire end. **D** Edwards releasing his pike unharmed after the careful removal of all hooks while the fish remained in the keepnet. This ensures the minimum of injury or trauma to the fish.

When striking, put a bend into the rod by winding the reel handle, at the same time lowering the rod tip sideways until it is about 0.6 m (2 ft) from the surface of the water. At this point a firm sweep to either side, and parallel with the surface, should result in the hooking of the pike. The rod tip should then be raised and the fish played out in the usual way. Playing a small pike is usually a short affair. If a larger fish has been hooked this may involve allowing the fish to run against the combined drag of the lightly set slipping clutch of the fixed-spool reel and pressure on the rim of the reel drum from finger or thumb. The fish is brought nearer to the landing net by clamping the finger on the rim of the reel and pumping the fish in with alternate dipping of the rod while leaning back and raising the rod tip so that the fish is drawn steadily nearer. An important point to watch while pumping a fish towards the net is that tension must be maintained, any slack on the line may mean the loss of the fish. A lively fish must be allowed to run against the slipping clutch if it gets a burst of energy on seeing the net, but to avoid putting kinks into the line the handle of the reel should not be turned while line is being pulled off the spool.

Working a deadbait is an efficient and enjoyable method of taking pike but the popularity of static dead-bait fishing increases year upon year. This style, too, is effective and often tempts the larger specimens. The range of deadbaits upon which the pike will feed is tremendous, it includes all of the freshwater fish species including eels, sea and estuarial species such as smelt, sardines, herrings, sprats, sandeels and mackerel.

If the static method of deadbaiting has a disadvantage it is that its use is more likely to lead to the deep-hooking of pike. This happens because the pike is conditioned to swimming round picking up dead or stunned victims from

D

E Allen Edwards keeps his rod at the correct angle while he fights a sizeable pike deep down. The water is the famed Shannon at Tarmonbarry, Co. Longford, Ireland.

Fig 3 Fan casting allows proper coverage of the water.

E

a previous driving attack. There are no sudden moves from the pike, just a stealthy and imperceptible scoop, turn and swallow. For this reason I prefer to use a float when laying-on with a deadbait and to strike immediately there is a movement from it, but other anglers prefer to use electronic bite alarms to signal a run from a pike.

For deadbaiting I keep my rig simple. The terminal tackle consists of a No. 8 treble hook which is whipped to the end of a 0.46 m (18 in) flexible wire trace. One point of this hook is nicked into the bait just behind the head. A No. 2 single carp hook is then slipped down the trace to act as a holding hook through the wrist of the bait's tail. The hook, secured to the trace by a couple of extra turns, is then pulled firmly through the wrist. The trace is run as closely as possible along the flank of the bait which should be kept straight. My rig is completed by joining the trace to the reel line with a swivel.

This tackle is used in conjunction with a slider float set a little over-depth and stopped with a knot, an arrangement which works well on hard-bottomed waters with gravel or clay ledges. It is less effective on waters which have a deep bed of fine silt because the action of wind, wave and under-currents usually pulls the bait through an arc, often burying it in the process. In these conditions I doctor my deadbait by pushing a small piece of polystyrene tile down its throat to give buoyancy. An alternative to this, and one which gives a head-down feeding look to the bait, is to cut a small slit behind the vent of the deadbait and to substitute some of the flesh with polystyrene. It makes sense to prepare these baits at home because they require sewing, using white cotton. On the bankside, I use a hypodermic syringe to carry out buoyancy building and perhaps to inject flavour or pilchard oil into the deadbait.

The deadbaiting style can be boring, so I temper this by using plug baits as well as spoons, fished as close as possible to the ledgered deadbait. This technique tends to draw the pike towards the static bait, which is sometimes taken in preference to the artificial lure.

There comes a time when the pike angler has to admit that spoons, plugs, static or moved deadbaits, allied to skilful presentation, will not tempt pike. Often, the smaller, male, jack pike will fall but the cunning, stony-eyed 'Jill' resists all temptation. Even the female, however, may fall to livebaiting tactics, and there is no doubting the attraction which the method holds for many anglers, those for whom there are no qualms about this form of fishing.

It is sensible to attract fodder fish such as bream or roach into the pike-fishing area, they will home in on the ground bait and loose-fed maggots or casters. The pike, in turn, follow their prey and will often take a tethered livebait.

Standard livebaiting gear in stillwaters includes a 3.3 m (11 ft) carbon rod with a test curve of 1.24 kg (2¾ lb) allied to a fixed-spool reel loaded with 5.5–9.0 kg (12–20 lb) b.s. line and a sliding float stopped at the correct depth setting by a knot made from nylon. Non-toxic weights, prevented from sliding down the line by a swivel, must be used. This rig is completed by a braided-wire trace and the armoury of hooks. I believe that most anglers overload their rigs with too many hooks, most of which are too large as well! In shallow water the old-fashioned Jardine snap tackle works well, permitting an instant strike; in water which is over 3.0 m (10 ft) deep I prefer a single treble hook. One point only is inserted under the dorsal fin of the bait which ensures that the livebait will stay active for a considerable time. It seems to me that pike strike with more confidence at these depths, often being cleanly hooked in the corner of the jaws, the area known as the 'scissors'. (Fig. 4)

For livebaiting in moving waters I use the two-hook rig, an invention by the late Captain Eric Parker for use on the Hampshire Avon. A single No. 2 carp hook is put through the top lip of the bait. The other hook, a treble, is attached to the trace with one point lightly nicked into the underside of the fish to act as a keel. When fishing the livebait it is essential to set it at the correct depth. The pike, unless it is on a feeding rampage, is usually low in the water. The bait should be set to swim 0.6 m (2 ft) above the bottom although it never bothers me if the fish is set over-depth and the bait is hard on the bottom, because it will rise from time to time and flutter in a half-circle, producing attractive vibrations on which the pike can home-in. (Fig. 5a)

In very deep water I dispense with the float and weights other than that of the swivel, trace and hook. Here, the technique of freelining is used. This involves using a short trace, a single treble hook through the dorsal fin of the bait and the patience to await the arrival of the fish in the depths. It also demands the angler's concentration on the rod tip, alert for bite detection to avoid the danger of gorge-fishing results. In known pike-holding areas, the simple static ledgering of the livebaits will often produce results but a float has its fascination and in these circumstances the paternoster allied to a sliding float comes into its own. (Figs 5b, 5c)

Late winter is a time of opportunity for the pleasure angler after pike. Reasonable deductions and sensible fishing are necessary in order to take the large specimens. It is a time when varying conditions dictate the skilful use of sporting methods. Females of most species are recognised as being the most deadly, a fact clearly demonstrated in the case of pike the females of which are not above making a meal of their suitors.

Ledger rigs for pike fishing are prone to tangling but this may be overcome by the judicious use of rig tubing. The trick is to use a swivel to connect the reel line to the

Pike rigs using either dead or livebaits (a practice which is losing favour) must present the pike with an acceptable food source and simplicity is all-important.
Fig 4 A livebait float rig using a single Size 8 treble, causing as little injury to the fish as possible, suspended from a slider-float.
Fig 5A For running water the bait must sit in the stream in a lifelike manner, attached by a single hook and a treble nicked into the belly. **Fig 5B** When a bait is freelined in deepwater the rig must be as simple as possible. **Fig 5C** The paternoster is very effective with livebaits, but the bait must be able to swim as freely as possible.
Fig 5D Ledgered rigs for pike can be very basic, or the hook-link separated by polythene rig tubing.

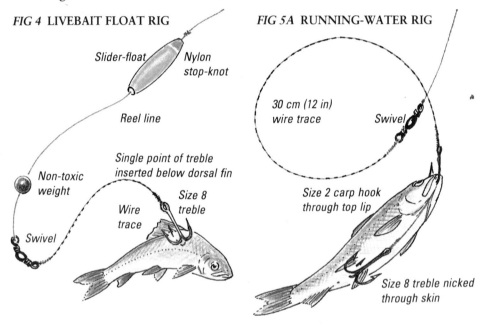

FIG 4 LIVEBAIT FLOAT RIG

FIG 5A RUNNING-WATER RIG

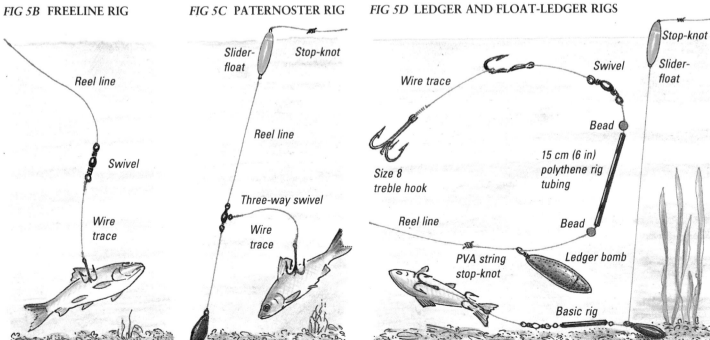

FIG 5B FREELINE RIG

FIG 5C PATERNOSTER RIG

FIG 5D LEDGER AND FLOAT-LEDGER RIGS

trace but to incorporate a short length of rig tubing between the swivel and the weight. Some anglers place a swivel some way up the line but I prefer to tie a stop-knot as devised by the late Billy Lane so that the rig becomes free-running. To do this, the stop-knot is tied with a piece of water-soluble PVA string, a substance which has a number of very useful applications in fishing. The angler makes the cast and after a few moments the knot dissolves. When the pike scoops up the bait the predator is free to move off without feeling any resistance. (Fig. 5d)

When ledgering it is never a good idea to let the fish run for very long before striking, because the pike will often take and begin to turn a static bait before moving off. A fish lost after a long run means that the pike was probably a small one; a bigger specimen likewise hooked indicates that the fish is deeply hooked, which is not good news for its survival.

A float used in conjunction with the basic ledger rig is a good idea. Once again, rig tubing is used to cut down the number of tangles. The basic benefit, however, comes

Plugs come in a fantastic variety of weights, shapes, colours and actions. A plug that has sufficient weight for adequate casting without the addition of further weight up the line is preferable for its better action. Whether used as a surface, mid-water or deep-diving lure, action is vital, it must trigger off an attack response from a feeding, predatory fish.

from the fact that a take from a pike is signalled as the float rises, lies flat, then begins to dive. I find it best to hit the fish with a sweeping strike the moment the float lies flat.

LATE WINTER: THE CHUB

There are those who will tell you that the chub is a fish for all seasons. It is not. True enough, the species may be caught at all seasons, for its greed is legendary. In the summer, chub swarm over the well-oxygenated runs and ripples to recover from spawning and may be taken easily, but at this time the species is not in good condition. Catch the same fish in the winter and it is a different tale. The chub is aggressive, bold, not too bright but with just enough awareness of danger to make its capture far from a foregone conclusion. Chub may be taken by a variety of methods, including fly fishing, but in the winter it usually comes down to a choice of presenting a bait with a float or ledger, perhaps even with a swimfeeder. There is no denying the satisfaction of watching and controlling a float to run a bait downstream to the feeding chub. Time spent in casting, trotting and retrieving a spoon speeds by and this is very therapeutic in itself.

My basic tackle when ledgering for chub consists of a three-section carbon-fibre rod, 3.45 m (11 ft 6 in) long, which has a built-in quivertip, weighs 255 g (9 oz) and was designed to cast a loaded swimfeeder. A fixed-spool reel is used loaded with 1.8–2.7 kg (4–6 lb) b.s. line. The rig is complete with split-ring, weights or swimfeeder and eyed hooks which may be as small as No. 12 or as large as No. 2. (Fig. 6, p. 18)

Ledgering used to be considered as the last resort on an unsuccessful day. In inexperienced hands this method, or series of methods, still qualifies for that denigration of a classic fishing style. There are two aspects which lift the method from the chuck-it-and-chance-it category. One is simply that of recording the bite when it comes, the other lies in making the correct choice of weight. The chub bite is often a smash-and-grab affair which puts a real bend into the quivertip; but there are times, especially in very cold conditions, when the fish will simply mouth the bait. In these circumstances touch ledgering, coupled with watching the quivertip, gives all the indication required to strike and to connect with the fish.

Concerning the choice of weight, the simple rule is to choose just enough to put the bait in front of the fish and to hold it there for as long as you wish it to stay.

Maggots, casters, cheese, bread, luncheon meat, tinned and fresh sausage, worms, shrimps and live and dead fish will all take chub. I have caught many fine River Trent chub on spinners and discovered that a deadly if somewhat expensive bait is a 19 mm (3/4 in) cube of stewing steak. For long-range ledgering I prefer lobworms, cheese and little cocktail sausages; I reserve bread-based baits for closer work.

Apart from the catching of fish the real pleasure from ledgering stems from the practised control and the placing of the bait where it should be. Late winter fishing for chub provides the perfect opportunity for indulging in the use of the rolling ledger, perhaps the most enjoyable method of presenting a bait to bottom-feeding chub.

Winter floods have cleared much of the weed growth and scoured the bottom of autumn leaf deposits. Now, the way is clear to roll or shoot the ledger and attendant bait across the front of feeding fish. The terminal tackle is made up of a split-ring which is slipped up the line and stopped from sliding down to the hook by a lead-substitute weight or small swivel. A piece of nylon, of lower breaking strain than the reel line, is tied to the split-ring. To this link, which should be about 25.4 cm (10 in) in length, is tied a non-toxic ledger weight and this may be of any weight from 0.035–57 g (⅛–2 oz) depending upon the strength of the current. An eyed hook is tied direct to the reel line. (Fig. 7)

The cast is made across and slightly downstream but the pick-up of the reel is not engaged at once. This is to allow the bait to move into the fishing area. An immediate engagement of the bale arm means that the bait will be swept round and away too quickly from the shoal-holding area. In the first instance the rod is held at an angle of 45 deg. while the bait is persuaded to move through the swim by gently lifting the rod tip; the pressure of the water on the line then sweeps the ledger downstream. The bait is thus alternately static and rolling and bites may be expected at any time. The take may come as a slight pull or as an honest-to-goodness thump in which the rod tip is slammed over.

Variations on the ledgering theme include upstream ledgering, especially useful in the summer for placing baits at the tail of long strands of water crowsfoot and ranunculus weed. With this style the bite is indicated by a slackening in the line. Snaggy waters may demand the use of the static ledger but the rolling ledger may be stopped in position by maintaining a fixed angle upon the rod.

Float fishing for chub is always a pleasure. Most of my fishing in this category is carried out with a 3.9 m (13 ft) carbon-fibre match-fishing rod and fixed-spool reel, but where the fish are at long range then a 3.6 m (12 ft) Avon rod is brought into play to enable a long, sweeping strike to be made, but the reel may differ. Some anglers maintain that it is not possible to trot a bait successfully while using a fixed-spool reel and prefer to use the traditional, free-running centrepin and there is real pleasure and satisfaction to be gained from the correct use of this kind of reel. The line strength should be the same for both, never below 1.5 kg (3½ lb) and up to 2.7 kg (6 lb) in snaggy and overgrown conditions.

Float selection is the key to successful trotting. It is a mistake to use floats which are too small. They must be visible for a long way and well able to support a lot of weight to get the bait down to the fish. Large balsa floats, or a combination of cane and balsa, are my choice for this style of fishing. (Fig. 8, p. 20)

A typical float-fishing session for chub includes the use of groundbait which incorporates samples of the hook-bait. For sheer convenience, therefore, bread baits, maggots, worms, wasp grub and shrimps are first-rate choices when float fishing. In the case of wasp grub and shrimp

Pharyngeal teeth of the chub

DACE

Leuciscus leuciscus

An active, delicate fish of the fast water, inhabiting shallows and aerated rapids. This silvery shoal-fish is often mistaken for an immature chub, but easy identification can be made between the species by comparing the concave dorsal and anal fins of the dace with the rounded, convex chub dorsal and anal fins. A small fish, the dace averages 226 to 283 g (8 to 10 oz).

Bait: Surface-fished bread and the smaller grub baits. The dace can also be caught by fly-fishing using both wet and dry flies in the smaller sizes.

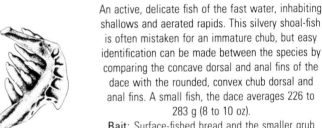

Pharyngeal teeth of the dace

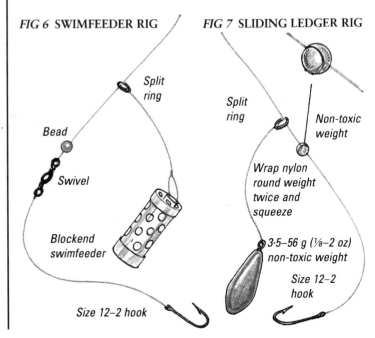

FIG 6 **SWIMFEEDER RIG**

Split ring

Bead

Swivel

Blockend swimfeeder

Size 12–2 hook

FIG 7 **SLIDING LEDGER RIG**

Split ring

Non-toxic weight

Wrap nylon round weight twice and squeeze

3·5–56 g (⅛–2 oz) non-toxic weight

Size 12–2 hook

CHUB

Leuciscus cephalus

Widely distributed in England, but absent from Ireland, most of Scotland, the extreme west of Wales and south-west Cornwall, the chub is found naturally in rivers but can adapt to stillwaters such as flooded ox-bow lakes and backwaters. A powerful, large-mouthed fish, the chub is reported to reach weights of 4 or 4.5 kg (9 or 10 lb) but a fish of 1.3 kg (3 lb) is regarded as a good specimen. At its best at the back-end of the season.
Bait: Plugs and spinners, most cereal and grub baits as well as artificial flies and livebaits.

Fig 6 One of the greatest innovations for the pleasure and matchfisherman was the swimfeeder carrying its own ledger weight.
Fig 7 Simplicity in terminal tackle is a way of avoiding tangles, and it saves a lot of time in tackling up. This rig is the simplest of sliding ledgers.

An unforgettable moment! Hundreds of mature chub spawning in a few inches of water, over shingle in the River Trent at Newark. The fish were totally oblivious of the photographer's presence, indulging themselves for many hours!

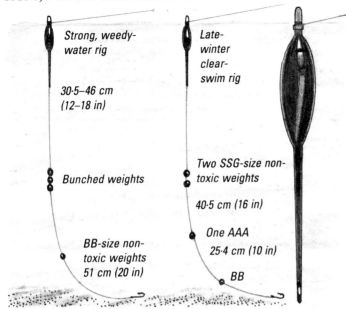

FIGS 8, 9 AVON TROTTING RIGS AND FLOATS

Strong, weedy-water rig

30·5–46 cm (12–18 in)

Bunched weights

BB-size non-toxic weights 51 cm (20 in)

Late-winter clear-swim rig

Two SSG-size non-toxic weights

40·5 cm (16 in)

One AAA 25·4 cm (10 in)

BB

Figs 8, 9 Weighting patterns will vary when fishing in different water conditions. Fig 8 More weight is needed in mid-water when the flow is strong and the weed growth is thick. Fig 9 As the water clears in late winter more weight is required nearer the hook.

A Flyfishing for chub with a minnow fly on the River Trent. Fast water running between gravel banks creates an ideal habitat and hunting ground for these marauding, large-mouthed predators.

A

baits nothing should be wasted. Every piece of the comb and every last bit of shrimp shell and whisker should be mixed in with the feed.

As always, hook size should be tailored to the hook-bait. A bunch of maggots on a Size 10 hook will take chub. A hook to hold breadflake or crust to be trotted through the same swim might be a Size 6 through to a Size 2 depending upon the size of the bait. I have taken good chub from the Upper Witham on a Size 12 hook baited with two kernels of wheat. The chub has a large mouth, so the criterion becomes the size of the bait to be fished. No hook is too big to use for the chub.

Much more important than hook size is the question of getting the bait down to the fish. Time is wasted if the bait is set too shallow and is swept through the swim well above the heads of the feeding chub. For this reason I usually fish over-depth when trotting and make sure of correct presentation by holding the float back slightly. The exception to this rule comes on those rare instances where a long, clear swim of even depth has been located. In this ideal situation the classic trotting method of setting the float at the exact depth may be enjoyed.

The chub has an almost national distribution, the exceptions being parts of the West Country and Scotland. It may be caught throughout the season, but for the pleasure angler seeking this big, brassy and beautiful fish, the best results come in the late winter.

LATE WINTER ROACH

The roach is the angler's most popular coarse fish species. Distributed from the approaches to the Scottish Highlands to the South Coast and in Ireland through the Shannon and River Erne systems, for many anglers it is the prime species to be fished for throughout the season. I prefer to fish for roach in the winter when the banks and river beds are clean and the fish are localised.

This classic fish has a mixed diet which includes algae, snails, freshwater shrimps and fly larvae, which means that the angler can use a wide range of baits to tempt the fish. In practice, however, most roach anglers are content to operate with variations of three: bread in diverse forms, seeds such as hemp and wheat and, most important to many anglers, the larval stage of the bluebottle, the maggot. For many the chrysalis stage (known to anglers as the caster) of the bait is more deadly than the wriggling maggot.

To fish the maggot or caster in running water I use a 3.9 m (13 ft) carbon match rod. It is light and has a tippy action enabling me to connect with the sometimes lightning-swift bite from the roach.

For roach fishing, the reel may be a centrepin or a fixed-spool loaded with line from 1.8 kg (4 lb) b.s. down to 0.45 kg (1 lb). A choice is made based upon the strength of current, the length of the swim to be fished and the size of the fish likely to be encountered. Problems with bait presentation or line-shy fish can be solved by adding a much finer hook link. Wind condition and the strength of the current dictate the choice of float but a combination of cane or balsa or cane and wire stem will be used for swimming the stream. A switch will be made to a peacock quill if a downstream wind is making fishing difficult. A Size 20 hook is used to present the caster or single maggot. A Size 12 hook, or larger, may be required to present a bunch of maggots or bread flake. (Fig. 9)

Crushed breadcrumb is best for groundbait now but is used sparingly in winter as in the cold water the roach are inclined to feed less than in the summer. A little groundbait and loose feeding of the hook bait concentrates the shoal and soon the fish begin to take the bait on the drop. In these circumstances a good combination is the stick float with an evenly weighted line below it to a Size 20 hook baited with a single caster. The bait is run through the swim over the groundbait and held back slightly every once in a while. The caster will rise and flutter in the water and often induces a take from the roach.

There are times, however, when the fish prefer a bait which is dragging or is laid on the bottom. Sometimes,

20

B

C

D

Three reliable lures: *B* Bushy floating fly, fished on a floating line or alternated with a live insect for dapping in overgrown river stretches. *C* Small spinner, a tiny fly spoon fished on a fly or light spinning rod.   *D* Freshly killed natural minnow or a quill minnow, fished on a light spinning outfit.   *E* Allen's leaded chub minnow fly, dressed on a long-shank hook. Tie on black peacock hurl with black silk, then thread on Mylar tubing. Make fast with a whip finish. Tie the Mylar down at the hookeye and dub on a collar of red, fluorescent wool. Complete the dressing with a black chenille head.

E

FIG10 ROACH FLOATS

Avon

Wire stem

Balsa and cane

Rubber grip-rings

F A superb 0.9 kg (2 lb) roach from Loch Lomond. The vast Scottish trout and salmon water is also home to Lomond's famous pike population.

Fig 10 Wind and water conditions can dictate what kind of float body is needed.

F

too, a downstream wind will dictate the use of the dragging-bait technique. For this I use a peacock quill waggler-type float fixed by a non-toxic shot at either side of the base of the float. In extreme conditions it may be necessary to attach a shot some 0.46 m (18 in) above the float and to plunge the rod tip below the water surface so that the line from tip to float is completely submerged. (Fig. 11)

Avon-type floats are my choice when fishing for roach at long range but in heavy water I prefer a balsa which has a wire stem. This combats the ripple and makes for better bait presentation. (Fig. 10, p. 21)

There comes a time when the roach, although present in the swim, are not responding to the trailed, trotted or held-back bait. A switch to straight ledgering tactics may produce results, but, especially in the winter, the roach is a shy biter, which means that intent concentration on the quivertip is critical.

Sometimes the fish cannot be taken on the ledger because it is not possible to be accurate in placing the bait in the groundbaited area. At this time a switch to pole-fishing tactics often proves successful. I use an 8 m (26 ft) carbon pole weighing 879 g (31 oz) or as many sections of it as are required to fish the chosen pitch. Using the pole permits accurate plumbing and pin-point accuracy with groundbaiting by use of a bait-dropper. (Fig. 12)

The pole may be used with ordinary running-through terminal tackle, but I prefer to use it as a specialist laying-on or stret-pegging technique. The baited hook is swung out and gently lowered into position over the groundbait and the float is then held back until a bite is registered. The line between float and rod tip is kept as short as possible but the length of line from hook to rod tip is never longer than the length of the pole.

Good bait preparation is important in all styles of fishing but for the roach it is vital. To prepare wheat, for example, large kernels of either the red or white variety should be washed in a sieve and soaked in a pan overnight. The next step is to bring the pan to the boil and to allow it to simmer until the kernels swell and split, showing the white, fluffy interior. Surplus water should be drained off and the wheat transferred to a cloth bag rather than a plastic one.

These preparations are basic for all seedbaits, including hempseed and tares, but care must be taken with the latter to soak overnight and to carry out the final rinsing with hot water. A dousing of cold water will split the bait, which is wrong for tares. Not that ruined baits should be thrown away, they should always be added to the groundbait. An addition to the boiling process for both hemp and tares is a pinch of bicarbonate of soda. This produces a dark, shining, clean and effective bait.

Wheat may be used on running-through tackle, but the deadliest combination is the pole, peacock quill float and laying-on set-up. There are a couple of problems associated with the use of seedbaits. The first is that it may take some time for the fish to respond to them. This should be overcome by loose feeding sparingly. The second, especially with tares and hemp, is that of false bites caused

A breadpunch makes neat hookbait the size of a grain of hemp that does not have to be handled and is ideal to present on a Size 20 or smaller hook. Other punch heads can be fitted to alter the bait size.

FIG 11 DRAGGING-BAIT

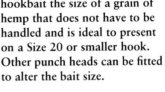

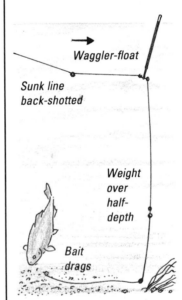

Fig 11 Sometimes fish can be tempted by a bait dragged along the bottom. To be effective, this rig must have the line sunk and back-shotted.
Fig 12 The pole offers extremely sensitive presentation, especially when laying-on. Fig 13 Quill floats have long been admired for their delicacy of presentation with the minimum of weight.

FIG 12 LAYING-ON

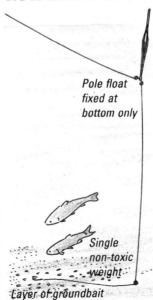

FIG 13 QUILL RIG

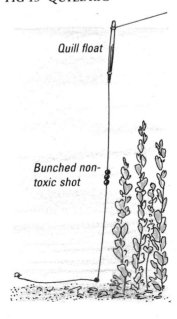

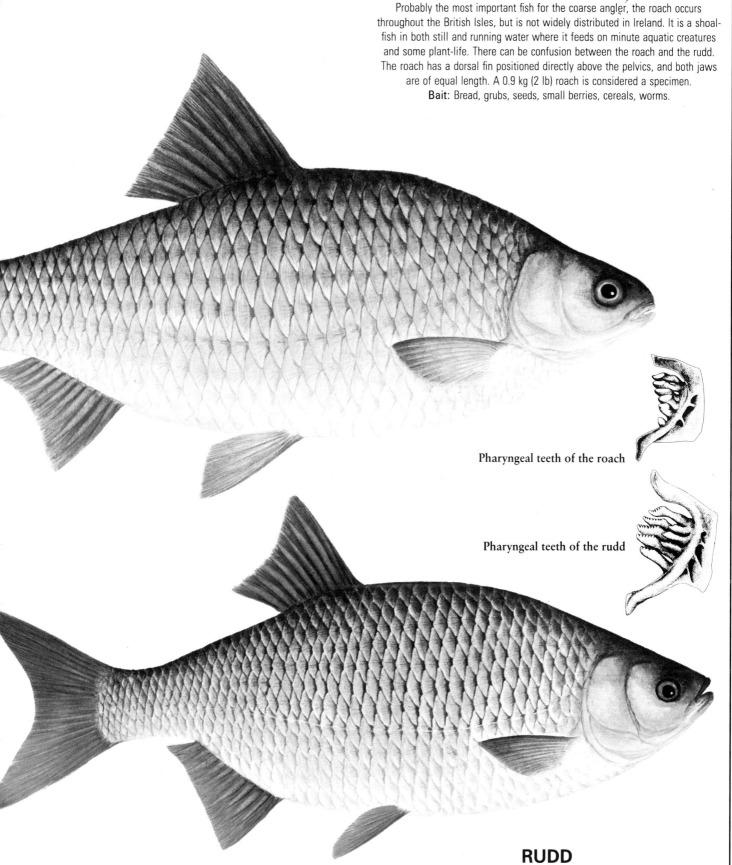

ROACH
Rutilus rutilus
Probably the most important fish for the coarse angler, the roach occurs throughout the British Isles, but is not widely distributed in Ireland. It is a shoal-fish in both still and running water where it feeds on minute aquatic creatures and some plant-life. There can be confusion between the roach and the rudd. The roach has a dorsal fin positioned directly above the pelvics, and both jaws are of equal length. A 0.9 kg (2 lb) roach is considered a specimen.
Bait: Bread, grubs, seeds, small berries, cereals, worms.

Pharyngeal teeth of the roach

Pharyngeal teeth of the rudd

RUDD
Scardinius erythrophthalmus
A deeper-bodied fish than the roach, with golden scales and bright red fins; the eyes have a brilliant red iris. The rudd's dorsal foredge begins from behind the pelvic fins and the lower jaw is longer than the upper. It is found in England, Wales and in Ireland, where confusingly it is often called the roach. The handsome rudd prefers stillwaters and quiet slacks and eddies of slow-running rivers. A 0.9 to 1.3 kg (2 to 3 lb) rudd is a specimen in any water.
Bait: All roach baits as well as a small dry fly.

when the fish mistake the shot for the bait. One way to combat this is to bunch your shot.

Bread, in all its forms, has been tempting roach since fishing began. To make a good, soft paste take the inside of a stale loaf, saving the crust for adding to the groundbait. Place the bread on to a large piece of clean cloth and, by picking up the four corners of the cloth, put the whole lot into a large bowl, cloth underneath and draped over the sides of the bowl. Add a few drops of water to the bread and, keeping the cloth between your hands and the bread, knead it. Keep adding water until a good, soft paste is made. Additives such as sugar, honey and aniseed are added by folding back the cloth but the angler can avoid leaving any hand scent if the cloth method is used.

Two other attractive bread baits are best taken from a new loaf: crust, cut into small squares, and flake from the inside make good, slow-sinking baits. Held back with a float or used on a long trail with a ledger, their fluttering movements often induce a take. I rarely fish bread baits on anything smaller than a Size 12 hook and often find that a Size 8 or 10 is needed to fish the bait properly. The exception to this is when fishing with fine tackle in gin-clear waters such as disused canals. In these circumstances I use a bread-punch to make tiny baits.

Such small waters present the pleasure angler with a challenge. I prefer to tackle them by using small balsa floats which have been fitted with a fine cane tip. In still conditions the floats are fixed top and bottom but if there is a wind or a surface drift the float is fixed at the bottom only. Maggots, casters, bread may all be used on this rig but there are others which are effective. These include woodlice and bloodworms. A fine-wire Size 20 hook is necessary to present these baits.

In coloured-water conditions the worm comes into its own. The tail of a lob or a couple of redworms will often tempt fish. I find that both these baits are the most effective when laid-on. To take the roach, then, requires patience, judgement and skill. A roach, whether it be a 152 mm (6 in) specimen from a polluted canal or a 0.9 kg (2 lb) fish from the Hampshire Avon, will not fall to anything but the finest tackle.

SUMMER FISHING: THE HANDSOME TENCH

In 1878, the Mundella Act imposed a close season upon freshwater fishing. For the coarse species, twelve weeks were set aside during which the fish might spawn without let or hindrance from anglers. But fish will spawn when the time is right for them and in the case of the tench this is often as late as mid-July. Despite this, the tench is the fish traditionally sought on June 16 when coarse fishing begins again. A handsome fish, strong, and found almost everywhere except the north of Scotland, the tench feeds on the larvae of midges, small pea-mussels and snails and spends much of its time head-down, sifting the silt. In doing this it creates areas of coloured water as from its gills the fish releases streams of tiny bubbles which are often the first indication that tench are in the swim.

It is possible to arrive at the water's edge and trust to luck that the tench will show up. It makes much more sense deliberately to create the disturbance made by feeding tench. This is done by dragging and raking the bed of the swim, freeing in the process myriads of midge larvae and water-hog louse. Tench will move quickly into such areas though the natural attraction is increased by ordinary breadcrumb groundbait laced with chopped-up worms and dried ox-blood. If maggot is to be the hookbait I add blanched maggots to the mix. These are produced by dropping them into boiling water for a few seconds, when they stretch and become white. This is an advantage on a freshly raked, silty bed where they are visible and still.

The choice of baits for tench fishing is large since they will take most of the angler's seed and animal baits. In practice, it usually comes down to a choice between bread, worms and maggots. My preference is for breadflake because its use solves most of the problems created by the feeding habits of the tench. When well and truly on feed they stand on their heads, and with tail-fins waving they pirouette, fanning pectoral fins and emitting streams of bubbles from the gills. All this makes for considerable disturbance of the silt, which buries heavy worms and bunches of maggots. On the other hand, breadflake tends to be wafted up by this movement and will tempt the tench which are moving in towards the baited area.

This is a strong fish which grows satisfyingly large and is rarely far from the cover of lily-pads and reeds. It means that the tackle must be capable of putting real pressure on the fish, and I use a 3.3 m (11 ft) carbon rod with a test curve of 0.56 kg (1¼ lb). With this I use a fixed-spool reel loaded with 1.8 kg (4 lb) b.s. line. Hook size is as always governed by the type of bait to be used. A big piece of breadflake sits well on a Size 8 hook. (Fig. 13, p. 22)

Bite detection is rarely a problem with tench and any of

A

E Certainly one of the strongest fighting coarse fishes in British freshwater, this specimen tench, hooked and fought in the half-light of dawn, severely tested Edwards and his tackle.

A The long stretch to a summer tench, coming to the net from a man-made coarse fishery, Sycamore Lake, at Skegness.
B This superbly conditioned and hard-fighting tench was taken on maggot bait.
C A positive lift to swing the fish out for the camera.   *D* A moment's care with the disgorger ensures that this fine fish is unharmed by its fight, capture and quick release.

E

B

C

D

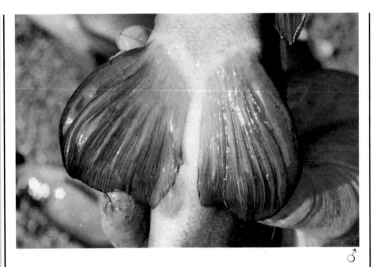

♂

♀

The tench is the only coarse fish in Britain which exhibits sexual dimorphism, an external difference between the male and female. Not, at first obvious, the differences are confined to the shape of the pelvic fins, those of the male being more solidly constructed. As shown in the two photographs on the left (top, male; lower, female), when spread sideways the male tench's pelvic fins show a

distinct hump in front, an external reflection of differences in skeletal structure between the sexes. Other examples of sexual dimorphism are the kype on the lower jaw of the male salmon and the white tubercles that develop on the heads of male cyprinids during the breeding season.

Pharyngeal teeth of the tench

FIG 14 BITE DETECTION METHODS FOR LEDGER FISHING

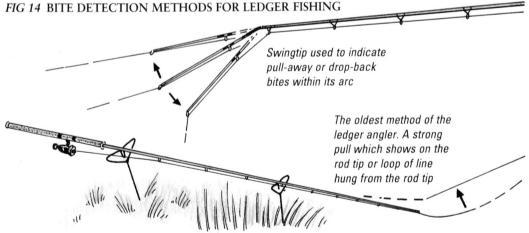

Swingtip used to indicate pull-away or drop-back bites within its arc

The oldest method of the ledger angler. A strong pull which shows on the rod tip or loop of line hung from the rod tip

Bite detection comes in many forms from finger-touch to today's highly sophisticated electronic systems with their flashing lights and buzzers. *Fig 14* In ledgering, watching for a pull on a loop of line was once the prime method, but the swingtip now gives a more positive indication as it drops away or makes a sudden movement.   *Fig 15* When float-ledgering for tench the weight should be kept away from the baited hook, which avoids the fish nudging the line and producing false bites.

FIG 15 FLOAT-LEDGERING FOR TENCH

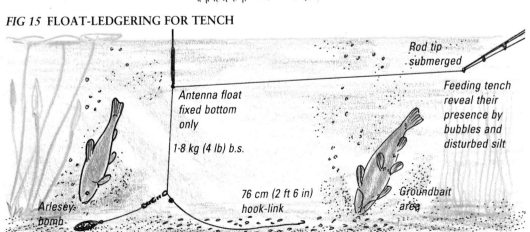

Rod tip submerged

Antenna float fixed bottom only

1·8 kg (4 lb) b.s.

Feeding tench reveal their presence by bubbles and disturbed silt

76 cm (2 ft 6 in) hook-link

Arlesey bomb

Groundbait area

TENCH
Tinca tinca

The tench is traditionally fished for on the opening day of the season. A handsome, thick-bodied, powerful fighter, found in stillwaters and sluggish rivers, the tench is a bottom-feeder down in the mud where it can find the small worms and insect larvae on which it feeds. The tench's tiny scales, covered in a thick layer of mucus, are embedded in the skin and tend to be overlooked. Two

barbules are present at the corners of the mouth. As the first of the winter frosts cools the water the tench move down into the mud and lie dormant until the coming of spring.

Bait: Worms, bread baits of all kinds, grubs and other water life.

the tip or butt indicators, or electronic bite-alarms, will be suitable. But tench fishing for me is wrapped up in the beauty of the summer dawn much of which is missed if all one's concentration is centred on a bite indicator, so I prefer to use a float. In still conditions I employ light float and laying-on tactics. If longer casting is required similar tactics come into play but I tackle up with a much larger float, fixed at the bottom-end only. Surface drift or a ripple is catered for by using a float-ledger set-up and here I use the lightest weight practicable. This is linked to the reel line by finer monofilament than the main one and is intended to break away in the event of my terminal tackle becoming snagged. The bomb sinks into the silt or weed but leaves the bait well presented. Again, the float is an antenna fixed at the bottom end only. (Figs 14, 15)

With either the float or float-ledger methods, the swim is over-cast and the tackle drawn back so that the hookbait is in the raked and groundbaited area. It is rare for the nearest weight to be closer than 0.76 m (2½ ft) to the hookbait. This removes the problem of false bites and hopes as the tench move about the swim, nudging the float in the process. The bite is usually a sail-away affair.

SUMMER: CARP

Much more than any other fish, the carp can transform a pleasure and leisure activity into an obsession, the reasons

for which are not difficult to find. The fish can often be seen shouldering their way through weedbeds as they prospect for food. They are strong and that strength, when apparent in the speed and power of the run of a hooked carp, leaves you in no doubt that you have a battle on your hands. For many anglers the first experience of this power is the catalyst which converts the pleasure angler into a dedicated carp-fishing fanatic. For these *Cyprinus carpio* worshippers the attraction of the carp holds fast throughout the year. I am not one of them, preferring to set aside the period from mid-June until October's end as the time when it is fun to catch a carp.

Thanks to the popularity of carp fishing, and to the efforts of club secretaries to cater for their members' interests, the numbers swell year by year. Except in carp-only waters (and these are few) the problem is to catch the carp while avoiding the tench, bream, roach and eels with which many waters abound. This problem is compounded by the fact that the carp appears to be more intelligent than the other coarse species.

I regularly fish a swim on the River Trent at Muskham, near Newark, Nottinghamshire. It is an unusual swim for that river in that it is relatively still and it is quite possible to groundbait heavily in a small area. My experience is that if a carp is hooked and either lost or landed from that swim then two hours is the average waiting time before another carp may be expected. The chub, bream and

LEATHER CARP
Cyprinus carpio

MIRROR CARP
C. carpio

WILD CARP
C. carpio

Pharyngeal teeth of the carp

COMMON CARP
C. carpio

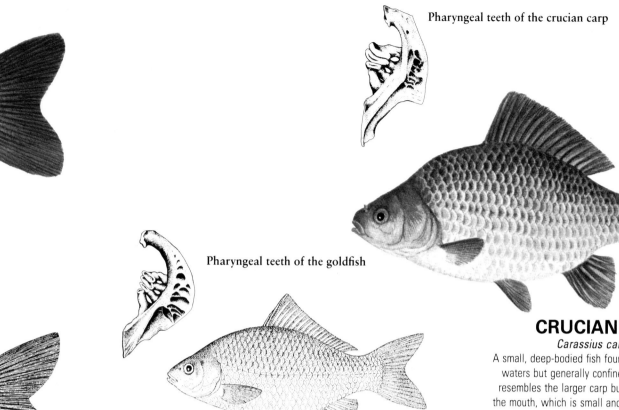

Pharyngeal teeth of the crucian carp

Pharyngeal teeth of the goldfish

CRUCIAN CARP
Carassius carassius
A small, deep-bodied fish found in a wide variety of waters but generally confined to small ponds. It resembles the larger carp but has no barbules on the mouth, which is small and blunt, with the upper jaw slightly longer than the lower.
Bait: Small pellets of bread, tiny worms and single grubs.

GOLDFISH
Carassius auratus
A carp relative that exhibits a fantastic variety of both colour and fins as a result of selective breeding by man. This is not an angler's fish, but in some lakes it can grow to considerable size. When both species are present, the goldfish and crucian carp may spawn together, producing fish with crucian coloration.

CARP
Cyprinus carpio
Carp live in stillwaters of all kinds natural and man-made, and also some slow-running rivers and drains. There are three varieties of the common carp, the fully-scaled, mirror (with large scales along the lateral line), and leather (having a total absence of scales). There are two distinct types of common carp, a huge, deep-bodied type that has been introduced to many stillwaters from a Continental-bred stock, and a slimmer, slightly-built fish known as the 'Wildie' supposedly derived from carp brought to Britain in the Middle Ages. The carp has four barbules, two from above the upper jaws and one at each corner of the mouth. The species prefers soft, muddy bottoms in which they find much of their food of small invertebrates and vegetable matter and into which they sink during the cold winter months. In the summer, carp can be described as surface feeders. Carp reach 22.8 kg (50 lb) or more.
Bait: Anglers have conditioned carp to accept most baits, including worms, grubs of many kinds, insects, bread in all its forms, meats, potatoes, fruits including cherry and banana, tinned animal foods.

roach carry on feeding over the groundbait but the more wary carp seem to recognise that this is a place of danger and keep well clear.

The standard gear for tackling the carp includes a carbon rod of 3.3 m (11 ft), with a test curve of 0.56 kg (1¼ lb). There are plenty of adequate carp rods on the market but many anglers, especially those who fish at a distance, prefer to step this tackle up and to use a rod with a test curve of 1.24 kg (2¾ lb). For my favourite Trent carp swim, a fixed-spool reel is used loaded with 1.8 kg (4 lb) b.s. line. This is employed in conjunction with an eyed hook. In unknown waters the line strength should be increased up to 3.6 or 4.5 kg (8 or 10 lb).

For carp, the basic tackle has changed little for many years but baits and terminal tackle-rigs certainly have. Simple baits such as bread are always worth a try but here the problem of attracting unwanted species must be recognised. The same may be said of worm baits for there is nothing more frustrating to the carp angler than to strike into a fish and then feel the sinuous backing-away of an unwelcome, unwanted eel.

The list of baits which will tempt the carp is endless. Cheese-flavoured pastes, banana, honey, sausage, tinned cat and dog foods, dried blood, minced worms, maggots and casters, all have taken carp. Current favourites in the armoury of dedicated carpmen are combination baits which have a high protein content. Known as boilies, they have the advantage of enabling the angler to switch flavours and textures so that the carp are not able to treat them all as a danger signal. (Figs 16, 17)

Most fishing tackle shops now carry a range of commercially made boilies but they are easy to prepare at home. The ingredients include casein (an extract of milk protein), Bemax (a wheatgerm health food), stock cubes of various flavours and a yeast product. These are mixed in a bowl with a couple of eggs and made into a smooth paste. This is rolled into bait-sized portions and dropped into boiling water for a minute or so, which has the effect of putting a shell on the bait, so helping to deter the smaller, unwanted species. Even so, the attentions of bream, tench and even eels must be borne philosophically. Boilie baits freeze well and can be taken to the water in a thermos flask, where a No. 2 hook can be slipped into the bait with the aid of a baiting needle. A long cast is made and after a few minutes in the water the bait will have thawed into a highly tasty, correctly textured bait to tempt the carp.

One does not need to fall into the trap of fanaticism to get pleasure from carp fishing. On many carp-holding waters the optimum feeding time is around dawn and a sensible evening-time pre-baiting session, coupled with the careful approach and tackling-up sequence of an experienced angler, is all that is required to take a fish or two before breakfast.

However, the 'carp bug' does bite many anglers and when that happens the addiction inevitably shows itself in a compulsion to be at the water's edge for 24 hours or more at a stretch. The variations which this produces in fishing techniques are minimal in the case of the angler

A

B

FIG 16 BUNCHED WORMS

Two lobworms hooked once on Size 2 carp hook

FIG 17 BOILIE STOPS

Size 2 carp hook

Boilies threaded on to hook with baiting needle

Hair-rig

Boilies can also be groundbaited – threaded on to PVA string and tied to trace swivel

Boilie

Boilie stops

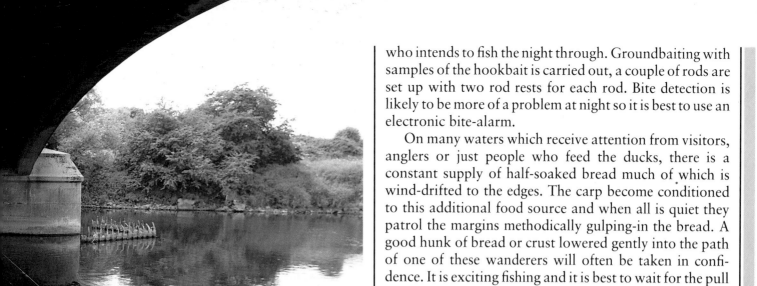

who intends to fish the night through. Groundbaiting with samples of the hookbait is carried out, a couple of rods are set up with two rod rests for each rod. Bite detection is likely to be more of a problem at night so it is best to use an electronic bite-alarm.

On many waters which receive attention from visitors, anglers or just people who feed the ducks, there is a constant supply of half-soaked bread much of which is wind-drifted to the edges. The carp become conditioned to this additional food source and when all is quiet they patrol the margins methodically gulping-in the bread. A good hunk of bread or crust lowered gently into the path of one of these wanderers will often be taken in confidence. It is exciting fishing and it is best to wait for the pull on the line before striking.

But, sadly, there are days when the best of groundbait carpets and the most cleverly presented hookbaits will be ignored while individual fish can be seen feeding and throwing up characteristic clouds of mud. These carp can be stalked and will often fall to a bunch of worms presented on scaled-down tackle. But be warned – landing such powerful, feeding fish is a very different matter indeed.

There is no denying the fascination which carp hold for the pleasure angler. Not the least of these attractions is the fact that the fish are often visible or give clear indications of their whereabouts and at times they are easy to catch. At other periods they can be totally infuriating as they cruise about like inviolate, fat-bodied submarines well

C   D   E   F

A Allen Edwards' carp-hunting ground, the dark water beneath a road bridge over the River Trent at Muskam.   B Roy Stevenson hooked his carp in the shadowy stream but the fish immediately ran out into the hard sunlight.   C After a tough battle Roy's fish nears the reeded bank, Allen is already standing by with the net.
D Success as another Trent fish slides over the net rim.   E A quick weigh-in which takes the balance down to a sound 5.5 kg (12 lb).   F A beautiful, fully-scaled carp from the River Trent's streamy water. The fast-flowing Trent has in recent years become one of Britain's best-known river carp habitats.

aware of the angler's presence and totally ignoring all hookbaits the angler presents.

On reflection, perhaps this is the greatest fascination of carp fishing. The water positively reeks of carp; the angler knows that the fish feed readily in the summer but he also knows that he will have earned every fish that he lands, for carp do not 'volunteer'.

There have been two revolutions in carp fishing in recent years. One has been in the increase in the technology associated with production of the baits used to tempt the fish; the other is in the terminal rigs used to present the ever-increasing range of baits, sometimes at extreme casting range. At great distances it is difficult to pick up line in order to strike into the fish but the bolt rig, designed at first to fool shy-biting carp, will generate runs which solves this problem.

The fish sucks up what is an apparently freely offered hookbait, feels the hook and tries to eject it, but is hooked as the back stop is pulled against the lead. A 57 g (2 oz) lead is used and to prevent snap-offs a shock leader of 6.8 kg (15 lb) b.s. is used. This should be twice the length of the rod and a little more to get a couple of turns of the leader on to the reel. The line is passed through the centre of a bead, through one end of a link swivel, through another bead and is tied to a swivel. The hook link is tied to the other end of the swivel. The stop-knot is tied on with Power Gum, a stretchy product more commonly used as a shock resister when fly fishing for trout on reservoirs.

Sometimes it is necessary to go down to very fine leaders when nymph fishing. The gum works well in cushioning some of the smash-takes from trout. The bead helps to cushion the shock as the lead flies up the line for the short distance between swivel and back-stop. A hook-link, which may be 152 to 203 mm (6 to 8 in) long, is passed through a short piece of silicone tubing to ensure that the bait, which may be anything from a single grain of sweetcorn to a large boilie, sits correctly. Sometimes the hair rig is simply tied to the bend of the hook.

A selection of baits can be dropped close to the hookbait by using water-soluble PVA string and a baiting needle. Some anglers prefer to bait the bolt rig by pushing the hook straight through the bait to leave the point of the hook exposed.

When they are cast into the middle distance many rigs are prone to tangles which can be overcome by using an anti-tangle tube rig. These may be used to produce a bolt rig by fixing the eye of the swivel well into the tube. If a running ledger is required then the tube should be cut flush with the eye of the bead which is on the tube and tangles can be avoided by making the hook link less than half the length of the tube. (Figs 18, 19)

If a water is not more than 1.8 m (6 ft) deep the carp are as likely to be taken on the surface as in the depths. Samples of the hookbait can include breadcrust, fried bread, cat and dog biscuits and air-injected worms, catapulted or drifted into the chosen pitch, which is usually in a reedy corner away from the bankside vibrations or on the edges of dense patches of water lilies. Carp 'feel' safe there, as they do under the over-hanging branches of

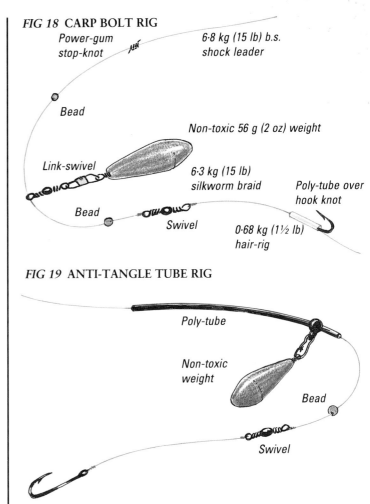

FIG 18 CARP BOLT RIG

Power-gum stop-knot

6·8 kg (15 lb) b.s. shock leader

Bead

Non-toxic 56 g (2 oz) weight

Link-swivel

6·3 kg (15 lb) silkworm braid

Poly-tube over hook knot

Bead

Swivel

0·68 kg (1½ lb) hair-rig

FIG 19 ANTI-TANGLE TUBE RIG

Poly-tube

Non-toxic weight

Bead

Swivel

A A group of small mirror carp from a tiny but prolific Nottinghamshire fishery. Seen congregating among dense surface weed, these sturdy mirrors were caught on the classic floating-crust bait and on something old-time anglers never knew about – sweetcorn.

Fig 18 When a strong fish takes the bait and runs, the bolt rig absorbs the initial stress on the tackle. Fig 19 This is one of the ideas for avoiding rig tangles. Fig 20 Keeping the bait away from the float is the objective here. Depth adjustment is crucial. Fig 21 The float prevents the weight sinking into the mud.

A

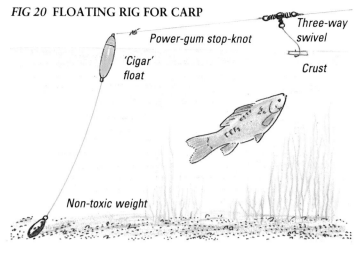

FIG 20 FLOATING RIG FOR CARP

Three-way swivel

Power-gum stop-knot

'Cigar' float

Crust

Non-toxic weight

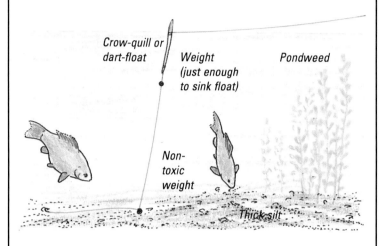

FIG 21 CRUCIAN CARP RIG

Crow-quill or dart-float

Weight (just enough to sink float)

Pondweed

Non-toxic weight

Thick silt

willows and providing they are not spooked by too much casting they will feed well.

One way to tempt carp is to float a bait at them, taking care to grease the reel line first, by using a silicone spray which the modern-day trout fisherman uses to ensure that dry flies stay that way. A more accurate method is carefully to plumb the depth, then to tether a suitable float at the correct depth. The reel line runs from this float up to the rod top and from this line is fixed, by way of a small three-way swivel and hook-link. The bait is lowered or raised from the surface by altering the angle of the rod, but of course, this is not a method for use at extreme distances. Any modern fishing tackle shop will stock commercially made boilies which float but if you prefer to make your own all you do is double the usual quantity of eggs in your boilie recipe and cook the mixture as you would a cake, in the oven for between 1½ and 2 hours. There can be fewer more exciting methods of catching carp than presenting them with a floating bait. It may – but should not – be a hit-or-miss affair. The fun may not be entirely from carp for all ducks will eagerly take a surface bait and tufted duck may become preoccupied with boilies – you have been warned! (Fig. 20)

SUMMER: CRUCIAN CARP

As we have said, the catching of large carp may so affect the psyche that the game is no longer fun. It becomes more like a religion to be practised with all the will and deter-

mination of a zealot. The crucian carp, which never grows very large, tempers this situation and is seen by many as presenting the opportunity for a little light relief. This species has a similar distribution to the larger carps but will exist in conditions which the barbuled carp and many other coarse fish cannot tolerate.

I have caught the crucian carp from the tiniest of farm ponds where they have shared perhaps 0.6 m (2 ft) of water over 0.3 m (1 ft) of silt, with a population of stunted tench and roach. Crucians have also come to the net as part of a mixed bag on the River Trent. A 0.9 kg (2 lb) fish is a good size for the species so it can be fished for with the lightest of tackle. This may pose a problem for the angler since crucian often share a large water with tench, which tend to grow much heavier. It is a mistake, however, to anticipate catching the bigger fish and so step up the strength of the tackle since this affects bait presentation for the crucian. They browse in the most delicate manner so it is better to scale the tackle to suit the crucian and to play a marauding tench with care when it does show up and takes your bait.

My tackle for the crucian consists of a 3.9 m (13 ft) match-rod or in blustery wind conditions the carbon roach-pole. For the match-rod I load a fixed-spool reel with 0.9 kg (2 lb) b.s. line but in very clear water it is not unusual to scale this down even further. In my experience, I find that a loaded canal-style float is satisfactory and the hook may be a No. 18 up to a 12 if breadflake is used as bait. This form of coarse fishing is great fun – fishing in miniature, with one or two anglers sharing the bank of a tiny farm pond. (Fig. 21)

The typical crucian-holding water has a soft, oozy bottom and worms and maggot quickly bury themselves. It is best to loose-feed such baits sparingly. Great care should be taken in plumbing the water before fishing, taking special note of the likely depth of the ooze. Your float tackle should be rigged so that any weight does not rest on the very soft bottom, the only variation to this rule being where the fish has been found in waters having a harder clay or gravel bed. In circumstances like these the lift method, which involves placing one shot on the bottom, will be effective.

Care is also required when groundbaiting for crucians. It should be done lightly on the little-and-often principle. Breadcrumb is satisfactory but I have found that crucians respond better when a little sugar is added to the mix or it has been possible to groundbait with biscuit-crumb. Samples of the hookbait should always be included and these include maggot or caster, tiny redworms or small pieces of breadflake. A breadpunch is useful in this respect since it produces standard-sized baits; the punch also makes it possible to nick the hook into the bait so that it is not touched by the hands.

While the angler is in action with ordinary float-fishing gear, a crucian will often mouth the bait without it registering a bite. For this reason I prefer to bait up a pitch which is close to broad-leaved pondweed if it is present. With a breeze and consequent drift it is possible to lay the line across the top of a strand of the weed and in this way to hold the bait in position. The pole is also useful in these conditions since the bait can be held in the baited area against the drift.

Fishing for crucians, then, is the essence of pleasure fishing. No one should have heart-failure from excitement when fishing for crucians, just a lot of fun.

SUMMER: THE GREGARIOUS RUDD

If asked to name the most handsome species on the British coarse-fish list I would nominate the rudd. It is true that the perch has its devotees but a big rudd, in good condition, has it beat. Short and deep-bodied, with vermilion fins, brassy flanks and a back topped off with dark green to black shading, the rudd makes a pretty picture. The fish is widespread in Ireland but has a patchy distribution in England and Wales.

Swarming as it does, the rudd is a relatively easy fish to catch in large numbers. It takes much of its food from the surface layer and in and around reedy margins, often betraying its presence by jostling competitively for emerging insects. Rudd will feed on the hottest of July or August dog-days and, in this respect, is very much a bonus fish. Specimens of 0.9 kg (2 lb) are quite common but there is always the chance of a larger fish turning up. I recommend an Avon-style rod and 1.3 kg (3 lb) b.s. line on a fixed-spool reel as the ideal tackle with which to fish. This tackle will set the hook in response to a sweeping strike. The rudd is shy and if approached in a clumsy manner it moves on to other reedbeds. Long casting is often necessary.

I prefer to fish for rudd from an old-fashioned, two-man punt. These craft make stable platforms and are not likely to set up rudd-scaring waves as can ordinary dinghies. The punt and long casting are just part of the equation in fishing for rudd. The third and probably most important need is to attract the fish into a comfortable fishing area. Rudd, and this applies particularly to the larger fish, spend a lot of time in the reedbeds where they browse away on the stems taking insects and little snails. They will also feed on the odd terrestrial casualty which is blown on to the water.

NECESSITY OF GROUNDBAITING

Groundbaiting is the answer to the problem; first to get the fish feeding on the intended hookbait and secondly to draw the fish to the front of the reedbed and into open water. Bread, maggots and casters are all good baits for rudd and it makes sense to use them as groundbait. The bread may be skimmed out or just drifted to the edge of the reeds where the rudd soon find it and, in feeding on it, break it into even smaller pieces. The angler can easily imitate these by pinching a piece of breadflake around the shank of a hook. Maggots and casters are most accurately delivered to the place where they will do the most good with the aid of a throwing-stick or catapult.

The rudd is not hook-shy unless it is spooked by clumsy casting and heavy movement from the boat. It will take a bunch of maggots on a Size 12 gilt crystal hook with

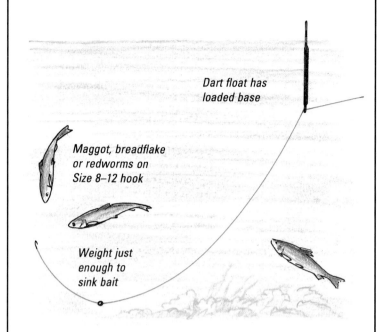

FIG 22 'ON-THE-DROP' RIG

Dart float has loaded base

Maggot, breadflake or redworms on Size 8–12 hook

Weight just enough to sink bait

confidence. A Size 8 or 10 will not be too large if breadflake is being used. Small redworms will also take rudd but whatever the bait it should be presented so that it sinks through the water as slowly as possible, which means that the weight must be bunched beneath the float or that a loaded float should be used. Rudd make a considerable disturbance at the surface when feeding which, I suppose, is the reason that they do not seem to object when a large float comes splashing down among them. It would scare off most species. (Fig. 22)

I get a deal of pleasure from angling for rudd with fly-fishing tackle, for it produces the slow-falling bait to perfection. Maggots are the best bait for this operation since a bunch on a hook will stand up to the false casting which is required. Not that it is necessary to use any bait other than an artificial fly, for the rudd will take both dry or wet patterns as used in trout fishing, but natural bait or artificial, the rule is to fish as close to the surface as possible. When using the wet fly allow it to sink a little, then impart movement with a steady pull on the line between the rod handle and the first rod ring, at the same time lifting the rod tip. This often induces a take. Flies that glitter are the most effective; silver- or gold-bodied offerings such as the Butcher, Wickham's Fancy, Cinnamon and Gold are favourites. For dry fly fishing, tiny Black Gnats work well with a finely tipped leader which is sprayed with silicone to ensure that both fly and the line float well on the surface.

Shoaling, gregarious fish, rudd are in competition with each other so the rise to the fly is often a nudging, scrambling affair. Whatever the method used to take them, a hooked rudd should be steered away from the shoal as quickly as possible. A fish which is allowed by a clumsy angler to thrash around on the surface will soon put the others down.

This small fish can trigger off a life-long addiction to fishing, for it is often found in small farm ponds, just the places where small boys can learn the ropes.

Much under-appreciated, the rudd is a deep-keeled, beautiful, plump species with majestic coloration. It is a fish which provides for a wide variety of angling methods on both lakes and riverbeds in the cooler months of the season. As the weather improves and the water warms the rudd rises to the surface in search of natural insects.

Three important ways of fishing for the fast-moving dace:

Fig 23 The line controller assists fishing at a distance where a float's action is impeded by the current.

Fig 24 A laying-on rig with maggot bait is a favourite style of dace fishing; while *(Fig 25)* fly fishing has always been popular.

The rudd is a fish of great beauty. It is found in the most beautiful of environments. To catch one – and of course return it unharmed – is always a pleasure.

SUMMER: DACE

The old English name for the dace is the *dart*, a title which paints an accurate picture of this little fish for which a specimen weight is 0.45 kg (1 lb). It is common, being found in the streamy runs of most unpolluted rivers in England and Wales. Often it rivals in numbers and, in the water, competes for habitats with the roach. It thrives too in small tributaries where differing techniques are required from those which take fish from the main stream.

I catch dace by using similar methods to those used for roach fishing in streamy waters. The range of baits is the same, with any preference given to casters, maggots, redworms and wasp grub, but both bread and hempseed are also effective. I have enjoyed splendid fishing for the dace on the white-water runs of the River Teme, which rises in Wales and meets the Severn in Worcestershire. The Teme and the Upper Severn push with white-fronted energy from side to side of the channels and the result of each succeeding run is a hollowed-out pool where the river regains its breath and the chub reign supreme. On many of these white-water runs there are dace-holding pockets of water looking like old stains on a freshly laundered baby's bib and the dace in these are superb, fine sporting fish of half the specimen size.

A method which I have used with success in these conditions has involved the use of an ordinary roach-action rod, a fixed-spool reel and 1.14 or 1.8 kg (2½ or 4 lb) b.s. line. A float will not register bites because of the press of the water. A 76 mm (3 in) length of cigar-shaped balsa, painted to make it water-proof, is used as a controller to present the bait. My controller is fitted with an eyelet at each end through which the reel line is passed. A stop-shot is pinched on to the line to ensure that the controller

does not pass down to the hook. Fishing is done by wading into the edge of the current, holding the rod-tip high and allowing the controller to run down-stream until the slightly darker water is reached. Here, the cigar is manoeuvred and held, for as long as possible, in the slightly slacker water. Ideal terminal tackle is a No. 12 hook baited with wasp grub. A steady trickle of bait is fed into the stream and each possible holding spot is tested. Bite detection is not a problem as the line is held between finger and thumb and the take is felt as a distinct pluck, but this is trout water and the attentions of unwanted browns have to be borne philosophically. (Fig. 23)

On broader shallows of large rivers such as the Trent the dace provides great fun on fly-fishing tackle. I use a 1.8 m (6 ft) old split-cane rod which casts a No. 5 floating line very well. The trick with this is to cast a fixed length of line while slowly wading up the shallows. Runs between islands are productive. Floating patterns, tied to No. 16 hooks, are Black Gnat and Red Tag. The cast is made up

FIG 23 LINE CONTROLLER RIG FOR DACE

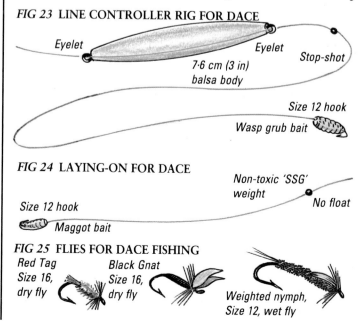

Eyelet

Eyelet

Stop-shot

7·6 cm (3 in) balsa body

Size 12 hook

Wasp grub bait

FIG 24 LAYING-ON FOR DACE

Non-toxic 'SSG' weight

No float

Size 12 hook

Maggot bait

FIG 25 FLIES FOR DACE FISHING

Red Tag Size 16, dry fly

Black Gnat Size 16, dry fly

Weighted nymph, Size 12, wet fly

and across and is allowed to drift only a short distance before the fly is lifted off and recast. (Fig. 25, p. 35)

For downstream work I use weighted nymphs which I tie on Size 12 hooks. A cast is made across and slightly downstream and movement is imparted to the nymph by a slight lifting of the rod tip. This gives the escaping-prey movement to the fly and the fish usually hook themselves in their eagerness to grab it. The dace is a free-riser in the summer months, though it is at its best in winter.

To catch dace in the winter I find that laying-on or very light ledgering tactics are best. An effective method on small waters such as the Little Alne, in Warwickshire, is to work quietly upstream flicking a maggot-baited hook, weighted with a single, non-toxic swan-shot into the run of the current. The rod is then held high so that the bait is carried down and under the near bank. This is particularly effective below hollow banks and tree roots. No float is used and the bite, which is generally deliberate, is felt as a pluck on the line. The sprightly dace is a fish for all seasons but because it takes the fly with such dash, for me it is a prime species for the summer. (Fig. 24, p. 35)

LATE SUMMER: THE GYPSY-LIKE BREAM

The bream is a roving, gypsy fish. Each year, if spawning has been successful, vast shoals of tiny fry gather and begin to move in a glittering mass around the perimeter of waters across Ireland, England and Southern Scotland. It is absent from the far West Country, West Wales and the far north of Scotland. These shoals represent food-on-the-fin for predators of all kinds, including the larger bream. Predation is great and large numbers of little fish are eaten. The search for food, aided no doubt by the herding action of predators, sets a wandering style of life on the shoal, which patrols a set beat and so its movements become predictable. Feeding as they go, each year-class moves off and, for the casual angler, the meeting points of these shoals of differing sizes of bream become hot-spots. It must be said, however, that the continual catching of small bream is a pleasure which soon begins to pall for the serious pleasure angler; for the matchfisherman, of course, it is a different matter.

The angler seeking quality bream must try to locate the feeding paths of the smaller shoals of much larger fish, and this is specialist's work. On large expanses of water, where its clarity is not always impaired by the feeding actions of the bream, the larger specimens can be found by observation. On the smaller areas, where the bream have coloured the water with their constant rooting for food, the job of pin-pointing larger fish becomes more difficult, although it is a good idea on the clear waters of canals to look for the roiled-up sections and I have prospected many miles of the Grand Canal in Ireland, where discoloration inevitably betrays the presence of bream.

Once the fish have been located the fishing becomes something of a ritual in which the sacrificing of large quantities of groundbait becomes an important part. This may be on the once-and-for-all principle of the casual angler but it is much more effective if fed in regular,

Pharyngeal teeth of the bream

smaller amounts. The aim is not to attempt to hold the bream in the swim but to condition the fish to finding an angler's bait in a set place at a set time. In both cases the groundbait should be the same: mix breadcrumb and bran then lace it with blanched maggots, chopped worms, sweetcorn or crushed hempseed.

The choice of hookbaits is wide and both flake and paste breadbaits are effective; so too are worms, maggots, sweetcorn and some of the mini-boilies. In the summer, bream will take large baits but as winter sets in it is better to fish with smaller offerings, and the single maggot or caster has accounted for plenty of large bream.

A bream does not fight strongly but its bulk will test out weak tackle. Add to the fish's slab-sided body the fact that it may be necessary to cast a long way to lay the bait before the bream and it can be seen that the use of very fine tackle does not make sense. In stillwaters, line with a minimum of 1.8 kg (4 lb) b.s. should be used. With running waters, where large fish may be encountered, this breaking strain may be too light. Hook size will vary with the bait but for breadflake and paste a Size 8 is not too large. Bunches of casters and maggots, or a couple of grains of sweetcorn, may be fished on a Size 12.

A 2.7–3.0 m (9–10 ft) ledger rod with a built-in quivertip is ideal when allied with a fixed-spool reel. The bream is not a shy biter, so a butt-indicator will work satisfactorily. When using this type of indicator it is an advantage to have two rod-rests. One of these should be

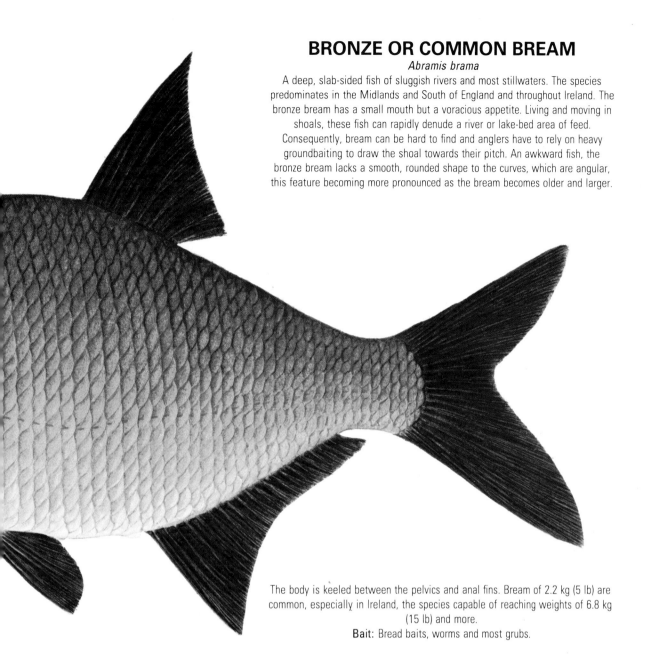

BRONZE OR COMMON BREAM
Abramis brama
A deep, slab-sided fish of sluggish rivers and most stillwaters. The species predominates in the Midlands and South of England and throughout Ireland. The bronze bream has a small mouth but a voracious appetite. Living and moving in shoals, these fish can rapidly denude a river or lake-bed area of feed. Consequently, bream can be hard to find and anglers have to rely on heavy groundbaiting to draw the shoal towards their pitch. An awkward fish, the bronze bream lacks a smooth, rounded shape to the curves, which are angular, this feature becoming more pronounced as the bream becomes older and larger.

The body is keeled between the pelvics and anal fins. Bream of 2.2 kg (5 lb) are common, especially in Ireland, the species capable of reaching weights of 6.8 kg (15 lb) and more.
Bait: Bread baits, worms and most grubs.

SILVER BREAM
Blicca bjoerkna
A smaller and more silvery fish than the bronze species and found rarely and locally in a number of waters in Eastern Britain. Although slab-sided, its body curves are more rounded and gentle than the bronze species. A fish of 0.45 kg (1 lb) is a specimen.
Bait: The silver bream will take all baits as for the bronze bream.

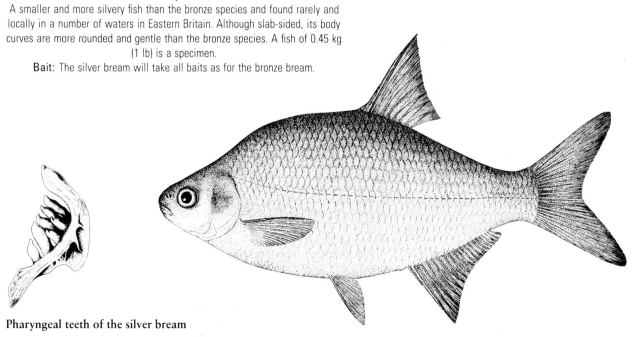

Pharyngeal teeth of the silver bream

A
FIG 26 THE LIFT-FLOAT

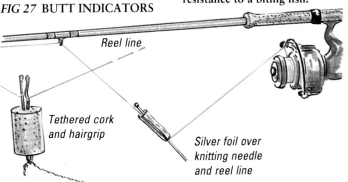

Bulk weight rests
on bottom with
1·5 cm (½ in) of
float showing
on surface

FIG 27 BUTT INDICATORS

Reel line

Tethered cork
and hairgrip

Silver foil over
knitting needle
and reel line

A The fenland lakes of East Anglia can provide some of our best bream fishing. *B* Quality fish from a fenland lake. Common bream to 3.2 kg (7 lb), a beautiful tench and a plump bonus roach.

Fig 26 The lift-float technique depends not on striking as the float dips but when it suddenly rises to lie flat on the surface, due to the fish lifting the bait (and the weight) off the bottom. *Fig 27* There are many highly complicated electronic bite-indicators, but the simplest are balls of dough, silver-paper twists, paperclips – anything that will supply just enough weight to create a sag in the line but which will give no resistance to a biting fish.

B

set directly behind the other with the front rest being set lower than the rear. The rod tip may then be set below the level of the surface and this helps to combat surface drag set up by wind and currents. (Fig. 27)

On stillwaters, the bait should be fished hard on the bottom and conventional ledger or laying-on float tackle may be used. Part of the attraction of float-fishing for bream lies in the leisurely way in which the fish appears to take the bait. It stands upon its head, lifts the bait, causing the float to rise and lie flat on the surface before submerging and sliding away. It is fascinating but it can be avoided, together with false line bites, by using a longer trail between the bottom weight and the hook. On moving waters a bottom-fished bait may take bream but there are times when the fish are taking on the drop. At such times careful plumbing of the depth is required to ensure that the bait runs through just tripping the bottom, or is just above it when the float is held back. (Fig. 26)

All of this presupposes that the bronze bream is the quarry. Ordinary roach-fishing gear will suffice for tackling the much smaller and rarer silver bream.

The bream, then, is an important fish for the pleasure

angler. It is not the greatest fighting fish in the world but it is abundant and accommodating. Be warned, however, the gypsy-like big, specimen bream is not that simple to catch.

LATE SUMMER: THE EEL

The eel is loved by a few and loathed by many. But this ought not to come as a surprise because most anglers' experience of the eel is based on the mini-mayhem created when tiny bootlace eels take the bait intended for other species and then knit-one-slime-one until the line is tangled into a horrid mess. Bigger eels, anything over 0.9 kg (2 lb), are an altogether different proposition and are worthy of respect.

There are few waters in the British Isles which do not have a population of eels. The fish may stay in a given water for 12 years or more, so most waters hold some large specimens even though anglers may not be aware of it. In waters where the eels become trapped because of falling water-levels, large eels become enormous and fishing tackle for these larger ones must be strong, with a capital 'S'. The hooked eel must be hauled up and away from snags as quickly as possible; a fish that is allowed to back away from the angler in its corkscrewing, sinuous manner is almost certain to be lost. This is because the eel lodges itself under rocks or roots or simply wraps its body round a snag. In these circumstances there is no point in being under-rodded, under-lined or at any other kind of disadvantage.

Lobworms are the most commonly used baits but on the tidal Trent eels have taken to boilies, of any flavour, with enthusiasm. The trouble with worms and boilies is that they are not selective and practically invite a confrontation with the smaller nuisance fish. A freshly killed roach, bleak or gudgeon is much the best bait to tempt the larger eels and the trick with these baits is to pierce the fish's swim-bladder so that it both rests on the bottom and also exudes traces of blood. Eels hunt by scent, in the way sharks can, detecting minute traces of blood at a distance.

The tackle for presenting the deadbait consists of a stepped-up carp rod, a fixed-spool reel loaded with 4.5–5.5 kg (10–12 lb) b.s. line, a light swimfeeder, a swivel and a flat-forged Size 2 carp hook. The technique is to use a baiting needle to thread the line through the bait from tail to head, then the hook is tied on and pulled back so that the point is just outside the corner of the mouth. A non-toxic swan-shot is placed on the line at the point where it enters the tail to prevent the eel from blowing the bait up the line as it attempts to eject it. The small swimfeeder is placed about 0.46 m (18 in) above the bait and is stopped from running down to the bait by a swivel. Dried ox blood, obtainable as fertiliser from garden centres, is packed into the swimfeeder. (Fig. 28)

When it comes, the take is usually felt by a few tugs at the bait, followed by a run. This run must not be impeded. The eel will stop for a moment or two and then begin with a second run, when a strike and instant bowed-rod pressure should be made. The fish must be kept on the move by maintained pressure and if it can be slithered up the bank so much the better.

Eels are nocturnal but I have had very exciting daylight sessions with them, particularly when thunderstorms have been building up. On one particular day dozens of big eels came to the net and it became quite impossible to take any other species. At one time almost every eel that was caught was killed but this is no longer the case. Most anglers return them, recognising that whether we love or loathe them they have their place in the natural scheme of things and should be treated with respect.

AUTUMN: THE BOLD AND PREDATORY PERCH

More than any other fish, the perch is responsible for the life-long pursuit, perhaps bordering on addiction, which fishing becomes for many people. This fish's bold stripes and flared vermilion fins, its pugnacity, fix a sense of wonder in the hearts and minds of small boys everywhere. The sharp spine at the front of its two dorsal fins and the sharp edges of the gill covers give the clumsy youngster good reason for an enthusiasm which he may never lose. A perch of any size looks exactly what it is: bold, boisterous and predatory. There are large shoals of small and medium-sized perch in most waters of the British Isles and they grow large on a diet of cyclops, mayfly larvae and small fish of any kind including their own offspring.

The appearance of the perch is its main commendation. Its tail is small compared, say, with that of the carp or pike, and its fight is usually a short-lived affair. The fun is in the chase and in the admiring of the perch's bristling good looks, rather like an old-stager which at last has been hooked.

Perch may be taken in many ways including fly-fishing but the better specimens usually fall to a fish bait, or lures that simulate fish. Worms, too, have their place in the perch fisher's armoury and many specimens are taken on the maggot. These accidental catches illustrate the readiness of the perch to dart in with dorsal erect and mix with (or feed upon) any shoals of gudgeon or other baitfish working over the angler's groundbait.

Cloudbaiting techniques are used to encourage small fish to feed in a concentrated area and so attract the bigger specimen perch. Sooner or later these predators move in to harry and feed on the small species. This is the time to use scaled-down livebaiting tackle to present a lip-hooked gudgeon or minnow on a single hook in Size 8 or 10, tied

FIG 28 DEADBAIT LEDGER FOR EELS

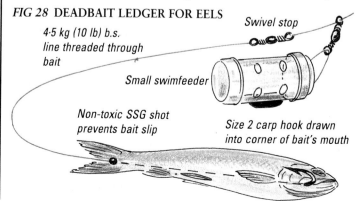

4·5 kg (10 lb) b.s. line threaded through bait

Swivel stop

Small swimfeeder

Non-toxic SSG shot prevents bait slip

Size 2 carp hook drawn into corner of bait's mouth

A

to monofilament line of 1.3 or 1.8 kg (3 or 4 lb) b.s. On stillwaters it is quite possible to present the baitfish beneath a small float with the bait being kept at the correct depth by a non-toxic swan-shot set about 30.5 cm (12 in) above the hook. Often, though, there is a pronounced surface drift which may move the bait away from the groundbaited area and in these circumstances it is best to use a paternoster rig, where the weight is placed at the end of the line. The hook-link is fished at right-angles to the main line by means of a three-way swivel. A paternoster is particularly useful for prospecting small, clear patches among dense areas of lilies. (Fig. 29)

The water in such gaps is often gin-clear and it is possible to watch the perch as it moves in to the attack but then, like a school-playground bully fearing a punch on the nose, backs off for a few seconds. Finally, however, it cannot resist the temptation of the little prey-fish, takes it, and down goes the float. There are times when a jack pike is in residence in these gaps and it is for this reason that I use an Avon-style rod for this branch of perch fishing. The rod may be a little too powerful for perch but will cope properly with a lively pike of 2.2 kg (5 lb).

In September and October the perch often become preoccupied with feeding on dense shoals of fry from the May or June spawning. When this happens the perch gather and drive in as a shoal. In the melee there are many

A A very sizeable eel from a fenland drain. Allen Edwards fishes the Great Ouse Relief Channel at Downham Market. Catches of prime eels can be made in the rivers and channels that drain the agricultural lands of the eastern counties and south Midlands.

B Prime indigenous predators of the British Isles, both pike and perch are in any water for a reason, if only to regulate the balance that nature has set. Our other major predator must be the brown trout. Old, lone male trout exist wholly on fish, including their own species.

B

casualties among the panicking fry and the perch pick them up from the bottom where they lie stunned or dead. When I see them I use a child's fishing-net to scoop out a supply of this handy bait from the margins; fished singly, hard on the bottom, they have accounted for many fine perch.

Locating the perch is the greatest problem on large waters. Mature gravelpits, for example, are perfect waters for the species but a lot of fishing time may be wasted in an area which, for reasons which may not be obvious, is devoid of perch. In these circumstances it is best to locate the fish by roving, spinning-rod in hand. Ideal tackle for this operation is a light 1.8 m (6 ft) spinning-rod with a fixed-spool reel loaded with 2.2 kg (5 lb) b.s. line. Small swivels and blade spinners complete the rig and with it every corner and every sand and gravel bar should be worked over.

The perch will respond to a steadier retrieve than the pike does and an even pace is an advantage. It is best to stand well back from the water's edge and care should be taken as the lure approaches the bank, where the perch will often be seen darting at the rear of the lure, making abortive and tentative attacks. Light spinning for perch is great fun.

Fly-fishing for perch comes into the same category as light spinning. Many fine specimen perch are caught from reservoirs by this style, often to the disgust of the game-fisherman who has paid good money in order to catch trout. The perch will take nymphs fished in a sink-and-draw fashion but they also respond to any of the fish-simulating lures.

The perch, then, is a fine sporting fish. Easy to catch as a youngster but difficult as a mature fish. A big perch is a real prize and looks, as I said earlier, bold, boisterous and predatory.

AUTUMN: BARBEL

Strength, fitness, tenacity and fun are the words which come to mind when the barbel season begins. The fish thrives in the strongest of flows and is to be found in the Yorkshire Derwent, Nidd, Wharfe and Swale. It is also present in the Trent, Severn, Nene, Bristol Avon, Hampshire Avon, Dorset Stour, Kennet and the Thames, as well as being found in their tributary streams. Barbel move in shoals feeding and browsing on the bottom and it is this habit which dictates the most popular fishing style for this powerful species.

THE OLD GROUNDBAITING RITUAL

In the old days it was considered necessary to prebait with a mixture of heavy crumb, bran and, most importantly, as many lobworms as could be obtained. This ritualistic procedure was followed through over several days so that the angler could begin to fish in the sure and certain knowledge that the barbel would be awaiting the baited hook. The trouble was that the barbel did not always oblige or, more likely, that the angler failed to put his hookbait in the baited swim. For the modern angler, swimfeeders have changed all this. The feeder, known to many anglers as the 'plastic pig' because of the speed with which it gobbles up the groundbait, ensures that a constant supply of bait is trickled downstream and round the hookbait. Sensing it, the barbel move upstream to meet this obliging food supply and sooner or later come in contact with the angler's hookbait.

The barbel's diet is catholic. Worms, sausage, luncheon meat, cheese, maggots, casters, hempseed will tempt the barbel and I have taken them from the Trent on tinned sweetcorn, but choice of bait determines the selection of swimfeeder. When using small baits such as maggots it is best to use the blockend feeder. An open-end feeder is more suitable for presenting stiff, cereal-based groundbait and in both cases I fix the feeder about 0.46 m (18 in) above the hook. A short link of lower breaking-strain line than that on the reel is used to connect the feeder to a swivel. The reel line is passed through this and is prevented from moving down to the hook by another swivel. In the event of snagging on the river-bed only the feeder and link line are lost. (Figs 30, 31, p. 42)

Correct hook selection is important for barbel fishing.

Fig 29 There is nothing like a simple paternoster rig to hold a small livebait over an area which has been groundbaited. Perch often lurk in lilybeds and the paternoster will hold the bait in the clear patches among the lilies in just the right way to induce perch to come out, inspect it and then take the offering.

FIG 29 LIVEBAIT RIGS FOR PERCH

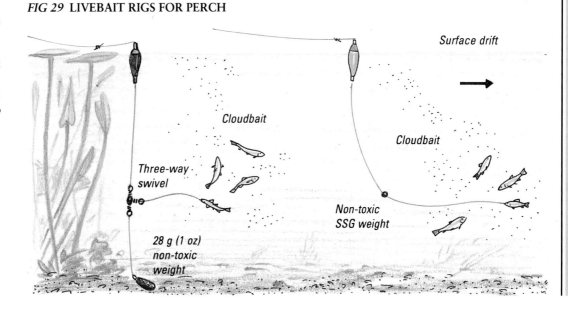

Surface drift

Cloudbait

Cloudbait

Three-way swivel

Non-toxic SSG weight

28 g (1 oz) non-toxic weight

The fighting power of this species is tremendous and they will soon straighten out all but the strongest of hooks. My choice is for flat-forged 'in-line' straight-eyed hooks, which can be bought with eyes that are no longer than a spade-end hook, size for size, and when tied directly to the reel line they will not let the angler down. The hook size should be tailored to the size of bait. A good-sized bait of sausage needs a hook of around No. 2; a single caster might be fished on a Size 16. Breadflake and chunks of cheese will call for an 8 or 10 and in each instance it is important to sharpen the point before fishing.

To cast a heavy swimfeeder into strong-flowing water and, more importantly, to stand any chance of hooking and landing the hard-fighting barbel, demands that the correct choice of rod must be made. A 3.4 m (11 ft 6 in) carbon-fibre rod is ideal and this should incorporate a quivertip. The outfit is completed by a fixed-spool reel

BARBEL
Barbus barbus
This is a fish of running water with a long, slender but powerful body. It possesses four barbules, two protruding from the tip of the upper lip and one from each corner of the leathery mouth.

The snout has a drooping shape indicating that the barbel spends much of its time rooting about on the river-bed among weeds and stones for the aquatic larvae, weeds and worms that form its diet. The presence of barbel in any water is an indication of the degree of purity of that venue, the species not being able to withstand polluted surroundings. Barbel have been introduced to a number of rivers in England where they did not occur naturally, with a concentration in the Thames Valley, southern chalkstreams, Yorkshire rivers and the Severn.

Bait: Bread, cheese, worms, grubs and tinned meats.

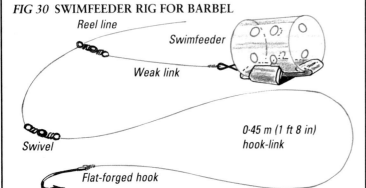

Pharyngeal teeth of the barbel

FIG 30 SWIMFEEDER RIG FOR BARBEL

Reel line
Swimfeeder
Weak link
0.45 m (1 ft 8 in) hook-link
Swivel
Flat-forged hook

FIG 31 TYPICAL LEDGER TERMINAL RIGS

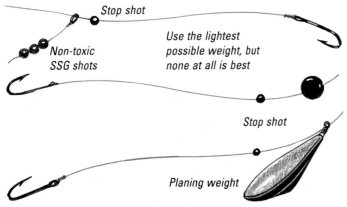

Stop shot
Non-toxic SSG shots
Use the lightest possible weight, but none at all is best
Stop shot
Planing weight

SPINY LOACH
Cobitis taenia
This is not a common little fish. The spiny loach has no angling value other than to small boys who want it

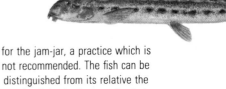

for the jam-jar, a practice which is not recommended. The fish can be distinguished from its relative the stone loach by the backward-pointing double spine below the eyes. There are six barbules.

STONE LOACH
Nemacheilus barbatulus
The stone loach is more widespread than the other species, the spiny loach (above). The stone loach prefers much cleaner water where it is found under stones and gravel in small streams and ponds. Look for the barbel-like snout that overhangs the fish's mouth. As with the spiny loach, this fish is of no interest to anglers.

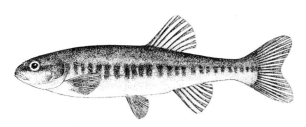

MINNOW
Phoxinus phoxinus
This is one of the small freshwater species used as a baitfish. It is silvery in colour, with occasional dots or black stripes. The minnow has an incomplete lateral line and averages about 7.6 cm (3 in) in length. The shoals feed in running water.

BLEAK
Alburnus alburnus
Easily recognised by its projecting, up-turned mouth, the bleak is used as a baitfish and also appears among the catches of match-anglers during contests on many major river systems. The silvery bleak can be caught on tiny hooks and single maggots, reaching 20 cm (8 in), with most specimens being very much smaller.
Bait: A maggot or tiny bread pellet fished near the surface.

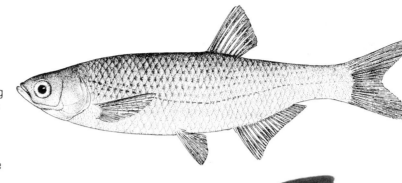

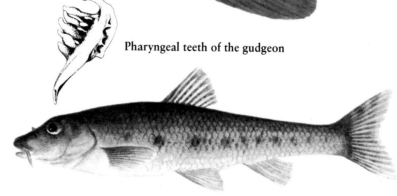

Pharyngeal teeth of the gudgeon

GUDGEON
Gobio gobio
A small, pugnacious fish showing certain external similarities in body shape to the barbel. The gudgeon has two barbules, one at each corner of the jaws, while the fish's body is almost straight from the mouth to the anal fin. The gudgeon prefers running water over gravel and sandy bottoms where it feeds on small animal life. It can withstand some pollution.
Bait: Maggots and small worms.

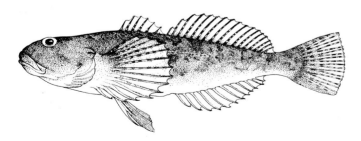

MILLER'S THUMB
Cottus gobio
This small fish possesses two dorsal fins, the first six to eight spines and the anterior dorsal has soft rays that are almost joined. This species has a broad, flat head with fewer than seven spines on the gill cover, or operculum. The miller's thumb is found on the gravelly runs in small streams.

loaded with monofilament of 2.2–2.7 kg (5–6 lb) b.s. but a centre-pin is necessary for long-trotting. The basic requirements for float-fishing for barbel are much the same as those for chub. A good Avon-style float capable of carrying sizeable non-toxic weights is required and you must ensure that the bait is well and truly down in the swim. Maggots and worms are easy to get down but breadflake, because of its buoyancy, should be fished well over-depth and held back a little to make sure of correct bait presentation to the bottom-feeding barbel.

KEEP CALM – DON'T PANIC!

Most anglers panic when a big fish is hooked. This is quite natural. The angler may have been at the waterside for a considerable time, there may have been blank sessions before. There may have been sown the seeds of self-doubt by the angler's inability to produce a genuine 'I caught a monster' story. Then, when the big fish is finally on, the panic sets in. This, however, is the time for calmness and self-discipline. It makes sense to remember that the fishing rod is in fact a spring and that providing it is kept at an angle of slightly less than 90 deg. it will absorb the force of the plunges of most species.

The most dangerous part of the whole operation comes when the fish sees the net. This should always be sunk into the water well in advance and it is absolutely vital that the fish should be brought to the net and that the net should not be poked at the fish. More fish have been lost at this stage than at any other as the fish is usually and quite simply knocked off the hook. Guide the fish over the rim of the submerged net and make a smooth lift to trap it. Remove fish and net from the water, using both hands if necessary. Once the fish has been landed it should be treated with care. Always have a wet cloth to moisten your hands and on which to lay the fish. If the fish is to be photographed and weighed do it quickly and then return it with care to its natural habitat to fight and give sport another day.

Once located, quite good bags of barbel may be made but it is a mistake to cram them into a keepnet. The spined ray of the barbel's dorsal fin often becomes entangled in the mesh, causing unnecessary discomfort and possible injury to the fish. A barbel which bites boldly and which always fights to the limit of its endurance cannot stand the additional stress of being cooped up in a net for long periods. It is better by far to unhook the fish, then to nurse it on an even keel until it is ready to swim away to fight another day. Tenacious, strong and fighting fit, barbel live in much the most attractive areas for the pleasure angler. To catch them is fun.

AUTUMN: ZANDER

Like the wels, the zander is not native to the British Isles. This species was introduced to the Great Ouse Relief Channel at Downham Market in 1963. From there it spread into the Great Ouse itself, the Old Bedford River, the Delph and the Cut-off Channel. The species is now

A

A This barbel, the first fish of the 1989 season, was a lucky catch. Mike Prichard was fishing seriously for a carp from a Trent hotspot! **B** Barbel from the River Severn, below Arley. They form a massive population in the river and result from a 'seeding' by an angling newspaper in the early 1950s. **C** The zander feeds best in dull, turbid water

B

firmly established across the whole of Fenland. Their colonisation continues. In 1988 small zander were taken from the screens in the inlet to a power station on the Tidal Trent. The fish is a rough, tough predatory survivor and is destined to spread right across the country. To say that this is regarded by many as a mixed blessing is to understate the case. In the first full flush of a population explosion the zander soon creates havoc among the fry and immature second and third year stages of a fishery's stocks of fodder fish which upsets the matchfishermen since they have been accustomed to winning competitions by building up large weights of small fish.

Following the introduction of zander the main concern of the pleasure angler was the effect which it might have on one native species of predator, the pike, but time has shown that this concern was misplaced. The pike haunt the margins in a solitary way, except at spawning time. On the other hand the zander move in packs in open water, so the element of competition between them and the pike is reduced.

The fish takes well in coloured water and dull light conditions and is definitely at its most active in the twilight. Zander do not grow to the same heavy weight as the pike and it is an advantage to scale the tackle down accordingly. This is because the zander is quick to eject a bait if it detects tension on the line so lighter running-time and terminal rigs produce more profitable runs. A good combination is a soft-actioned rod with a test curve of 0.7 kg (1½ lb), a fixed-spool reel loaded with 2.7 kg (6 lb) b.s. line and the terminal tackle which is based on the use of very fine multi-strand steel wire to combat the needle-sharp teeth of the fish. I have known zander to be caught on both worms and maggots and they have also fallen to spinners but in general the bait should be a fish of some kind. Fishbaits, live or dead, are a matter of conscience for the angler but deadbaits are as good as live ones in attracting the feeding zander.

This predator will feed at all levels in the water and it is

conditions. It takes live and deadbaits, fished at all depths, but is wary of line drag and quickly drops a bait if it feels any resistance to its attack. Small hooks are vital. Zander can be found in Norfolk waters, into which they were introduced in 1963 and have rapidly spread to many East Anglian rivers and fenland drainage systems.

a mistake to concentrate on one method of angling. An effective and simple style is the ledgered deadbait slightly off the bottom. The bait, which should be slit open so that it exudes blood and scent, is injected with air or lifted off the bottom by the use of a small polystyrene ball; 2.7 kg (6 lb) running line is first taken through the eye of an Arlesey bomb and stopped with a swivel. The bomb's size is chosen to suit water-flow conditions so that when the rod is lifted the bait and bomb will move a short way downstream. It is illegal, however, to use a lead weight of less than 28 g (1 oz). A 30.5 cm (12 in) long trace of monofilament is then joined to the swivel and then threaded through the buoyant ball to another swivel. To this is attached the fine-wire trace on to which two Size 12 or 8 treble hooks are placed 76 mm (3 in) apart. The deadbait is hooked through the lips and into the wrist of the tail, with the bait being kept straight. Some anglers choose to reverse the position of the hooks but I believe that it does not matter a great deal since the zander is usually moving quickly. The fish is in competition with fellow-members of the pack and the take is very much a smash-and-grab business so there is little time for the zander to inspect the bait. Even though the fish is in a rush it will drop the bait instantly if it becomes aware of drag. For this reason I prefer to sink the rod-tip well into the water and to use a butt indicator, striking at the first sign of a bite. (Figs 32, 35, p. 46)

There are many variations on the terminal rig. Float-fished livebait will take its share of zander; link-ledgering with live or freshly killed baits hard on the bottom are effective. Very slow twitch-retrieving along the bottom catches zander too. Baits in the 57–113 g (2–4 oz) size are ideal and should be as fresh as possible. (Figs 33, 34, p. 46)

The British list of freshwater fishes is short when compared with that of many other countries. The zander, in the short term, creates problems; in the long run it is my belief that this fine fish is welcome to our waters and that old mother nature will keep it in check.

EUROPEAN CATFISH OR WELS

In October 1880 70 'cats' were released into the lakes in Woburn Park, Bedfordshire, the home of the Duke of Bedford. These fish thrived and in 1951 when the fish stocks were thinned out, fish in excess of 27.2 kg (60 lb) were killed, with one weighing over 31.7 kg (70 lb). Since that time the fish has been introduced, illegally for the most part, into about two-dozen good fishing waters, mainly sited in the Bedfordshire/Buckinghamshire area, but there are catfish to be found in Shropshire too.

The fish is a predator and can be caught on small live and dead fish, as well as lobworms and freshwater mussels. The fishing can be dour but the truly repulsive catfish becomes active in periods of high water temperature. The species has two long feelers on the upper jaw, four short ones under the lower jaw, small eyes, a single very small dorsal fin and a very long anal fin. There is a growing band of specialist anglers interested in catching the catfish and there is much lobbying to persuade the authorities to extend its range. But remember – a Danube specimen is recorded as having reached the alarming weight of some 317 kg (700 lb)!

AUTUMN: THE GUDGEON, RUFFE AND BLEAK

In the eyes of the non-angler the pleasure angler is a fool, dozing the hours away beneath a green brolly with mind, and sometimes eyes, closed to the harsh necessities of life. Non-anglers imagine that the thought processes grind to a halt once the waterside is reached but they are wrong. The pleasure angler is never rendered insensible by his sport. Indeed, many anglers put more concentration into their fishing than they do while earning a living. The hours flash by as the angler asks himself countless questions, ranging through bait presentation, weather conditions, water flow, the strength of tackle, anything that affects his prospects for sport. Some anglers ask and answer these questions by instinct and are called lucky by the envious

ZANDER
Stizostedion lucioperca

A predatory species that came to British freshwaters over 100 years ago as an introduction from Eastern Europe. The zander has some of the appearance of both the pike and the perch, some anglers referring to it by the species couplet pike-perch but the fish is not related to either and is a separate species. The first dorsal fin is composed of sharp spines with the second formed of soft rays. Some specimens exhibit broad, dark vertical bars along the flanks. The species grows to 11.4 kg (25 lb) weights in Europe, but a fish of 4.5 kg (10 lb) is good for the East Anglian waters throughout which it is spreading.

Bait: Zander take live or deadbaits that are worked to attract the predator. On the Continent, small artificial spinning lures are used by fishermen with great success.

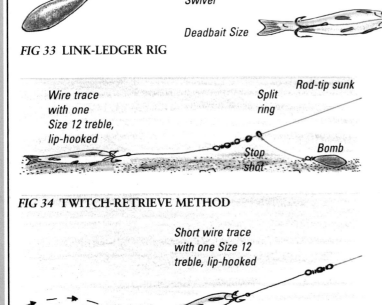

FIG 32 BUOYANT LEDGER RIG FOR ZANDER

Bomb
Swivel
Monofilament
Polystyrene ball
Wire trace
Deadbait Size

FIG 33 LINK-LEDGER RIG

Wire trace with one Size 12 treble, lip-hooked
Split ring
Rod-tip sunk
Stop shot
Bomb

FIG 34 TWITCH-RETRIEVE METHOD

Short wire trace with one Size 12 treble, lip-hooked

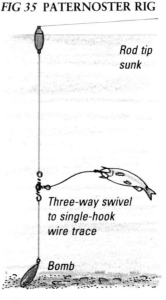

FIG 35 PATERNOSTER RIG

Rod tip sunk
Three-way swivel to single-hook wire trace
Bomb

Since the zander is not wholly a bottom-feeder any rig should be capable of fishing the bait off the bottom. *Fig 32* This is a buoyant rig for zander, the polystyrene ball acting to keep the deadbait just off the bottom. *Fig 33* With this rig an Arlesey bomb is free to slide on the reel line, while the ledgered bait is mounted on a wire trace. *Fig 34* Often, zander will be enticed to take if the bait is twitched, so a direct contact is kept by use of a short wire trace and a lip-hooked bait. *Fig 35* The classical float-paternoster again, ideal for mid-water roving zander.

46

RUFFE OR POPE
Gymnocephalus cernua
This small fish can easily be distinguished from the much bigger perch by the presence of two dorsal fins which are virtually joined together. The spiny little ruffe, rarely sought by anglers, is considered a specimen at 57 or 85 g (2 or 3 oz). It shoals in deepish water that is coloured or shaded from direct light.
Bait: Those who want to catch the ruffe should use small worms, fish fry and insect larvae.

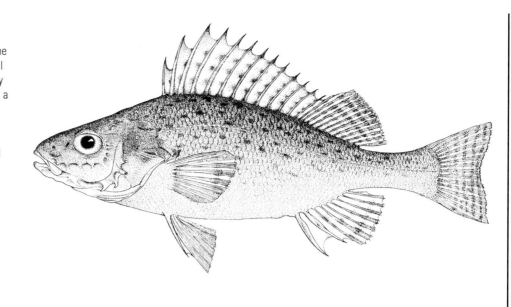

PERCH
Perca fluvialitis
This is a striking predatory species possessing two separated dorsal fins, the first bearing 14 stiff spines and the second a few short spines followed by 14 soft rays. There are often one or two black spots on the base of the first dorsal. Perch are probably found in every water in the British Isles, with a preference for the slow-running stretches of rivers and streams where there is cover from over-hanging trees and banks. The species adopts a more brilliant coloration for the spawning period. The species does not reach massive weights, a fish of 1.8 kg (4 lb) being regarded as a specimen.
Bait: The perch will take almost anything edible that the angler, or nature, offers – fish fry, insects, freshwater molluscs, worms, maggots and grubs, and bread. This fish will also rise to an artificial fly and many forms of twinkling spinning lures.

majority. Others build up a computer-bank of experience and are happy to take their modest share of fish. For the pleasure angler, fishing means constant thought and subsequent action, but there is a group of little fishes whose capture is of little significance so the mind may wander at will; they are the gudgeon, ruffe and bleak.

In Victorian and Edwardian times the gudgeon was an excuse for family parties to take their punts on the Thames. Careful groundbaiting and the raking of the bottom by the boatman assured a steady feeding shoal and fishing was a pleasure. Times have changed, but the gudgeon still abound and are best taken by tripping maggots or a small redworm along the bottom of a gravel-bedded swim. Tackle should be scaled right down with the float so weighted that just the tip is above the water. But it still makes sense to muddy the water and a simple method of creating this is to wade about in the shallows stirring up the silt and gravel by shuffling the feet.

In these circumstances the angler's mind can wander to other aspects, perhaps of trouble and concern to the sport. What, for example, about problems generated by anglers themselves? It is reckoned that more than four million people participate in angling and of these, 50 per cent are below the age of 25. Today's anglers have been raised in a throwaway age and this, in itself, creates problems.

LOST WATERS

Waters are lost to fishing because anglers open and discard luncheon-meat, corned beef and sweetcorn tins and leave them on the bank. Their sharp edges cause injuries to cattle and the farmer can hardly be blamed for stopping the anglers using his land. The same may be said about plastic bags, which are a constant and possible lethal hazard to cattle and should never be left behind on the bank, although the presence of fertilizer sacks suggests that farming people, in their turn, add to the problem.

Some anglers forget that the cover of vegetation at the front of a pitch is a good rather than a bad thing. It is a mistake to hack about with landing-net handle or scythe to clear the ground completely. But there are more serious pollution problems than the litter left and damage caused by too many unthinking fishermen.

The angler may have difficulty in finding a clear patch of gravel from which to fish. He may have to contend with a thick carpet of blanketweed which prospers to the detriment of the fish, because of the over-enrichment of the water. Quite literally, the weed is fertilized by the run-off of nitrogenous fertilizers applied to the land by farmers. Its growth is also boosted by sewage effluents from inefficient treatment works. The odd gudgeon may be missed while it occurs to the angler that in 1988 742 sewage works broke the law by pumping illegal discharges into Britain's waterways. In some areas, and the South West is a good example, rivers are in decline because of a devastating combination of the effects of farming practices and poor sewage treatment. Thirty per cent of the sewage treatment plants set among the lush farmlands of the South West Water Authority's area were not comply-ing with the law in 1988. Fish will be missed, too, while the angler considers that too many discharge consent conditions are set at the capability of the treatment works and not to the requirements of the receiving stream.

No fish can survive the fearful effects of pollution imposed upon the environment by the farm industry. In 1977, pollution by farmers was rare, it is now, sadly, common. The pollutants are slurry and silage, the latter being used as foodstuff for livestock. Silage is made from grass, cut and stored when fresh and green, and it produces a strong liquid. Stored properly, this causes no problems but too few farmers cover their clamps to exclude rainwater or to drain the liquid into sealed tanks for disposal. The effects of a silage pollution have to be seen to be believed. A typical 400-tonne silage clamp produces the same pollution load as one day's untreated sewage from a town of 150,000 people. Even small quantities of liquid silage kills the fish.

Slurry is the manure of pigs and cattle and has become a problem because of the growing practice of keeping animals under cover and together. Farmers are adept at placing feed in front of rows of penned animals; but in too many cases they are not so clever at dealing with what comes out at the other end of their livestock. On some farms, slurry is stored in vast quantities. In one instance a farmer kept 40,000 gallons behind a wall some 29 km (18 miles) up from the mouth of the River Axe, in Devon. The slurry weakened the foundations of the wall and it finally collapsed to send the whole stinking mass on a sinister slither down a slope and into the river. The Axe was very low and it took this evil plug of pollution three days to kill everything in its path to the estuary. And so, in those waters in which fish can survive, and to return to the gudgeon, here is a fish which is often sought for bait and can hardly be bettered as a perch and chub bait.

GREEDY LITTLE RUFFE

Another small species which might feature in the often mixed bag of the pleasure angler is the ruffe. This is a greedy little fish the appearance of which in the swim is dreaded by some anglers because they know that its capture and removal from the swim will not be taken as a warning to other ruffe. Catch one and you will probably catch dozens. The ruffe shares the double dorsal fin characteristic with the perch. In coloration it is a pale ghost of the larger, more sought-after species but does not have its bold stripes. The ruffe differs from every other species in the colour of its eyes, which are violet. Care should be taken when handling this fish as the edges of the gill cover are sharp.

The ruffe falls easily to the presentation of maggot, casters or small worms. The fishing is easy, with bites impossible to miss. There is little skill needed or pressure felt by the angler in this kind of fishing and the thinking fisherman has plenty of time to consider the national situation of the over-abstraction of water from our rivers, thus compounding some of the pollution problems. The angler may also consider the ill-effects which the growth of fishing-farming is having. A clear example of this is the West Beck in Yorkshire. This is a beautiful chalkstream, but within the space of a few miles it is reduced from a Class 1 water, the home of mayfly and trout, to a Class 2 water, the home of midges and coarse fish. And it is due to the insidious polluting effect of fish-farm effluents.

There are those who consider that a decline in the quality of the fishing on the Hampshire Avon is attributable to abstraction. Time will tell, as the National Rivers Authority begins the task of 'policing' the 'burglar-style' activities of those who take good-quality water from the environment, use it to make profit, then return it to the watercourses. Even the 'unmissable' bite from the greedy little ruffe may well be missed as the significance of the problem of abstraction sinks into the angler's mind.

More anglers are appearing on the scene with each successive season. In May 1989 the Angling Foundation published the results of an independent survey undertaken on their behalf. The main findings from this showed that the angling population had shown a 3.5 per cent increase since 1986 and that 8.2 per cent of the total population of Great Britain fished for pleasure. Statistically, within the bounds of errors with such surveys, it is possible to claim that four million people go fishing. Of these, three-quarters are below the age of 35. This increase in anglers has to be set against the prospect of a decline in the quality of our rivers but, fortunately, an increase in the availability and quality of our stillwaters. Not one angler can afford to be complacent about the future of his sport.

No discussion of the pleasure angler's small-fish quarry would be complete without a mention of the bleak. This silvery little fish is regarded by many as an out-and-out pest. It swarms to attack the maggot, caster, flake or paste intended for the roach, chub and rudd. There are times, however, when the catching of a bleak assumes an importance not to be compared with its size. For example, there can hardly be a better fish for use as a live or deadbait. The competition angler, too, may bless the bleak which he sees topping in large numbers on a rapidly rising river.

To catch bleak intentionally means that one's tackle must be scaled right down to the finest of lines, the most sensitive float and the smallest of hooks. These fish are easily gathered into a surface-feeding shoal by the use of cloud-groundbait, casters and maggots. On a near-fishless day there can be a kind of repetitive pleasure in building up a catch of these little fish.

If any fish can be said to symbolise the ever-growing army of pleasure anglers it is the bleak. It is restless and sometimes infuriating; it is mobile and constantly trying to get into what it believes is the action. Taken singly the bleak has a character and an attractiveness of its own.

When raised in a sustained clamour the voices of four million very concerned anglers must be heard. The shouts must be directed at those who influence the environment by pollution and ill-considered abstraction. If the anglers will not do this, then so far as this country's rivers go he must face the fact that not for long will he be able to claim 'Angling is a pleasure!' And the sport will have died.

B

A A fish found in relatively few waters. This wels, or European catfish, took the scales down past 9 kg (20 lb) when it was caught at Jont's Point, Leighton Buzzard, Bedfordshire.
B The laid-back angler, his stall is set out, his tactics thought about and decided upon.

A

| | | | Perch | | Pike | |

TROUT **SALMON** **PARR** **Minnow** **Stickleback** **Miller's Thumb**

GRAYLING

BARBEL **CHUB** **Dace** **Gudgeon** **Bleak**

Roach

Every river has a defined gradient from source to the sea. The illustration depicts a classic highland, snow-fed river and its steep gradient. In broad terms almost all rivers of the British Isles can be divided into five zones: trout, grayling, barbel, bream and tidal or estuary. The zones cannot be regarded as clearly defined areas for there will always be overlaps, often many miles in length, where zones merge. Fish respond to basic, life-supporting conditions appropriate to their species.

TROUT ZONE

GRAYLING ZONE (Minnow zone)

BARBEL ZONE (Chub zone)

Increase in bank and riverbed vegetation

BOTTOM-SPAWNING FISH

OXYGEN CONTENT OF WATER

| **Extremely high to very high** | **Very high** | **High in surface waters, decreasing with depth – especially during warm weather** |

AVERAGE TEMPERATURE DURING SUMMER

| **Rarely above 10°C (50°F)** | **Rarely above 15°C (59°F)** | **Frequently above 15°C (59°F)** |

Perch   Pike

Salmon,   Sea Trout,   Eels migrate to headwaters of river

Roach

BREAM

Tench   Carp   Rudd   Silver Bream

Zander   Ruffe

Flounder, Smelts, Shads, Grey Mullet, Bass

The oxygen content and temperature of the water, variety and type of vegetation, depth and speed of current all have a bearing on the species in residence. The chart tells an outline story of a river. To learn where to fish for specific species one must refer to the coloured bands at the top of the illustration.

Select a fish, then move vertically down to the lower colour bands for information about the river zoning, vegetation on riverbed and bankside, spawning behaviour, oxygen availability and average temperatures.

There must always be an overlap of zones, but a knowledge of the broad rules governing fish survival in the various conditions that a running water undergoes will be invaluable to the angler.

BREAM ZONE

TIDAL ZONE and ESTUARY

FISH SPAWNING ON VEGETATION

Sufficient oxygen in surface waters, frequently insufficient to support fish life in bottom layers of deepest parts

Frequently up to 20°C (68°F) and higher

Frequently above 20°C (68°F)

MATCHFISHING TO WIN

I do not consider myself to be another Ivan Marks or a Billy Lane, they were products of a different and certainly a much better era so far as the sport of angling is concerned. If Billy Lane could return from the grave and fish the way he always used to he would not win many matches until he had adapted to the many changes in technique and method which have taken place since his heyday.

Ivan Marks, of course, is still with us and still a masterly match angler. In Sweden in 1988 he stepped back in time to lead my Barnsley team to victory in the DFDS Seaways Challenge final. He did it with a superb display of long-range bream fishing, using the tactics and knowledge he had acquired decades before.

When Ivan Marks and Billy Lane were at the peak of their powers all the competitors in virtually every match had the chance to make big weights. Contests were fewer but much better then, especially in the Fenlands. If the angler did not take a big weight, usually of bream, he did not win — it was as simple as that. Ivan and Billy were adept at drawing the bream to their swim, making them feed, keeping them feeding longer than anyone else and then catching most of them. One felt that these two giants could think like bream, or whatever other species they were after. These two master fishermen were attackers; plunderers of fish shoals the presence of which were taken for granted. The top anglers of that decade were fish-catching machines.

Billy Lane reached the pinnacle of matchfishing fame

Master matchman and world-beater Tom Pickering at work with the pole on the River Trent at Stoke Bardolph.

by preaching and practising the use of enough weight to achieve perfect control of his tackle in any given situation. With the fish invariably present in numbers, and willing to have the feed piled in on them, that was virtually all he needed to do. But it is very different now, for the matchman of today has to live with the consequences of what was happening, undetected, when earlier generations were enjoying their matchfishing bonanzas. While they were winning matches our rural waterways were being poisoned with agricultural chemicals, and in so doing impairing the abilities of fish to reproduce in their former numbers. Cyprinid populations suddenly crashed on every fishery where Marks and Lane, and many others, earned their reputations.

For a few brief years the more urban rivers were improving as rural waters declined. Clean-up campaigns by industrial and sewage plants to eradicate pollution worked wonders for such rivers as the Trent and we enjoyed a decade of plenty which deflected our attention from what was happening in the Fens. Now all that has gone into reverse due to a lack of investment and the political will to fight pollution. The authorities now tell us that they are making the investment which will safeguard our future. Maybe, but today's matchman has to live with current reality.

Hopefully, one day someone will say that my approach to matchfishing is no longer relevant; that it *is* possible to fish heavier and to attack more. If he or she is correct it will signal the fact that our waterways are much better than they are today. Pollution, in all its pernicious forms, will have been conquered – if it happens.

But the reader must not misunderstand these words: the picture I have painted is not one of total disaster. Of course, there are fewer fish and drawing the right peg has become far more important than it was in the past. We have had to lower our sights and use a different approach. The name of the game is now finesse: we are no longer attackers and plunderers of huge shoals of fish because they are no longer there in such profusion.

In our favour is the fact that we now have superb fishing tackle with which to perform; our carbon rods have taken us light-years forward in ten years; and reels, line and hooks have never been better. Reel failure is almost a thing of the past and we have deadly methods about which our angling fathers and grandfathers knew little or nothing – pole fishing and the swimfeeder to name just two methods that Ivan Marks barely knew about and in fact he did not mention the feeder at all, probably not realising that here was a method which, once perfected, would negate so much of his skill. This will be understood when we discuss bream fishing.

Stillwater fisheries and some canals have escaped the ravages of pollution, and even the waters which have been affected are still quite good fisheries, but have to be approached in a different way. While the match-weights are different, the main objectives are precisely the same as always – to catch more fish than anyone else and win! I go out to win every match I fish and I don't care whether I do it with 0.9 kg (2 lb), 9.0 kg (20 lb) or 18 kg (40 lb). It is very nice to catch a lot of fish, and we often do, but the most important thing for the matchman is the winning of fishing competitions.

When I enter a match my first rule is to decide in advance what weight is likely to win on the venue and then I set out to achieve it. Follow me through a typical Tom Pickering season and you'll see how it's done.

SUMMER TACTICS

For me, a new season always starts on the Stainforth and Keadby Canal. I am aware that all the readers of this encyclopedia will not be able to fish it but this venue introduces several methods which are relevant to many similar waters up and down the country. There is not enough space here to give comprehensive details about every single method, but I hope to cover as many different and effective styles as possible.

The 'S. and K.' is a real fisherman's water. We who fish it regularly do not expect big weights in matches but it is dependable, with 0.9 kg to 1.8 kg (2 to 4 lb) on every peg, and if you weigh-in 1.8 kg (4 lb) or more you are usually in contention. The three basic methods are waggler float, light ledgering and the pole, and sometimes we employ all three during the course of one match. I have caught a lot of fish here with what are possibly the newest methods in matchfishing. Certainly it employs the newest equipment, a 2.7 m (9 ft) 'wand' ledger rod, very slim and light, and usually equipped with two or three different quivertips, all

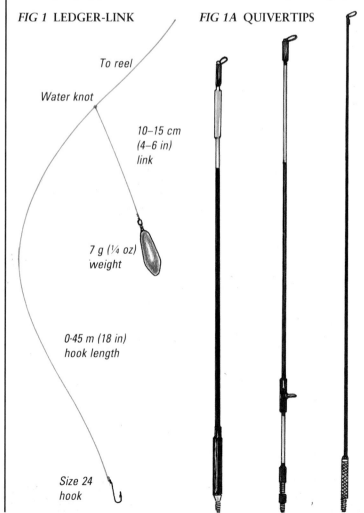

FIG 1 LEDGER-LINK   FIG 1A QUIVERTIPS

To reel

Water knot

10–15 cm
(4–6 in)
link

7 g (¼ oz)
weight

0·45 m (18 in)
hook length

Size 24
hook

of them extremely sensitive by previous traditional standards. (Figs 1, 1a)

I rig mine up with a 7 g (¼ oz) weight and, usually, a maggot on a Size 24 hook to 340 g (12 oz) line. The weight will be on a 10 to 15 cm (4 to 6 in) link with a hook length of about 46 cm (1 ft 6 in). The bait is cast to a ledge on the far bank to catch mostly small chub and roach, although we can expect skimmer bream and other species.

Many anglers think that this is a method for the slightly cooler days of autumn, but it also works on those summer days when the wind is a bit too strong for easy float-fishing. With the 'wand' ledger rod you can drop the bait in exactly the right place and dip the tip under to sink the line. Dunking the reel-spool in washing-up liquid helps to sink the line quickly, without dislodging the bomb from the far shelf. Then all you do is prop the rod low and to one side, out of the wind, and watch for the bites. It is amazing how those little chub whip the quivertip round! These tips are so sensitive that they will register the tiniest of bites, but the early chub bites tend to be both spectacular and unmissable.

Every few minutes, loose-feed a few maggots with a catapult and for a while you will catch quite a few fish. It is surprising how many small roach, as well as eels and perch, will be taken on the wand, fish which would never register a bite on stronger ledger tackle. The fine, soft tips were designed to register all manner of bites and I deal with them all the same way, striking at the first indication, be it a big pull or a tiny tremor. Only if I miss a couple of bites do I consider ignoring the first slight indication and wait for something more positive.

THE WAGGLER

Sometimes it is as easy, if not easier, to hit the small-fish bites on the ledger as it is on the float, though I prefer to use the waggler float if I can, at least for a while. On the narrower sections, which are about 15 m (50 ft) wide, I use a 3BB or 2AAA peacock-quill waggler with the fine insert in the tip. This float is weighted down so that only part of the insert is showing on the surface, and it will be cast to the far shelf, the same place as the ledger tackle. (Figs 2, 2a, p. 56)

Virtually all the weight the float takes is on the line, either side of the float, with very little down the line. If by plumbing the depth I find I have 0.9 m (3 ft) of water I will place a tiny No. 10 weight about 0.3 m (1 ft) from the hook. Any deeper and I will have a second No. 10 set at about half-depth, with the other still 0.3 m (1 ft) from the hook. Again, it is important to treat the line with washing-up liquid to help it sink. Immediately after the cast I let a little bow develop on the surface, and then without moving the float off-line chop the line under with a sharp sideways movement of the rod.

A lot of fish, especially chub, will be taken as the bait sinks slowly down along with the loose feed, although some bites will also come after it has reached bottom. The main reason for the float out-scoring the ledger is

Fig 1 Matchfishing is a specialised and hard-learned skill based on much sensitivity of fined-down rigs. See how the bait on the Size 24 hook can act naturally. *Fig 1A* The lightning speed of quivertips aids the matchman to an extent unknown not very long ago. In all matchfishing, speed and accuracy are total necessities.

Tom Pickering strikes powerfully into a chub while ledgering on the Trent.

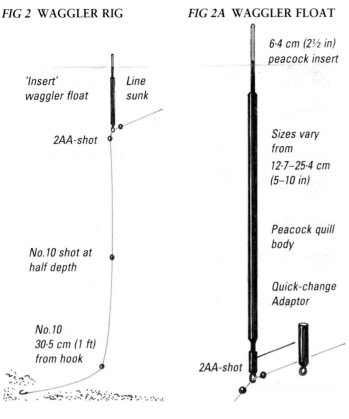

FIG 2 WAGGLER RIG

'Insert' waggler float
Line sunk

2AA-shot

No.10 shot at half depth

No.10 30·5 cm (1 ft) from hook

FIG 2A WAGGLER FLOAT

6·4 cm (2½ in) peacock insert

Sizes vary from 12·7–25·4 cm (5–10 in)

Peacock quill body

Quick-change Adaptor

2AA-shot

Figs 2, 2A One of the most sensitive float patterns, the waggler comes in many sizes. All are attached to the line by the bottom end only. Most are made from peacock quill.

Fig 3 Groundbait and fish the far shelf at first. Some will trickle down the slope to the foot of the shelf. Fish here when bites begin to drop off from the original target area.

FIG 3 FISHING THE FAR SHELF

Begin fishing on shelf

When fish stop feeding try fishing down the shelf

Groundbait area

Some feed falls here

Shelf

Loose maggots

Float fishing is the most used matchfishing method although in big rivers, where the feeder has proved a winning technique, ledgering has almost taken over.

that you can twitch the float slightly, causing the bait to lift and drop down. This small movement often provokes a bite, but when you try this with the ledger the bomb will be pulled out of position. You are also likely to hook rubbish.

When you sprinkle loose maggots on the far shelf some will drop short, into the deeper water at the bottom of the shelf. This is quite all right, for I have found that the fish will find them and come down from the shelf, and then the bites will slow down. When that happens I deepen the float to fish right at the bottom, which usually produces a few more fish. It is surprising how many roach and skimmer bream are congregated down there, and at times chub can be found in the same place.

When the bites stop coming from below the ledge, shorten off again and go back to the ledge. On this water, and on a great many others, never persist too long with a method which has stopped working. Keep switching around and work for your fish. This basic approach will be the same on wider sections of the canal, but I might need a bigger float and more weight. (Fig. 3)

Do not seek for variations of the waggler float method. It works on a variety of waters, from canals, ponds and lakes to drains and slow-to-medium-flowing rivers, but it is virtually always used in the same way. You need enough weight locking the float on the line to cast the required distance, and very little weight down the line. It is a method for catching fish on the drop at any depth.

The wagglers are a big family of floats, all attached bottom-end only, which range in weight-carrying capacity from a couple of No. 4s right up to three swan and more. But I do virtually all my waggler work with peacock-quill floats taking from 2AAA to 3AAA lead-substitute weights.

THE POLE

The third method which is vital on the S. and K. Canal is the pole, a style of fishing which can take thousands of words to describe. Here I can do little more than summarise why the pole is so deadly within a range of 15 m (50 ft), and give a few examples of the method in action.

The pole offers the angler a chance to fish with light tackle under close and perfect control. The bites are easy to hit, partly because the little floats offer very little resistance and partly because the end of the pole is directly above the float and a gentle lift is all it takes to set the hook. The pole fishes the float in exactly the same place every time, although you can go up to a metre (about 3 ft) farther out or in by adding or removing a section. Short poles can be rigged up with a length of line which allows a hooked fish to be swung directly to hand. With a longer pole you have to feed some of it behind you – usually using a roller – and take it apart ('unshipping') at the right length to either swing to hand or net your fish.

There are ingenious systems employing elastic, running through the tip sections of the pole, which act as a shock-absorber when you strike and play a fish. There are different grades of elastic to suit the sizes of fish you are expecting to catch and you have got it right if the fish you are catching are heavy enough to pull a bit of elastic out of the end of the pole. The stronger elastics are absolutely brilliant at controlling and playing out big fish. Even quite sizeable carp are in trouble against the stronger elastic but you see the system at its best, probably, when you hook a bream. The progressive power of the elastic will usually take the fight out of the bream on its first run, then the fish slows down, stops, and comes back to the angler's net, on its side and quite unresisting. Species such as carp and tench take a lot longer, many making ever-shorter runs before they are beaten.

Many anglers who took one look at the pole and decided they wanted nothing to do with the method are now dedicated converts. It grows on one, it's addictive, but the bottom line is that it is often *the* best way of catching the fish. The case for the pole is so overwhelming in the match-angling context that virtually every match-man now has at least one. Poles can cost several hundred pounds for good-quality carbon, with some reaching four figures, but as always in fishing, go for the best tackle you can afford. My advice is to aim for an 11 m (36 ft) carbon pole. Don't start with a glass pole, they are cheap but

Modern, ultra-lightweight poles, even 14 m (46 ft) long, can be held throughout an average match. Perfect balance is vital.

heavy, and you will end up buying a carbon in the long run. But let us get back to that canal!

The pole methods I use for the S. and K. Canal are fairly standard for a lot of waters. On all canals, drains, still-waters and even slow rivers one of the most effective pole methods is the slow-falling bait, just as described for the waggler on the canal. The big difference between pole and waggler, though, is that the waggler has to be reeled in and re-cast at regular intervals. With the pole you can just lift out and lay the line down again. It becomes an endless routine which puts the bait to the fish and keeps it where they are for vastly longer periods than can be achieved with the waggler. The equation is thus: More effective fishing time equals more bites, which equals more fish!

Within the limitations imposed by its length the pole is virtually unbeatable in many situations, though on the S. and K. it tends to be part of a varied approach. One rig I use has a small float taking three No. 8 shot, and a second float a bit heavier, taking three No. 6 shot. That is the overall capacity of the floats, anyway, but both are rigged with a No. 10 shot near the hook and an 8 above it. Whatever else is required to sink the float down on to the bristle tip is strung out evenly along the line above the No. 8. As before, the hook length will be 340 g (12 oz) and the hook probably a No. 24 or 22. (Figs 4, 4a)

I loose-feed maggot or caster to the 9–10 m (30–32 ft) mark and fish as described with the slow-falling baits. As before, the feed will be a bit scattered, so when the bites cease at, say, 9 m (30 ft), I either add another metre (or a few feet) and go farther out, or perhaps detach a pole section and fish nearer.

I share the time between the pole, the ledger and the waggler, trying all the variations I have described and in this way keep busy. I'm feeding pole and far bank swims constantly – an absolute must – but by switching from one method to another after catching two or three fish I rest one of the swims and increase my chances of keeping the fish coming to the net. Very low weights usually make the difference on this canal and the winner is usually the angler who keeps the fish coming to the keepnet right to the end of the match.

THE RIVER WITHAM

The Witham, one of the waters which has declined through pollution, has a long and glorious history as a prolific bream and roach water and it still holds these species. For the matchman, at certain times and certain places the winner will need weights of one or the other of these shoaling species.

I watch the summer Witham match results in particular for bream catches, noting from where they have been taken. If bream have been winning recently and I have drawn a peg in the right place I will fish for them but I have to admit that I hope the bream have not been showing. When they are absent in summer the scene is set for my favourite summer sport – Witham eel fishing.

If the reader copies my Witham method on any water where eels can influence the outcome of a match he will

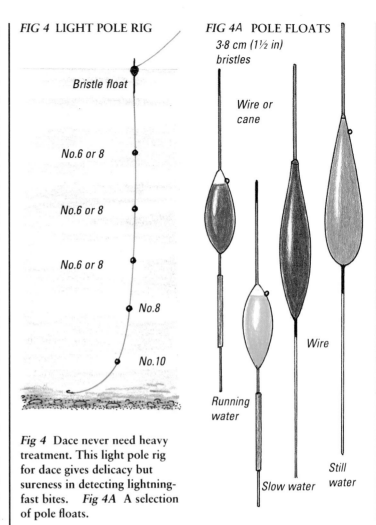

FIG 4 LIGHT POLE RIG

Bristle float

No.6 or 8

No.6 or 8

No.6 or 8

No.8

No.10

FIG 4A POLE FLOATS

3·8 cm (1½ in) bristles

Wire or cane

Wire

Running water

Slow water

Still water

Fig 4 Dace never need heavy treatment. This light pole rig for dace gives delicacy but sureness in detecting lightning-fast bites. **Fig 4A** A selection of pole floats.

find them easy to catch. In my experience fishing for eels is only difficult on the River Witham. After years of hard thinking I am not a lot nearer to understanding why this is so, but I do know a lot about the problems and how to overcome them.

The main difficulty lies in hitting the bites. While I am reasonably confident about virtually catching every eel that takes my bait on other waters it is totally different here. If I hit one in three I feel that I am doing very well. Sometimes I get it wrong and will be driven to despair, missing nine out of ten or even 19 out of 20. Why? Because the bites vary so much. Bites which come on the drop are rare, but hittable. So are the few which take the float under and keep on going.

More difficult is the bite which takes the float under and holds it there for a few seconds. You have to wait until it comes up and goes down again, and keeps on going before you can strike with any hope of success. One essential therefore is a float you can see under the surface. It must have a brightly coloured top or bristle insert, to be precise, for I almost always use the pole to fish for Witham eels. There is one impossible type of bite which takes the float under a short way and just holds it there. This bite is caused by tiny bootlace eels and if I get a lot of these bites I start to feed heavily, trying to fill these little nuisances with food and, at the same time, to attract bigger eels into the swim.

The tackle is simple enough; a pole rigged with No. 5 elastic, 0.9 kg (2 lb) main line, 5 kg (11 lb) hook-length

and a small hook, usually a No. 22, but it can be a 24 if I am having more than the usual amount of trouble with the bites. Part of the trouble, I believe, is that the eels take the maggot sideways in their mouths and the smaller the hook the better is the chance I have with the strike.

The hook is usually a Mustad 90340 barbless, which is light but quite strong. I use barbless hooks because when they can be seen they are easier to remove. Taking a leaf out of the big-eel specialist's book, I break the line if the hook is not visible, because it is better to cut the line than to risk damaging the eel by poking around in its mouth with a disgorger. Eels can swallow hooks without harm and eventually get rid of them.

Float selection depends upon whether the water is still or moving. It will either be a river-float designed for slow flows (round-topped, tapering body) or a stillwater float (pointed-top body which fattens towards the base). In perfect conditions I prefer to use one taking about 0.5 g (1/50 oz) of weight overall, though it could be as big as a 1.5 g (1/20 oz) if the wind is tricky.

The half-gramme float is perfect and I use the equivalent weight in split-shot, three or four No. 6 shots together about 1 m (3 ft 6 in) from the hook, with a Size 10 0.3 m (1 ft) from the hook and a No. 8 0.3 m (1 ft) above that. There is also a No. 10 just under the float as a depth marker and it is all rigged to fish about 152 mm (6 in) over-depth. (Fig. 5)

At times this rig will catch eels when the bait is allowed to trundle slowly through with the flow, but I usually hold the float dead-still. When a bite starts to develop I move the pole toward the float to create a bit of slack line, for if the bite develops quickly the eel will feel the resistance and let go. That applies anywhere and to any species, but it is particularly important with Witham eels. Usually I have 0.9–1.2 m (3–4 ft) of line between pole tip and float which, given the average depth of the Witham, allows me to fish with a long-enough length of line overall, suitable for a 5 m (17 ft) pole.

Any more length I need is added to that and I unship the pole to 5 m (17 ft) to land the eels. As always in match-fishing it pays to feed two lines, whenever it is possible. When fishing the River Witham I feed at 11 m (36 ft) and 8 m (26 ft), expecting to catch the majority of eels from the far swim. The close swim is mainly used to give the far swim the occasional rest. It always produces a few fish, but on some occasions, for some reason, the near swim can yield more than the far line.

Feeding, always the key to match-angling success, is critical for Witham eels, but the formula is fairly simple. When you are catching eels go sparingly with the loose-fed maggots, for there is no point in giving them too much and filling them up. I have had my biggest totals, including four eel catches into double figures, by feeding only 1.1 l (2 pints) of bait over five hours.

Conversely, if the fish are not there, or are there but not feeding, I will feed much more heavily to attract them into the swim or to encourage them to have a go. Once they are feeding, I cut back to a rate of about 20 to 25 maggots per cast. The heavier feeding disposes of more than 1.1 l (2

Within the limitations imposed by its length, the pole is virtually unbeatable in many situations. Bait can be put out and held in a position where the fish are far better than could be achieved with a conventional rod.

FIG 5 WITHAM EEL RIG

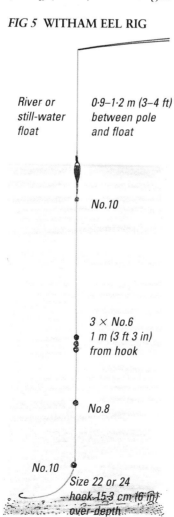

River or still-water float

0.9–1.2 m (3–4 ft) between pole and float

No.10

3 × No.6
1 m (3 ft 3 in) from hook

No.8

No.10

Size 22 or 24 hook 15.3 cm (6 in) over-depth

Fig 5 Tom Pickering finds eel bites on the River Witham vary so much they are difficult to hit, they differ all the time. So he devised this simple rig and now has no trouble in adding eels to his match-weight.

pints) so it pays to carry 2.8 l (5 pints) altogether. And do not forget the closer-in swim, it needs feeding too, at about half the rate chosen for the far swim.

DACE ON THE WARWICKSHIRE AVON

If there is one summer activity which rivals eel fishing for sheer enjoyment it is dace fishing on the Warwickshire Avon at or near Evesham. I have always loved dace fishing of course, but doing it on my favourite river is a pleasure doubled. I find plenty of excuses to fish this river, even making the trip for mid-week match series and taking the family along for the ride.

Some of the biggest successes early in my career came on the Avon and it would not worry me if I had to fish there and nowhere else for the rest of my time. It is so much like the Stainforth and Keadby Canal in two key ways – you need to keep really busy to win, and to use several key methods. Indeed there are four which are all relevant: the pole, the waggler, the float and the feeder. I rig all four up, every time, and usually use them all, feeding a line for each method I want to use, relatively close in for the stick-float or pole, farther out for the waggler and farther out still for the feeder, endlessly switching about between them.

Just like the S. and K. Canal, the winners on the Warwickshire Avon are not usually more than a little weight ahead of the place-men. The keys to success are exploiting each method to maximum potential, and knowing when to rest each swim. Usually I start close in, with light pole tackle, a string of evenly spaced No. 8s and a 10 nearest the hook. If you are going to catch fish close-in it is usually early in the match and on the pole I expect to take them on a slowly falling bait.

As soon as the tackle has sunk to full depth I lift out and lay the tackle on the surface again. It should be dropped in a straight line downstream, with the baited hook sinking among constant loose feed.

You can expect a bite anywhere in this river, from right on the surface to the full depth, so keep the eyes firmly fixed on the float, which will slowly cock as each weight registers and finally settle down so that only part of the bristle shows up top. Strike if the behaviour of the float differs in any way from the norm. It may not settle as soon as it should at any given point: it may flicker slightly or simply zoom away. Strike at any indication. Dace are fast biters which do not give too many chances. (Fig. 6)

I fish with the pole until the bites cease, then take up the rod and the stick-float rig to explore the same line but farther down, in the area which I cannot reach with the pole. The shotting pattern will be the same, aimed at catching on the drop until the rig sinks to full depth, and from the bottom or close to it. (Fig. 6a)

Success in stick-float fishing depends on several factors, including correct casting and good control as the float progresses down the swim. The aim should be to cast so that the tackle lands in line downstream, as described for the pole. If it lands in a heap the bait sinks too quickly and less naturally.

FIG 6 AVON RIG   FIG 6A STICK FLOAT

Fig 6 The Warwickshire Avon is scene of many of Pickering's wins and this rig explains why. Fig 6A The stick float demands accuracy in casting.

At one time the need to slow the float down below the spread of the current was stressed, but I do not know a water these days which does not respond best to speed of current presentation. Just let the float run through, watching for bites on the drop, or lift-and-go-under bites after the tackle has sunk to full depth. The only control required is to keep the line as straight as possible between rod tip and float – tricky, sometimes, in a wind.

If you allow the bow in the line to develop the float will eventually skate off-line and you will not get a bite. Bows in the line are corrected by trapping the line as it comes off the spool and quickly lifting the line to straighten it. If you cannot correct a bow by doing that the chances are that you need a bigger float carrying more weight, a stick-float variation, one which has a wire stem instead of heavy cane, or an alloy-stemmed float such as the John Allerton stick. The wire stem is more stable, but designed really for more turbulent waters than the Warwickshire Avon offers and Allerton's float has a small shoulder near the tip which grips the current better.

Go for more weight or greater stability whenever stick-float control becomes more difficult. Always shot right down so a mere pimple of the tip is showing, for with too much sticking up you will miss bites. One tactic which unfailingly attracts bites is to check the float now and again by stopping the line coming off the reel spool, causing the bait to rise and often provoking a take. A pattern begins to emerge when you are catching plenty of fish on the stick.

Building a catch is all about rhythm: feed the swim, bait up, cast out, fish through and repeat the sequence, all the time noting the catch rate to build a bag continuously through the match period.

You will get to know where in the swim the majority of bites are coming from and checking the float at that point can be absolutely deadly; the float will stop and go under in the same instant.

It is doubtful, however, whether you will reach that situation in the near swim on the Avon, but it should be possible to add a few fish to those taken on the pole. Sooner or later you will be struggling for bites, and now is the time to switch to the waggler-float line, which should be fed by hand or catapult all the time you are feeding and fishing the near line.

The longer I can catch fish close-in the happier I am, for the waggler swim will be building up nicely with dace and, hopefully, species such as skimmers and chub feeding with ever-growing confidence. This is from where the bulk of the catch is going to come and I always feel a thrill of anticipation when I finally make the switch.

Although the methods are totally different there are similarities in the way the fish are caught on waggler and stick-float. While the latter float is attached top and bottom with silicone rubber sleeves it is rigged to fish a fairly slow-falling bait. The waggler, always attached bottom-end only, is rigged to fish an even slower fall. On the Avon it will probably be carrying no more than a No. 10 near the hook and one or two BBs above it.

The line is usually sunk when I am waggler fishing on stillwater and canals. On most rivers, it can pay to leave the line up on the surface, for this ensures a cleaner and more effective strike. Small-to-medium-sized bows which

develop are not enough to drag the float off-line and they do not hamper the strike if the angler does it properly. It takes a long, smooth sweep of the rod to take up the bow and hit the fish. Sometimes you have to take the rod through a full 180 deg. and quite often you do not know if you have hooked the fish until you start reeling in.

Only if there is a very strong wind, especially one blowing downstream and in, is there a need to sink the line, but on the Avon this is rare. My float is not usually in long enough for bad bows to develop. In effect I am fishing similarly to the way the pole is used here, with a re-cast the moment the tackle has sunk to full depth. For some reason, Avon dace rarely take a bait at full depth, so for them one has to be constantly casting and striking. Occasionally I let the bait trundle through on the bottom in the hope of picking up another species, perhaps a roach, chub or skimmer bream.

All the time I am fishing the waggler line I will be trickling loose feed into the near line, preparing to give the main swim a rest if I sense that the fish are starting to become shy. Leaving the swim alone for a while rebuilds their confidence.

On the Warwickshire Avon and, indeed, the majority of other rivers, it is wrong to flog one swim to death, but it is a common-enough error. Only if I am struggling to catch enough from the first two swims will I resort to the feeder in the hope of connecting with some bonus fish such as chub, but this is a method I will deal with at some length, under different headings, starting with the next section which concerns summer bream.

SUMMER BREAM

I like to think that a typical Tom Pickering summer will include at least one chance at a shoal of good-sized bream. With great respect to bream enthusiasts, however, I reckon this is the easiest game in fishing, though it used to be vastly more skilful than it is today. The great equaliser has been the swimfeeder.

Billy Lane and Freddie Foster could throw large balls of bait, packed with feeder maggots or casters, with pin-point accuracy out to the distances often required on waters such as the Welland, Middle Level and Relief Channel. They therefore had to temper their accuracy with caution. Dropping big balls of groundbait on to the heads of feeding bream usually drove the fish away, so they tried to put the feed in when the bream weren't there and to get as much on the bottom as they could in order to attract and hold a wandering shoal.

Bream fishing in those days was a game of chess played by grand masters, usually with the pawns just there for ritual sacrifice, that plus the hope of becoming king one day, just as soon as they found out how it was done.

But almost overnight the pawns stopped being rookies, due to the arrival of a simple tube of plastic, dotted with holes, weighted with a strip of lead and rigged to fish on a link in place of the once universal Arlesey bomb. Enter the swim-feeder, and suddenly everyone who could cast with any accuracy was able to place feed in the right place, and for some reason the bream did not object to a falling feeder as they once did to a big ball of bait. Instead, the fish seemed mesmerised by the constant arrival of food.

Nowadays it is the matchman who can draw the bream, not he who can keep them the longest and catch the most. Everybody is a bream angler, with the quivertip usurping the role of the swingtip, which effectively died with Freddie Foster. Some still use the method which Freddie did more than anyone to popularise, and it is still deadly in the right hands and in the right places. But casting with the quivertip is easier, and it can do everything which the swingtip could do and more besides.

I cannot see what is difficult about bream fishing these days, certainly on still and slow waters. For good-sized bream of, say, 0.9 to 1.8 kg (2 to 4 lb) all you need is an open-end groundbait feeder on a 23 cm (9 in) link fixed to the main line, a hook length of 1.2 to 1.5 m (4 to 5 ft) and the patience to wait for the action. The long tail ensures that the bream will usually have the bait well inside its mouth before it swims far enough for a bite to register on the quivertip. By that time the strike is a mere formality. If you fish with a short tail for sizeable bream you will miss bites and even lose some of the fish you manage to hook. (Fig. 7)

Since bream do not fight very hard, light line of 0.45 to 0.7 kg (1 to 1 lb 8 oz) is all right, and hooks should be small. Size 20 or 22 are now the norm, with 24s if the fish are a bit on the shy side. Many of the modern Continental groundbaits are formulated for bream, so you can choose whichever takes your fancy. In my opinion they all work best used as half-and-half mixes with ordinary breadcrumb groundbait, the effect is the same and it is more economical. The ration of feed to groundbait is no longer critical, nor is the consistency of the mix, because feeders no longer break up in the air in the way those badly constructed balls of groundbait once did! Today, most anglers seem to mix feeder groundbait on the dry side to make sure that it is washed out more quickly. There is now no need for really heavy mixes to get it down fast.

Where to cast the feeder demands thought. If I do not know the swim I will cast around with an empty feeder, counting as it sinks to find a slightly deeper area or a shelf. If I do find some kind of feature, a hole or ledge, I will settle on that area and then concentrate on laying a carpet of feed on it. You can do this just by casting and retrieving a packed feeder for a while, and unlike those old-time matchmen I do not worry whether there are bream in residence to start with because these fish accept feeders as part of the scenery. (Figs 8, 8a)

If these bream were there at the start of the match they are there for a reason; they got to the peg long before I did and they are likely to stay. The constant casting and bait delivery simply encourages them to feed, and they no longer react adversely to a splashy bombardment of biggish balls thrown in by hand. On most bream venues I mix about six orange-sized balls packed with casters, unless I have reason to believe the bream on a given water do not like this bait. Most bream do, but there are some places, Holme Pierrepont, Notts, is one, where they prefer pinkies

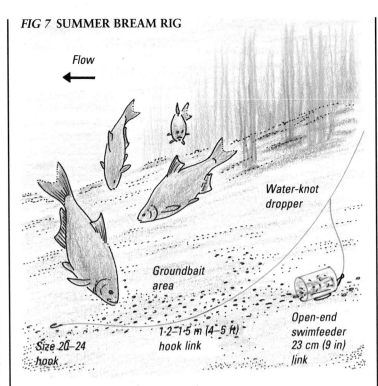

FIG 7 SUMMER BREAM RIG

Flow

Water-knot dropper

Groundbait area

Size 20–24 hook

1·2–1·5 m (4–5 ft) hook link

Open-end swimfeeder 23 cm (9 in) link

or squatts. I like a bit of everything as a rule, including samples of the hookbait.

Do not overload the groundbait with feed or it will not throw without breaking up. One useful insurance against this possibility is to wet the hands before throwing. Re-moulding the balls with wet hands seals the outside and helps it hold together through the air. If you have a good-enough arm, throw them, or make the balls the right size to be catapulted if you know that you cannot make the distance by hand.

Pin-point accuracy may be the aim but you will never achieve it, nor is it desirable. After all, you will not get 22.8 kg (50 lb) of bream off a small pile of bait. A good shoal occupies quite a large area of water and it does no harm to spread the bait over a reasonable area.

Once the area is baited you will be adding to it with every cast with the feeder, but do not get too busy with casting. It is a matter of patience and we are looking, initially, for some positive sign of the presence of bream. As a rule, the first sign is a line bite – a quick rattle of the quivertip as a bream swims into the line. Try to avoid the temptation to strike at this, but you probably will, quite instinctively. To strike at the first movements is automatic, but when you have missed a couple and noted that the bait has not been touched you know what is going on. From then on you can ignore the little plucks and tweaks and wait for something more positive to develop.

When the fish are feeding well there is no mistaking the genuine bites. The tip will go round and stay there, whereas the line bite will take it round and let it spring back again just as quickly. One of the main attributes of a good bream angler is having the patience to watch the tip go and to wait for it to stay or spring back. Thanks to that long hook-link he will know that he is going to get the fish if he waits. He also knows that it is a time-wasting re-cast if he strikes too soon and misses. Recognising the true bites, and hitting them all, is what matchfishing is all

Fig 7 The matchman who can draw the bream can win the match and the quivertip will play its part. But the terminal tackle and particularly the feeder must be right. Keep the groundbait coming and include some hookbait with it. Bream nudging the line can cause the senses to flutter, but resist the temptation to strike at each pluck.

FIG 8 GROUNDBAITING TECHNIQUES

Far bank

Angler C adopts a different line to the other competitors

Flow

XXX

XXX

XXX

XXX

A

B

C

D

E

Angler C is free to collect fish moving either up or down-stream

FIG 8A A DEFINED 'KILLING GROUND'

Balls of feed

Loose feed

Flow

'Killing ground' 6·4 m (7 yards)

Figs 8, 8A Aimlessly hurling in balls of groundbait will achieve little. Watch what the pegs either side are doing, then select your own spot. Their groundbait can well bring fish to your hook.

about. Just as small weights win canal matches, one extra bream wins a lot of big-weight matches.

Given a swim full of feeding bream the foregoing is just about all there is to it, but if I have been sitting at the peg for a long time without any indication of the presence of bream I will try to attract some on to feed by adding one or two hand-thrown balls of bait. Sometimes the sight of groundbait clouding down will attract a passing shoal, or a single fish which may have been hanging about on the edge of the action.

Another tip is to fill the feeder from the bottom of your groundbait container rather than from the top, for the feed maggots work themselves down below the upper layer. Conversely, take it from the top for hand-throwing or mix it all up thoroughly. You can have too many feeder maggots falling in a ball for throwing but it can pay to add lots more to groundbait used through the feeder. Sometimes the extra feeder maggots falling through the water persuade the bream to feed. Often it only takes two or three to start feeding and then the others join in. Whoever compared bream with sheep was not far off the mark.

WINTER BREAM

While the method described in the previous section is about right for summer bream it needs scaling down for autumn and winter, when these fish become more finicky. Very probably they will not take the arrival of six big balls of bait without being spooked. Instead, I usually have six casts with a large-capacity swimfeeder.

These bream do not usually feed so voraciously in the colder months, so overdoing the baiting can give them so much choice that your hookbait has less chance of being taken. You need to be in with a chance when a hungry bream is looking for food, but you have to tailor your approach and expectations to the venue.

You might be on a winner with two or three bream.

What many anglers do not realise is that a bite every half-hour means, if you hit them all, ten bream in the net in five hours. If they are 0.9 to 1.3 kg (2 to 3 lb) fish the weights will total about 9 to 13.6 kg (20 to 30 lb), weights which are not usual in winter. Ten bites in a match is slow going, but it is usually a great deal fewer.

In winter, bites can be a lot less emphatic, too. You might just get the odd spectacular pull-round, but more likely is a tiny pluck. Do not worry about identifying line bites, the winter rule is that you strike at any indication. The fish do not move about as much, so the winter approach involves using a hook-length of about half the summer length and usually a shorter link-length as well.

FAST-WATER BREAM

By fast water I mean rivers with more pace than the slow-flowing Fenland rivers such as the Witham and the Lower Welland. The classic example is the Trent, which on current form stands a chance of becoming the finest bream river we have seen for generations. Just about every match reported on the Trent on the opening weekend of the 1989–90 season was won with bream. The weights included 25 kg (55 lb) at Holme Marsh, 20 kg (44 lb) at Winthorpe, six weights over 13.6 kg (30 lb) and two over 12.3 kg (27 lb) in one match at Winthorpe/Holme Marsh and 21.5 kg (47 lb) at Shelford. Few matches were won with less than 9 kg (20 lb).

Virtually all these weights were taken on groundbait feeders, fished very much in the way I have described, except for one small detail: you have to be able to cope with the fact that the feeder needs to carry enough weight to just hold in the flow. It could be 14 g (½ oz) of lead strip (under legislation, lead is legal as an integral part of a feeder) for the non-tidal Trent in normal flow to 85 g (3 oz) plus in the tidal river or in heavy flows on the non-tidal. The light-to-medium feeder rods which cope on

A Probably the most significant advances in matchfishing have been the ledgering techniques applied and the use of swimfeeders, accessories which provide a continuous baiting process ensuring that both feed and hookbait lie in the same position on the riverbed.
B Removable weights of various sizes allow swimfeeders to be weighted to exactly suit the speed of current and casting distances needed to get the bait among the fish.   C Fish clear up the feeder maggots but are still capable of sucking out the body juices of the hookbait.
D Tom connects and holds his chub at an alarming distance of 27 m (30 yards), drawing it carefully and with the minimum of excitement away

A

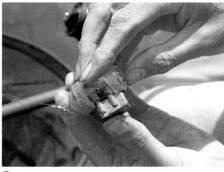

B

C

stillwaters and slow rivers are no use for casting more than 28 g (1 oz), so you need something with more power and a stiffer tip.

There are so many feeder techniques that the method rates a book on its own, something that I would like to do. In this book there is room only to discuss one or two methods ranging from the mere crude to the deadly clever. In the former category is the use of a very heavy feeder and a small hook to a shortish tail of about 0.6 m (2 ft). The idea is that when a fish of whatever species or size picks the bait up and turns downstream it is stopped immediately in its tracks by the weight of the feeder.

When fish feel resistance, they usually eject the bait, but in the case of the heavy feeder they have no chance. The combination of heavy weight and small, sharp hook ensures that the fish hook themselves. They rattle the quivertip and then get reeled in. It is effective, but whether is it proper fishing is a matter for debate! The method has accounted for some huge match totals of chub, bream and barbel, but it works better in the faster swims than in the slower sections. The main problem with this method is the smash-take from bigger fish which can break the hook-length against their weight. This led to the introduction of power gum shock-absorbers into the terminal rig.

The main, and more enjoyable alternative is to use a longer tail and a feeder which is more balanced to the flow. I cast-in with an empty feeder, trying to find what weight is just enough to hold bottom. There are clip-on weights of varying sizes if the feeder is too light, or trim weights down if it is too heavy. Do not make feeder selection with a loaded one. You need to know that the feeder will not move when its groundbait load has washed out, and that when it does move the probable cause is a bite. This can only be found out if the feeder is empty.

To some extent the type of bite registration is dictated by the flow. In the slower sections of a swim it is likely to be a pull on the tip, which could be slight or pronounced.

Strike at either indication, but wait for more positive pulls if you miss when striking those little knocks. In the faster sections the bite is likely to dislodge the feeder, causing the quivertip to wag like the tail of a dog, and these bites are hard to miss.

In theory, the fish should feel resistance and let go the hook, but it does not seem to if the feeder is properly balanced to the flow. This is because the feeder is dropping downstream with the fish, which either does not feel it or cannot get rid of the hook anyway, due to the tension between hook and feeder making the bait impossible to eject. Whatever the reason, there are no smash-offs with this method, for there is not enough resistance for the fish to exploit.

WINTER CHUB

Up to now we have discussed groundbait feeders only, and while chub sometimes turn up among the bream-attracting groundbait this feeding is usually a chub deter-rent. The species does not like it, responding better to feed in the form of loose maggots. When the chub were more widespread in the Trent than they are today the killing method was blockend feeder with a maggot/hemp/caster mixture. This is virtually the same as the groundbait feeder but is sealed at the downstream end, with a remov-able cap at the upper end to enable the feeder to be filled.

When used properly the maggot feeder is deadly in its efficiency and it is just as effective in the streamier areas into which the chub seem to have retreated. They also congregate in slower areas where snags abound, and for the matchman drawing the peg adjoining a shoal of resident chub tends to be a frustrating experience. The fish will seldom take any interest. Barbel, too, have their preferred areas, though the experts say the fish will move around as the river rises and falls, looking for the pace of water which best suits them.

D

E

F

from the feeding shoal. Letting the fish splash about in the feeding area would result in fish rapidly leaving the swim.
E With a finger poised to check any last frantic dash and with

the net well sunk, a chub is eased towards the net rim.
F A small chub, but they all count and if kept coming out at 0.34–0.45 kg (12 oz–1 lb) can contribute to a winning total.

The blockend feeder, preferably loaded with casters, is the best way to catch Trent barbel, and most of what I have to say about chub on the maggot feeder is also applicable to barbel. Indeed the method applies to both species in summer as well as in winter. Sadly, I do not get round to the Trent in summer these days, mainly because I am too busy fishing elsewhere, mostly with the all-important National Championship, invitation matches and other team events.

What feeders essentially do is to provide the matchman with the opportunity to place bait accurately in one place, while at the same time attracting fish from downstream. A feeder starts to lose maggots as soon as it hits the water and continues to do so all the time it is sinking. The bulk of the maggots stay in until it hits bottom but the early escapees drift to the end of the peg and beyond, bringing new fish to replace those being caught.

On good days this is an endless procession of fish. They will sometimes come right up to the feeder itself and shake it to release more bait! In the early stages, therefore, the fish can be caught on a very short hook-length, but you must be prepared to lengthen it if the bites slow down. That usually means that the chub have become wary and have dropped downstream. You need to get the hookbait farther away from the feeder, and a longer tail gives the bait a more natural fall and some bites will come before it hits bottom.

I usually cast to about a third of the way down the peg. It can pay in the later stages of a match to make the last few casts farther downstream to take the fish which have dropped right down. Do not try this too soon, for it eventually kills the swim, but the tactic is usually effective for a late burst of top-up fish.

Bites will vary from savage pulls on the short hook-length to less impressive indications on the longer lengths, but you should hit most of the genuine bites without much difficulty. You may get a few line-knocks when the fish are

milling around the feeder early on, but most tip movements after that are caused by genuine bites.

Once again it can pay to balance the feeder to the flow to encourage drop-back bites caused by a dislodged feeder. In fact, this type of bite can be encouraged in the faster swims if you cast directly in front with a balanced feeder and allow a biggish bow to develop in the line between rod tip and feeder.

By experimenting with the weights and the size of the bow you can make a feeder bump straight downstream, holding and then moving. You are sending it in search of fish and the quivertip will move slowly in tune with each movement and when the bite comes the feeder dislodges completely, causing the quivertip to waggle madly. That is another unmissable bite. Those sportsmen who say the feeder is nothing but a crude method for crude anglers are quite wrong.

CHUB AND ROACH ON THE FLOAT

Given anything like the right conditions in autumn and winter I much prefer to catch my chub on the float, and since roach demand a virtually identical approach I shall deal with both species at once. I have described stick-float fishing in the context of the Warwickshire Avon, and it is not all that different on the Trent and elsewhere.

The Trent was the river where the stick-float was first used, with caster the key bait. Later it proved adaptable for maggot fishing too and that is now the main approach. The basic shotting pattern has never changed, it is still the old 'shirt-button' style, evenly spaced shot gradually decreasing in size towards the hook.

Whatever size of stick-float I am using the bottom three shots are always the same, a No. 10 near the hook, an 8 above it and then a 6. What happens above that depends on float size and depth, but it could be one, two, three, even four No. 4s strung out evenly. The float itself will

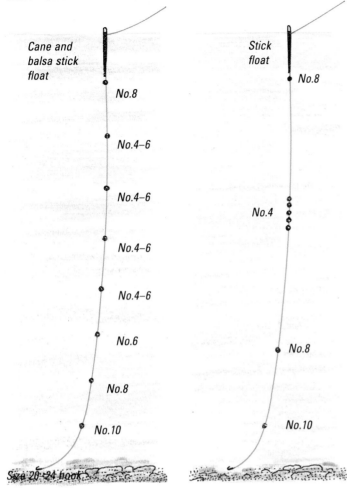

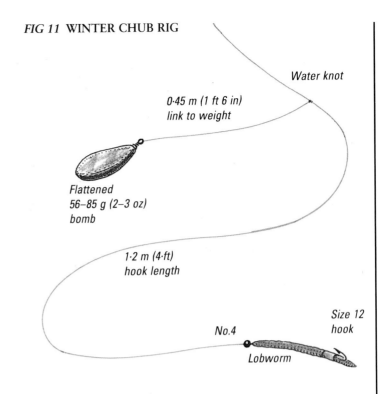

Fig 9 The weight runs down the line evenly, ensuring that the bait drops evenly.   *Fig 10* But chub take in middle or deeper water, so the weight is in the middle and towards the hook.   *Fig 11* This worm rig takes winter chub.

Tom Pickering 'whipping' bleak at speed. Two top sections of a pole, a fixed line length and a small float which gives enough weight to cast the bait. Catch enough and many a match has been won with this tiny but prolific fish.

usually be the traditional cane and balsa model for the smooth, even-paced swims, or something a bit more stable for more turbulent water. Some anglers use the Allerton sticks with alloy stems all the time, but I think they are better for 'boily' swims. (Figs 9, 10)

Hook sizes have changed over the years. We used to think that 20s were small for the Trent and considered ourselves daring if we dropped to a 22. Now a 28–340 g (1–12 oz) line is standard for many Trent anglers, though I never start that fine. I begin fishing with a Size 20 to 0.45 kg (1 lb) line and catch what I can with that, and only when the bites stop will I scale down, but the move always works. It is very obvious that the fish are harder to tempt than they once were.

The stick-float is best fished at the speed of the current, with slowing down a useful tactic when you are struggling for bites. It is the feeding which is really important and that has to be constant, a given amount of maggots at every cast. A dozen at each cast used to be the recommended amount, but I feed double that nowadays, although it can depend on the situation. If I am not catching fish I will feed much more heavily, trying to make the fish feed or to attract fish. I use more feed when I am struggling to find fish than I do when I am catching them.

As soon as the fish start to bite I cut back on the feed to the standard feed-rate of about 20 maggots per cast and dropping the tackle into the feed in a straight line downstream, allow it to run through. It becomes an almost mechanical exercise after a while, although it pays to keep

alert, I always try to work out what I will do if the bites stop coming.

One tactic which works (apart from checking the tackle and slowing down the speed of presentation) is to try casting farther down the swim. It is surprising how often this produces more fish, probably because the bait is sinking through a different, undisturbed area. Trying a little closer out or in also works well, as does the odd slight change to the terminal weighting. I find it mysterious how quite small alterations to weight patterns can lead to fish coming to the net.

Only change the weighting pattern when chub are in the swim. Roach like the evenly falling bait achieved with the 'shirt-button' shotting style, but chub are usually to be caught lower down or on the bottom. For them I try bunching the No. 4 weights where the 6 is, which makes the rig sink a lot faster, and fishing a little more over-depth.

Dragging the bait over the rocks is an effective tactic for chub, and another dodge which can pay on the Trent and elsewhere is to start hammering loose feed in towards the end of a match. This often catches good bonus chub in swims which have been producing only roach. It also seems to switch them back on, sometimes, when they have become wary. If you have a dying swim in the later stages of a match you have little to lose and potentially much to gain from trying it.

If conditions permit I always bait two swims on rivers, one close in for the stick and one farther out in the stream

underground and retract like lightning if disturbed by a heavy footfall or too bright a light. The trick is to grab them as far back from the head as you can just hold on. The worm will contract its body, trying to get back down its hole, but after a few seconds the contractions stop and the worm can be pulled out without further resistance.

In the right conditions it does not take long to collect a few hundred lobs, which can be kept alive for use weeks or even months later. I put mine into an old bath, sunk in the garden and filled with ordinary soil. Whenever collecting conditions are right I go out and top up the supply.

It may seem a lot of trouble to go to but I enjoy it, and when the time comes for lobworms to decide match and team results I am never at a loss for this bait. How to fish them is a matter for endless debate. Hitting lobworm bites seems to be as complex for some anglers as those baffling bites from Witham eels. But I think I have found the best way, certainly for Trent chub in winter floods.

At one time these fish used to come close-in to the bank in high-flow conditions but this is no longer the case, not as often anyway. The fish are more likely to be out in the flow, which demands the use of quite a big weight to hold the bait and tackle where you want it.

I usually hold it there with a 57–85 g (2–3 oz) bomb, flattened to help it hold bottom. This weight needs a strong rod to cast and of course stronger line than we would normally use. I have 1.3 kg (3 lb) reel line with a 2.2 kg (5 lb) shock-absorber tied onto it. This should run from the reel to about 0.6 m (2 ft) beyond the rod tip when the tackle is in the casting position. It ensures that I can cast the heavy gear without risking a break, but I still have fairly thin line offering little resistance to the flow.

The terminal tackle is fairly simple, a fixed bomb link of 0.46 m (1 ft 6 in) with a 1.2 m (4 ft) hook-length and a Size 12 hook. Critical to the success of the method is how the worm is mounted on the hook. We might be waiting for just one or two bites and when they come they must be hit. Some anglers have the self-control to sit there watching the little nods and bobs on the quivertip, waiting for the tip eventually to slam round and stay there. But sometimes they get nothing but the warm-up act and find that the main show has been cancelled! (Fig. 11)

This is puzzling, but I rationalised it this way: every movement of the tip is caused by a chub mouthing and testing the bait. If you reel in after several little movements which do not develop you invariably find that the tail of the lob has been chewed, the end missing, or there are several damaged areas along the worm's body. I decided that it should be possible to hook a chub if it has my bait in its mouth long enough to cause this kind of injury to the bait. Putting the hook in the worm's tail was the obvious answer, but if you do that the bait fishes head-downstream and loses its attraction.

What was needed was a method of rigging the lob with the hook in the tail and the tail pointing downstream. The problem was solved as shown in the tackle illustrated in the drawing. The hook is passed through the head of the worm, which is then pushed up the line. Depending on the length of the worm, a Size 4 shot is pinched on and the

for either the stick-float or waggler style, fished as previously described.

HARDER CONDITIONS

While we often get normal flow conditions in winter, and, with luck, some mild weather too, we cannot always depend upon it. Very often matchmen find themselves struggling on rivers which are a bit out of sorts. It can be cold, with some extra water, or well up in near-flood. Some of our Winter League fishing seems to take place in such conditions too often for comfort and catching fish in team events is vital.

When the more normal approaches fail we have to try something else and there are one or two tactics which are well worth considering. In flood conditions, the first idea is a bait-change to the lobworm and at times it is that last-chance method!

A very important point here is to be sure that you have this bait when you need it. The conditions for collecting lobworms are often hopeless when you come to need them and I get mine in the autumn when the weather is both mild and damp. The lobs come up on to the surface of lawns, flower-beds and vegetable plots, beginning to emerge as darkness falls and the later you leave it the farther out they come.

On very warm, wet nights the lobs come out all the way and you can locate them with a shaded torch and simply pick them up. More often, though, they keep their tails hook is put through the tail of the worm. The shot stops the worm sliding down the hook length and the bait is strung out, with the tail end waiting to be nipped by a chub. Striking with this rig is not at all complicated: watch for a tap and ignore it, but strike the second tap, and in the majority of cases you have your chub well-hooked and on the way to the net.

If you miss the bite you sometimes find that the worm is in two halves. That tells you that the bite did not come from a chub but an eel – and there is not much that you can do about that. I stick with the system of striking at that second tap. Very often it is no more positive than the first. It can be quite a tiny movement, but hit it anyway, it is surprising how often you will connect. It is also possible, though, to get a very positive first pull. You have to be ready to hit it, which is why I always ledger with my hand on the rod.

The reason for the long tail and the long bomb-link is that it creates a bit of slack in what is basically a crude and heavy method. It allows the chub to pick the bait up without feeling much initial resistance from the heavy bomb. In flood conditions and powerful streams, a shorter, tighter rig would be as taut as piano wire, and bites would be a lot more difficult to hit.

It is unusual to get many bites on lobworm, a bait which probably works in high and coloured water simply because worms are naturally washed into rivers in these conditions. Here, more often than not, we are fighting for bites and one useful tip is to try a switch-bait such as cheese. It is surprising how often a change to cheese, especially a smelly one – Danish blue is an example – will attract a bite.

I say 'a bite' deliberately, for that is what it usually is. Very often, in fact nearly always, cheese provokes a single bite and it usually comes straight away if it is going to come at all. I do not know why cheese is a one-bite wonder, and cannot even come up with a theory, but I have learned from experience that after hitting or missing a cheese bite I might as well go back to lobworm, there will be no more action with the cheese.

THE BOMB METHOD

There is a stage between a normal river and high water/flood conditions. In winter the water can be up just a little, or normal but a bit cold. It can be fishable with a stick-float or waggler, but the fish are not active enough to chase or intercept a moving bait. In this situation a method of straight ledgering can produce a fish when nothing else will.

I use a weight as small as possible, usually 10.6 to 14 g (³⁄₈ to ½ oz), fished on a short link of 76 to 100 mm (3 to 4 in) and a 0.46 m (1 ft 6 in) tail. Many match anglers resort to this tactic without really understanding what makes it work properly, and in my view it is the feeding method which goes with it that is the key. I feed the swim as though I were float-fishing, and that can be very difficult when you are not actually float-fishing! (Fig. 12)

It is so easy to trickle maggots in at every cast with the

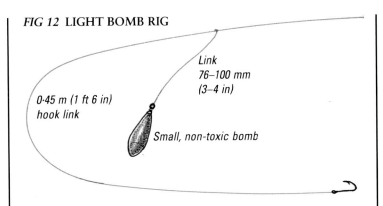

FIG 12 LIGHT BOMB RIG

Link
76–100 mm
(3–4 in)

0·45 m (1 ft 6 in)
hook link

Small, non-toxic bomb

Fig 12 With this light ledger the swim is fed as in float-fishing and it works!

float, but it is a different thing altogether to maintain the same kind of frequency while watching a quivertip. Nevertheless it has to be done. Denis White and I have a saying which applies to several angling methods, 'Fish ledger, think float; fish feeder, think float'. The float is the ideal way of catching fish because it is completely in tune with the feeding which goes with it. When we cannot fish the float, or cannot *catch* fish on the float, therefore, we still try to feed as though we are float-fishing and in some instances make the terminal tackle behave at least for part of the time like float tackle.

For example, a few moments after a feeder has hit bottom the hook-length is falling among feed just like a float-rig in the last 0.6 or 0.9 m (2 or 3 ft). Thinking this way helps us to imagine what is going on below and assist us to anticipate events. Sometimes, we are quick on to a ledger bite because we are expecting it at the exact moment when it comes.

In the case of the bomb method we assume that regular feeding, while not attracting float bites, is necessary because the fish are cleaning it up after it has hit bottom. They want it still, or moving more slowly than it can be presented with a float. They will take the bait 'nailed down' with the ledger tackle, but the fish need to be attracted and held in the right place.

I fish with my maggot bait in a side-tray, trickling it in all the time with the free hand. The other hand holds the rod, which is propped on a rest set just upstream of straight out. That way, bites register only on the quivertip. If the rod is angled downstream bites go through the tip and register on the rod, giving the angler much less chance of hitting the bite.

Usually, the right place to cast is about halfway down the swim. Close the bale arm of the reel as soon as the bomb hits bottom, and be ready for a bite in the next few seconds as the bait sinks to the bottom. The odd suicidal fish will take it on the drop but in hard conditions the bites are more likely to come after the fall of the bait.

I like to fish a line as tight as possible with as slack a tip as possible, which does not sound easily achieved. I am aware of this, but what I do not like is for my line to be too direct to the bomb, which causes much of the bend to be taken out of the tip. The current puts a bit of a bow in it, which eases the pressure on the tip. In effect, it creates a bit of slack for a biting fish to take up, which ensures that it has the bait well inside its mouth when the bite registers.

This may seem an immobile and boring way of fishing but I do not find it so, I am thinking all the time, concentrating on the feeding and watching the tip for bites. It is hard work for five hours and one obvious essential on cold winter days is to keep warm. If you are not wearing the correct clothing you will be too cold to concentrate properly. I sometimes wonder how the old-timers managed, sitting on a freezing, snow-covered bank without the benefit of good waterproof clothing and, above all, the modern thermal vests, longjohns and boots.

Matchfishing is tough in winter, but if you have a choice do not make it any tougher than it needs to be. In team events such as the winter leagues you have to take what comes, but it makes little sense for the accomplished match-angler to choose difficult and patchy winter venues. I hate matches in which anglers drawn in half or even three-quarters of the pegs have no chance of catching a fish.

While I love the River Witham in summer I loathe it in winter, when roach or bream are concentrated in one or two areas and the majority of anglers have no chance. I recall qualifying for one big competition final by catching a single stickleback on the Witham. It made more headlines than some of my big wins!

When the average matchman gets a plumb draw, a patchy venue does offer him the occasional chance to shine, but the ultimate aim of the ambitious matchman should be to compete regularly against the top performers. Watch them carefully when you get the chance. Learn from them and one day you will beat them. Angling is a truly great sport and the only one I can think of in which the newcomer can turn up and have a crack at a world champion. You can turn up and fish peg-to-peg with world champions Tommy Pickering or Kevin Ashurst, and you *might* beat them. Lots of anglers do and are inspired enough by their achievement to try even harder the next time.

Never take defeat hard: just try to analyse why it happened and learn from it. However good they are, no one is immortal on a riverbank. The real measure of a top matchman is how often he wins when the chance presents itself. Mastery of all the methods is the key and if you can absorb everything you have read here you will be a long way down the right road.

A

A Matchfishing is all about total familiarity with tackle and techniques. Complete mastery and control over rod and reel are absolute requirements.
B Completely different from the streamy River Trent, this placid stretch of the Grand Canal, at Ticknevin, in Co. Kildare, produces very good quality bream, tench and rudd in a more relaxed match atmosphere.

B

MICHAEL PRICHARD

BOAT FISHING

Many times have I been asked why I chose the sea as the arena for my sport, but there is no simple answer. Undoubtedly my choice had a lot to do with the sheer vastness of the ocean. And I like open horizons. When fishing freshwaters, as I often do, I tend to see myself as by the riverside or lake but when I fish the sea I become part of it. Bouncing along over wind-whipped waves in a sturdy offshore craft, in the knowledge that below the surface lie many potential habitats and marine creatures, has been my choice.

Knowledge is the key to successful sea angling: knowing something of the mood of the sea and a little of the life-style of fish that live in it is vital. To talk of vast oceans is easy, to comprehend their vastness is mind-boggling. Some two-thirds of the earth's surface is covered by water; north of the Equator there is more land than water, and a reverse situation exists in the Southern Hemisphere.

Not all of this water is available as a sportfishing resource, for most of the ocean is far too deep for rod and line, so the sea angler must find his sport over the Continental Shelf. The British Isles enjoy a larger area of shallow West Atlantic Continental Shelf than its European neighbours and as most fish species live over this shallow ground the share is greater, although the richer seas round Britain have become a hunting ground for practically every commercial fishing nation of the Northern Hemisphere.

The Continental Shelf was formed by a constant flow of silt, carrying minerals and other fertilizing ingredients

Mike Prichard fishing over a World War One wreck off the coast of Co. Cork. During previous winters, skipper Brian Byrne spent many weeks carefully documenting the offshore waters of this Irish coastline using video echosounder cross-referenced to satellite navigation equipment. He now knows everything about the seabed there, its contours, wrecks, reefs and fish-holding areas and can take anglers direct to the most favourable marks at the very times when they are fishing well.

With such carefully plotted marks good conger, ling, pollack and other species that inhabit wrecks and haunt the crevices and weed-covered reefs are not difficult to find. Attention to detail in every aspect of sea angling, finding marks, making up rigs, baiting up, proper clothing, plus experience, brings its reward with quality catches.

71

FIG 1 CONTINENTAL SHELF AND BAIT ZONES

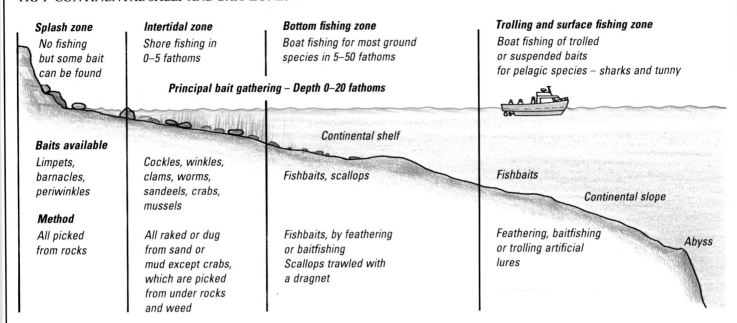

Splash zone
No fishing
but some bait
can be found

Intertidal zone
Shore fishing in
0–5 fathoms

Bottom fishing zone
Boat fishing for most ground
species in 5–50 fathoms

Trolling and surface fishing zone
Boat fishing of trolled
or suspended baits
for pelagic species – sharks and tunny

Principal bait gathering – Depth 0–20 fathoms

Continental shelf

Baits available
Limpets,
barnacles,
periwinkles

Cockles, winkles,
clams, worms,
sandeels, crabs,
mussels

Fishbaits, scallops

Fishbaits

Continental slope

Method
All picked
from rocks

All raked or dug
from sand or
mud except crabs,
which are picked
from under rocks
and weed

Fishbaits, by feathering
or baitfishing
Scallops trawled with
a dragnet

Feathering, baitfishing
or trolling artificial
lures

Abyss

out from the rivers. Erosion of the coastline by wind and wave action also adds to the fine material that forms the seabed. These continuing functions ensure that the littoral and shallow waters are incredibly fertile, supporting a growth of marine flora that provides both shelter and food for invertebrate life. This area is the grazing ground of most fish, whether they live by feeding on lesser creatures or predate on their own species. (Fig. 1)

Not all marine fish are resident in our seas throughout the year. Many come and go according to an availability of food or the urge to reproduce. Most of these annual migrations are along well-known paths and at regular seasonal periods. Many factors define when and whither their travels begin, one of the most important of these being the availability of warm water. There are many warm currents north of the Equator though the most important, passing close to the western coasts of the British Isles, is the North Atlantic Drift. A spur of the Gulf Stream, this current stream brings many of the pelagic species such as mackerel, bass, pilchard and sardine, with the larger predators, the sharks, swordfish and tunny following in their wake. At the same time the higher temperature of the Drift encourages shoals of demersal species such as Mediterranean breams, which hug the seabed as they range northward.

Tide is the most important influence on all marine animals. This twice-daily phenomenon brings a cleansing action to the littoral waters; carries fresh food supplies in the form of drifting plankton while stimulating a regular pattern of underwater activity. Sea anglers will many times have heard the skipper say: 'The tide's about to turn, look to your rods, now we'll get fish!' The ebb, or slack-water, generally creates lethargy among marine creatures, leaving the angler little to do but wait for the freshening of the tide. All life in saltwater reacts to the tidal phases, even human beings are in many ways affected by the moon and its gravitational effect on the ebb and flow of the tides.

Fish leave their resting places to meet the new force that brings food and those species that are strongly territorial

Fig 1 Light, depth, shelter, whether the ground is composed of mud, sand, shingle or rock all provide a habitat for animal life which the sea angler can use as bait. But many baits taken from the splash zone will attract fish even when offered in deep water. Whatever bait is used, it must be fresh and presented on a hook of the right size.

will patrol their patch, redefining their rights. They are keyed into feeding and pugnacious behaviour, the time when fish are most vulnerable.

TIDE

There are two high tides in every 24-hour period, but there are a few places round Britain which experience two high rises in each tidal phase. The high tide does not arrive at the same time every day and neither does it always reach the same height. Both tide and its height are dictated by the gravitational pull exerted by the moon, which exerts a pull at that point on the earth directly below it. While the water cannot rise from the earth's surface toward the moon, water from round the world is drawn in the direction of the point of influence of that satellite, thus creating a highwater phase. At the same time, on the other side of the world, there is a similar high tide and water lying between these two high points experiences a low-tide area. As the moon passes round the earth the high tide times change.

Many factors complicate the tidal heights: the seas vary from vast deeps to shallows, land masses are not equal, with enormous areas jutting into the oceans; all these natural features affect the movement of water, producing complex tidal patterns and a lack of regularity in tide times and heights.

It is not necessary for the sea angler to calculate tide times or heights, the Admiralty issues lists of annual predictions which are available for almost any harbour round the British Isles. Anglers need to know about tide-time variations because they tell them when to go fishing. Small-boat owners use local knowledge so that launching and recovery times coincide with the availability of sufficient water to get afloat and ashore.

WIND AND SALINITY

The effects of wind and the salinity of the water are two important things which must be considered by sea anglers when deciding where to fish and for which species. Excessive wind, producing a broken sea, can be dangerous for the dinghy angler. Wind also affects the height and strength of the tide, particularly when it is blowing in the same direction as the tidal flow. A gale blowing in a restricted channel, the Straits of Dover for instance, where the tide is running with it, will produce a much higher tide than that predicted and there will be an extended period of high water, held up by the gale. Shore fishermen are more likely to notice this effect than boat anglers.

The temperature of the wind has an effect too. A cold east wind will chill the surface and put fish off their feeding, whereas a warm, moist south-westerly, especially in the evening, creates a frenzied feeding period that continues into the twilight.

Salinity, the amount of dissolved mineral salts present in water, establishes the range of species that can occupy a certain area. Some species are more tolerant of a freshwater inflow into the sea than others. Bass, mullet and flounders live and feed in estuaries into which rivers discharge freshwater, though this must be clean and pure. Where there is severe pollution from industry or farming both fish and other marine life will be driven from the area or become diseased.

Offshore, where freshwater and suspended matter from the landmass have less effect, are found the sharks and other oceanic travellers, for it seems that these species keep to water undiluted with that from the land. Both in British waters and overseas, skippers have said that these fish stay beyond the blue-water line, defined as the clear border between the greyish inshore and clean oceanic

A

A A traditional sea angling craft crossing the Blasket Sound, in Co. Kerry. These tough charter boats have been the backbone of sportfishing for many years. *B* The new generation of sea angling craft. A fast and stable 'Orkney 19 Fastliner', built by Panda Boats, in Ireland, to meet the demand for private, group and club ownership.

B

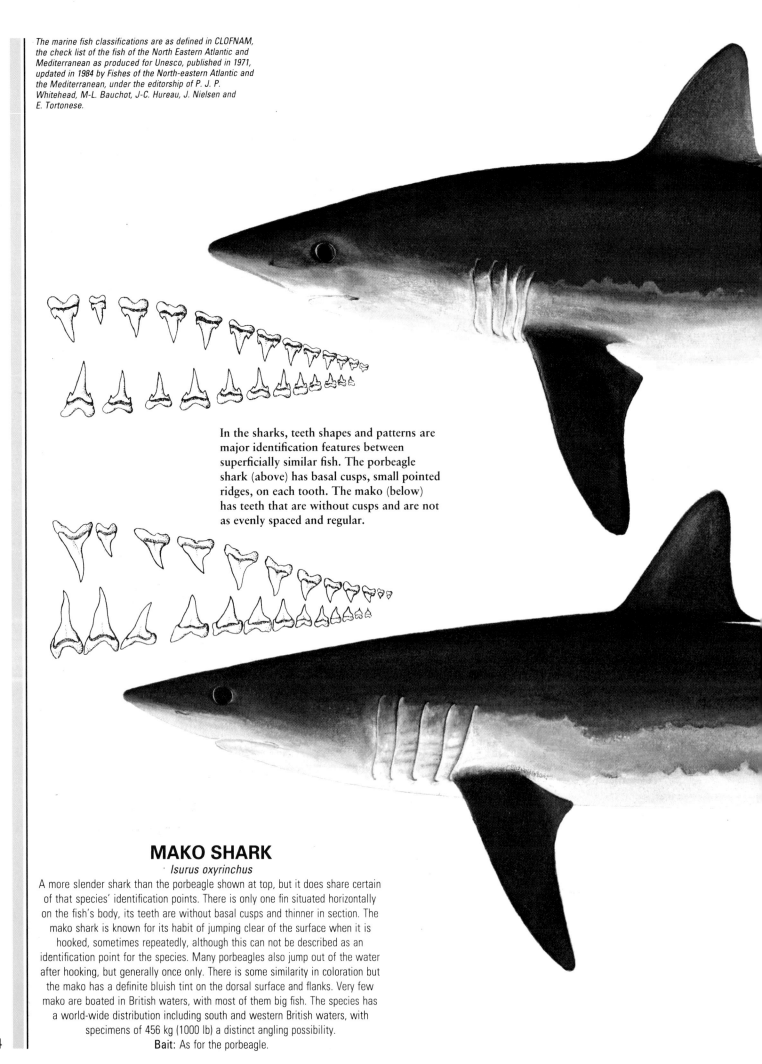

The marine fish classifications are as defined in CLOFNAM, the check list of the fish of the North Eastern Atlantic and Mediterranean as produced for Unesco, published in 1971, updated in 1984 by Fishes of the North-eastern Atlantic and the Mediterranean, under the editorship of P. J. P. Whitehead, M-L. Bauchot, J-C. Hureau, J. Nielsen and E. Tortonese.

In the sharks, teeth shapes and patterns are major identification features between superficially similar fish. The porbeagle shark (above) has basal cusps, small pointed ridges, on each tooth. The mako (below) has teeth that are without cusps and are not as evenly spaced and regular.

MAKO SHARK
Isurus oxyrinchus

A more slender shark than the porbeagle shown at top, but it does share certain of that species' identification points. There is only one fin situated horizontally on the fish's body, its teeth are without basal cusps and thinner in section. The mako shark is known for its habit of jumping clear of the surface when it is hooked, sometimes repeatedly, although this can not be described as an identification point for the species. Many porbeagles also jump out of the water after hooking, but generally once only. There is some similarity in coloration but the mako has a definite bluish tint on the dorsal surface and flanks. Very few mako are boated in British waters, with most of them big fish. The species has a world-wide distribution including south and western British waters, with specimens of 456 kg (1000 lb) a distinct angling possibility.

Bait: As for the porbeagle.

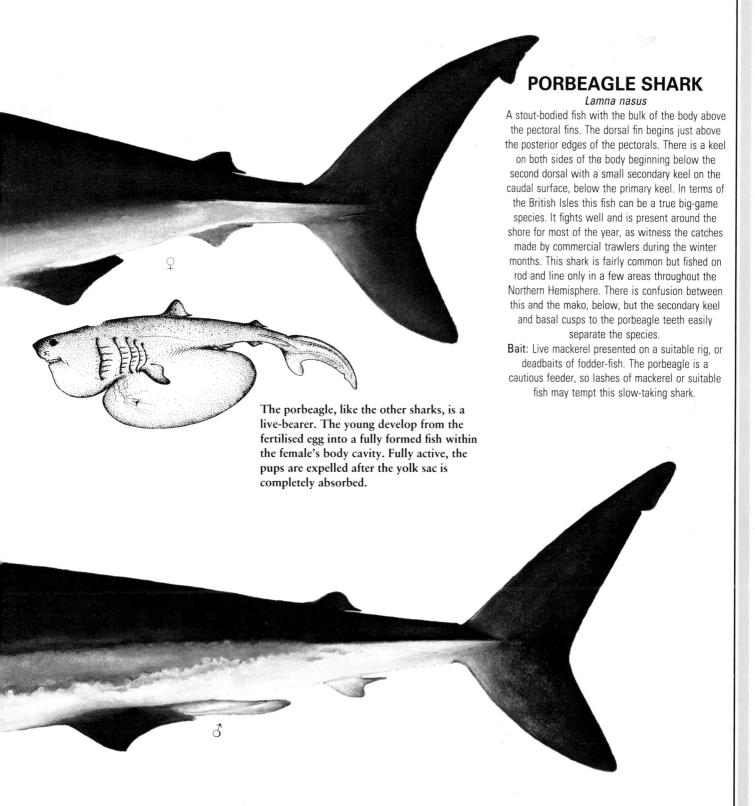

PORBEAGLE SHARK
Lamna nasus

A stout-bodied fish with the bulk of the body above the pectoral fins. The dorsal fin begins just above the posterior edges of the pectorals. There is a keel on both sides of the body beginning below the second dorsal with a small secondary keel on the caudal surface, below the primary keel. In terms of the British Isles this fish can be a true big-game species. It fights well and is present around the shore for most of the year, as witness the catches made by commercial trawlers during the winter months. This shark is fairly common but fished on rod and line only in a few areas throughout the Northern Hemisphere. There is confusion between this and the mako, below, but the secondary keel and basal cusps to the porbeagle teeth easily separate the species.

Bait: Live mackerel presented on a suitable rig, or deadbaits of fodder-fish. The porbeagle is a cautious feeder, so lashes of mackerel or suitable fish may tempt this slow-taking shark.

The porbeagle, like the other sharks, is a live-bearer. The young develop from the fertilised egg into a fully formed fish within the female's body cavity. Fully active, the pups are expelled after the yolk sac is completely absorbed.

BLUE SHARK
Prionace glauca

This is a streamlined, slender shark possessing large wing-like pectoral fins and an elongated, sloping caudal fin. The colour is a brilliant blue as the fish leaves the water but this vivid coloration quickly dulls to a drab black. Blue shark have tearing teeth, extremely sharp and with a saw edge with which they strip long gouges in a bait that is attacked but not taken. Due to over-fishing in British waters this species has shown a marked decline in average weight, with numbers of small fish of 13.6 kg (30 lb) caught off Cornwall and 22.8 kg (50 lb) off the southern coast of Ireland. Blues should now always be put back alive. The blue shark has a world-wide distribution with fish weighing over 196 kg (430 lb) coming from New Zealand waters. There would appear to be a shoaling factor as this shark hunts in packs.

Bait: Fresh deadbaits, mackerel, herring and other fodder fish.

HAMMERHEAD SHARK
Sphryna zygaena

This shark is an oddity, with its flattened head bearing eyes set out on the tips of two wing-like protuberances. It has a small mouth in comparison with the body bulk and has not been taken in large numbers by anglers presumably because it cannot take whole-fish baits with any speed. This shark, properly named the black hammerhead, has a number of similar species distributed round the world, mostly in tropical waters, where it reaches 300 kg (650 lb).

Bait: Fishbait, lashes rather than whole fish.

76

THRESHER SHARK
Alopias vulpinus
The thresher shark is unmistakable, with its outrageously elongated caudal fin shaped like a scythe. The body is fairly short and sturdy with large pectoral fins, the second dorsal and anal fins are very small and the mouth is crescent-shaped with small triangular teeth. The thresher is not an uncommon shark in British waters but is rarely caught by rod and line angling. As it circles fodder-fish, its huge tail is used to 'herd' the prey into a small area before charging into them. The tail is also known to be employed in stunning swimming sea-birds. Fish of over 456 kg (1000 lb) are known to live in tropical seas, with a British record of 147 kg (323 lb).
Bait: As for the other sharks.

SPURDOG
Squalus acanthias

Taking its name from the two spurs or spikes present at the leading edge of the dorsal fins, this is the most prolific member of the shark family found in the waters of the British Isles. There is no anal fin. The spurdog moves in huge shoals cropping fodder-fish of the sea as do sheep the grass on land. They stay on the bottom during the winter months but 'doggedly' follow baits and hooked fish to the surface in warmer times. A voracious fish, the spurdog can provide good sport on light tackle and reaches up to 1.2 m (4 ft) long and 9.6 kg (21 lb) plus.
Bait: Fish strips or small whole fish such as 'joey' mackerel or pouting.

TOPE
Galeorhinus galeus

The most sporting fighter of the smaller sharks, the tope can put up a tremendous struggle when hooked in shallow water or when fished on suitable tackle that allows the fish to show its speed. The dorsal fins are spaced far apart with the pelvics exactly midway between them. The lower lobe of the caudal fin is deeply notched in an unmistakable identification pattern. A tope's teeth are large and sharp, with a slight serration to the inner edges. The species has a wide distribution, being present throughout the year in British waters, although the winter months see them out in the deeps. Fish of 13.6 to 18 kg (30 to 40 lb) are the average, with the possibility of one weighing 31.7 kg (70 lb).
Bait: Fish as whole-baits or lashes. Elasticated thread should be used to tie the bait to the hook because tope otherwise will tear it off the hook.

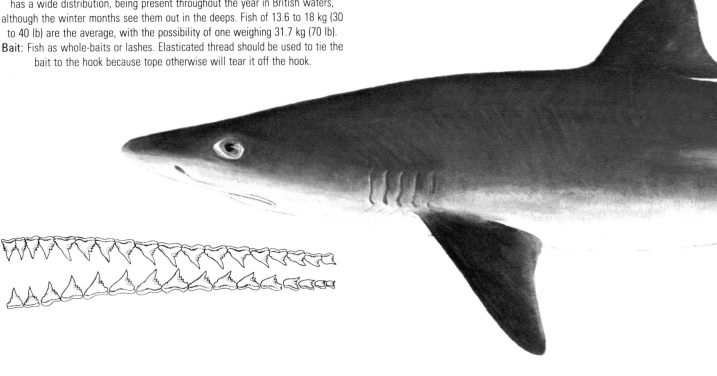

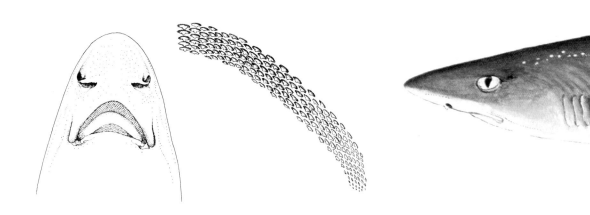

The underside of the smooth-hound jaw showing the teeth rows and pattern.

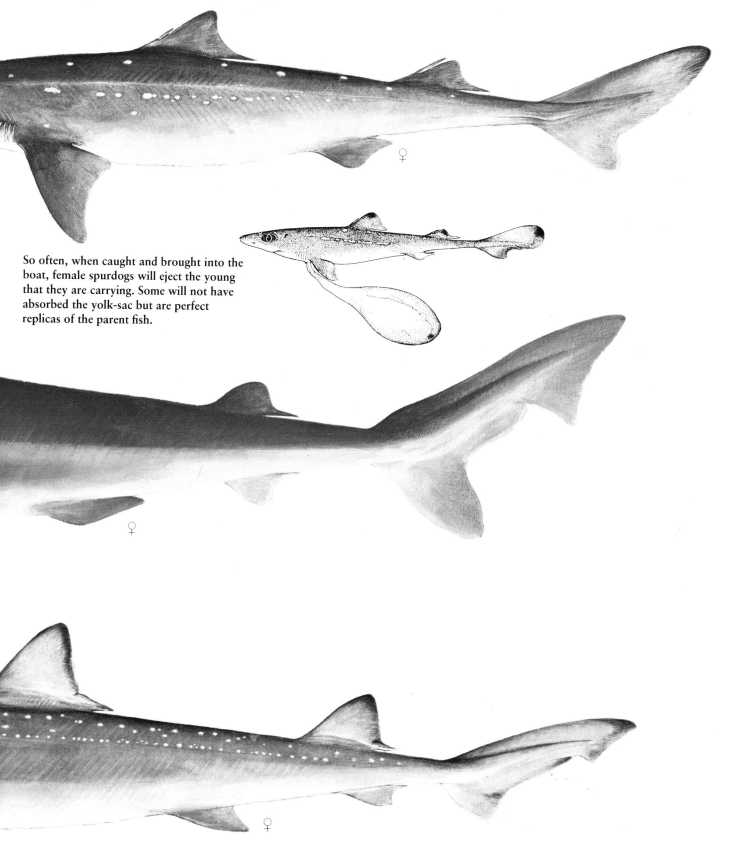

So often, when caught and brought into the boat, female spurdogs will eject the young that they are carrying. Some will not have absorbed the yolk-sac but are perfect replicas of the parent fish.

♀

♀

♀

SMOOTH-HOUNDS
Mustelus mustelus and *M. asterias*

These small sharks are often mistaken for small tope, but have much larger dorsal fins and the pectorals have a more square shape. Both species are grey dorsally with a diluted coloration on the belly. The pectoral fins begin at a point under the fourth gill-slit. *M. asterias* has a number of light spots along the flanks of the adult fish. Both species have grinding, skate-like teeth used to crush food such as crustaceans, cephalopods and fish. Specimens of nearly 1.5 m (5 ft) are known but the average is about 1 m (3 ft). Both species come inshore during the warmer months, at times swimming well up into brackish estuarial waters.

Bait: Fish-strips, squid and crab.

MONKFISH
Squatina squatina

An ugly fish, perhaps better known as the angel shark, the monkfish is half skate and half shark with a wide, flattened body and large paired fins. The dorsal fins are the same size and far to the rear of the body along the 'tail'. The mouth is large and situated on the extreme fore-edge of the head, unlike the sharks to which it is related. The monkfish can reach considerable weights of 80 kg (176 lb) and feeds over known flatfish grounds, but eats crustaceans and molluscs too. The monkfish cannot be said to be a sporting fish and due to its alternative name of angel shark it is often confused with the angler fish (below), which is a totally different, bony, species.

Bait: Fish-baits, although most worm/squid cocktails will be taken.

ANGLER FISH
Lophius piscatorius

A true bony fish, the angler fish has an enormous mouth full of sharp, curved teeth some of which are hinged, and on top of the head there is a modified first dorsal ray which can be twitched to act as a fishing lure. Small fish, invertebrates, crustaceans, cephalopods are its food. The angler fish lacks scales and there are rows of bony flaps which run along the body at the junction of the dorsal and the under-body. This is but one of the many species that can be regarded as very deepwater fishes, those that are found at depths of 1000 fathoms or more. In British waters it reaches weights of over 43 kg (94 lb) but it is not considered to be a serious angling quarry.

Bait: Fish-baits as lashes or whole fish.

Camouflaged by disturbed sand and mud, the wide, cavernous mouth of the angler fish contains rows of backwards-pointing teeth. Attracted by the waving 'lures' on the fish's head, fish of many species are drawn towards the jaws and are quickly sucked in as the angler fish lunges forward.

water. Depth, too, plays its part in keeping fish such as sharks out deep.

THE SEABED

A soft sea-bottom predominates round the British Isles, interspersed by patches of gravel, sand, shell, chalk, clay, outcrops of rock and pavements of flat rock-shelf. Most areas comprise a mixture of two or more of these materials. Fish live permanently in or migrate to areas that provide two things, food or a spawning ground. The quality of the water and light that filters down dictates whether marine life is present. Turbidity, caused by suspended material in the water from strong coastal currents or silt out of rivers that spill into the sea, has a marked bearing on the amount of light that penetrates through to the depths. With no light there will be little if any vegetation. Lack of light means few invertebrates, so the fish will not be present.

Fortunately, fish do not depend for food solely on plantlife or its associated small animal populations. Many marine fish graze on a continuous crop of crustaceans and shellfish living on or under the mud or sand forming the seabed. Other fish feed on zoo- and phyto-plankton that come with each floodtide. Many, probably most, marine fish predate on lesser species or immature fish of their own kind. The food chain in the sea can be described as every creature forming food for another animal species!

HABITAT RECOGNITION

Unlike freshwater anglers, who have relatively few fish species to locate, the sea angler has about 400 species of fish in his environment. Fish species are not found spread evenly through the seas, they move into conditions that suit them. The predator will be found where its preyfish are, including species which the angler seeks.

THE SEA ANGLER'S MARKS

When sea anglers find a hot-spot, a place where fish congregate and can be caught regularly, it is called a mark. This mark is usually a feeding area that fulfils a demand throughout a season, or part of one. The mark is there as the result of some shipping disaster such as a wreck or the result of wartime operations; it may be a reef of rocks, a fertile sandbank or a shellfish bed. Each of these can support a larder of vertebrate and invertebrate food either in the lush weed growth on the mark or in the sea surrounding it. Feeding fish gain two advantages from staying in the vicinity of the mark, food and hiding places where they can rest secure from predators. (Fig. 2)

Occasionally a mark will be found that seems to have none of the natural advantages. The seabed may be flat and devoid of marine life. This type of mark may be a 'meeting place' where certain species congregate at spawning time, for the moment ignoring the danger from predators while intent on reproducing their kind. This mark will not always fish well, only being productive at certain times of the year.

A

FIG 2 ECHO-SOUNDER TRACE

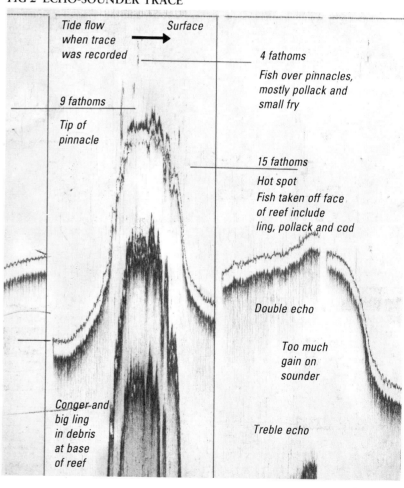

Tide flow when trace was recorded → Surface

9 fathoms
Tip of pinnacle

Conger and big ling in debris at base of reef

4 fathoms
Fish over pinnacles, mostly pollack and small fry

15 fathoms
Hot spot
Fish taken off face of reef include ling, pollack and cod

Double echo

Too much gain on sounder

Treble echo

A This type of echo-sounder gives a continuous readout, as the boat moves across the sea, on a paper chart. Its main advantage is that paper rolls can be stored and compared when on future expeditions to the same reef or wreck mark.

Fig 2 To get the best from an echo-sounder printout one has to know how to interpret the reading. Fish can be seen as tiny smudges, but double and triple echoes may mislead. There is some lateral contraction to be considered.

Why is it necessary to be able to recognise a mark? The skipper of any charterboat is relied on to find his customers the best fishing, but a successful angler needs to know something of the seas' life-cycle and the behaviour of his quarry. The skipper may say that he is anchored over a sandbank, but more importantly, in order to assess the situation one should know on which side of the bank you are relative to the tide. Some flatfish habitually lie on sandbanks, turbot and brill wait on the downtide side waiting for small preyfish, particularly sandeels. The knowledgeable angler will use a rig and bait that simulates the behaviour of the preyfish. More and more sea anglers are becoming dinghy-owners and these anglers must understand the inshore waters, the tides and potential seabed factors that create marks.

HOLDING GROUND

More than any other, one kind of seabed fulfils the sea angler's demand for a consistent, fish-producing mark — broken ground. Inshore, the marks can easily be recognised, such as places where cliffs have been constantly eroded, the broken rocks dropping and spilling into the littoral waters. If the sea is shallow the mark will normally hold only small fish even though there may be plenty of food, but larger fish will come and go. Offshore, the same ground will give better results, because deeper water means less light, creating ideal conditions for ambush by predators. Many species of fish haunt offshore broken ground both for the security it gives the predator and the chance to hide and pounce on preyfish. For the angler, finding this kind of mark can be difficult. A charterboat skipper might provide the information or an Admiralty chart can be studied and the plotted mark found in conjunction with an echo-sounder.

Inshore broken-ground provides crabs, worms and shellfish as food for small fish. Big fish move in to feed on each tide and often disperse to rest during the tides' powerful phases. The offshore counterpart holds all the food potential, a population of resident species as well as a never-ending migration of fish using the ground on a short-stay basis.

OFFSHORE BANKS

There are many famous sea-fishing areas round the British Isles where rivers have spilled vast amounts of silt into the sea. Strong currents and tidal action move this material to areas of lesser current-flow, creating huge banks of sand and mud. More often than not the tide pressure is still too strong to allow any vegetation to take hold, but food for fish is there in plenty beneath the mud and sand. Worms and some fish species are adapted to living under the surface, lying dormant during strong tides and merging when the tide slackens.

Many flatfish and members of the skate family pursue a similar life-style. They drop down into the gullies or to the base of high banks when the tide is at its strongest, returning to the killing ground when water pressure puts their fodder species at a disadvantage. From half-tide on, their body shape allows them to hug the sand while the current sweeps over them, giving free movement over the bank. Cod and tope also range the sandbanks and both species being opportunist feeders they scavenge for food-fish in trouble.

Offshore banks pose a problem in seamanship for boat-owners. During a tidal phase, water flow will switch from one direction to another. Fish then move over a bank to areas of least disturbance and greatest feeding potential, so the angler must follow their movements while taking heed of the danger of strong water flowing across comparatively shallow ground.

PINNACLE ROCKS

Rising vertically from the seabed, pinnacle rocks and the associated reefs nearby provide another of the sea angler's most promising habitats. Here, of the most importance is the absence of commercial fishermen, who do not want to lose expensive nets. Only lobster-fishermen will be interested in this ground, although netsmen might attempt to get close-to, seeking to scoop up quality fish that use the rocks as a base from which to range over surrounding areas. A few years back, long-lining might have taken the best fish but few commercial boats use this system today.

Most pinnacle rock, often the underwater continuation of a landmass, is to be found off the west and north-west coasts of Britain and Ireland. Here, bulky reefs cause massive alterations to tidal flows, creating a variety of holding habitats. Over the pinnacle peaks are found many smaller fish, pouting, breams and pollack, feeding either on plankton or fry that move in pelagic layers. Slightly deeper in the water, alongside the sheer wall of the pinnacle, are bigger specimens of these species as well as cod, coalfish and ling, all rising to predate on the lesser fish above them. Specimen fish tend to populate the lower, darker regions of the rock where a multitude of crevices and debris provide resting places and ideal ambush points. Below, at the base of the pinnacle, are the scavengers, conger eels, skate and the slow-moving species that expect animal detritus to drop down from above. Often oceanic sharks and the smaller ground sharks will take up positions round the reef, aware that here is a prized larder. This, then, is a prized angler's mark.

Finding good marks becomes a lifetime's task with some anglers. Those who can read a chart, plot a course and handle a boat are in the forefront of successful sea angling. Knowing the requirements of fish is the key to it all: what they feed on, at what depth and at what time of the year and recognising a possible habitat, whether it is a small reef, a wreck, a gully between sandbanks or a patch of worm-bearing mud between rock and weed-growth.

THE BOAT ANGLER'S SPECIES

There are some 400 marine fish species inhabiting or visiting the coastal waters of the British Isles. Not all are sufficiently large to arouse the interest of anglers and of the 40 to 50 species that do receive serious attention, about 10 per cent are seasonal visitors. Our inward migratory species, although fairly regular in appearance, do not necessarily come each year or to the same offshore locations. Warm currents, offshoots of the North Atlantic Drift, exhibit a wide variation of strength and penetration of the colder North Atlantic waters and it is within these streams that our seasonal visitors swim.

There are periods which seem to become more noticeable as one grows older, when species all but disappear from the angler's catch. For some reason or other the red bream virtually disappeared from off the South Coast and are just beginning to show again, although the closely related black bream appears to visit our shores as regularly as ever.

Commercial fishing ('over-fishing' is the better term) is a major threat to herring, mackerel and other pelagic species. Deepwater hake, once a mainstay of trawling and lining boats operating in the Irish Sea and round the Hebrides, are now rarely seen by anglers.

The mako shark seems to be a sporadic visitor, whereas blue sharks are reasonably constant in their visits and there is always a resident population of porbeagles. Nevertheless, when shoalfish do not arrive, neither do these larger predatory fish that follow in their wake to feed on them.

The marine species that illustrate the sea angling section of this bok are those that have most interest for both boat and shore anglers, plus some of the more interesting small fishes. Ideally, any marine-fish illustrator would choose to paint fish exactly as they were when taken from the water and before colour fades on a dull, lifeless skin. In this volume we have tried to faithfully reproduce what the sea angler sees as his fish breaks the surface film.

Some anglers find that the colour varies between fish they have caught. This is perfectly possible because fish in the sea, like the freshwater species, adapt their coloration to suit that of the surrounding habitat in which they exist. A few species adopt sexual colour variations, while immature fish often display diluted adult hues.

A

A Sea angling can be a tough game, without the often back-breaking and very tiring task of playing and boating fish from deepwater. Just maintaining balance throughout the day can be exhausting if the sea is anything but flat calm. This lady angler is about to find out the hard way. B This is the prize that makes it all worth the effort, a superb ling for Joyce West, fishing a deepwater wreck off the southern coast of Ireland.

B

TACKLE FOR BOAT FISHING

Sea angling is fairly new as a sport. The rod and reel came into use in the latter half of the 19th century and I doubt whether a sea fisherman of those times really looked on a rod as a sporting extension, or as a spring that allowed him to lighten his line. More likely, he regarded the rod as being less rough on his hands than the traditional cutty-hunk handline. Together with a wooden centrepin reel, his rod allowed a more gentlemanly approach to what was described by the unknowing as a 'chuck-it-and-chance-it' sport!

We have moved on from the clumsy whole- or built-cane rod towards exceptionally light and responsive kinds made from a variety of mineral fibres bonded with phenolic resins. But we still share one factor that the rod brought to the earlier sea fisherman – vibration. The sensation of movement below the keel, of a straining, fighting fish that we cannot see until the fight is almost at an end, is what our sport is all about – and we can eat what we catch, even share it with friends and family. But that sensation of multiple tremors transmitted through rod and forearms cannot be shared!

Modern sea fishing was born when anglers understood that dragging a fish to the surface was reasonably easy and that there could be far more subtlety in methods as well as tackle.

Manufacturers have tried many rod materials in an effort to increase sensitivity and playing power. We have had tubular-steel that rusted from within, lighter built-cane stiffened by a steel core, solid glass, hollow fibre-glass tubes and now we enjoy featherlight carbon and boron rods. The quality of design and the material used makes the rod – but it cannot make the angler: only the way in which the rod is used will do that!

ROD VARIANTS

There are two basic sea-fishing rod lengths; the first is the traditional weapon of about 2 m (7 ft) used in an up-and-down fashion or when trolling a natural or artificial lure. It is of a manageable length when one considers the confined space in the average cockpit of a charterboat. This rod will be used by boat anglers the world over, whether fishing for the smallest dabs or the largest of big-game species.

In the past two decades a modern 2.7–3.0 m (9–10 ft) rod with both playing and casting action has emerged. This new-style instrument comes into play in uptide fishing, when baits are cast up to 45.7 m (50 yards) to a position on the seabed ahead of the anchored boat. Both forms of boat rod have their uses, each acting in a different way and neither out-performing the other.

What is important is that the rod should be well finished; its rings and handle appropriate for the kind of fishing undertaken and that it balances with the angler's line. There is a formula, expressed as a test curve, which enables the fisherman correctly to load his reel with line

Some powerful and most IGFA-class rods have a gimbal fitting. This prevents the rod twisting by having grooves in the end of the handle. This groove locates in a similar fitting on a strong butt pad or fighting chair.

Handles are important on any boat rod but one that slips is a menace. A cork top grip which both hands can grasp is perfect. Beware of a grip that is too thick. A hand that cannot close around it loses power.

Not all boat rods require roller guides but there is a need at times for a low-set cradle-type ring that is braced and hard-chromed for the heavy work that general purpose boat rods are subjected to.

A fast taper 13.6 kg (30 lb) light tackle boat rod, 2 m (6 ft 9 in) long with hard-chrome intermediates and a roller tip ring.

TWO BOAT ANGLER'S RODS

A IGFA 22.8 kg (50 lb) class rod, compound taper, 2.1 m (7 ft) long with roller guides.

A modern grip from modern material – a form of plastic/rubber composite. It does not become slimy and with a subtle resilience in the material gives a positive handhold. Unfortunately, for the angler, it can be expensive.

On a light boat rod a rubber butt cap or threaded button will finish the handle nicely. Make certain that the diameter of the butt cap is large enough to spread the load associated with fighting a big fish, or use a belly pad.

Most important – the winch fitting. Essentials are quality material and positive locking so that the guides always align. Threads should be cut and not rolled allowing wide adjustment, between the two collars, for fitting different reels.

that suits the rod. American authorities have further simplified this, the International Game Fish Association nominated a line breaking strain to suit each rod class. This is a good starting point to arrive at the correct line to use, for the line will always be the weakest link between angler and fish. The established line classes are:

IGFA line ratings

2.7 kg (6 lb)	22.8 kg (50 lb)
5.5 kg (12 lb)	36 kg (80 lb)
9 kg (20 lb)	59 kg (130 lb)
13.6 kg (30 lb)	

Most rods now carry an IFGA line rating rather than the older test-curve information. Decide what fishing suits you, buy the rod and use it with the correct line breaking strain. Obviously, it is not simply a matter of assessing the fighting power of the species that predominate in your part of the coast. The added pressure of strength of tide and weight of sinker needed to counteract it all put a strain on the rod blank. A correctly selected class-line rod should take all three factors into account.

Class lines are makes of braided Dacron, Terylene or monofilament nylon that fulfils the demand that they break at a defined strain, at the same time balancing perfectly to the rod's blank and its fighting curve. There is no point in vastly increasing the line breaking strain to a point where it cannot be broken by excessive power from rod or fish, all that happens then is that the rod is pulled over in an arc to a point where it cannot apply any more power and a stalemate exists between angler and fish. Far better would be a situation where the tackle is balanced correctly, with the fisherman recovering or giving line according to the state of play between him and the fish. An infinitely better struggle develops, with both angler and fish giving of their best: this epitomises good fishing.

Rods have a variety of inbuilt actions. Their taper can be fast, medium or slow. I prefer the first two types because a fast-tapered blank has an extremely sensitive tip. This aids bite detection with added power from about a quarter of the tip's length as the rod is pulled over and the stronger, less flexible mid-section comes into play. Such a rod is ideal for general fishing; species such as cod, ling, pollack and others that do not exhibit sustained fighting qualities. My medium-actioned rod, where the real power comes into play a third of the length from the tip, is reserved for those fish that either run for long distances, fight with a series of arm-shattering lunges, or give a long-drawn-out and dour battle; in this category come tope, shark, skate and big conger. This kind of rod has a lot of spring power which absorbs much of the sudden fish movement that might be my undoing.

THE IRONMONGERY

Rods must have rings and reel fittings that suit the blank and the fishing style. The rings need to be neat, sufficiently

Hard-chrome bridge guides are ideal for light tackle boat rods, although a bracing strut might be necessary. Providing a rod has enough rings to support the line stress imposed, these rings can withstand playing quite big fish. They are also suitable for casting and spinning rods.

A type of non-strutted double roller tip guide found on 13.6–22.8 kg (30–50 lb) class rods. It can just about withstand the use of wire line, is neat and adds little weight as well as being made to close tolerances.

Stand-off, strutted end rings of this kind are suitable for both nylon and braided lines. Pull a piece of nylon stocking through the seamless centre of the ring to find whether there are any high spots or rough edges left by the manufacturing process.

An AFTCO-type double roller butt guide with rollers of hardened steel within a stainless steel, chromium-plated, cage.

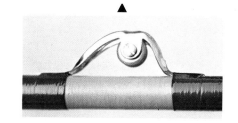

AFTCO roller guides are used as single roller intermediate units between double roller butt and tip roller guide.

A strutted double roller tip guide. With care it can be used for wire line.

LESSER-SPOTTED DOGFISH
Scyliorhinus canicula

This small shark is known by many anglers as the small-spotted catshark or the rough hound, due to its habit of wrapping the body round the arm when a hook is being removed, the extremely rough skin quickly abraiding the angler's flesh. This fish is very easily distinguished from its relative the greater-spotted dogfish, or bull huss, by the single, simple nasal flap and the front of the second dorsal fin is in line with the end of the base of the anal fin. This small, prolific member of the shark family is a bottom-feeder, mainly on crustaceans and small fish. Its egg cases are narrow with thin arms and spiral filaments. Those who like 'rock salmon' from fish-shops might be surprised if they knew they were eating this small, plentiful shark!

Bait: Practically any bait, but worms and fish-strip work best to attract the lesser-spotted dogfish, fished over open ground.

strong to support the line along the curve of the blank and not too heavy in construction. Every time a ring is whipped to a rod it places a stiffened area on that section of the hollow tube, creating a series of flats. This is particularly noticeable on the two lighter classes: 2.7 and 5.5 kg (6 and 12 lb) though not so important on heavier rods as the blank gets stiffer around the 13.6 kg (30 lb) class.

I am especially fond of quality hard-chrome and ceramic-lined rod rings, both are light, strong enough to stand up well to a bruising fishing session and are kind to the lighter lines. I am not convinced that a ceramic-lined ring gives less line wear by minimising friction because fishing line is being lubricated continuously by water and there is no vicious casting involved that might increase line surface abrasion. On 13.6 kg (30 lb) rods and above, a tip roller ring can be very useful as there is always a right-angled change in direction for the angler's line to take and if there is any wear on the line it is made at the tip.

Sea angling becomes specialised at the 22.8 kg (50 lb) class. The rods are subjected to heavy work either from deepwater fighting fish or those enormous game specimens that can rip a lot of line off the reel. Also, many anglers use braided Dacron, Terylene or nylon lines which can suffer badly if the rings do not allow a smooth flow of line. Both intermediate and butt roller rings now have their place on the blank.

One other form of bottom fishing calls for rollers or a reinforced rod ring; it is when a wire line is being used to get the bait down to the seabed in a strong tide. Roller rings will markedly reduce the possibility of kinking in these heavy conditions. Very little servicing of roller rings is necessary, just a wash in freshwater after each fishing session, with regular lubrication to ensure that the outer roller and its inner bearing move freely.

A good handle is vital to a rod that has to work hard. In earlier times, makers used cork foregrips with a wooden butt section. It is now mostly composite material which is kinder on the hands, does not become so slimy and also gives a rod a better appearance. The reel fitting must be capable of locking the reel seat and its position must be

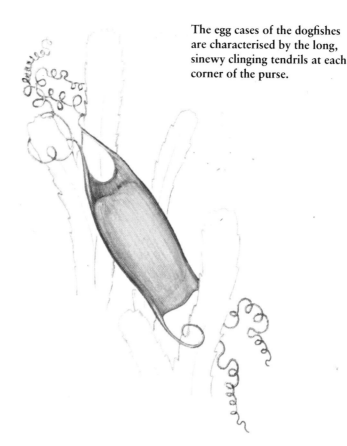

The egg cases of the dogfishes are characterised by the long, sinewy clinging tendrils at each corner of the purse.

Underside of the head of the lesser spotted dogfish (above). The nasal flaps are joined in this species but distinctly separated in the larger bull huss (below).

GREATER-SPOTTED DOGFISH

Scyliorhinus stellaris

A thick-bodied fish of the rocky, deepwater marks, this species is also called the bull huss or nurse hound. This fish is quickly differentiated from the lesser-spotted species by its two separate nasal flaps which are clear of its mouth and the anal fin extends to the middle of the second dorsal fin. The greater-spotted dogfish can reach over 1.5 m (5 ft) long and 10 kg (22 lb) and is credited with displaying much better fighting qualities than the lesser species (above). The greater-spotted dogfish feeds on bottom-living molluscs, crustaceans and demersal fishes. Again different from *S. canicula*, the egg cases are similar but stouter in build with stronger spiral filaments.

Bait: Fish baits are probably the best attractors, but the species will accept shellfish and marine worms.

correct for its owner. Ideally and assuming the use of a multiplying reel, the centre of the reel should be about 40.6 cm (16 in) from the butt cap. My preference is for the left-hand side plate against the inside of my forearm when reeling in, it helps to prevent a rock-and-roll action as the handle is turned.

TWO BOAT REELS: MULTIPLIER AND CENTREPIN

There are only two forms of the boat-angler's reel, the multiplier and the centrepin; fixed-spool reels cannot cope with the heavy weights of lead and fish common to sea angling, though they have a use when spinning on the surface is necessary.

Boat anglers' reels must all have a number of qualities: first-class spindles and bearings, machine-cut gear-trains, a clutch system that operates over a wide variation of applied drag and a spool that will not collapse or spread when line, especially nylon under great pressure, is wound

back. This is a lot to ask of a reel and there are many which do not fulfil these requirements.

There is not much to choose from between the effectiveness of multipliers and centrepins, they both function well, although I believe that their uses are different. The multiplier is generally lighter and neater to work with; it winds line back through a gear-train that gives x-turns of the spool to one of the handle. This gearing demands that the cog and meshing must be sound.

Of the smaller reels, the clutch plates are sometimes tiny, giving very little drag adjustment, described by sea anglers as 'Either all on or all off'. Multipliers carry a lot of line on a spool that one can touch with the thumb, a fact which may not sound important, but it is. Applying thumb pressure is another way of adding drag to the line as it is pulled off by a strong fish. Thumb pressure is infinitely quicker and more sensitively applied during the play than any amount of fiddling with the clutch star wheel. Lever-drag multipliers, most of which have a large braking area, are many times easier to adjust while playing a fish but they are much more expensive. In summary, the quality multiplying reel is first-class for general fishing and in its larger, specialised sizes has proved the most capable big-game reel for really powerful species.

There are, of course, countless situations where the sea angler fishes straight up and down, or nearly so, for fish that do not rip line off the reel. The competitive sea angler particularly needs a fast line-retrieve both when changing bait and to get small fish inboard. This is one occasion when the centrepin will out-score a multiplier.

At one time, as a running fish took line the spool on a centrepiece revolved under direct drive. This was a danger when an unwary angler tried to grab the handle as it spun round. Modern centrepins can now be bought that possess a clutch system, divorcing the winding handle from a direct drive to the revolving spool. Another advantage of the centrepin is its simplicity of construction: no gear-train to mesh, reasonably large bearings on a chunky

spindle, both of which give a certain robustness in use.

Using either reel, the only major problems will be those caused by abuse or lack of simple anti-corrosion maintenance. Forcing the handle round to recover line when a fish is obviously not ready to come to the surface can only lead to a worn-out clutch washer or, worse, a bent spindle. Giving line by using the inherent spring in the rod blank and taking time will serve the reel well and give more satisfaction with the fight.

Wash saltwater off reels after every trip, never throw them into a saltwater-soaked tackle-box to corrode. Relax hard-wound nylon by trailing it over the boat's stern on the way back, it eases pressure building up on the spool and takes out line twist that has built up during the day — but make sure your line stays well clear of the boat's propellor. Take heed of the manufacturer's instructions concerning where and with what to lubricate the reel. Avoid too much oil on or near the clutch, most are

THE ANATOMY OF SKATES AND RAYS

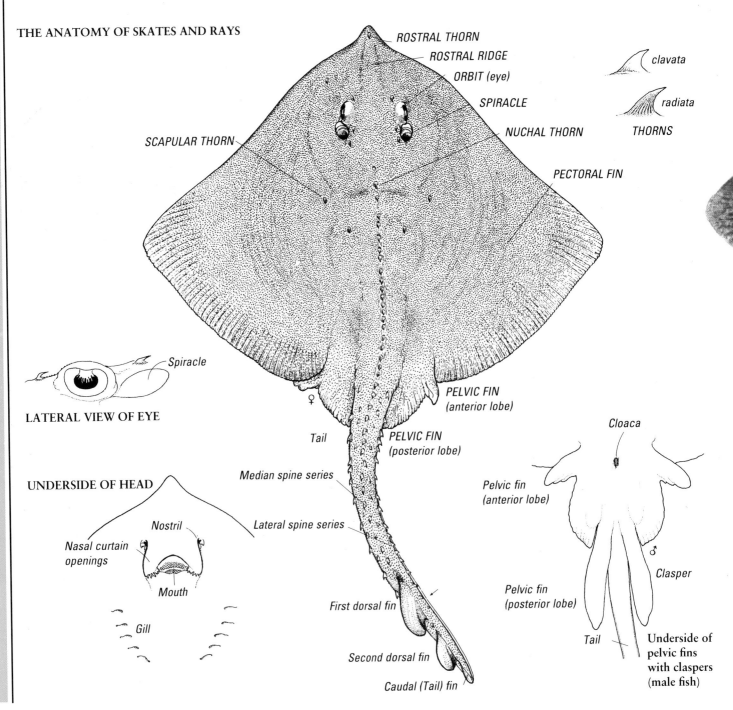

ROSTRAL THORN
ROSTRAL RIDGE
ORBIT (eye)
SPIRACLE
NUCHAL THORN
PECTORAL FIN
SCAPULAR THORN

clavata
radiata
THORNS

LATERAL VIEW OF EYE
Spiracle

Tail
PELVIC FIN (anterior lobe)
PELVIC FIN (posterior lobe)
Median spine series
Lateral spine series

UNDERSIDE OF HEAD
Nostril
Nasal curtain openings
Mouth
Gill

First dorsal fin
Second dorsal fin
Caudal (Tail) fin

Cloaca
Pelvic fin (anterior lobe)
Clasper
Pelvic fin (posterior lobe)
Tail
Underside of pelvic fins with claspers (male fish)

THE THORNBACK RAY
Raja (Raja) clavata

Many variations in coloration and thorn position typify thornback rays. The short snout has a pronounced wave in the anterior edge of the sharp-angled wings. There are two dorsal fins, the posterior reaching the tiny caudal fin. Most specimens have spines along the back and tail in two rows curved on the wings' upper surface with a final row along the dorsal surface of the spine and tail, or an irregular pattern on the wings but clearly defined on the tail. There may be spines on the under-surface of the wings. The belly is white, with a brown-grey mixture with dark or light patches on the upper surface. Thornbacks frequent shallow inshore waters where they grow to over 9 kg (20 lb), feeding on many marine animals.

Bait: Marine worms and fish-baits.

Some colour/spine variations found on thornback rays. Two males and two females are illustrated.

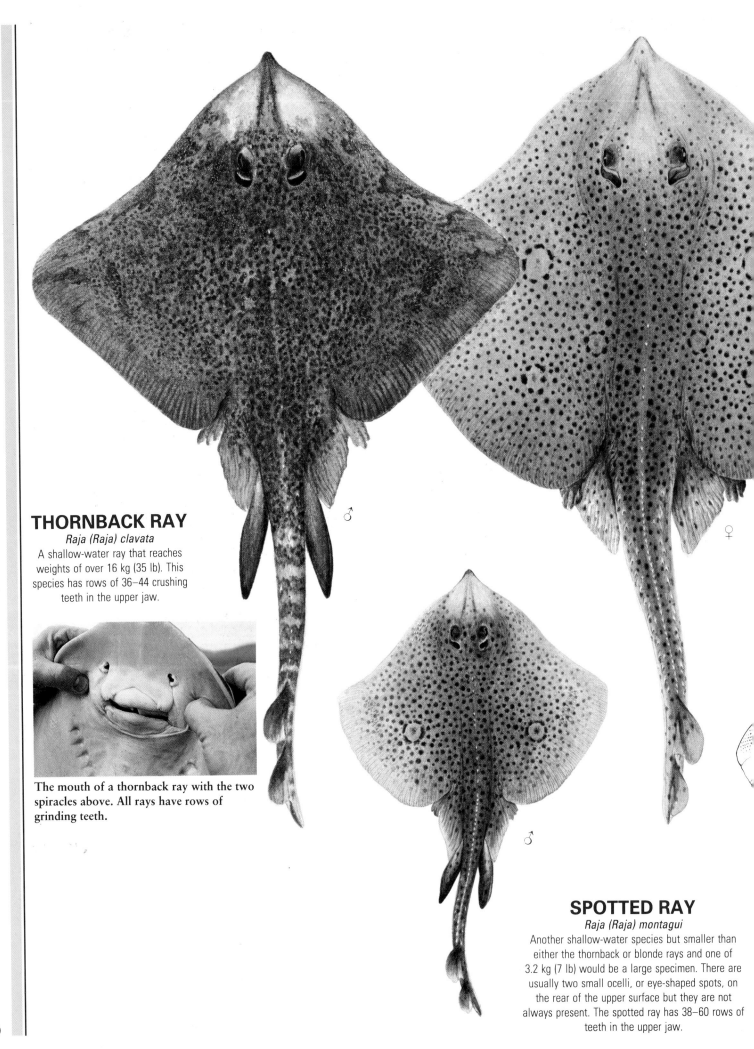

THORNBACK RAY
Raja (Raja) clavata
A shallow-water ray that reaches weights of over 16 kg (35 lb). This species has rows of 36–44 crushing teeth in the upper jaw.

The mouth of a thornback ray with the two spiracles above. All rays have rows of grinding teeth.

SPOTTED RAY
Raja (Raja) montagui
Another shallow-water species but smaller than either the thornback or blonde rays and one of 3.2 kg (7 lb) would be a large specimen. There are usually two small ocelli, or eye-shaped spots, on the rear of the upper surface but they are not always present. The spotted ray has 38–60 rows of teeth in the upper jaw.

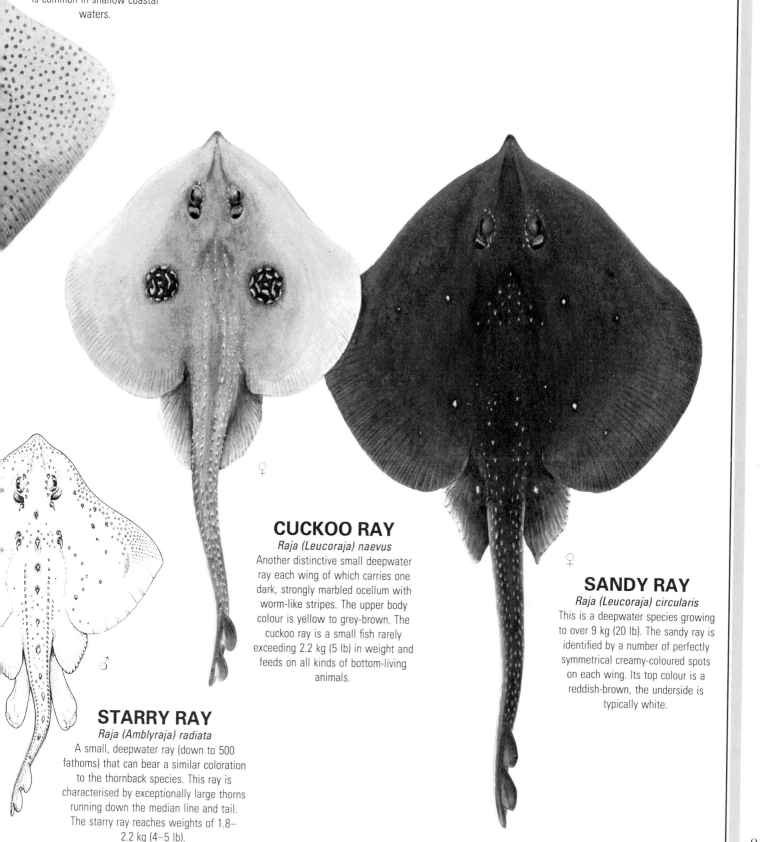

BLONDE RAY
Raja (Raja) brachyura
Largest of the rays sought by anglers the blonde grows to about 18 kg (40 lb). It has more teeth than the other ray species, between 60–90 rows in the upper jaw. Confusion between the blonde and spotted ray can be avoided by comparison of the wing spots, which in the blonde ray reach to the wing margins. This ray is common in shallow coastal waters.

GENERAL NOTE ON THE RAYS
Relatives of the sharks, with cartilaginous bones, all the skates and rays are internally fertilized. The males are easily identified by a pair of stiff, sharp claspers, extensions of the pelvic fins, which together enter the cloacal aperture of the female and deposit the seminal fluid. The females produce a number of eggs that are enclosed within an oblong pouch, known popularly as the 'Mermaid's Purse'. The young rays develop within the pouch and eventually swim free through a slit, emerging as fully formed although miniature versions of the parent stock.

Bait: Most fish baits will take rays while marine worms and shellfish are also readily accepted. Alternative baits are crabs and other crustaceans.

CUCKOO RAY
Raja (Leucoraja) naevus
Another distinctive small deepwater ray each wing of which carries one dark, strongly marbled ocellum with worm-like stripes. The upper body colour is yellow to grey-brown. The cuckoo ray is a small fish rarely exceeding 2.2 kg (5 lb) in weight and feeds on all kinds of bottom-living animals.

SANDY RAY
Raja (Leucoraja) circularis
This is a deepwater species growing to over 9 kg (20 lb). The sandy ray is identified by a number of perfectly symmetrical creamy-coloured spots on each wing. Its top colour is a reddish-brown, the underside is typically white.

STARRY RAY
Raja (Amblyraja) radiata
A small, deepwater ray (down to 500 fathoms) that can bear a similar coloration to the thornback species. This ray is characterised by exceptionally large thorns running down the median line and tail. The starry ray reaches weights of 1.8–2.2 kg (4–5 lb).

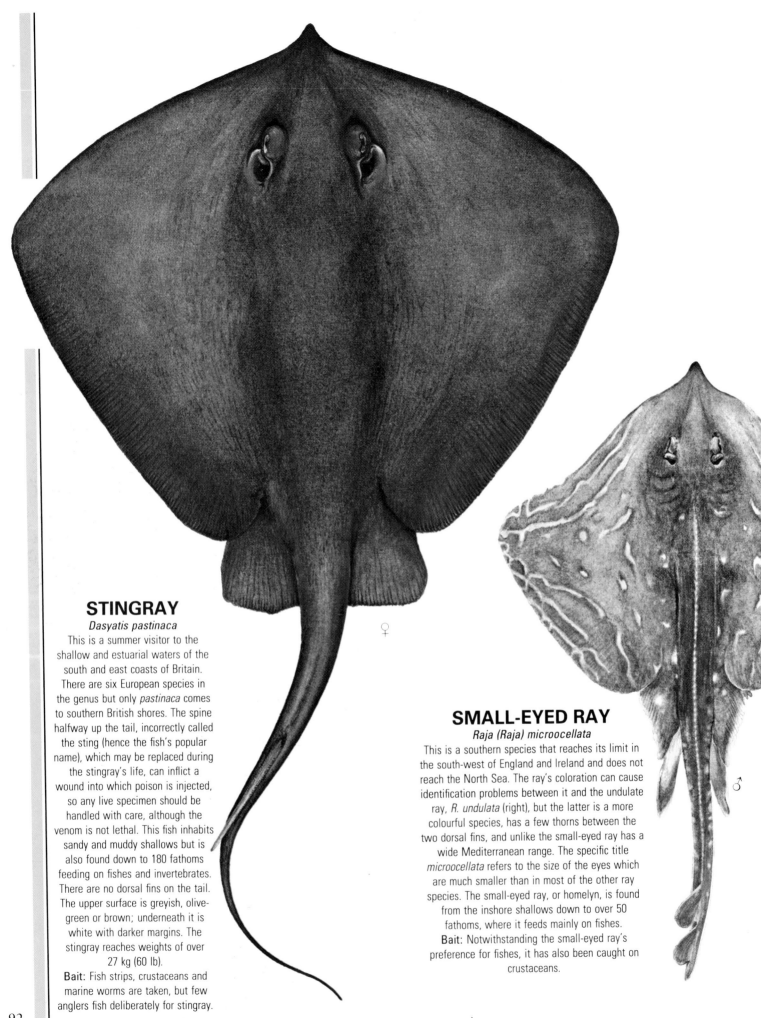

STINGRAY
Dasyatis pastinaca

This is a summer visitor to the shallow and estuarial waters of the south and east coasts of Britain. There are six European species in the genus but only *pastinaca* comes to southern British shores. The spine halfway up the tail, incorrectly called the sting (hence the fish's popular name), which may be replaced during the stingray's life, can inflict a wound into which poison is injected, so any live specimen should be handled with care, although the venom is not lethal. This fish inhabits sandy and muddy shallows but is also found down to 180 fathoms feeding on fishes and invertebrates. There are no dorsal fins on the tail. The upper surface is greyish, olive-green or brown; underneath it is white with darker margins. The stingray reaches weights of over 27 kg (60 lb).

Bait: Fish strips, crustaceans and marine worms are taken, but few anglers fish deliberately for stingray.

♀

SMALL-EYED RAY
Raja (Raja) microocellata

This is a southern species that reaches its limit in the south-west of England and Ireland and does not reach the North Sea. The ray's coloration can cause identification problems between it and the undulate ray, *R. undulata* (right), but the latter is a more colourful species, has a few thorns between the two dorsal fins, and unlike the small-eyed ray has a wide Mediterranean range. The specific title *microocellata* refers to the size of the eyes which are much smaller than in most of the other ray species. The small-eyed ray, or homelyn, is found from the inshore shallows down to over 50 fathoms, where it feeds mainly on fishes.

Bait: Notwithstanding the small-eyed ray's preference for fishes, it has also been caught on crustaceans.

♂

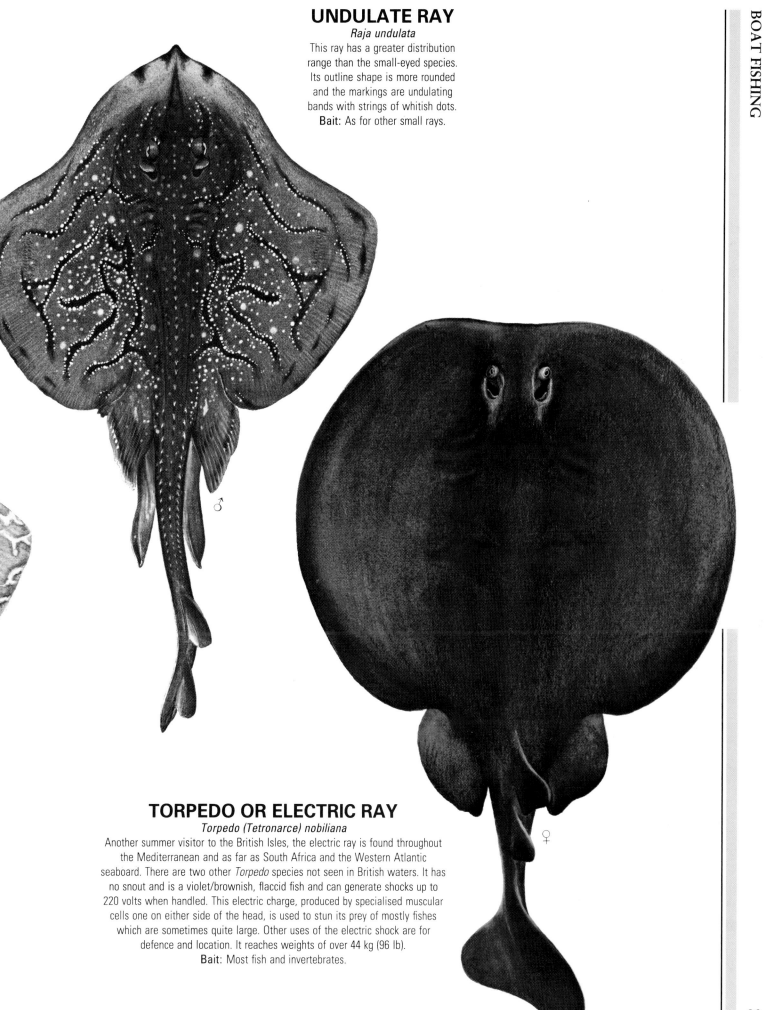

UNDULATE RAY
Raja undulata
This ray has a greater distribution
range than the small-eyed species.
Its outline shape is more rounded
and the markings are undulating
bands with strings of whitish dots.
Bait: As for other small rays.

♂

♀

TORPEDO OR ELECTRIC RAY
Torpedo (Tetronarce) nobiliana
Another summer visitor to the British Isles, the electric ray is found throughout
the Mediterranean and as far as South Africa and the Western Atlantic
seaboard. There are two other *Torpedo* species not seen in British waters. It has
no snout and is a violet/brownish, flaccid fish and can generate shocks up to
220 volts when handled. This electric charge, produced by specialised muscular
cells one on either side of the head, is used to stun its prey of mostly fishes
which are sometimes quite large. Other uses of the electric shock are for
defence and location. It reaches weights of over 44 kg (96 lb).
Bait: Most fish and invertebrates.

intended to operate dry. These are all simple things, yet they add years to the life of your reel.

LINES AND TERMINAL TACKLE

Over the years, three types of line have emerged as those most used by boat anglers: monofilament nylon is by far the most popular, then there is braided line, which could be of either nylon or Terylene make-up, and wire in either single or multiple strands. (Fig. 3)

Nylon is cheap, reliable, strong for its diameter and relatively tough in terms of abrasion toleration. Some makes have more stretch than others, though this is sometimes regarded as an added safety factor for the newcomer to angling. Low stretch is also offered as a strong selling point, but be careful. While it may be better to detect bites by keeping a good contact with the fish, low-stretch line demands that knots are the correct ones and perfectly tied. In terms of colour, I have yet to find any fish-catching differences between nylon in various colours. In deep water there is little light penetration to make any colour discernible and I doubt if fish react to any particular colour.

Class-line fishing came to Britain from the US as do most of the available braided lines. I was informed by one manufacturer that to achieve a stated and guaranteed breaking strain it is easier if the line is built up from a number of strands, each one capable of withstanding a known pull. When the strands are put together the single-strand breaking strains are multiplied into a number of graduated class-lines.

Braided Dacron or Terylene does not stretch but the nylon alternative does, although not as much as a monofilament of equal breaking strain. This absence of stretch in braided lines in very important to game and bottom-anglers; it gives a precise contact with the fish when it takes so that detection is far better. When trolling a lure, striking is more positive and a fish will tend to pull the hook home as it turns away against the tension of the line.

A possible disadvantage in braided line, one especially experienced by bottom anglers, is that of abrasion, because this line has not the natural lubrication quality of nylon; lack of stretch means that it is taut as a bow-string when near to breaking point – a mere touch on the keelband of a boat can mean disaster. But for me braided line gives a perfect contact right down to the hook.

Sometimes wire lines are necessary. Cutting through extremely strong tides is often the only way to get the bait down to the fish. Nylon and braided line will do this but their larger diameter and lack of weight mean that the terminal rig is a long way downtide from the boat, lessening contact and muting striking power. Wire, on the other hand, has a very fine diameter and carries weight along its length, which gets the terminal tackle down, allows the use of lighter weights and gives fantastic bite-detection, with each small pluck being felt at the rod tip.

Naturally, there is a price to pay! Wire can be dangerous at sea, drawn taut it can slice fingers through to the bone. I always connect my weight with a piece of weaker

FIG 3 THEORETICAL CURVES OF REEL LINES IN TIDE

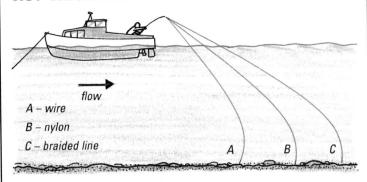

flow

A – wire
B – nylon
C – braided line

Fig 3 Wire line will offer less resistance to tidal flow than nylon or braided line.

nylon, called a 'rotten bottom', so that if the lead is stuck fast on the seabed a heave on the main line will break the nylon and all that is lost then is the weight. It is also a sound principle to have a length of nylon between the wire connecting link-swivel and the hook trace. This acts as an elastic buffer, a precaution against over-vicious striking or the snatch bite. Probably one of the best accessories for the wire-line angler is a pair of industrial gloves, they can save the hands from injury.

THE HOOK, A MOST IMPORTANT CONSIDERATION

The choice of hook patterns is legion, many varied shapes, sizes and barb conformations have been produced over the years, each purporting to do one particular job for the sea angler or his commercial counterpart. I tried many hook patterns before settling on only four kinds for all my sea fishing. (Fig. 4)

For flatfishing my choice has to be a Viking hook, forged straight with an extra-long shank, from Size 1 down to 10; these cope handsomely with flatfish from dabs to turbot. Most flatfish mouth a bait for a long time before taking it inside the mouth, so judging the moment to strike is vital; leaving it too long will probably mean that the fish has got the hook right down, and to unhook it the hook must have a shank that can be firmly gripped. Furthermore, if you want to return the fish alive, a long-shanked hook will allow a clean unhooking. This is more easily done and with far less injury to the fish than probing about inside its mouth with fingers or pliers.

General deepwater fishing requires a strong hook. Of

FIG 4 HOOK PATTERNS

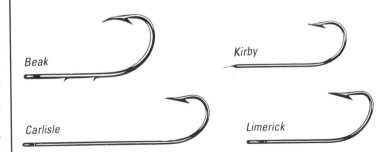

Beak

Kirby

Carlisle

Limerick

O'Shaughnessy

Seamaster

Tarpon

Viking

A secure hook-hold means that this is one wreck-caught cod that did not get away. The size of the hook was relative to the bait, disregarding the well-known enormity of the cod's capacious mouth. Rory Jackson was the angler who caught this fish, just one of the splendid catch that were reeled in while fishing over the wreck of a tanker.

95

WHITE SKATE
Raja (Rostroraja) alba
This skate has a pronounced snout projecting from a convex leading-edge to the wings. The upper surface is a greyish-blue and the underside is white, with dark markings at the edges. The pores are not fringe-marked with brown or black as in the common skate, *Raja (Dipturus) batis*. In Ireland, where the latter species is often caught, it is admitted that some have been white skate and a similar incorrect species identification has probably been made by anglers in Scotland.
Bait: Whole fish or lashes.

COMMON SKATE
Raja (Dipturus) batis
In all the skates, rays and sharks there are anatomical differences between the sexes and the common skate is no exception. The female has pelvic fins divided by the tail whereas the male has elongated fleshy appendages called the claspers, those in the common skate being long, some two-thirds of the length of the tail. All skates lack anal fins though they possess two dorsal fins set back on the tail, which carries a single row of spines, and a caudal fin which exhibits great variance between the various species. There is usually a patch of spines towards the edges of each wing. As the female reaches maturity prickles develop on the grey-brown upper surface. The lower surface is a pale blue-grey. The common skate is found mainly at about 100 fathoms, but is known down to 320 fathoms where it favours broken ground composed of a mixture of mud, sand and rocky outcrops. The young of the common skate feed on all bottom animals but the larger specimens predate on live fish.
Bait: Fish, as lashes or whole.

LONG-NOSED SKATE

Raja (Dipturus) oxyrinchus
This species has a long, pointed snout and the fore-edges of the wings are deeply concave, the trailing edges near-straight. A row of 4–11 spines runs along the tail, but there are none on the body. The upper surface is dark brown or grey in adult fish, the underside also dark brown to grey. This skate is known to reach depths of 500 fathoms and feeds on a wide range of bottom-feeding fish.
Bait: As for other skates.

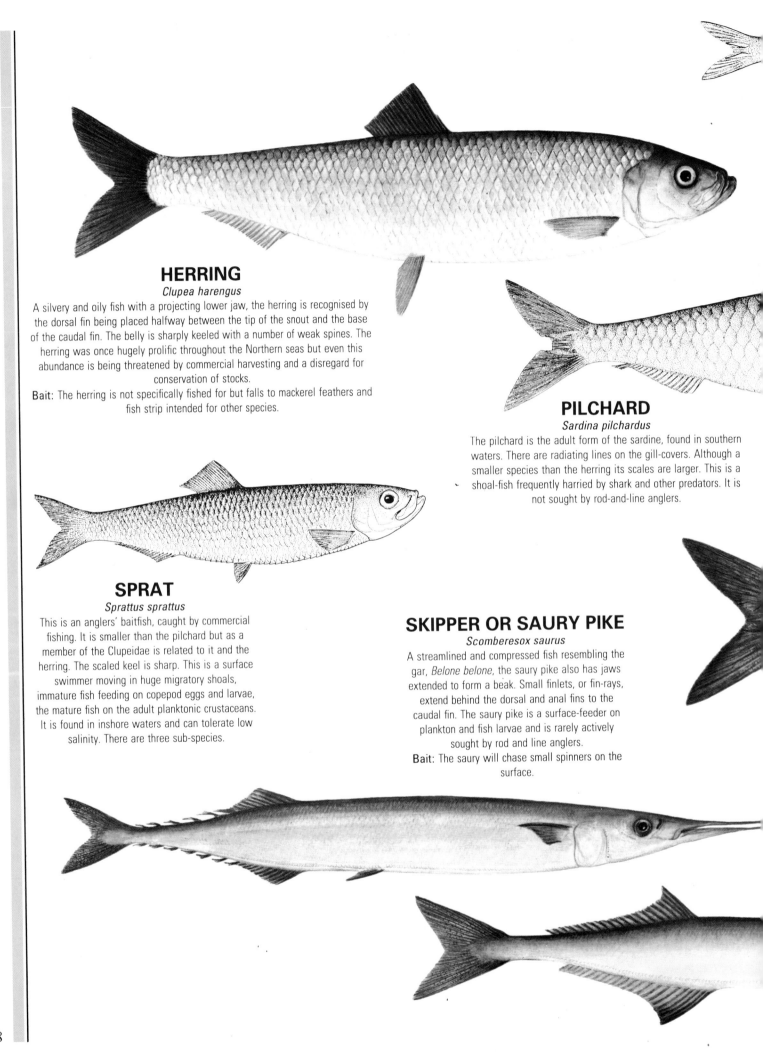

HERRING
Clupea harengus

A silvery and oily fish with a projecting lower jaw, the herring is recognised by the dorsal fin being placed halfway between the tip of the snout and the base of the caudal fin. The belly is sharply keeled with a number of weak spines. The herring was once hugely prolific throughout the Northern seas but even this abundance is being threatened by commercial harvesting and a disregard for conservation of stocks.

Bait: The herring is not specifically fished for but falls to mackerel feathers and fish strip intended for other species.

PILCHARD
Sardina pilchardus

The pilchard is the adult form of the sardine, found in southern waters. There are radiating lines on the gill-covers. Although a smaller species than the herring its scales are larger. This is a shoal-fish frequently harried by shark and other predators. It is not sought by rod-and-line anglers.

SPRAT
Sprattus sprattus

This is an anglers' baitfish, caught by commercial fishing. It is smaller than the pilchard but as a member of the Clupeidae is related to it and the herring. The scaled keel is sharp. This is a surface swimmer moving in huge migratory shoals, immature fish feeding on copepod eggs and larvae, the mature fish on the adult planktonic crustaceans. It is found in inshore waters and can tolerate low salinity. There are three sub-species.

SKIPPER OR SAURY PIKE
Scomberesox saurus

A streamlined and compressed fish resembling the gar, *Belone belone*, the saury pike also has jaws extended to form a beak. Small finlets, or fin-rays, extend behind the dorsal and anal fins to the caudal fin. The saury pike is a surface-feeder on plankton and fish larvae and is rarely actively sought by rod and line anglers.

Bait: The saury will chase small spinners on the surface.

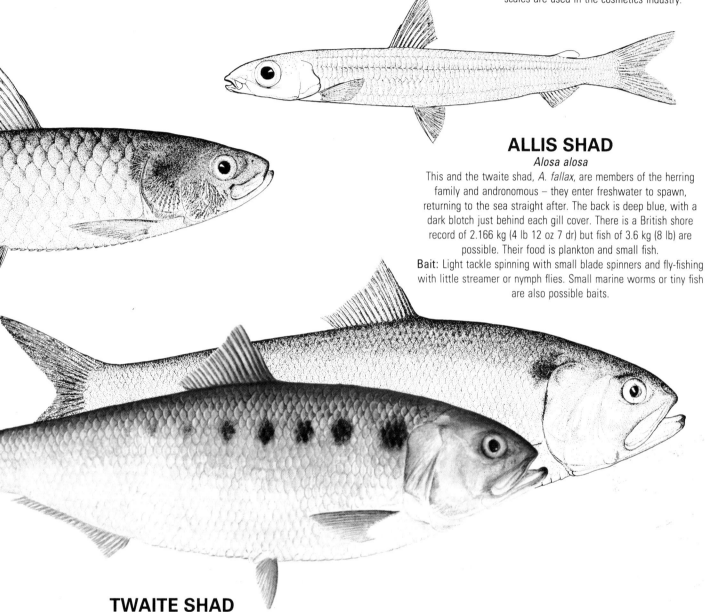

ANCHOVY
Engraulis encrasicolus
A small, big-eyed fish the head of which has a projecting snout. The dorsal fin rises directly above the pelvic fins and the elongated anal fin is midway between the pelvics and caudal fin. The anchovy feeds on planktonic animals.

ARGENTINE
Argentine sphyraena
A tiny fish found in the warm waters off the western coasts of Britain. With its large eyes as an identification feature, this is a shoal-fish taken commercially from depths down to 200 fathoms. Apart from its food value, argentine scales are used in the cosmetics industry.

ALLIS SHAD
Alosa alosa
This and the twaite shad, A. fallax, are members of the herring family and andronomous – they enter freshwater to spawn, returning to the sea straight after. The back is deep blue, with a dark blotch just behind each gill cover. There is a British shore record of 2.166 kg (4 lb 12 oz 7 dr) but fish of 3.6 kg (8 lb) are possible. Their food is plankton and small fish.
Bait: Light tackle spinning with small blade spinners and fly-fishing with little streamer or nymph flies. Small marine worms or tiny fish are also possible baits.

TWAITE SHAD
Alosa fallax
Like the allis shad, the twaite also ascends rivers in order to spawn, but at a later period in the spring, with May the usual time. This fish is very similar to but smaller than the allis shad, A. alosa, and is distinguished by a row of six or seven dark spots running back from behind the gill-covers. Its food is similar to that of the allis shad described above.
Bait: Most effective are the methods and artificial lures as used for the allis shad described above.

GARFISH OR GARPIKE
Belone belone
This is a more slender and longer fish than the skipper, Scomberesox saurus, and has no finlets behind the dorsal and anal fins. The upper jaw is sharp and finely pointed and may be used as a weapon; the lower jaw is longer, with a soft end. The garfish is found in company with shoals of mackerel skipping and jumping on the surface. The bones are greenish and as bait the flesh does not seem attractive to other species.
Bait: Artificial lures and mackerel feathers.

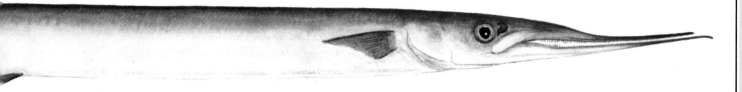

course, we all set out to catch a particular species but we also know that anything can come along and take the bait. For this reason I prefer to use strong but small hooks on the basis that they take hold easier and can be well hidden within a bait, both these factors increasing the chance of successfully hooking and boating whatever comes along – but the hook must be of the best. There must always be a relationship between hook and bait, a big fish can be successfully caught on a smallish hook, but it is impossible to mount a small bait on a large hook!

For most of my boat fishing I use the Mustad 7780c pattern, made from forged wire, bronzed, with reversed superior point and a down-tapered eye. It comes in sizes from 6/0 down to No. 1 and will cope with conger, tope, the heaviest winter cod and rays; and the smaller sizes handle wrasse, whiting, bream and lesser species.

When light-tackle fishing for small fish on home-made lures, feathers or tiny natural baits I prefer the spring of a fine-wire Aberdeen hook. It is the same pattern that can be used for bass fishing from the shore. When using light gear, the advantage is that the hook is neatly hidden, the barb chemically sharpened for superb hooking and if it becomes tangled in weed or rocks I can exert enough pressure to open the bend and release it rather than losing the lure or, worse, the whole terminal rig. With such a fine-wire hook it is also an advantage to be able to mount a sliver of fishbait or a lugworm without tearing it to pieces, not possible with a stout hook pattern. When fishing with Redgills or similar large rubber eels I use larger sizes of long-shanked flatfish hooks. They can easily be inserted into the bait and bent to give action to the lure.

My final hook choice concerns fishing for the giants. Any angler who elects to fish for big sharks, skate or ocean billfish is not going to get many offers because strikes do not come once an hour! Apart from the cost of travel and boat-hire, it is madness to pay a fortune for rod, reel and line and then save further expense by using an inferior hook. Here, the Mustad Seamaster in Sizes 1/0 to 10/0 have never let me down. The late Leslie Moncrieff, one of the sport's thinking anglers, introduced me to the pattern some 25 years ago. They are hand-made, forged hooks with a brazed eye and a small offset to the point and barb that ensures efficient penetration of a tough jaw. Such a hook has to stand up to incredibly sharp, sometimes grinding teeth during a fight that might last for hours.

Here I must comment on the modern fashion for chemically sharpened hook points. There have been instances when I have lost a fish after a few minutes playing it, although it seemed to be well hooked. Whether the points are sometimes too sharp, with an edge that saws its way out from a hookhold is hard to say, but. . . .

Keep hooks dry in a wooden or plastic box and never let them rattle about in a metal tin. It will ruin the points and the barbs. A dab of fish oil will keep rust at bay, and a quick rub with a sharpening stone puts a keen edge to the point. It is worth doing that task after a few fish have been landed, for the point of any hook can turn if it hits a bone in the mouth of a fish. Check all hooks before tying them into the rig, occasionally one will be far too rank in the barb, making it difficult to pull home. Give the barb a quick sharpen and then tap it a little closer to the shank.

SINKERS

I see no reason for using a variety of lead weight shapes when boat angling. The most efficient weight must be a streamlined one that gets down fast through the water, has enough weight to hold, presents little interference surface to the tide and is then easy to retrieve. Shorecasters' bombs in larger sizes serve me well, they can be pulled out from snags far easier than a portly, conical or round watch-type sinker.

I use Breakaway and Sandfast grip-leads when uptide fishing, they take a perfect hold on the seabed with the fold-back wire-grips of a Breakaway easier to pull out from the bottom. Sandfast weights are cheap to cast at home from a simple mould, but remember to insert a length of wire with an appropriate eye protruding at least

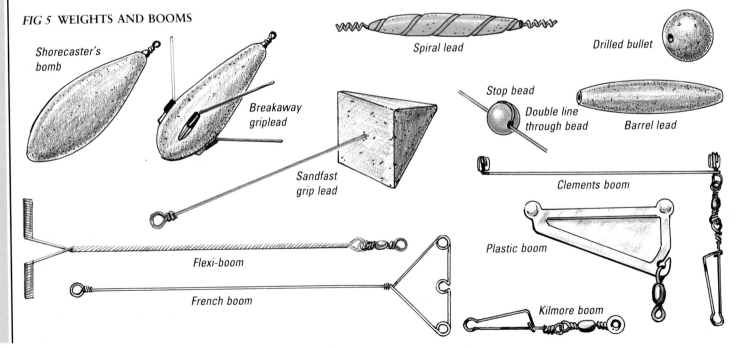

FIG 5 WEIGHTS AND BOOMS

Shorecaster's bomb

Spiral lead

Drilled bullet

Breakaway griplead

Stop bead

Double line through bead

Barrel lead

Sandfast grip lead

Clements boom

Plastic boom

Flexi-boom

French boom

Kilmore boom

15.2–20.3 cm (6–8 in) out from the weight. Make the cast, feel the weight hit bottom, then apply a slight rod pressure to pull a corner of the sinker into mud or sand with the wire, which should lie horizontally, keeping a point always digging in.

The only other sinker I use is one that adds weight to a spinning lure, takes a float-fished bait down or keeps a trolled lure below the surface. Casting them in a variety of sizes, I bend some into a banana shape, the 'keel' helping to prevent line twist when spinning or trolling. The sinker is provided with eyelets at each end of a connecting wire, moulded through the weight for line attachment or cast plain and then drilled through for use as a float-fishing sinker. They are similar to the freshwater angler's Wye lead, but larger. (Fig. 5)

THE BITS AND PIECES: METAL AND PLASTIC

Most anglers collect a mass of small items in their tackle boxes, some are handy though many are of dubious value. Basically, the useful ancillary items are:

- Booms to set paternostered hooks away from the reel line
- Running booms to make ledger weights slide freely on nylon
- Swivels to prevent line twist
- A connecting piece for joining reel line to trace material
- Connectors between wire and nylon lines

PATERNOSTER BOOMS

Offset, flexible booms can be tied direct on to a nylon trace as blood loops, or stiffened by the addition of a polythene tube. Adding the tubing keeps the hook-link well clear of the trace when the bait is lowered. I use 2 mm (0.07 in) internal-bore plastic tube in fluorescent orange, making it easily seen by the fish, which might add to its attractiveness on the seabed. Tackle-shops sell metal

French booms and a variety of plastic ones. The idea is the same, to offset the baited hook and at the same time give the angler an easy way to adjust the boom's position on the line. They are cheap and functional and easily made from stiff, stainless 18 SWG gauge wire. (Fig. 5)

RUNNING BOOMS

The most famous of these are the Clements and Kilmore booms, both with and without the porcelain inserts. The porcelain eyes are said to make these booms slide freely; perhaps so, but lack of care such as allowing the booms to rattle about in a tacklebox is likely to crack the inserts and if this happens the boom will increase wear on the line and not lessen it. Stay with the plain metal kind, a bead placed between the boom eye and its stopping swivel will prevent the metal from wearing away the knot.

A functional and, incidentally, cheaper running boom can be made by pulling a 15 cm (6 in) length of stiffish polythene tube through the eye of a link swivel, but make sure that it is tightly held. The polythene becomes well lubricated when it is in water, sliding perfectly freely along nylon line. The tube extension acts as a means of booming-off the hook from the reel line and when being dropped down, for nothing is more disconcerting than a well-presented hookbait becoming wrapped round the line as it spirals down to the bottom. (Fig. 5)

SWIVELS

Swivels are an important item for easing line twist yet a constant source of trouble. Swivels cease to turn either because they become packed with filament weed, or the wire twisted to form the eye jams in the body. Some swivels break because the manufacturers did not use wire strong enough to form the eyes; and there are many swivels that pull open at very low strains. I prefer open box swivels where the wire, flattened to form the eye, can be seen. Small ball-bearing versions are fine for spinning and in the much larger sizes are suitable for extremely heavy forms of sea angling. (Fig. 6)

Always test swivels before use. Look at the snaplinks, some have a quick-fastener that can *and probably will* open under the weight of a big fish. The best link-swivels have a safety catch that gives added security.

TRACE CONNECTORS

I use just one kind of connector between trace and reel line: a boom; quality link-swivels perform all the other connecting functions. My choice is an L-shaped boom, easily made, incorporating two swivels, one for the reel line and the other to the hook link, together with a snap-link to attach the sinker. This is known as the Arran rig and was shown me by Neil McLean when we were on a haddock-fishing trip in the Firth of Clyde. This rig will function for a wide variety of bottom-feeding species whatever their size. I have found that it aids lowering a bait down fast, never tangles and also functions perfectly using a grip lead in uptide fishing. All that is needed to

FIG 6 LINKS AND SWIVELS

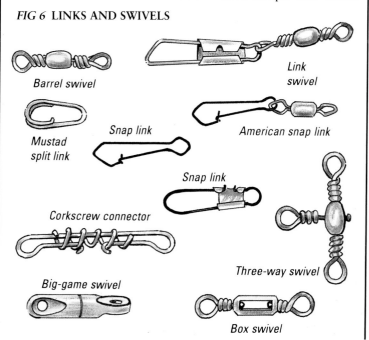

Barrel swivel

Link swivel

Mustad split link

Snap link

American snap link

Snap link

Corkscrew connector

Big-game swivel

Three-way swivel

Box swivel

COD

Gadus morhua

This is the most important member of the Gadidae, the cod family, both from the point of view of angling and commercial fishing. It is found throughout the North Atlantic and associated seas and has been fished for and caught as far south as Spain. There are two clearly defined types; the yellow cod, deep in the belly from rich deep-water feeding, and the red or rock cod (not the rock cod of the *Ephinephelus* spp) that inhabits British littoral waters. Both are true cod, the yellow fish of any size tending to migrate annually in shoals of the same size between Arctic waters and the British Isles. The red type remains in the latter waters for an indeterminate period, its colour dependent on its habitat where brown and red weed predominate on rocks and reefs. It may be that the rock cod will merge with migratory shoals of the yellow kind and adapt their coloration. There are local names for cod of different sizes, a codling being a small fish or one up to 2.7 kg (6 lb). Many cod over 27 kg (60 lb) have been taken from British coastal waters, and the IGFA lists a record weight of 44.79 kg (98 lb 12 oz) from the New Hampshire, US, coast. At least one cod weighing 91 kg (200 lb) has been netted by commercial fishing but present-day trawling methods, which are detrimental to stock conservation, do not allow fish to reach maturity. Of all demersal species the cod has suffered most from commercial fishing.

Bait: Anything, fish flesh, marine worms, shellfish, artificial lures will attract cod.

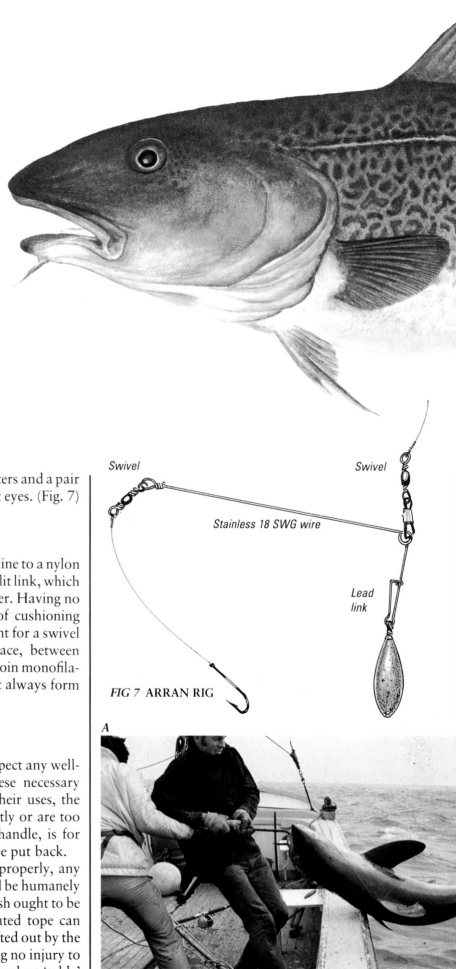

FIG 7 ARRAN RIG

make this rig is some stiff, stainless wire, cutters and a pair of pliers to twist tight the swivel attachment eyes. (Fig. 7)

WIRE CONNECTORS

It only remains to discuss joining a wire reel line to a nylon trace. For this, again use a link-swivel or a split link, which is my choice because it is likely to be stronger. Having no stretch, wire line offers little in the way of cushioning sudden pulls from a big fish. Any requirement for a swivel can be incorporated farther down the trace, between lengths of nylon. On no account attempt to join monofilament direct to wire, a metal connector must always form this junction.

BRINGING FISH ABOARD THE BOAT

I never carry a landing-net or a gaff, for I expect any well-equipped charterboat skipper to have these necessary accessories already on board. Both have their uses, the gaff to boat heavy species that twist violently or are too large for a net. The hoop-net, on a long handle, is for flatties and those fish that are intended to be put back.

Gaffing is often said to be cruel. Done properly, any unkindness is momentary for the fish should be humanely killed immediately. The decision to return fish ought to be made before anything is even caught. Boated tope can then be tailed and returned, small dogfish lifted out by the rod, skate gaffed only in the wingtip, causing no injury to vital organs, sharks are best tail-roped. Succulent 'table'

A A porbeagle shark of 50 kg (110 lb), gaffed neatly in the lower jaw and being brought inboard. This was a fish to be killed and eaten. All fish to be returned should either be secured by a tailing rope to have the hook removed at the boat's side while the fish is restrained, or tailed and brought aboard if the unhooking is a more difficult task. But leave this job to someone with a deal of experience.

B Taking a landing-net to a rare fish, one intended for unharmed capture or for the frying-pan is a sensible thing to do. *C* Pat Auld, from Portpatrick, makes certain that the plump haddock he has hooked arrives safely in the boat, such a delicacy is a must for the table. *D* Neil McLean with a cod from the open ground of Whiting Bay, Isle of Arran. The cod taken here are clean, well-made North Atlantic fish, firm fleshed and tremendously rich in coloration.

species such as cod, mackerel, turbot, plaice, bass, should all be boated with care, killed immediately, gutted, taken home and eaten.

FISH OF WINTER

THE COD

Winter is a time when beaches are busy with anglers seeking the arrival of the cod; boat fishermen are launching their dinghies from discrete hards and charter skippers know that a time of plenty is upon them. Winter gives anglers space: there are no holidaymakers scampering in the shallows and dodging round the lines that stretch seaward; boat anglers are not hampered by windsurfers and those irresponsible speedboat owners, who insist upon having an audience as they tow skiers across our anchor ropes.

Winter is just the sea, sky and call of birds as they, like the angler, seek fish. Bright colours have gone with fading ·autumn, the inshore water is a brownish grey bringing comments of 'Looks a good cod sea!' from men who have waited months for the magic of winter codding. As Alan Yates will tell, the cod's fecundity ensures a constant species, always arriving with the November gales to feed toward the shore. Boat anglers do not always have to travel far, for the winter cod hug the coastline while following herring shoals. With enormous appetites, each shoal demands a massive food availability as they graze across the inshore feeding grounds like lowland sheep.

Codling will push right into the surf although much larger fish tend to stay in deeper water, particularly where there is cover of broken ground, rocks and other prey-holding habitats.

Lugworm have been dug from a muddy estuary in the early morning by the do-it-yourself angler, for codmen know that cod change their diet to one of small crabs and marine worms as they approach the shoreline. Worm is a bait shared by both shore and boat anglers, with fishbait, squid-strip and a variety of artificial lures more useful in deep water. Cod seem to be attracted by colour, a flash of red or gleam of a silver spoon attached to a rig adds another hooking possibility.

Cod rigs are simple to put together; there are only two variations, a paternoster when the tide is slackish and a ledger, running or fixed, when the tide pulls through. I prefer to use the paternoster whenever possible for it gives direct contact with the fish, an advantage when bait-stealing codling and whiting, adept at tearing baits away from any hook, come on the tide. Paternosters should be fairly short between sinker and hook booms because cod feed hard on the seabed, they are not interested in rising up to find baits. (Figs 8, 9, 10)

In the murky sea conditions found along the south and east coast of Britain, the fish are hunting by scent, feeling their way along just above the bottom. Baits strung high in the water will probably attract the attention of whiting and pouting, not the species the codman is after, but fish nevertheless. There is a strong argument for adding flashers of some kind to the hook link, even in murky conditions a metal flasher will give a hint of flash and vibration that might prove attractive.

Ledgered baits offer the best presentation when there is strength in the tide. The baits wave about in the current right where the cod expects to find food – on the bottom. Keep the rig simple, either a fixed ledger such as the Arran rig, or a running ledger using a sliding sinker attachment. One hook is enough to cope with and the bait should be fairly large and securely fastened. (Fig. 11)

Cod can give all kinds of bites, slack water cod generally produce nibbling tweaks, and in both cases the angler's reaction must be positive. Lift the rod sharply and take in a few winds on the reel to tighten the line down to the fish. Do not strike and then wait to feel if the fish is there, for if you relax the tension this is the time when the fish will twist off the hook. Striking does not necessarily mean pulling the hook right home into the fish's jaw because stretch in nylon dampens much of the strike force. Only when a cod 'knows' that it is tethered and begins to pull away against the hook does the barb penetrate and take hold. Even a big cod cannot be said to fight hard, a constant arc in the rod, coupled with a steady winding pressure will bring it to the surface. Pressure change is lethal to most members of the cod family, making it unnecessary either to pump hard or drag a fish up at speed.

Detecting a bite when the bait is ledgered in a strong current is sometimes difficult. The cod swim about everywhere searching for food, so we cannot always assume that a biting cod is pulling the bait away from the boat. The fish often picks up the bait while moving toward the craft and the angler does not feel the bite, but senses movement on the sinker. Most cod will have hooked themselves, and that is the secret of success of uptide fishing. It is a waiting game that does not appeal to me. There are times when I like nothing better than to fish downtide, using a ledger rig where the sinker only just balances the flow of the tide. A lift of the rod tip, allowing a few yards of line to run off the spool, takes the bait to new ground. I like to search for fish rather than wait for them to signal their arrival.

FISHING UPTIDE

When fishing the uptide style, anglers rely on a weight, equipped with gripwires that take hold on the bottom and

FIG 8 HOOKING LUGWORM

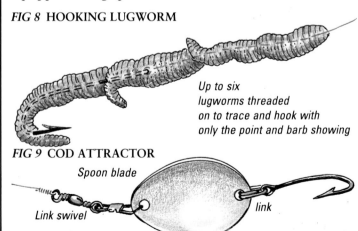

Up to six lugworms threaded on to trace and hook with only the point and barb showing

FIG 9 COD ATTRACTOR

Spoon blade

Link swivel

link

FIG 10 PATERNOSTER

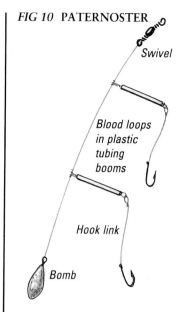

Swivel

Blood loops in plastic tubing booms

Hook link

Bomb

FIG 11 COD LEDGER

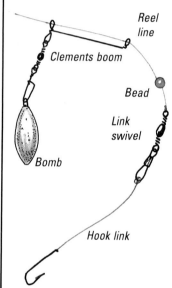

Reel line

Clements boom

Bead

Link swivel

Bomb

Hook link

Fig 8 Lugworm is a major cod bait, but correct hooking is essential.   Fig 9 An additional attractor on a cod rig often tempts the wary fish.
Fig 10 A two-hook rig with one above the other takes cod which are hunting at different depths.   Fig 11 In a strong tide, a ledgered bait will snake about attractively.   Fig 12 Once considered quite impossible, the uptide technique is now a proven, entertaining style and prevents too many lines streaming back from the stern and tangling.
A Scotland is renowned for its cod fishing. Late in the year the species moves into the North Sea. Sea anglers have relied on this one species for the best of their winter fishing, so without the cod most sea anglers would have a lean time. Mike Shepley displays a fish of nearly 13.6 kg (30 lb).

A

FIG 12 UPTIDE TECHNIQUES

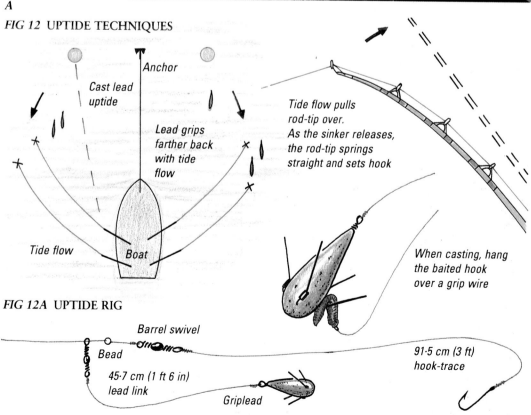

Anchor

Cast lead uptide

Lead grips farther back with tide flow

Tide flow

Boat

Tide flow pulls rod-tip over.
As the sinker releases, the rod-tip springs straight and sets hook

When casting, hang the baited hook over a grip wire

FIG 12A UPTIDE RIG

Barrel swivel

Bead

45·7 cm (1 ft 6 in) lead link

Griplead

91·5 cm (3 ft) hook-trace

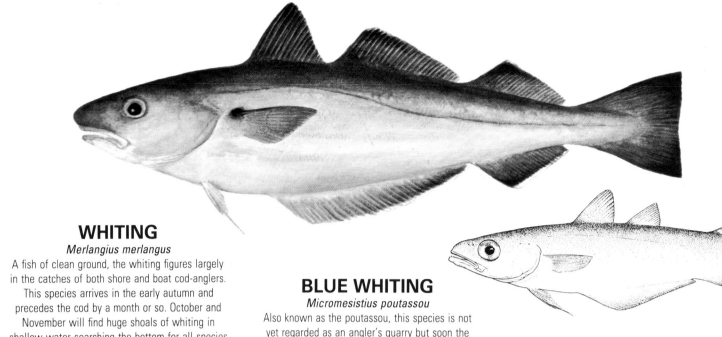

WHITING
Merlangius merlangus
A fish of clean ground, the whiting figures largely in the catches of both shore and boat cod-anglers. This species arrives in the early autumn and precedes the cod by a month or so. October and November will find huge shoals of whiting in shallow water searching the bottom for all species of small fish. In late winter they leave for deeper waters. This species can only be regarded as sporting when fished for on light tackle that will allow them to put up some kind of struggle. Whiting average 0.45 kg (1 lb), but the larger 'channel' whiting are known to 2.7 kg (6 lb).
Bait: Fish strips such as the oily herring and mackerel; baited feathers and marine worms.

BLUE WHITING
Micromesistius poutassou
Also known as the poutassou, this species is not yet regarded as an angler's quarry but soon the blue whiting will come into prominence as a food source, for the stocks of this edible species are sufficient to provide much of Britain with its fish-food requirements. This fish is found at far greater depths, down to 500 fathoms, than other members of the cod family. It is distinguished from the whiting by the unequal distances between the dorsal fins.
Bait: Small fish fry and fish strips.

POLLACK
Pollachius pollachius
The pollack is to be found in most of the coastal waters of Britain and Ireland with the possible exception of the south-east corner of England. This is a fish of summer, being seen in catches from April right up to the late autumn. Of the Gadidae, the pollack is by far the most sporting species. The smaller members of the species inhabit harbours in inshore rocky situations, the larger specimens are found over off-shore reefs and wrecks. Its natural food is mainly sprats and herrings.
Bait: All kinds of fish-bait, shellfish, marine worms and artificial lures, any flashy lure with movement. Fly-fishing takes surface-feeding pollack.

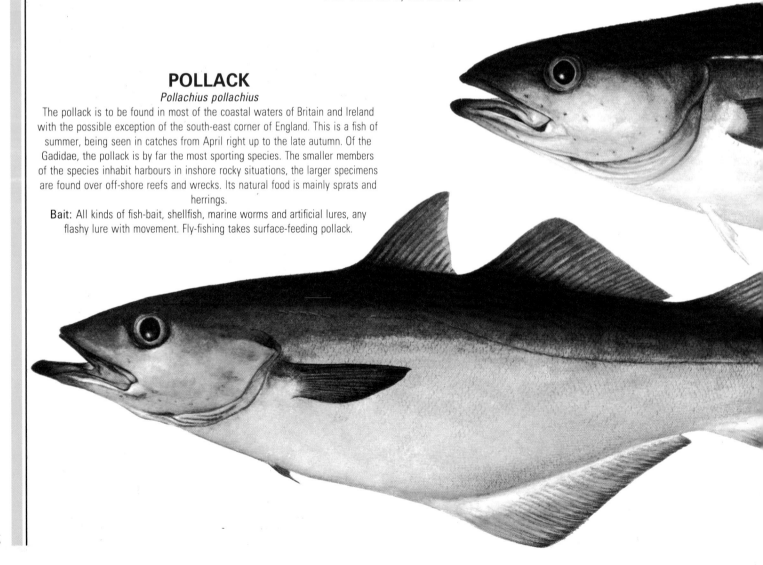

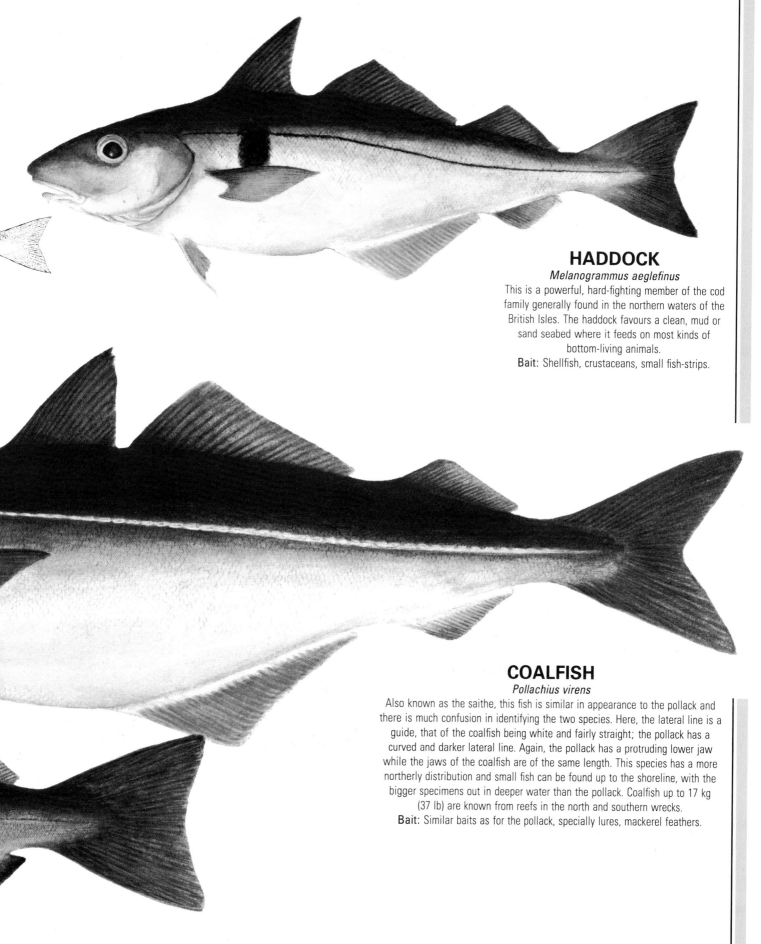

HADDOCK
Melanogrammus aeglefinus
This is a powerful, hard-fighting member of the cod family generally found in the northern waters of the British Isles. The haddock favours a clean, mud or sand seabed where it feeds on most kinds of bottom-living animals.
Bait: Shellfish, crustaceans, small fish-strips.

COALFISH
Pollachius virens
Also known as the saithe, this fish is similar in appearance to the pollack and there is much confusion in identifying the two species. Here, the lateral line is a guide, that of the coalfish being white and fairly straight; the pollack has a curved and darker lateral line. Again, the pollack has a protruding lower jaw while the jaws of the coalfish are of the same length. This species has a more northerly distribution and small fish can be found up to the shoreline, with the bigger specimens out in deeper water than the pollack. Coalfish up to 17 kg (37 lb) are known from reefs in the north and southern wrecks.
Bait: Similar baits as for the pollack, specially lures, mackerel feathers.

POOR COD
Trisopterus minutus

This fish looks rather like a pouting and is found from similar fishing grounds, but it is smaller and less colourful, lacking the black spot at the base of the pectoral fins and vertical bars of the pouting, *Trisopterus luscus*. The poor cod is a small fish rarely exceeding 23 cm (9 in) and has a British record of 311 g (11 oz). It feeds on small fish and shrimps.

Bait: As for the pouting.

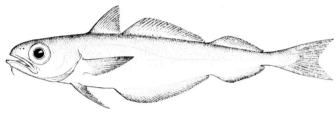

NORWAY POUT
Trisopterus esmarki

A small pouting-like species but less bulky. Its large eyes and protruding jaw distinguish it from the poor cod and pouting. This fish has little if any real angling significance.

do not change position unless something drags them out of the sand. The bait is cast to a feeding ground uptide in an arc either side of the anchor. The rod is rarely held, often being leant against the gunwale with the tip slightly bent under the tension from the tight reel line. Fish moving across the seabed grab the bait and swim on to pull up sharply against the sinker. This gets dragged out of its hold, releasing tension on the line, which allows the rod tip to straighten. Bite detection is more positive, but uptide fishing has one major advantage, other than bite detection, for the angler can cast and hold ground away but at near right-angles from the boat, which conventional paternostered or ledgered bait cannot do. (Figs 10, 11, 12)

PIRKING

Cod fishing alters away from the south-east corner of England. There is less murky water, so the fish are more able to feed by sight. Natural baits, with taste and smell to appeal to the cod's olfactory senses, are less important. The artificial lure now comes into play. For many years, commercial fishermen and anglers used a string of cod-sized feathers and it was a very good system, especially when there were huge shoals of cod about and all that mattered was fish in the boat. Farther north in the Atlantic, Norwegian and Scottish professionals favoured using what they called the 'Ripper'. It was a chunk of lead almost smothered in treble hooks – and not very sporting, but it was successful. This idea has gradually become

Fig 13 Pirks, descendants of the 'Ripper', are now firmly established in the sea angler's tackle-box. They provide their own weight and account for many fish.

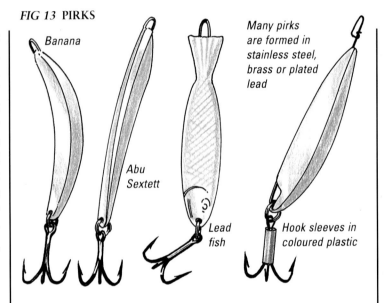

FIG 13 PIRKS

Banana

Abu Sextett

Lead fish

Many pirks are formed in stainless steel, brass or plated lead

Hook sleeves in coloured plastic

adapted to a point where the modern alternative, the pirk, has all but taken over from conventional bait-fishing. A simple rig, just the reel line tied direct to a sinker which might have a banana shape, or one with facets cut into a stainless steel bar. The asymmetrical form gives the lure an erratic action as it is jerked up and down above the seabed. Cod probably see it as a small fish trying to escape, or injured. Hooking is very positive, though some fish when boated are found to have the treble hook outside the mouth, or even in the body. This possibly comes about when a fish strikes at and misses the falling pirk, only to be snagged in fin or body as the angler raises his rod for the next sweep. Rods and lines for pirking have to be of the

POUTING
Trisopterus luscus

Another cod-family species, the pouting is present all round the British Isles and particularly off the south and western shores. This species favours rough ground, wrecks and reefs. As with young pollack, the pouting is taken close-in to the shore, harbours and from under piers. These fish fall largely to young anglers and sea matchmen fishing with small hooks and baits. The British record is a specimen of 2.5 kg (5 lb 8 oz).

Bait: Strips of fish, mussels, cockles, small worms close to or on the bottom.

It is sad to say that many members of the cod family will not survive being brought to the surface hurriedly or from a great depth. They die because their swim, or gas, bladder expands fatally, not able to adjust to rapid changes of depth and therefore pressure.

best, both they and the angler work very hard indeed. And since pirks can weigh up to 0.9 kg (2 lb) their loss can be expensive. (Fig. 13)

WINTER FLATFISH

ESTUARY FLOUNDERS

This season can be a time of gales, a time when the wary angler avoids the open sea. I am fond of estuary fishing when a stiff north-easterly heaps tides up in great lumpy waves, uncomfortable yet unavoidable. The more sheltered estuary waters give me the opportunity to attack the fleshy flounders, they in their prime having grown fat on a diet of worms and crabs.

Tackle and tactics are light and satisfying. In shallow water I use a sea spinning rod coupled with the lightest shorecasting multiplier or fixed-spool reel with a 4.5 kg (10 lb) line. The fixed-spool is easiest to use with small weights. A single-hook rolling ledger, weighted by a drilled bullet of 28 g (1 oz) or so, is cast across the flow to roll round and down into the gully to where most food is swept to waiting flounders by the flooding or ebbing current. Begin with gentle casts fairly close to the boat, lengthening each successive cast so that your bait explores every part of the channel.

Sometimes the rolling ledger will snag on its arc of travel, but wait a few moments before giving the rod tip a lift. If the sinker was trapped by weed it will jump and continue swinging, but a biting flounder will be indicated

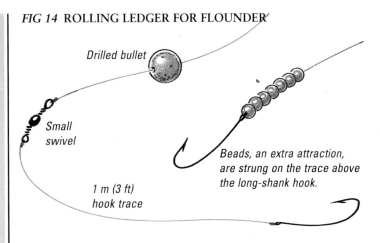

FIG 14 ROLLING LEDGER FOR FLOUNDER

Drilled bullet

Small swivel

1 m (3 ft) hook trace

Beads, an extra attraction, are strung on the trace above the long-shank hook.

Fig 14 The secret of enjoyable flounder fishing is fishing light. A lift of the rod-tip sometimes tempts an inquisitive flattie to take the bait before it escapes.

TORSK
Brosme brosme

A fish of northern waters, the torsk is separated from the ling and hake (to which it is related) by the lack of a second dorsal fin. Boat anglers catch it off the Shetlands and Orkneys and off the Pentland Firth. It can reach weights of over 9 kg (20 lb).
Bait: Fishbaits are best with pirks a possibility.

LING
Molva molva

This predator is one of the hardest fighters in the large cod family. The ling haunts wrecks and rocky grounds, either broken or as defined reefs. The best of the inshore ling fishing is in the northern waters of the British Isles, but in recent years the specimens have come from the deepwater wrecks off the West of England. There are two dorsal fins, the first short, the second long; there is only one anal fin. The ling's teeth reflect its predatory nature, being many and sharp but they are not as prominent as those of the hake. The ling can reach weights of over 27 kg (60 lb) and a length of over 2 m (7 ft).
Bait: Fish, squid and artificial lures.

by a series of trembles back up the line. A good idea is to hold the nylon between the fingers of your left hand, because touch ledgering is far more sensitive than waiting for a thump at the rod tip. Do not strike too quickly, a flounder nudges at the bait with its mouth. Lift the rod tip gently if a bite does not develop, this will ease the bait towards you, perhaps just enough to encourage a cautious fish to make a positive snap at the baited hook. (Fig. 14)

This form of boat fishing can be exciting sport, flounders give their best fight on extremely light gear in shallow water. It is much better fun than the same fish hooked on a beach rod in winter where the fish probably have to tow a 170 g (6 oz) grip-lead to give any indication of a bite. Flounders are easy fish to catch, so do not take too many, just sufficient for the pan, for at this time of the year flounders are in their prime.

OFFSHORE FOR TURBOT

Some may not consider the turbot a winter fish, but it is. When the sea is calm over the offshore sandbanks, showing a glassy smoothness with just a trickle of tide, it is time

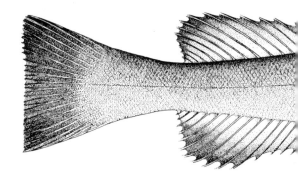

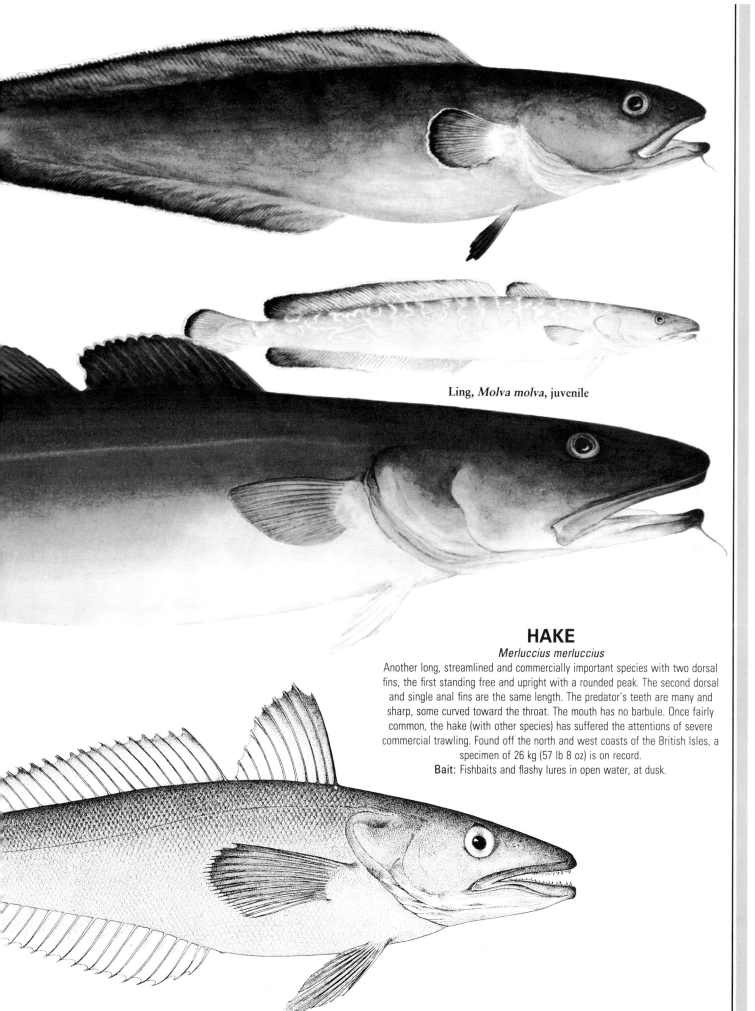

Ling, *Molva molva*, juvenile

HAKE

Merluccius merluccius

Another long, streamlined and commercially important species with two dorsal fins, the first standing free and upright with a rounded peak. The second dorsal and single anal fins are the same length. The predator's teeth are many and sharp, some curved toward the throat. The mouth has no barbule. Once fairly common, the hake (with other species) has suffered the attentions of severe commercial trawling. Found off the north and west coasts of the British Isles, a specimen of 26 kg (57 lb 8 oz) is on record.

Bait: Fishbaits and flashy lures in open water, at dusk.

FIG 15 THREE-HOOK TURBOT RIG

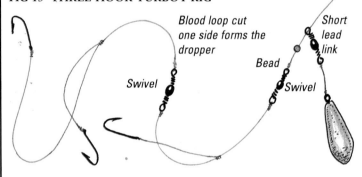

Blood loop cut
one side forms the
dropper

Short
lead
link

Bead

Swivel

Swivel

Peter Collins, a former editor of 'Sea Angler', with a magnificent turbot from the sandbank that surrounds many offshore wrecks.

Fig 15 In the three-hook turbot rig the swivels are necessary for three twisting baits will soon tangle unswivelled traces.

to seek this larger flattie. Cod anglers fishing gullies between offshore sands often return with a turbot among their catch, proving that they had their baits on the edge of the bank and that there were still enough sandeels or other small fodder fish for the turbot to remain.

A standard cod ledger rig will do for turbot fishing, though there are many fishermen who make-up a multi-hook ledger rig, contending that where there is one turbot there ought to be another. Such a complex of hooks and connecting snoods necessitates a number of swivels to remove line twist, because each hookbait will twirl in the tide and give a propellor action, which puts knots under a lot of strain. Only on a very slack tide can a multi-hook rig be dropped down without bait-twist. (Fig. 15)

Some smaller species inevitably appear when winter fishing. Pouting favour broken ground or weeded reefs, whiting like clean sand and a mud bottom. Neither fish is a fierce fighter, though both can give good sport on small paternostered fishbait. Watch out for the damage to nylon snoods by the teeth of whiting. This fish is essentially a

predator on small fry, but it will take an angler's worms and shellfish baits. Fished as a deadbait on a flowing trace, whiting make an exceptionally attractive lure for the larger cod.

Anglers tend to think of this or that species as being a winter, spring or summer target, but the appearance, or disappearance of fish is not always the result of an urge to migrate. More often, fish leave because of a shortage of food. Some species do not like the colder, troubled inshore waters when being lashed by a gale. All that happens is that the fish move out to slightly deeper water where there is less disturbance, a more even sea temperature and a constant food supply. Some species change their diet as worm and soft crabs become impossible to find, taking fish instead. The first hint of spring will bring these species back inshore for the dinghy angler and the beachcaster.

SPRING: THE AWAKENING OF A YEAR

HADDOCK IN THE NORTH

Spring does not come in with a bang for the sea angler, rather it creeps slowly upon us. The cod have departed and apart from those fortunate anglers who have access to deepwater wrecks which fish well the year round, all anglers await the arrival of rays, flatfish and bass. It is not until early in April that the season freshens and we can get to grips with the influx of a different species.

At one time I used to stretch the winter fishing period

THE ROCKLINGS

There are five species of consequence among the rocklings, members of the Gadidae, the cod family. Habits and habitat vary widely between these species, but there are only slight anatomical differences.
Bait: Small fishbaits.

THREE-BEARDED ROCKLING
Gaidropsarus vulgaris

This rockling has two barbules on the upper jaw and one on the lower. It is a larger fish than either the four- or five-bearded rocklings and is known to have a southerly distribution, the British Isles being the limit of its northward migration. It is found in depths from the littoral zone down to 100 fathoms. The three-bearded rockling feeds on fish and crustaceans and can reach weights of over 1.3 kg (3 lb).

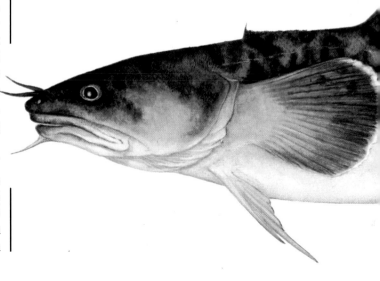

FIVE-BEARDED ROCKLING
Ciliata mustela

This rockling has a leading dorsal in the form of a spine followed by a low fringe, mostly neatly folded into a narrow cleft running along the dorsal area.

Only one anal fin is present. The fish has five 'beards' or barbules, four protruding from the front of the upper jaw and one on the lower jaw. The species favours a mixed ground of shingle, sand and rocky patches. As with the other rocklings, this is a small fish, the British record being 340 g (12 oz).

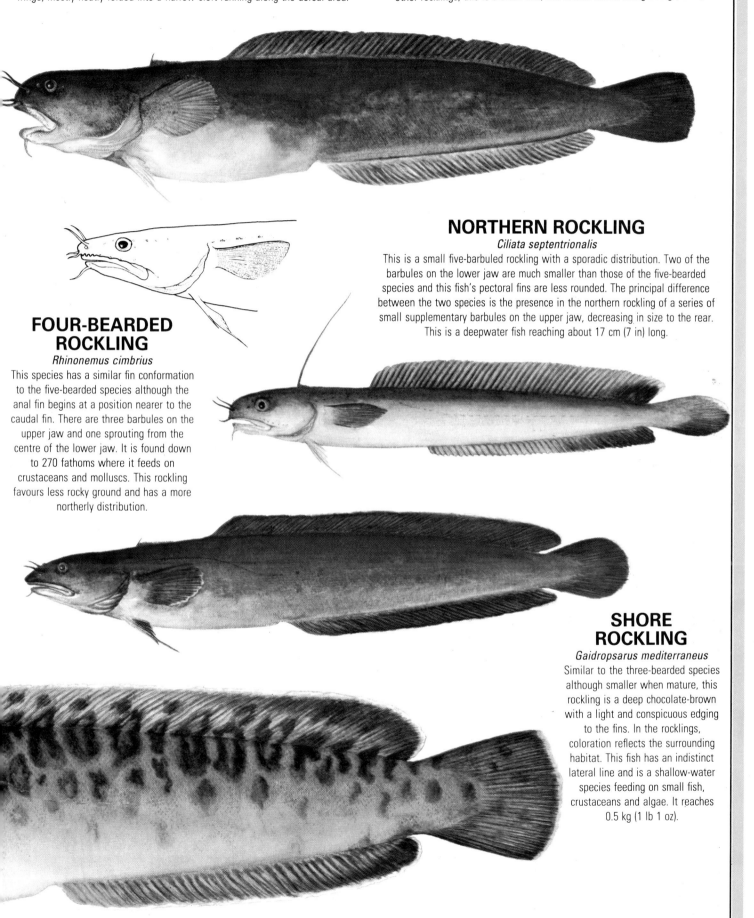

FOUR-BEARDED ROCKLING
Rhinonemus cimbrius

This species has a similar fin conformation to the five-bearded species although the anal fin begins at a position nearer to the caudal fin. There are three barbules on the upper jaw and one sprouting from the centre of the lower jaw. It is found down to 270 fathoms where it feeds on crustaceans and molluscs. This rockling favours less rocky ground and has a more northerly distribution.

NORTHERN ROCKLING
Ciliata septentrionalis

This is a small five-barbuled rockling with a sporadic distribution. Two of the barbules on the lower jaw are much smaller than those of the five-bearded species and this fish's pectoral fins are less rounded. The principal difference between the two species is the presence in the northern rockling of a series of small supplementary barbules on the upper jaw, decreasing in size to the rear. This is a deepwater fish reaching about 17 cm (7 in) long.

SHORE ROCKLING
Gaidropsarus mediterraneus

Similar to the three-bearded species although smaller when mature, this rockling is a deep chocolate-brown with a light and conspicuous edging to the fins. In the rocklings, coloration reflects the surrounding habitat. This fish has an indistinct lateral line and is a shallow-water species feeding on small fish, crustaceans and algae. It reaches 0.5 kg (1 lb 1 oz).

by making an annual trip to Scotland in March or April in order to fish for haddock in the Firth of Clyde, but sadly that fishing has gone. Whether it was just over-fishing or the fact that the scallop beds were dragged out, removing the reason for the haddock being there, we are not likely to know. Of course, haddock still arrive in many other areas off Britain and, thankfully, cod still put in an appearance round the Isle of Arran along with some good coalfish, but it was the haddock that drew me; there was something special about the way they fought, weight-for-weight haddock make cod look sedate!

Neil McLean was my mentor in those waters. An expert at haddock fishing, he developed a good system for this shy-biting species. Using a paternoster with two fairly long hook snoods, his idea was to bait with whole scallops, lower them to the seabed and wait. The difference in the technique lay in the fact that he then rested the rod on the gunwale of his boat. Neil explained that most big haddock are lost by premature striking and he always waited until the rod tip was pulled over – and it had to stay that way – then he made a firm lift, never a full-blooded strike. The bigger haddock have relatively smaller and much softer mouths than cod and are finicky feeders, tending to mouth the offering for a long time. When holding the rod, one felt the first tremble, instinctively struck, and the result was a lost fish.

It took me a long time to come to grips with Neil's style. I have had haddock off the Scottish west coast and from the North Sea, particularly off Whitby, and the small fish gave an entirely different bite indication, fast and hard. I assumed that the larger Arran fish were feeding over shellfish beds, becoming selective and taking time in their feeding. In other areas, haddock shoal over open ground in fierce competition for whatever food is available, forcing them to grab eagerly at baits. (Fig. 16)

EARLY POLLACK

As the weather warms, pollack show among the catch. Early spring brings fish but it is not long before a better class of pollack move in to take up residence on rocky or heavily weeded areas. This is a time for sink-and-draw or slow trolling tactics over the foul ground. One thing about pollack is that they respond to artificial lures, rising fast in the water to strike at an attractive bait. Attraction is the key to this fishing, the baits must have movement simulating a live fish, colour is not too important because these fish attack from low in the water to a bait passing over them, so they see most lures in silhouette. Pollack also fish superbly on natural bait using conventional rigs, yet I much prefer to take the opportunity to do something different and exciting.

Using either a Redgill, a rubber eel, a long streamer fly or even a lash of mackerel, mount the bait on a long trace of about 2.4 to 3 m (8 to 10 ft) long. Tie in a swivel to act as a stop for the sinker, usually a drilled trolling weight. These baits can be trolled from a dinghy over the peaks of rocky ground or along the outer edge of a kelp-bed. Pollack are territorial, you have to find them and rarely

FIG 16 TWO-HOOK ARRAN RIG

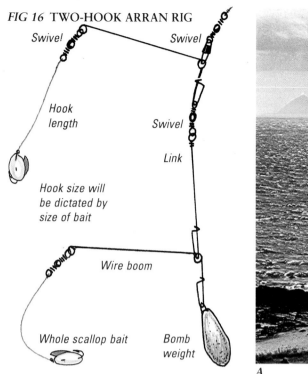

Swivel
Swivel
Hook length
Swivel
Link
Hook size will be dictated by size of bait
Wire boom
Whole scallop bait
Bomb weight

A

A Pladda, the lighthouse isle at the south end of Arran, a haddock and pollack mark of note. B Open, broken seabed will provide many resident pollack and codling of average size. C The nearer one gets to a reef, the larger the pollack become. Fishing into the twilight hours brings good fish on this Baltimore mark.

Fig 16 With the Arran rig, wait for the haddock to hook itself, otherwise a 'snatch' strike will result in a lost fish.

B

will they leave the habitat to feed over nearby open ground. Take the boat over a zig-zag course so that the lure gives a rise and fall motion each time the boat turns; this creates an undulating action in the lure that has a fatal attraction for pollack. (Fig. 17)

SINK-AND-DRAW TACTICS

Fish sink-and-draw from a boat anchored over a rock mark. It is quite simple, just lower the bait until you feel the weight touch kelp or bottom. Wind in a few turns immediately to make sure that you do not snag-fast the rig. Then as you raise the rod take in about two turns of the spool, then lower the rod back to the horizontal. This movement is followed progressively until the lure nearly reaches the surface. Most strikes come as the rod tip is raised; sometimes fish follow the lure almost to the surface, striking at it hard if the 'fry' looks as if it is escaping.

The weight of sinker can be decreased to allow the lure to be worked back downtide, although line stretch can make striking difficult. The most efficient hooking

C

FIG 17 TROLLING RIG FOR POLLACK

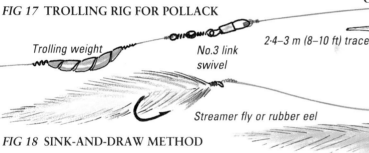

Trolling weight

No.3 link swivel

2·4–3 m (8–10 ft) trace

Rubber eel made from gas tubing, a No.3 swivel and long-shanked 4/0 hook

Streamer fly or rubber eel

FIG 18 SINK-AND-DRAW METHOD

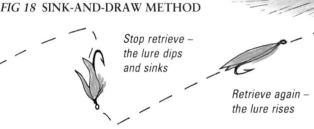

Stop retrieve – the lure dips and sinks

Retrieve again – the lure rises

Streamer fly made from white cock cape and any bright-coloured dressing feather, a long hook and a swivel

method is to let the pollack take the bait and turn down while you hold the rod high; the fish's vertical flight will tighten the line and pull the hook home. (Fig. 18)

BASS IN THE SURF

Surf is not only for shore anglers, there are a number of areas round the British Isles where offshore sandbanks dry out as the tide ebbs, leaving gleaming white sands slashed by deep-cut channels threading between the mounds.

Essex, Suffolk and Norfolk all have a coastline riddled with ever-moving, offshore sands. Early in the spring, long before the shore angler begins to sort out his tackle, splendid, silver-scaled fighting bass appear over the outer sands. Their prey is usually sandeels disturbed from the sand whenever there is enough breeze to create a turnover in the wave pattern. It can hardly be called surf, in the same way that the East Coast sandbanks cannot be termed storm-beaches.

Off East Anglia, dinghy anglers anchor close to the banks or at the sandbar which is found to the south of

FIG 19 BASIC BASS RIGS

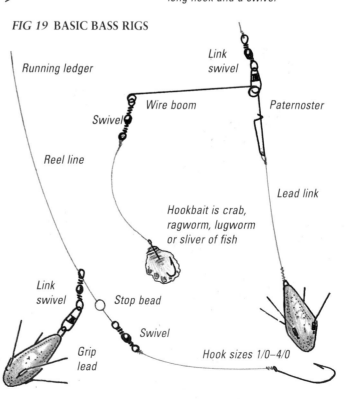

Running ledger

Reel line

Link swivel

Wire boom

Paternoster

Swivel

Hookbait is crab, ragworm, lugworm or sliver of fish

Lead link

Link swivel

Stop bead

Swivel

Grip lead

Hook sizes 1/0–4/0

115

most of the area's rivers. They cast their baits to the surfline, using a simple running ledger or paternoster with grip-lead, and with ragworm, soft crab, lugworm or slivers of fish, all ideal baits. As the tide strengthens bass and anglers move along the sands to where the white water is most evident.

Bass might not be the only catch from these sandbanks, there are thornback rays moving over them too and, later in the spring, stingrays arrive for the feast of sandeel. Alter the rig described above by attaching a 13.6 kg (30 lb) wired trace. Where there are gullies to create a crab environment I expect to find smoothhounds before the beginning of May, with the offchance of catching a tope searching out a flatfish nursery.

DEEPWATER IN MAY

Off the wild west coasts of Britain and Ireland temperatures are a great deal higher and when the stormy months and the usual winter Atlantic winds have died away bottom fishing begins in earnest. Fish that inhabit broken ground are foraging hungrily, with small ling and conger the two rocky-ground species moving into the coastal areas. (Fig. 19, p. 115)

Large ling and conger are essentially 13.6–22.5 kg

Famous West Country skipper John Trust swings in a sizable conger for the late Leslie Moncrieff. Leslie was fishing one of the many World War Two wrecks that occupy the seabed off Brixham, Devon.

MACKEREL
Scomber scombrus

This is a species of fast-moving, oily fish related to the tunny and is probably the best-known of the British sea fishes. It is a prolific fish the vast shoals of which move into British littoral waters in the late spring, providing both food and excellent bait for sea anglers. Swimming in the pelagic layers of northern Atlantic waters it feeds on plankton and the fry of other fish species. The mackerel has no swim-bladder and the tail is forked with two barely noticeable keels on each side of the wrist. In the cold months of the year the mackerel moves to deep water but here it is not safe from massive predation by man, whose commercial fishing operations have for some years taken vast quantities of mackerel by deep-water trawling in the middle of winter. It is noticeable that the mackerel shoals are now much smaller.

Bait: A string of feathers is all that is needed when gathering mackerel for bait. But to experience the fight in a mackerel it should be fished for with light spinning gear or fly rod with a minute streamer fly.

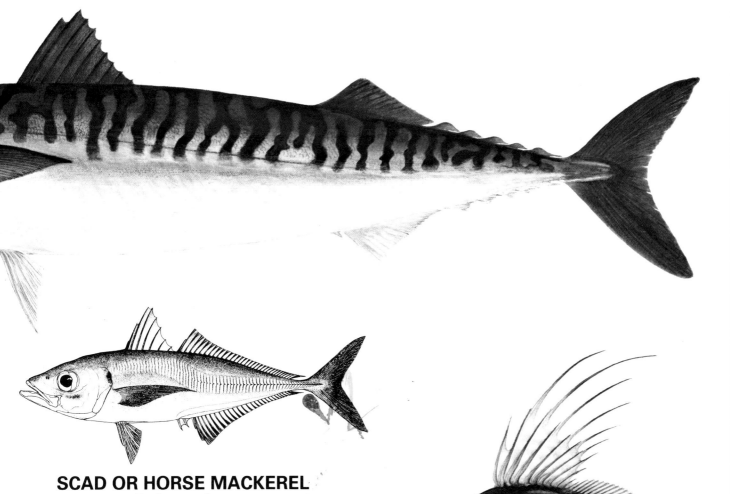

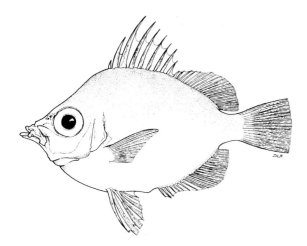

SCAD OR HORSE MACKEREL
Trachurus trachurus

While superficially similar this species has no relationship to the mackerel. The scad has a wide distribution and is sometimes found in large shoals, but has no value either as an angler's species or for the table. There are two separate dorsal fins, the first with spines and the second with a single leading spine followed by soft rays. The anal fin also carries spines at the leading edge. The lateral line is clearly marked with a number of bony scutes more noticeable towards the caudal fin.

Bait: Small strips of fish, marine worms and feathered lures.

JOHN DORY
Zeus faber

This is a unique fish with the dorsal fin divided into two sections composed of spines intersected by delicate filaments running along half its length followed by soft rays that run back to the caudal fin. The very long pelvic fins are nearly twice as long as the pectorals. There are two anal fins, spined in the first and soft-rayed behind. The dory, with its sad-looking down-turned mouth, has a deep body compressed almost as high as it is long with a large head and protrusible mouth. A solitary fish, it is found close inshore and down to over 200 fathoms, using its fast-acting tube-mouth to feed on a wide range of fishes and crustaceans. The dory's colour varies from browns to green-greys, with a large yellow-rimmed black egg-shaped blotch at mid-flank, providing it with ideal camouflage. The species is not deliberately fished for.

BOAR FISH
Capros aper

Another fish with a compressed, deep body and similar in shape to the dory, with spines in the first dorsal and anal fin with soft rays in both the secondaries. When feeding on many species of worms, crustaceans and molluscs, the mouth extends to form a short tube. The eyes are very large when compared with the size of the mouth. A small species rarely caught by anglers.

117

FIG 20 HEAVY-DUTY LEDGERING

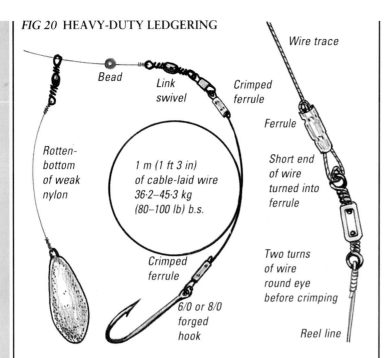

(30–50 lb) line-class rod fish and seriously to attempt their capture means finding an early mackerel shoal to provide fresh bait, otherwise frozen fish will have to do. Really large specimens of both species favour deepwater with its security, which probably means finding a wreck, pinnacle rocks or an underwater reef. Tackle up with a wired trace for both fish, using about 0.9 m (3 ft) of cable-laid wire, 36–45.4 kg (80–100 lb) b.s. between a 6 or 8/0 forged hook and a quality swivel, or fixed ledger boom. The rocky seabed will entail attaching sinkers via a weak link of nylon – the rotten bottom. When the ground is foul the angler will lose some gear and if he doesn't he can be sure that he is fishing in the wrong place! (Fig. 20)

ANCHORED OVER ROCKS

When at anchor, baits can be lowered and the bottom make-up felt through the rod tip, keeping the angler always aware of hazards. Do not give fish too long to mouth a bait, they will try to back into whatever crevice they emerged from and there is no way that a big conger, once back in its hole, can be extracted. Get the hooked fish moving immediately after striking; it is the first few fathoms that are important, for only when a fish is fighting in open water and up from the bottom does the angler have the advantage.

FISHING ON THE DRIFT

Drifting the boat over this kind of rocky mark can be more productive because much more ground can be covered, but extreme care must be taken. Ideally, the same terminal rigs as described above can be used. They are lowered, hit bottom, and then have to be raised by at least a couple of metres (6 ft) or so, which is about three winds on the multiplier handle. This action keeps the sinker and hook clear of rocks, although the tackle could drag into an outcrop at any moment during the drift over the mark. This is hard work, demanding the angler's total attention.

Ling, cod, pollack, coalfish, bream and many other species will come to the baited hook. A big conger is not likely to be caught because the species only takes bait hard on the seabed and rarely will come up to grab at something moving over its head.

OFFSHORE IN SUMMERTIME

This is the time of the year when our sport becomes crowded as holidaymakers and occasional anglers add their numbers to the regular sea anglers going out in boats. There is a far greater variety of fish to catch which, added to the extra number of anglers fishing, always makes summer appear a time of plenty. But I doubt whether this is true, it is probably what the carp-anglers term the 'rod-hour factor'. The strictly summer species have arrived, breams from the Mediterranean, mackerel are shoaling to be hounded by seabirds and sharks which follow them from tropical waters. For the inshore fisherman in his small craft, many fish will have left the deepwater and its security and freedom from storm surge to come close into

A Joyce West, editor of 'Seafood News', holds her well-hooked conger in mid-water against its plunge back into the safety of the wreck from which it had been tempted. **B** It was a long way up and the conger put up a protracted fight to the surface. This muscular fish, drawn up from seabed darkness into the sunlight, begins a vicious spiralling that so often tears a hook free. **C** The beaten conger comes back up-tide, steadily drawn to the skipper's waiting gaff.

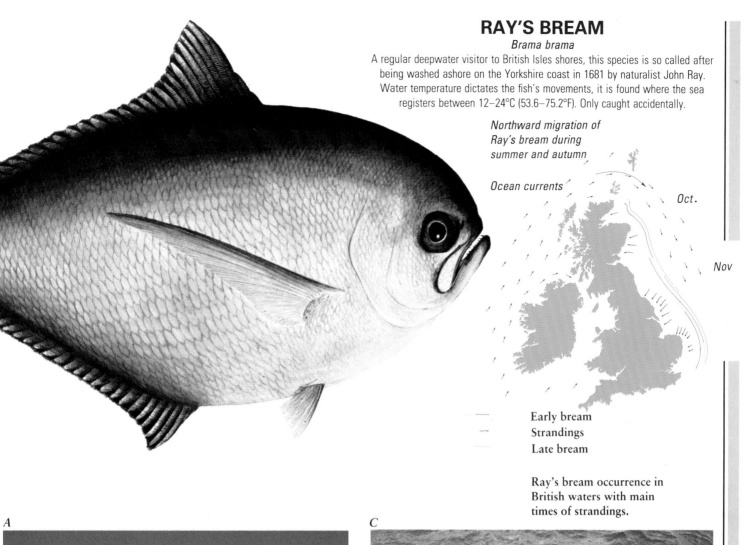

RAY'S BREAM
Brama brama
A regular deepwater visitor to British Isles shores, this species is so called after being washed ashore on the Yorkshire coast in 1681 by naturalist John Ray. Water temperature dictates the fish's movements, it is found where the sea registers between 12–24°C (53.6–75.2°F). Only caught accidentally.

Northward migration of Ray's bream during summer and autumn

Ocean currents

Oct.

Nov.

— Early bream
— Strandings
Late bream

Ray's bream occurrence in British waters with main times of strandings.

A

B

C

119

BOGUE
Boops boops

A Mediterranean species that comes on the warm drift to the western shores of the British Isles. While related to the sea-breams it does not have their general shape, being elongated and slender and only slightly compressed. There is a small dark spot near the base of the pectoral fin. Carnivorous when young, it is omnivorous thereafter. It is not specifically fished for.

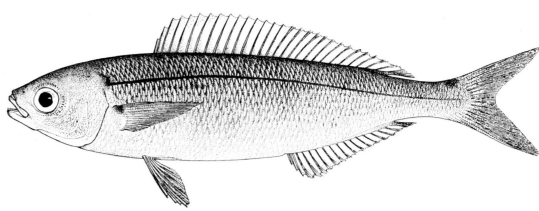

BLACK BREAM
Spondyliosoma cantharus

A deep, boldly coloured bream that comes to British waters each year about May. This once hugely prolific species was taken by anglers during competitions held from English South Coast marks, notably Littlehampton, where the migratory drive brought the bream into tight concentration. Due to this angling predation, the numbers have dropped. The superb fighting qualities of this species are often masked by the heavy tackle used in conventional bottom fishing. The fish should be sought on light tackle. The species has an hermaphrodite element and can grow to at least 3.1 kg (6 lb 14 oz).
Bait: Small marine worms on small hooks; fish strip, squid, feathers, lures.

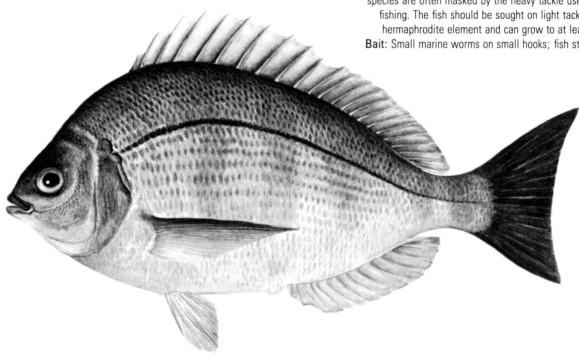

rich feeding grounds within 2 or 3 kilometres, a mile or so, of the shore.

WRECKING

The serious boat anglers now range far out to sea as weather conditions are far more settled, extending the number of marks and species available to them. Far-offshore wrecks are safe to voyage to, undisturbed for months they will have a rich harvest for the rod and line. Success in pin-pointing wrecks and offshore reefs was made certain through the rapid advances in electronic technology. The echo-sounder, and lately the far-more advanced video fish-finder, together with satellite and radio beacon navigation systems allow skippers to find their offshore marks with perfect repeatability. (Fig. 21)

Wrecks litter our seas, their positions fairly well docu-

Video scanners have changed the face of sea angling. They produce a visual picture that outlines rocks, seabed, weed and fish in a colour pattern. Shoals of fish show clearly, their movements easily seen. Large specimens give a defined image and the picture can be zoomed in to magnify a chosen area on screen.

Fig 21 A section of an echo-sounder chart revealing a wreck on rocky ground in deep water. The wreck shows as a sharp trace standing on the left-hand side of the centre underwater hill. Weed growth on the wreck shows in a paler image.

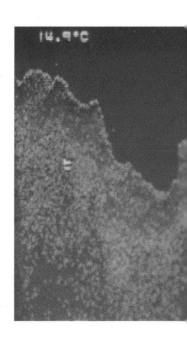

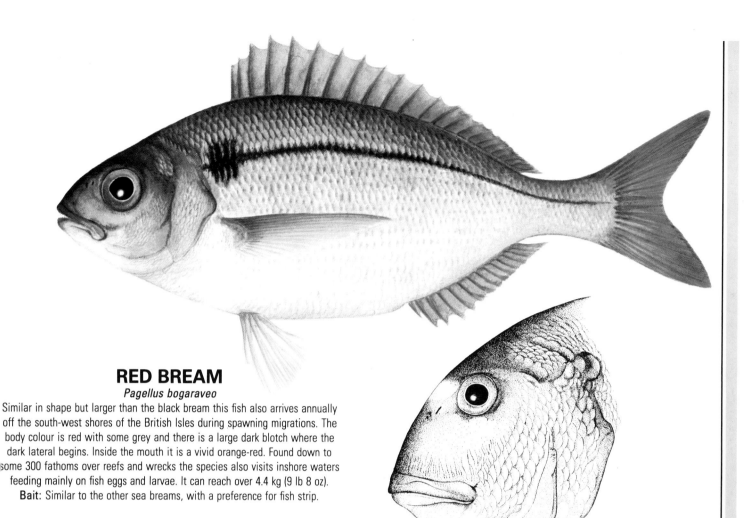

RED BREAM
Pagellus bogaraveo
Similar in shape but larger than the black bream this fish also arrives annually off the south-west shores of the British Isles during spawning migrations. The body colour is red with some grey and there is a large dark blotch where the dark lateral begins. Inside the mouth it is a vivid orange-red. Found down to some 300 fathoms over reefs and wrecks the species also visits inshore waters feeding mainly on fish eggs and larvae. It can reach over 4.4 kg (9 lb 8 oz).
Bait: Similar to the other sea breams, with a preference for fish strip.

GILTHEAD
Sparus aurata
The gilthead is seen more and more in British waters, but perhaps this is due to the increase in fishing deepwater reef and wreck marks that has taken place. It is similar in shape and colour to the black bream but has a distinct golden bar across the head between the eyes and patches of bright gold-orange on each gill-cover. It feeds on crustaceans and algae, reaching over 3.6 kg (8 lb).
Bait: As for the other sea breams.

FIG 21 ECHO-SOUNDER READING

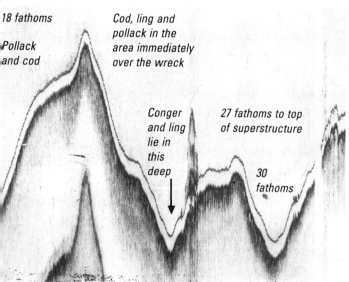

18 fathoms

Pollack and cod

Cod, ling and pollack in the area immediately over the wreck

Conger and ling lie in this deep

27 fathoms to top of superstructure

30 fathoms

mented, so they can be found. All that remains is to be able to anchor up in a way that allows us to drop baits on to them with accuracy. Wreck and reef fishing can be highly selective. Fish over the wreck and the mid-water species such as pollack, pouting, cod, coalfish and breams will come to the bait. Touch the top of the wrecked hull and one either catches bigger specimens of those fish, with perhaps ling as well; one may well also snag fast in broken superstructures and rigging. For conger, the ideal place for the hookbait to be is alongside the wreck, within the trough that has been scoured out by strong currents. The chance of losing gear is always present, for the sand can be littered with debris torn from the ship's superstructures.

The message is that wreck fishing, like drifting over broken ground, is very demanding of the angler's total concentration. He must avoid getting snagged but at the same time must put, and keep, his bait on to ground where

121

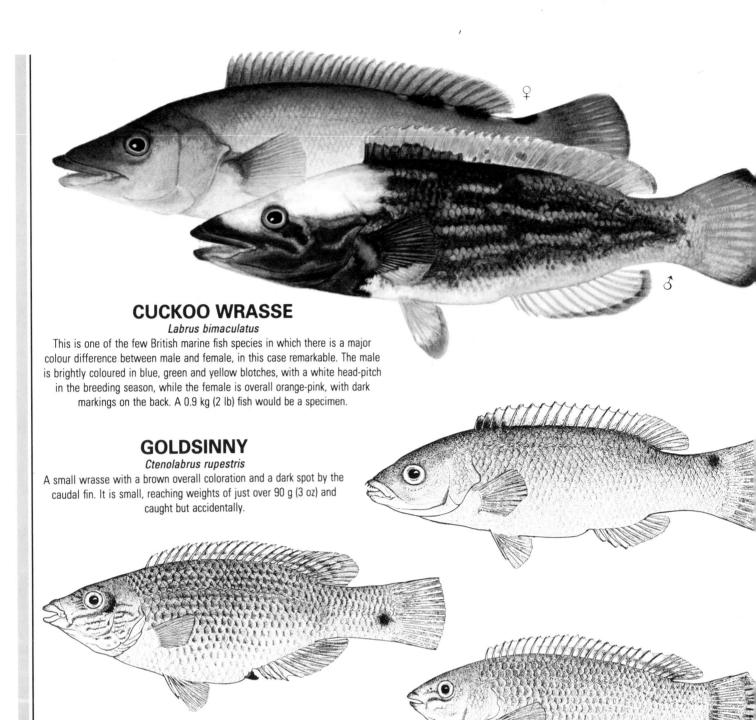

CUCKOO WRASSE
Labrus bimaculatus
This is one of the few British marine fish species in which there is a major colour difference between male and female, in this case remarkable. The male is brightly coloured in blue, green and yellow blotches, with a white head-pitch in the breeding season, while the female is overall orange-pink, with dark markings on the back. A 0.9 kg (2 lb) fish would be a specimen.

GOLDSINNY
Ctenolabrus rupestris
A small wrasse with a brown overall coloration and a dark spot by the caudal fin. It is small, reaching weights of just over 90 g (3 oz) and caught but accidentally.

CORKWING WRASSE
Symphodus (Crenilabrus) melops
The body is rather deeper than that of the goldsinny and the dark spot is lower down on the wrist of the caudal fin. The head and jaws have variegated colour bands. Found in the same habitat, this small wrasse is slightly heavier than the goldsinny, attaining over 310 g (11 oz).

SMALL-MOUTHED WRASSE
Centrolabrus exoletus
Also known as the rock cook, this wrasse species differs from the others by having more dorsal fin rays. It has a very small mouth.

Upper and lower jaw of the ballan wrasse

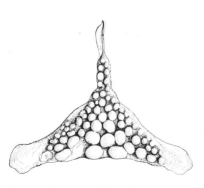

Pharyngeal teeth of the ballan wrasse

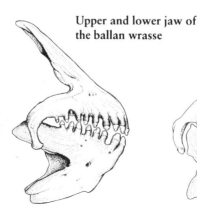

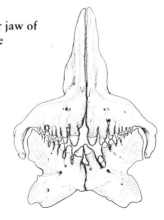

RAINBOW WRASSE
Coris julis

A fish of 0.45 kg (1 lb) would be an exceptional weight for this small wrasse. Though small, its coloration is brilliant, the sexes having different hues. Rare north of Biscay, this is an occasional visitor to southern British inshore waters, but Gibraltar has recorded one of 0.14 kg (5 oz). So far it is not established as an angler's species.

GENERAL NOTE ON THE WRASSES
(Labridae)

All members of the colourful wrasse family are found on very rough ground that suits their feeding and breeding behaviour. Their dentition is adept at removing limpets and other molluscs from rocks in the intertidal zone. This indicates that wrasse are generally found in inshore waters where the water is deep close to rocks. Here they establish some form of territory unaffected by the rise and fall of the tides. The wrasses are nest builders. Primarily day-time feeders, they hide-up in rock crevices at night or bury themselves in soft sand to 'sleep'. Some species are known to exhibit sex-reversal, changing from female to male.

Bait: All marine worms, molluscs, crustaceans and tiny slips of fish flesh.

Lips of the ballan wrasse

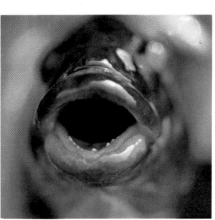

BALLAN WRASSE
Labrus bergylta

This is the largest of the wrasse species found in the waters round the British Isles and is considered the shore-angler's quarry. Thought of as a summer fish by most anglers, the ballan wrasse can be caught throughout the year in south and western areas. In both sexes the species is subject to a wide variation in coloration which reflects the habitat. These fish are also able to adjust skin colours to match those of their mineral and vegetable surroundings. There is no colour difference by which to distinguish the sexes. This fish is capable of reaching 4.5 kg (10 lb) and can live for some 18 years.

the fish will find it. Simplicity is vital, the less complex the rig the fewer chances there are of becoming snagged – and there is far less gear to lose. When over the wreck, consider using a long-flowing mid-water trace which puts such a life-like action into a fish-strip or artificial lure. This rig can be allowed to touch the wreck just once, to establish a perfect depth setting, then it must be taken up a fathom or two before the hook or part of the rig snags. (Fig. 22)

Down below on the seabed, or right on top of a wreck or reef, a 0.9 m (3 ft) wire trace is best, with a crimped-on loop to a quality link-swivel for its quick-release facility. The weight, a sliding sinker attached on a rotten-bottom, must be heavy enough to hold the ground without moving in the tide. It helps to completely shroud the hook with the bait. Fishing into a wreck can be troublesome, any movement of the lead, apart from that induced by a taking fish, will ensure that it finds its way into a snag. This can be annoying when you know that a good fish is hooked and will be lost because of the obstruction below. (Figs 23, 24)

Many conger are lost when they reach the surface. This species spins hard on the way up and thrashes about as it comes up to strong light. Here, gaffing discipline is vital. If there are a number of anglers, all with hooked fish coming up, try to time the arrival of your conger to match the skipper's gaffing schedule. Do not let big fish lie thrashing about, it is easy for them to shed the hook. Having that quick-release trace is useful when fishing for conger and ling. The skipper will be busy bringing writhing eels aboard, so make life easy for him. Let him dump the fish and the trace into a sealed fish-well. The trace and hook can be recovered later when the fish has quietened. And have a number of traces prepared and ready for use, this is something to do when the boat is making its way out to the mark.

The tide will change within hours of your anchoring over a wreck. This means up-anchoring and altering the boat's position relative to the wreck and the new tidal flow. There is a period, between the boat lying in one direction and the other, when the craft will swing away from the wreck. This moves the baits out on to a clean seabed, and the species change immediately. There could be turbot, bull huss and possibly sharks feeding on the smaller fish that avoid the predators which live their permanent existence within the hulk. These off-wreck species can be a terrific bonus to the catch, though this clean-bottom fishing will not last very long, only between the periods of slack-water.

I find the heavy work involved in conger fishing needs breaking up into sessions, I begin by fishing heavy, then take up the lighter tackle for half-hour or so, to see what species are in mid-water. Alternating my fishing system regularly takes away much of the strain that depletes an angler's ability to concentrate.

INSHORE FOR SMALL FRY

Boat fishing need not always be a heavy affair. There are so many species, though not enormous in body-weight,

FIG 22 MIDWATER RUNNING LEDGER TRACE

Fish strip or lure

Bomb weight

SSG freshwater shot (not illegal in sea fishing) prevents trace wrapping round the reel line

Stop bead sets the length of trace

2–3 m (6–9 ft)

Tie fishbait to the nylon or wire trace with elastic thread
Hook size will match bait size, usually 1/0–6/0

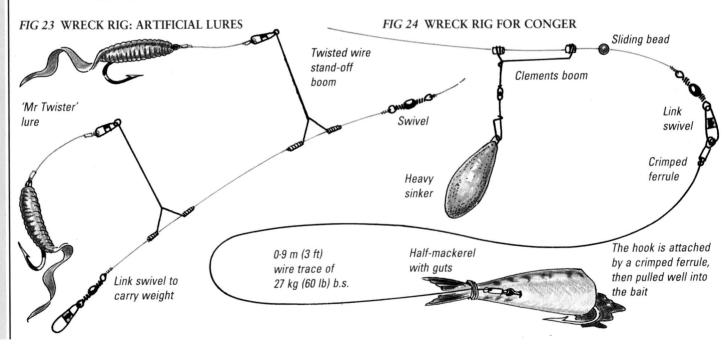

FIG 23 WRECK RIG: ARTIFICIAL LURES

'Mr Twister' lure

Twisted wire stand-off boom

Swivel

Link swivel to carry weight

0.9 m (3 ft) wire trace of 27 kg (60 lb) b.s.

FIG 24 WRECK RIG FOR CONGER

Sliding bead

Clements boom

Link swivel

Crimped ferrule

Heavy sinker

Half-mackerel with guts

The hook is attached by a crimped ferrule, then pulled well into the bait

that can give marvellous sport provided that the tackle is balanced to their ability to fight. Plaice are often found frequenting musselbeds, dabs on open ground, the highly coloured gurnards, smaller members of the rays, flounders and mackerel – while not including all the species that can be found in the shallower water, they give the angler a lot of fishing.

My award for the most sporting species would go to the mackerel, for sheer speed there cannot be many fish to touch it! Sadly, most boat anglers look upon mackerel only as a potential bait for better things, and do not take kindly to one of the party choosing to spin. This is a pity because this fish has a lot to offer and should not become a sport solely for the dinghy owner.

Give mackerel their chance on light tackle, a spinning rod with a fixed-spool reel, 2.7–4.5 kg (6–10 lb) line and a spoon-bait with a small treble or, better still, a single, short-shanked hook. Perhaps additional casting weight will be necessary but only enough to get the lure away from the boat and just below the surface. Mackerel are related to the tunny family, which says it all! Once hooked, mackerel move at an incredible speed, changing direction rapidly and are slow to tire. Among a shoal of summer mackerel there are often garfish, again extremely fast swimmers, they leap out over the water, even turning somersaults in an effort to shed the hook. Sometimes they are difficult to hook, their long bill and very small mouth making it awkward for the fish to get hold of the lure. They slash at it, giving many false bites. And they have green bones, but do not let that put your wife off cooking the garfish, because they are delicious. (Fig. 25)

I use a short trace for plaice fishing over known holding ground, and a running ledger of a metre (about a yard) is all that is required between hook and sinker and a Size 1 hook, always a long-shank, tied leaving a whisker of nylon over which a worm is pulled. The whisker serves to prevent taking fish sucking the worm off the hook without giving any indication of the bite. I sometimes mount a bait on a two-hook Pennell rig, the lower hook tied on with a

tucked half-blood knot and a smaller hook fixed above it, on the nylon, using a little piece of polythene tube. This rig does the same thing as preventing the bait being torn off, but has the added and useful facility of allowing adjustment to accommodate larger or smaller baits. (Fig. 26)

A dab is no fighter unless it is fished for on spinning rod and very light line, but it can prove very tasty in the pan. I enjoy the ultra-light sport this little fish gives, though it is really a matter of knowing that there are dabs below the keel! Similar terminal rigs to those used in plaice fishing will do, but the hook should be smaller and mounted with a 5 cm (2 in) sliver of fresh fishbait. The species will also take worms but fish is more productive.

THE DOGFISHES

It may seem strange that I lump three species together, for they vary tremendously in size. It is true, but there is little difference between their performance. Bull huss grow

A

FIG 25 SPOON BAITS FOR MACKEREL AND GARFISH

Single hook replaces treble

Spoon

Short nylon leader

Swivel and anti-kink vane

FIG 26 RIGS FOR PLAICE

All hooks are Size 1 long-shank

Nylon whisker left on knot

Reel line

Sliding plastic sleeve for hook

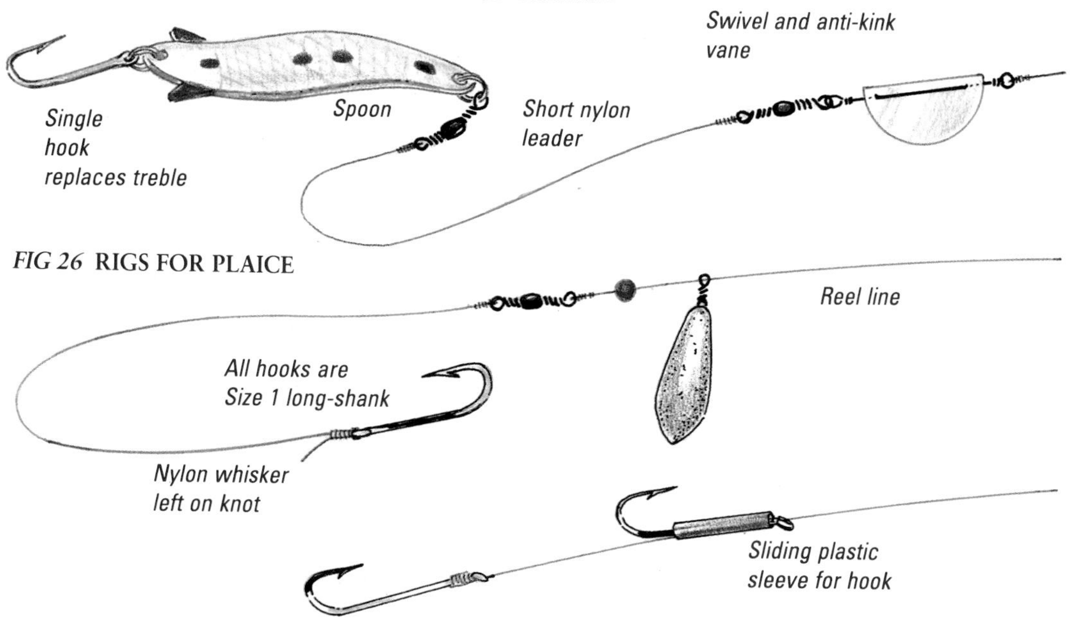

Prime dabs from one of the best marks Mike Prichard has ever fished, Porturlin, on the North Mayo coast of Ireland. Lady angler Hilda Cavanagh, from Westport, organised an angling foray for nothing but this small and very succulent species. Two dabs on each retrieve of the terminal tackle was the order of the day. These small flatties must have been lying ten deep on the clean ground alongside the rugged cliffs. *Fig 25* Mackerel and garfish can give great sport but the tackle must be light. For these species a treble hook is not necessary. *Fig 26* The two-hook Pennell rig is a very old freshwater idea that has found uses in all kinds of fishing.

fairly large and give the best fight, nothing startling but still demanding skill in the hooking. Huss can be infuriating, playing with a bait and coming up, after a strike, as though they are well hooked. Then, seeing the change in light above their heads, the fish simply let go of the bait. They can hold it in their mouths like a playful puppy while being hauled to the surface, then let go. I have lost many really large huss this way. Now, if the species is about (and that means seeing several hooked and boated) I change the hook size radically, down to a well-sharpened 1/0–3/0, fished on a tough trace of heavier 22.8 kg (50 lb) nylon. A small hook, well hidden in a lash of mackerel, invites less mouthing and gives faster hooking, without reducing holding ability inside the tough jaw. (Fig. 27)

The problem is even worse with the lesser-spotted dogfish. This species not only steals bait intended for more highly prized fish and gets your tackle in all sorts of tangles while giving a 'nothing' fight, but then has the audacity,

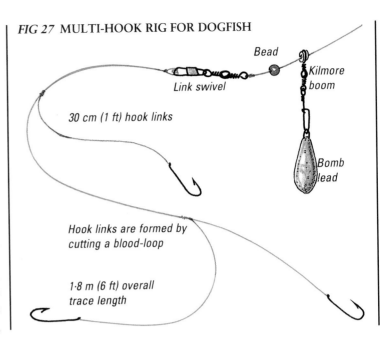

FIG 27 MULTI-HOOK RIG FOR DOGFISH

Bead

Link swivel

Kilmore boom

30 cm (1 ft) hook links

Bomb lead

Hook links are formed by cutting a blood-loop

1·8 m (6 ft) overall trace length

VIVIPAROUS BLENNY
Zoarces viviparus
One dorsal fin extends to a position just above the gillcase back to the caudal fin. The soft rays forming the dorsal fin have a depression near the caudal fin and here the finrays are spine-like. Soft rays are equal in length with the spines shorter. Like many fish species, its skin is able to adopt a coloration that enables it to blend into its surroundings. This species has small scales on an elongated body and lives inshore among weedbeds and rock outcrops where it feeds on a variety of fish fry and eggs, crustaceans, gastropods and other small animals. A small inshore species, the viviparous blenny reaches 368 g (13 oz) and is not seriously fished for by anglers.

Dogfish can be rough on humans! If carelessly held the small shark's tail wraps round the forearm, resulting in a painful 'sandpapering'. Immobilise the fish by trapping head and tail and when held against each other this prevents sudden movement.

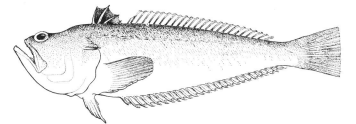

LESSER WEEVER
Echiichthys vipera

A small fish found widely in the sand of shallow water on British Isles beaches, the lesser weever is considered by Unesco to be the most dangerous of the European weevers for its potentially lethal poison and its numbers inshore. The poison glands are situated on the rear of the operculum (gill-case) and on the first dorsal fin; paddlers are those most likely to fall victim and should be given immediate medical treatment. The fish gives birth to live, fully active young. Not surprisingly, it is not actively sought by anglers.

GREATER WEEVER
Trachinus draco

Since this is a deep-water species it is the boat-angler's version of the lesser weever and is just as venomous. It is only caught by bad luck.

COMMON CATFISH
Anarhichus lupus

Also called the wolf fish, this is an ugly brute with an enormous mouth and canine-like, backward-curving teeth in the jaws and behind them are grinding molars for crushing the crustaceans that this fish feeds on. No relation to the freshwater catfishes, this species haunts the rocky ground in deepwater. Many tons of this fish are netted by commercial fisheries each week and, filletted and headless, they become welcome and wholesome food. It grows to over 21.5 kg (47 lb) but does not appear often in anglers' catches.

Bait: Perhaps a mixture of worm, fish and shellfish.

when being freed of the hook prior to being returned alive, to wrap its sandpaper-like body round your forearm and remove the skin like a rasp! But they are easily caught. They have one saving grace, when all other fish have disappeared off the mark you can bet your rod that these endearing little monsters will remain, and that at least is something.

One dogfish, found mostly in the deepwater of our western seas, can exhibit something close to being called a fight. This is the spurdog. Gathering in huge shoals in summer but more so in the autumn, the spurdog move in to predate on anything that swims. They will clean out a productive mark in no time at all. If you meet them, change to a wire trace to combat their very sharp teeth and keep to a single hook. Their presence is often given away

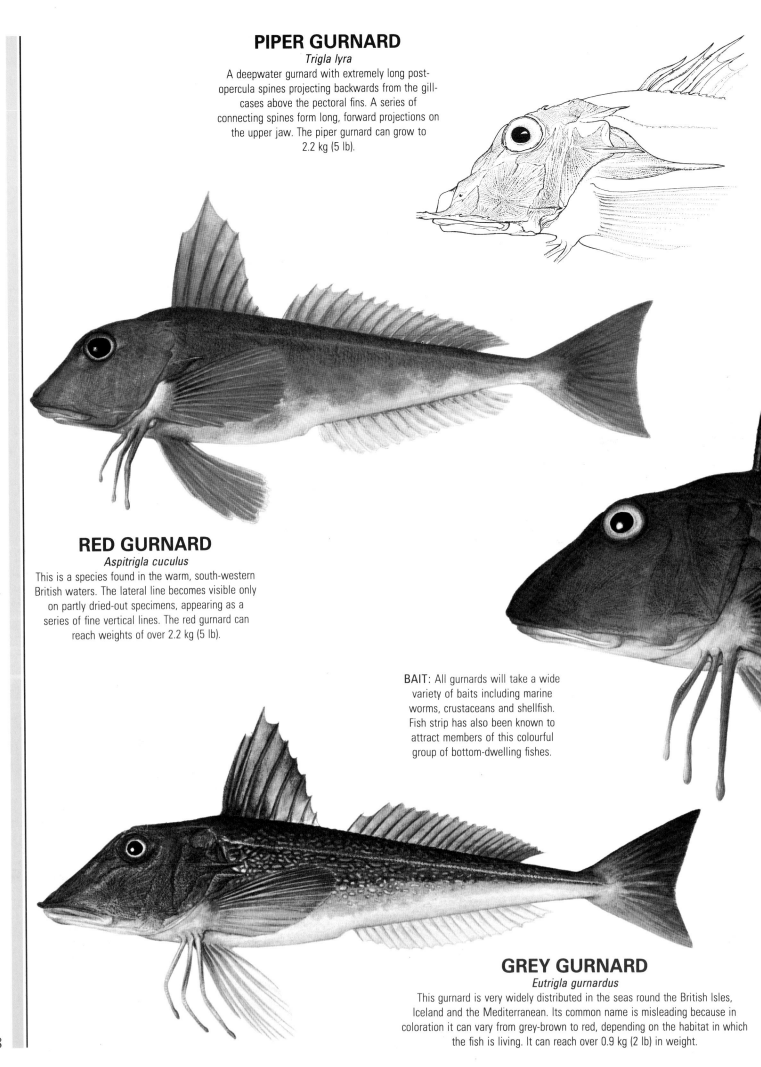

PIPER GURNARD
Trigla lyra
A deepwater gurnard with extremely long post-opercula spines projecting backwards from the gill-cases above the pectoral fins. A series of connecting spines form long, forward projections on the upper jaw. The piper gurnard can grow to 2.2 kg (5 lb).

RED GURNARD
Aspitrigla cuculus
This is a species found in the warm, south-western British waters. The lateral line becomes visible only on partly dried-out specimens, appearing as a series of fine vertical lines. The red gurnard can reach weights of over 2.2 kg (5 lb).

BAIT: All gurnards will take a wide variety of baits including marine worms, crustaceans and shellfish. Fish strip has also been known to attract members of this colourful group of bottom-dwelling fishes.

GREY GURNARD
Eutrigla gurnardus
This gurnard is very widely distributed in the seas round the British Isles, Iceland and the Mediterranean. Its common name is misleading because in coloration it can vary from grey-brown to red, depending on the habitat in which the fish is living. It can reach over 0.9 kg (2 lb) in weight.

STREAKED GURNARD
Trigloporus lastoviza

This gurnard has a far wider distribution than angling accounts would suggest. The species is often confused with both the red and tub species but the blunt shape of its head and the vertical streaks on the flanks are unmistakable. Its colour is red on top, pale below, with dark blotches on the head and back. The streaked gurnard can grow to about 1.3–1.8 kg (3–4 lb) in weight.

TUB GURNARD
Trigla lucerna

This fish, also known as the yellow gurnard, is the largest of the family and can be immediately identified by the deeply embedded scales along the lateral line. A sizeable fish, it can reach weights of over 5.5 kg (11 lb 7 oz).

LANTERN GURNARD
Aspitrigla obscura

This is a deepwater fish that must be regarded as an angling rarity in British waters. Usually red with pink flanks, it has a lateral line of plate-like scales. Little is known of its feeding or breeding habits. It can reach weights of 0.9–1.3 kg (2–3 lb).

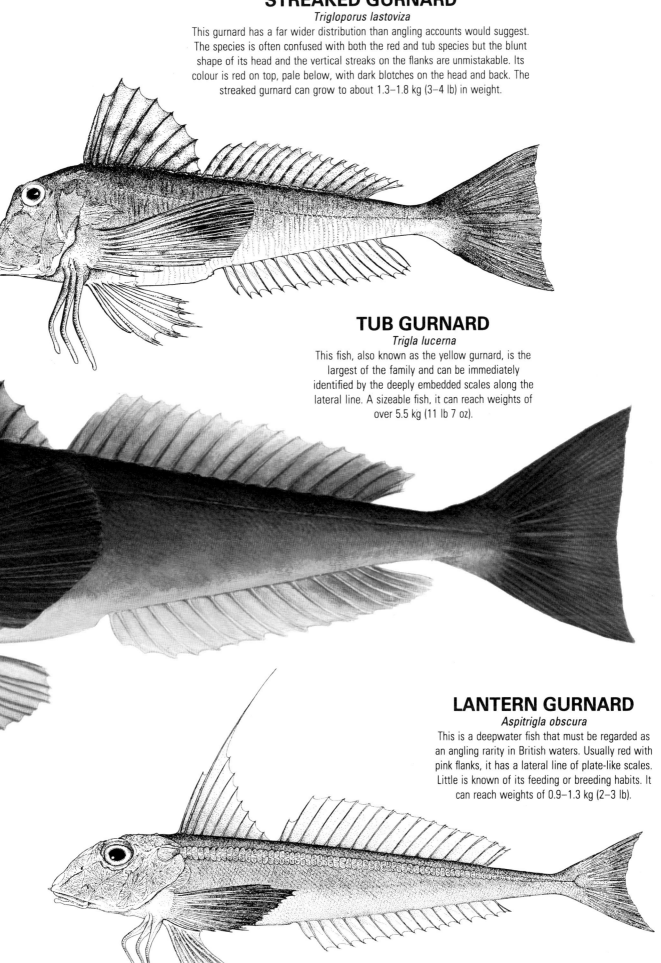

by gannets, kittiwakes and fulmars following the spurdog as they chase mackerel up to the surface, causing great mortality and leaving a trail of bloody debris for the birds.

FISHING THE BLUES

As regular as clockwork each season, blue sharks arrive off the South and West Coasts of Britain and Ireland. It has never been established, so far as I know, whether their migration northward has anything to do with the urge to breed; more likely these fish move up in the warm water of the Drift purely as a seasonal feeding behaviour, harrying mackerel and other pelagic species as they go.

As the boat drifts on the tide, anglers trigger the sharks into a feeding mode by laying a trail of fish oil, bran and pulped fish. A sackful is suspended over the side of the boat to bump against the side in the swell, slowly spilling its contents into the water. Why this noisome mess is called rubby-dubby I have no idea, but it does work as an attractor of sharks with their fantastic olfactory sense. Along with the oily, bloody smear spreading out on the surface there is a constant falling through the water of minute pieces of rubby which can be seen by sharks swimming at depth.

Shark baits are usually fished suspended from a float. Baited 8/0–10/0 hooks are attached to a 113 kg (250 lb) b.s. wire trace about 3.6 m (12 ft) long. A quality swivel with quick-release facility joins the trace to the reel line. I usually put another swivel in the middle of the wire trace,

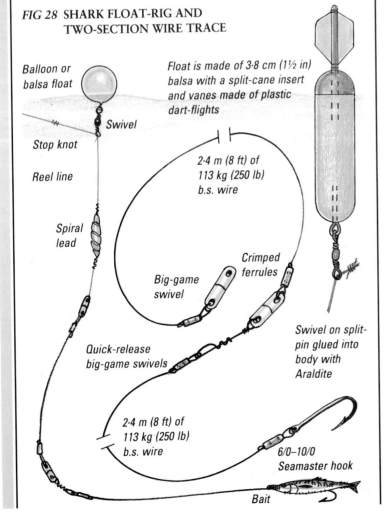

FIG 28 SHARK FLOAT-RIG AND TWO-SECTION WIRE TRACE

Balloon or balsa float

Float is made of 3·8 cm (1½ in) balsa with a split-cane insert and vanes made of plastic dart-flights

Swivel

Stop knot

Reel line

2·4 m (8 ft) of 113 kg (250 lb) b.s. wire

Spiral lead

Crimped ferrules

Big-game swivel

Big-game swivel

Quick-release big-game swivels

Swivel on split-pin glued into body with Araldite

2·4 m (8 ft) of 113 kg (250 lb) b.s. wire

6/0–10/0 Seamaster hook

Bait

LONG-SPINED SEA SCORPION
Taurulus bubalis

A fairly common species round Britain, found in deep water with a rocky, broken ground. It grows to 226 g (8 oz), slightly heavier than the short-spined species.
Bait: As for the short-spined species (opposite).

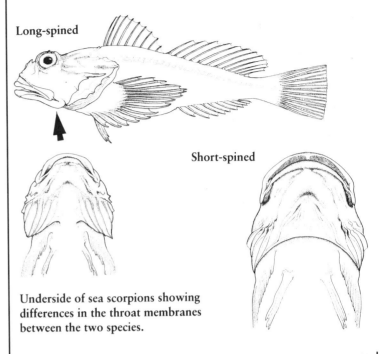

Long-spined

Short-spined

Underside of sea scorpions showing differences in the throat membranes between the two species.

A

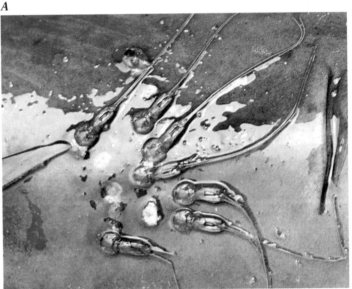

A Most creatures have parasites that attach themselves to the host. These are sea lice that prey on porbeagle and other sharks. Called *Lepeophtheirus sp.* they are found forward of and at the base of the tail. *B* A male tope comes quietly up to the surface. At the boat's side the conservation-minded angler can boat the fish by grasping the dorsal fin and tail wrist.

it helps to relieve line twist brought about as the hooked shark spins while being drawn to the surface. The float, generally a balloon, is tied on to the reel line at a depth setting decided upon by the angler. When four anglers are fishing they agree on different bait settings until shark appear. The bait that gets the strike first tells everyone the depth at which fish are swimming. It is a good theory which does not always work because sharks will be

SHORT-SPINED SEA SCORPION
Myoxocephalus scorpius

A fish of the northern waters of the British Isles. Highly colourful and with much variation between specimens from different habitats. Sometimes called the

father lasher, or bull-rout, it can reach 0.3 m (1 ft), but 15–17 cm (6–7 in) is average. When hooked it inflates the throat area.

Bait: Almost any of the conventional baits will be taken.

B

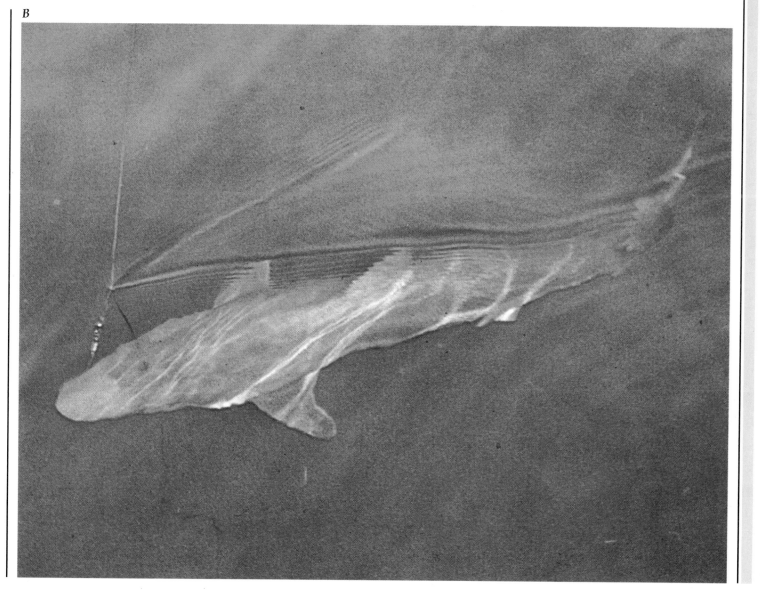

gradually brought nearer the surface by the trail of rubby-dubby. As a float, the balloon can be improved on, it offers too much resistance to a taking fish. I use a coloured balsa-wood float, rather like an over-sized pike bung. It supports a mackerel-bait well and is easily pulled under by a shark. And I always know from the colour of the float which float is mine! (Fig. 28, p. 130)

A run usually starts with a series of bobbing movements of the float; then the float dips and the line begins to run off the spool, which has already been set at a firm-strike drag, but out of gear with the ratchet on to avoid over-runs. Blue sharks make an initial run, then they stop to turn and swallow the bait. I strike as the second run gets under way, for if you strike too soon the hook will probably be dragged out from the bait. A strike left too long after the shark is making its second run will often result in a gut-hooked shark which will have to be killed. It is best to strike early, chancing a lost fish, than strike late and cause serious injury – and death.

Some anglers still gaff blue sharks, when there is little need to do so. A small blue can be lifted out by the tailfin. With strong gloves, one man grabs the wired trace as the swivel hits the top ring on the rod. He then handlines the shark, which should have been well played out, until it lies at the boat's side. Another angler lifts the fish by its tail. Once the tail is out of the water a shark has no forward drive, it can only thrash about.

Be careful as the shark comes aboard, though tired it can still bite! Restraining the fish is a two-man job, one holding the fish above the gills, the other angler keeping a tight hold on the tail, then the successful angler slips a hard-wood block between the fish's jaws so that the hook can be extracted. Heavy-duty pliers will give the right purchase for this task. With the hook free, the two men can return the shark to the sea, one holding the tail, the other taking charge of the head behind the pectoral fins. It may seem difficult, but it isn't!

Tail-roping is the only way to subdue and bring in a large shark. This is done by using a rope, with a small, spliced loop, around the angler in the latter stages of the fight. When the trace-man sees the shark coming, the rope is formed into a lassoo, taken over the angler's body and on up the rod. As the shark is pulled in against the side of the boat by the trace the noose is shaken down the trace and round the shark's body. As the loop gets past the pectoral fins the noose is quickly pulled tight and the tail lifted high out of the water. A turn of rope should be taken round the nearest bollard. Everyone can now relax while they work out whether the fish comes aboard or has the hook extracted while it lies alongside. There are no rules for this, it has to be sorted out at the time.

AUTUMN: A FAVOURITE TIME OF YEAR

I have three favourite fish of autumn, the first a fast-swimming shark relative, the others are sea-angling heavyweights. All three can be caught much earlier in any year, depending upon where you live and fish, yet autumn has always given me the best fishing for these species.

TOPE: THE SPEED-MERCHANT

Dingle Peninsula grew to fame on its bass catches from the shore. Few fishers bothered to fish for anything else in Dingle Bay until a few years ago, when there came a demise in the bass shoals. Perhaps the shortage of charter-boats made offshore angling difficult to get, although the tiny port of Fenit, on Tralee Bay, has always had sea-going craft available.

The rock-strewn coastline of Kerry is interspersed with beautiful, gently sloping surf-beaches. Golden strands slope on out underwater offering a clean sand bottom, with occasional outcrops of reef and pinnacle rock. There are tope here, sometimes in great schools, moving leisurely over the seabed they feed on immature flatfish in both bays, as well as depleting the mackerel that shoal towards the Blasket Islands.

I believe the tope to be a proud fish, one that gives us a lot of sport and deserves to be handled with respect. Doing this involves using the correct tackle bearing in mind that tope should always be returned to the sea. Start with your 13.6 kg (30 lb) class rod, or even a 9 kg (20 lb) class model if you feel confident with light gear, the appropriate nylon or braided lines carrying a sliding boom with a sinker that just stems the tide. Make sure that the boom slides easily and that the weight selected is only enough to get the bait down and holding.

The trace is in two parts; a multi-strand wire of 45.4 kg (100 lb) b.s. or so, about a metre (a yard) long joined to a length of tough nylon, say 36 kg (80 lb), of 1.8 m (6 ft) long, by a good swivel. Another swivel joins the reel line to the thicker nylon. The reason for the two trace materials is sound: the wire guards against the tope biting through the hook trace, whereas the heavy nylon absorbs abrasion from the fish's extremely rough skin. Some anglers bait up with whole mackerel, I don't because I find that after the tope's run one has to wait so long before striking. And even then you can get it all wrong. It is better to use only a lash of mackerel, shrouding the pre-sharpened hook as best you can. Adjust the striking drag on the reel, flip it out of gear, but remember to apply the ratchet mechanism. Lower the bait downtide slowly, if the drop is too fast you may get the bait twisted around the reel line. (Fig. 29)

FIG 29 TOPE RIG

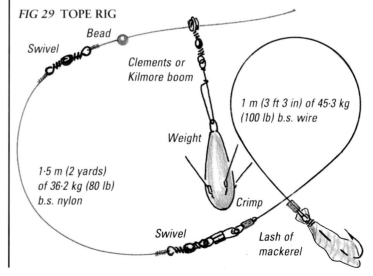

Swivel

Bead

Clements or Kilmore boom

1 m (3 ft 3 in) of 45·3 kg (100 lb) b.s. wire

Weight

1·5 m (2 yards) of 36·2 kg (80 lb) b.s. nylon

Swivel

Crimp

Lash of mackerel

A

A feeding tope will come on the bait, inspect it, then take it up and mouth it and very little of this is felt at the rod. What you might see, if there is any sort of tide run, is a gentle dipping action at the tip. The fish should then take off fast, particularly when the bait is lying in shallow water. It will run for anything up to 27.4 m (30 yards), although it seems like a hundred! Pick the rod up, ease the ratchet off and control the revolving spool with the thumb, this stops the possibility of an over-run. The tope will stop, then go again, and as the second run starts slam the reel into gear and strike simultaneously with the rod held high. A lot of line stretch has to be overcome.

It is not possible to determine what size the tope will be, so I tend to set the clutch fairly loose, adding further pressure with the thumb as I pump. Let the fish run, do not drag it to the surface before it is ready, this way you can enjoy the battle and have a subdued fish on the surface when the job of removing the hook has to be faced. This can either be done by using long-handled pliers while holding the trace, while a friend holds the fish's tail; or the tope can be tailed into the boat. Keep a secure hold on the tail when removing the hook, for loose on the cockpit floor a lively tope can create havoc among tackle boxes, feet, and the usual angling gear.

SKATE: THE BACK-BREAKER

I have decided that skate fishing is no longer for me. My biggest specimen, one of 78 kg (172 lb), nearly put me in

A Jim McLanaghan prepares to return this tope, unharmed, to its environment. Conservation is a priority if we sea anglers want our sport to have a future. *B* The finest reason for ensuring that your rig is formed from quality components: a huge common skate can easily rip a weak trace apart during the fight, and the fish should only be gaffed in a wingtip where it will not injure the internal organs.

B

bed for a week, but I'll explain how to catch one. You will need to do a lot of research, for skate are not as plentiful as they once were. The west coast of Ireland is still a likely area, with the Minch and other parts of Scotland's North West coast having the right ground. Now check the 36 kg (80 lb) rod, reel and line. Then buy the best swivels, hooks, crimps and some multi-strand wire. A butt pad will be handy too, for the skate is a formidable opponent. Skate are not speedy predators, they feed by cautiously moving over open ground, finding a bottom-living fish and flopping over it. The mouth of the skate is under the body and a long way back from the tip of the snout. It is probable that the fish's binocular vision enables it to gauge how far over the preyfish it has to be before covering it. It is this feeding action that is the clue to bite detection.

Make up a stout wire trace, something about 68–91 kg (150–200 lb) is right. Mount an 8/0 Seamaster or similar hook, locking it into the wire with a crimp. Form a loop at the other end of the trace wire, 30.5–38 cm (12–15 in) is long enough, then lock this firmly with another crimp. The reel line should carry a sliding boom and be tied to a sound swivel with quick-release. I have always used a heavier-than-necessary sinker because it is vital that it does not move in the tide. (Fig. 30)

When a skate arrives it will flop on to your bait. Its nose passes over the reel line, making the rod-top dip. That movement tells you that a skate is on the bait. Now you wait, ignoring any trembles up the line, an indication that the fish is adjusting its body to engulf the bait. Having taken it, the skate will move away, giving a definite pull on the line. Feeling that movement, the angler has something to strike at. (There is a nuisance skate that starts to digest its meal while lying on your line and no amount of tugging will move it. When this happened, Leslie Moncrieff used to twang the reel line hard, like a guitar-string, hoping that the vibration would make the skate swim off.) But one has to get the fish moving and it is important that one gets some water between the skate and the seabed. Once it is about a fathom up, the fish cannot hump its back to create a vacuum on the bottom, this is something that is very difficult to release.

Skate are not fast but they are powerful swimmers. The motion is slow, each wing-beat registering as an undulating action on the rod tip. The fish must be made to swim

against the pressure of rod and tide to tire it. In a textbook fight, the skate is supposed to 'kite' upwards in the tide as the water flows under the fish's flat belly. It is hard on angler, rod and line and can be a protracted, dour battle if there is any strength at all to the current. Once on the surface, even a large specimen can be 'skated' across the surface towards the boat. A strong gaff is needed to pierce the outer edge of the wing and then the fish can be lifted into the boat – if there are strong anglers to help!

PORBEAGLE SHARK

This portly shark offers the nearest thing to big-game fishing that sea anglers of the British Isles can find. A cold-

A The key to good fishing; a charter boat skipper who does his homework and understands the whims of the sea angling fraternity! *A* Brian Byrne, fishing out of Cork, with the MFV 'Lagosta' believes in disciplined conservation fishing. *B* A superb charter boat, 'Carbery Marlin', out of Baltimore, skippered by Paddy Cotter. With such deck space, it is like fishing from a pier, so stable and comfortable is this multi-hulled vessel. Safety comes first when the coast is inhospitable.

B

FIG 30 SKATE RIG

Reel line

Bead

Snap-link swivel

Sliding boom

Crimp

Heavy grip lead

68–91 kg (190–200 lb) b.s. wire trace

8/0 Seamaster hook

Crimp

water species, the porbeagle stays around our rocky coasts for most of the year. There are places where these shark seem to gather in deep trenches, although this is often in areas devoid of broken ground. Porbeagle will take up residence on habitats that hold a consistent food supply. Pinnacles and huge areas of rock are instances of porgie terrain, sometimes a number of them will stay on a reef for weeks. One hotspot for this species is found under the cliffs of Moher, off the Clare coast, Ireland.

I had great fishing there, using both float and trolling methods. The float-fishing style was exactly that used for blue shark with the simple precaution of an increase in wire trace breaking strain, that on the hook section going up to 226.7 kg (500 lb), the strength of trace dictated by

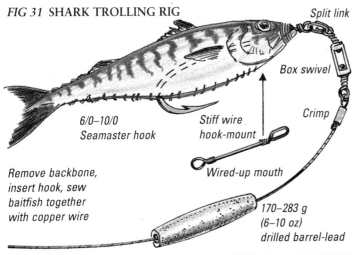

FIG 31 SHARK TROLLING RIG

Split link

Box swivel

Crimp

6/0–10/0 Seamaster hook

Stiff wire hook-mount

Wired-up mouth

Remove backbone, insert hook, sew baitfish together with copper wire

170–283 g (6–10 oz) drilled barrel-lead

the need to combat teeth and a rough, tough skin. The amount of trace is also important, enough is needed to exceed the length of a potential porbeagle shark with a few metres (yards) over. This length guards against the shark wrapping itself up in the wire and smashing the reel line with its tail. I prefer to float-fish on a day when there is little wind, so that a slow drift can be made across a reef, putting the bait over the peaks of the pinnacles. Surface rubby-dubby is not very much use and a better attractor is chum, which is a lot of mackerel cut into small chunks. These are fed continuously over the side of the boat where they drop through the water on to the reef. There is not enough food value in chum to feed sharks, but the arrival of oily pieces will be detected, possibly leading porbeagles to investigate the source.

An alternative idea is to troll a bait, it is a very successful and exciting way to fish, where you really do see the chase and strike as a shark drives on to the bait. The rig can be a duplicate of the float gear with a 170–283 g (6–10 oz) drilled weight slipped on to the reel line. Slit a mackerel open, take the backbone out and then insert the hook through the mouth. Sew the bait up with soft copper wire, leaving only the hook bend showing. Then wrap copper wire round the mouth of the baitfish and lash it firmly to the trace wire, which prevents water entering the bait and tearing it off the rig. At a boat speed of about 2–3 knots, the bait should be drawn along just under the surface. A slightly different rod–reel set-up is needed for trolling, so leave the reel in gear but with a low drag-

The eye of a porbeagle, size infers fantastic vision in the depths.

setting and the ratchet on. Should a fish strike at the bait it will partially pull the hook home as it turns away, and the angler's strike is in no danger of breaking the line before the boat slows to a halt. Increased fighting drag should be applied after the shark's initial run. Porbeagles struck on the troll are always hooked cleanly in the jaw. (Fig. 31)

There can be no justification for killing any of these species. The sea is not all bountiful and we need to preserve all we have. There are far too many global pressures on marine life, such as pollution and over-fishing. Let us be responsible as sea anglers, handling fish with consideration and ourselves with pride in our sport.

ALAN YATES

SEA ANGLING FROM THE SHORE

The realities of sea angling from the shore arrive with the first on-shore Force 8 gale the angler tries to fish in, and 142 g (5 oz) of lead are tossed aside by the wind to land 36.5 m (40 yards) away. The line sinks in a tide-towed bow, draped in weed and resembling a washing-line. The lead struggles to grip under the pressure of the line and is towed ever nearer to the breaker line where it becomes buried in sand and shingle. The angler has no choice but to retrieve and cast again but now the line is so loaded with weed that it breaks at the leader knot.

Choose to fish from the shore and you encounter the most hostile of angling environments. The options to be a fine-weather angler are there: a deck-chair on the pier in July catching small pouting could be a retirement dream. Choose your fishing spot with consideration for comfort only and you are almost certainly to fail, although you may enjoy doing it. These are the options, for sea angling from the shore offers regular discomfort, many problems and if success is your demand this comes out of effort. Luck, thankfully, has its influence but on many occasions the angler makes his own.

If I had to label a department of angling as being the most important it would be within casting. The skill to cast a baited hook over a long distance solves the shore angler's foremost problem. No matter how good your bait, if you cannot put it near fish you are doomed to failure. Casting is a skill that can be learnt with comparative ease, a few hours with an instructor will iron-out problems and ensure the angler has the basics right.

Alan Yates, a lone angler on an Atlantic surf beach in the West of Ireland. Gone are the schools of bass of yesteryear that flashed along the breakers, though the occasional fish may happen along. On open strands, from early spring to late in the year flounder and rays will cooperate.

Trying to teach yourself while you are fishing is a mistake because the angling takes priority. It is better to spend time practising casting in a field where you can concentrate on casting and nothing else.

A great deal of rubbish is written and talked about casting and with the British record approaching 274.3 m (300 yards) such long distances are becoming impracticable in angling terms. The most powerful casts make it difficult to retain bait on the hooks, while the increase of tidal pressure on a far greater length of line in the water makes holding the bottom in tide more difficult.

The facts are that any angler who can cast a baited hook over 91.4 m (100 yards) is capable of catching fish anywhere. Those anglers who lack distance-casting skills are not totally lost, there are piers where a short cast is often all that is needed to get results, while there is always the sea angler's trump card: to fish at night when they come closer to the shoreline under cover of darkness. Whatever your casting skills, the ability to cast a long distance is no guarantee of success, which comes if you overcome ego and cast to where the fish are, even if it is only 18.2 m (20 yards) from your feet. (Fig. 1)

Tournament-casting distances are achieved in perfect conditions of wind, with the competitor casting from a flat surface. It is easy to sky a plain lead dragging nothing but the line up into the air where the wind will assist it. On the beach, the angler is often casting across or even against the wind, or from a cramped position. Sky the lead here and the wind will take the line in a large bow along the beach and drag the lead with it. Cast into the wind, a lead towing a large baited hook will slow rapidly, causing an overfull multiplier to over-run. A distance of 137 m (150 yards) with several baited hooks is still beyond all but a handful of Britain's shore anglers.

RODS AND REELS

We are all individuals and the tackle market reflects this with a host of rods and reels. As a basic guide, quality is governed by price and the buyer will not go far wrong if a decent price is paid for the essential rod and reel. This does not mean that there are no cheap bargains available, although I would advise against buying a 'cheapo' unless one has first-hand knowledge of its ability and quality. Rods for shore angling come in a range of lengths and materials with carbon, boron and Kevlar currently in favour with the manufacturers.

There are three categories of rods: the ready-made rods, including most of the cheaper imported rods and blanks from Japan, Taiwan and so on, some sold under a UK label. These offer a degree of risk, many blanks having thin walls which might crack under pressure and it pays to stick to the most reputable makes. The second category, the blanks which are offered by various manufacturers who only make rod blanks, can be made up by the angler and are specially favoured by the matchman or specialist angler because they can be customized to suit the individual. The third category are rods constructed by tackle dealers from blanks under the Customized tag. They vary greatly in the quality of the finish and are generally expensive in terms of value for money when compared with the cost of making up your own blank.

Most shore-fishing rods are about 3.6 m (12 ft) long, with models up to 4.6 m (15 ft) preferred by pendulum casters using the reel-at-the-butt styles. The majority of rods are made for pendulum casting, which includes swinging the lead in almost a 260° circle, and the simple, off-the-ground or 'overhead-thump' styles do not put enough compression into the blank to get the best from it. The reel at the butt and the longer rod allow for slower, smooth casting and an increase in distance because of the extra rod length, even for off-the-ground casting styles.

Since the introduction of lightweight materials such as carbon, Kevlar, and so on, longer rod lengths have become practical. The only other consideration the angler might have over a rod's length is in the break-down section. Mostly favoured are the 2.6 m (8 ft 6 in) tip, 1.2, 1.5, or 1.8 m (4, 5 or 6 ft) butt, although equal-length sections are available. The longer tip length offers a more constant action throughout the working section of the rod, while the equal-length two-piece rod offers easy transportation.

Some things to look for when buying a rod include making sure that the spigot joints have a slight gap between male and female when they are pushed together, allowing for wear of the carbon material. Spigots which fit

THE DEVELOPMENT OF THE FLATFISH

All flatfish species are either left- or right-handed, i.e. the eyes are both to the right of the mouth (left-handed) or to the left of the mouth (right-handed). Exceptions do occur, when a species shows the opposite condition to the normal, as in a right-handed turbot (very rare) or a left-handed flounder (very common).

1 The embryo within the egg.

2 The newly hatched flatfish (a symmetrical larva with yolk sac).

median fin fold

3 The larva with characteristic concavity on the underside of its body, caused by absorption of the yolk sac.

median fin fold

developing fin rays

4 The larva with frilled body cavity showing a deepening of the embryonic (median) fin fold. The caudal fin is beginning to develop.

median fin fold

snugly have no room for wear and the joint will become loose with use. Ring quality is important, as sand carried on the line can quickly groove cheap chrome or wire rings. The best are Fuji and Seymo lightweight rings which have hardened inserts. Whichever rod you select it is worthwhile fitting a hardened chrome tip-ring of a good diameter. It will prevent grooving and the leader knot jamming with weed. Ready-made rods come in two versions, being rigged for fixed-spool or multiplier reels. With the multi-plier, the rings are used on top of the blank; for the fixed-spool they are underneath and therefore, for the latter, fewer rings are required. Larger-diameter rings are usually preferred for fixed-spool reels.

The most popular methods of fixing a reel to the rod-butt include the screw winch fitting, the clip and the coaster type of reel clamp, which are pipe-grip clamps as used on water-hoses. These have grown in popularity from the tournament-casting field, but a word of warning:

FIG 1 CASTING SEQUENCE

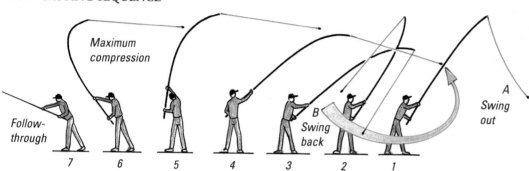

Follow-through 7 6 5 4 3 2 B Swing back 1 A Swing out

Fig 1 Distance in beachcasting is achieved by practice and more practice. The perfect control of the spool of the multiplier reel is the secret of success. Brute strength has no part to play in casting sinker, terminal tackle, baited hook to distances of some 137–183 m (150–200 yards). But the fish are not always that far out!

PIGMENTATION IN FLATFISH

Flatfish larvae show varying degrees of pigmentation during their development. The pigment cells are developed and distributed over the body surface, patches of coloration appearing in later stages which reflect the deeper and larger colour patches exhibited in the adult fish.

With the adoption of a bottom-dwelling mode of life, and as the eye migrates from one side to join the other, one side of the fish will become darkly coloured. The blind side of the flatfish remains a drab white or grey, but some species have a distinct grey coloration to the blind side.

There are exceptions, where dark colouring shows on the blind side, either as variously sized patches or over the whole body area, with the head remaining white. This occurs mostly in those species exhibiting reversal of body shape. The commonest examples are to be found among flounders and has been termed ambi-coloration.

REASONS FOR AMBI-COLORATION

Partial coloration of the blind side may be due to the light reaching it, as in individuals living on a hard bottom where they cannot bury themselves. Piebald pigmentation of the blind side, seen as a series of colours, is assumed to reflect striping in ancestral species.

Totally ambi-coloured fish showing a white patch on the head often have a 'hooked head', a notch along the top of the head and under the dorsal fin.

REVERSAL

Most species metamorphose over to the 'correct' side, but some individuals in British Isles water are reversed, the most common species being the flounder. Rarely, the plaice and halibut will also reverse, a phenomenon common in some species of the world where 50 per cent are normal and reversed.

Many features describing the flatfishes also apply to the soles but reversal is almost unknown. Soles are not directly related to the other flatfish species.

ALBINISM

The condition of albinism, a deficiency of pigmentation, is not unknown in fishes, but it exposes the individual to predation so the mutation line usually becomes extinct. Individuals with a white 'coloured' side are also known but such fish will nearly always show a small patch of colour on the head, in front of the eyes.

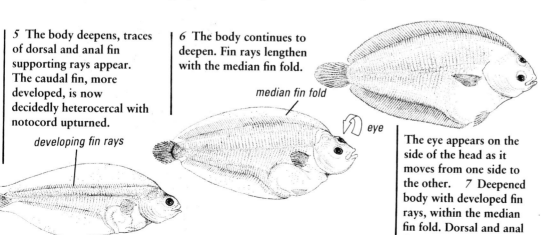

5 The body deepens, traces of dorsal and anal fin supporting rays appear. The caudal fin, more developed, is now decidedly heterocercal with notocord upturned.

developing fin rays

6 The body continues to deepen. Fin rays lengthen with the median fin fold.

median fin fold

eye

The eye appears on the side of the head as it moves from one side to the other. *7* Deepened body with developed fin rays, within the median fin fold. Dorsal and anal fins separate from the tail; the eye continues to migrate.

The eggs and larvae of flatfishes are pelagic, they float in the upper layers of the sea, and are transported by currents. At stage 5 of their development (left) the fish begin to sink down towards the seabed to adopt their eventual mode of life. Fully developed, they are benthic flatfish.

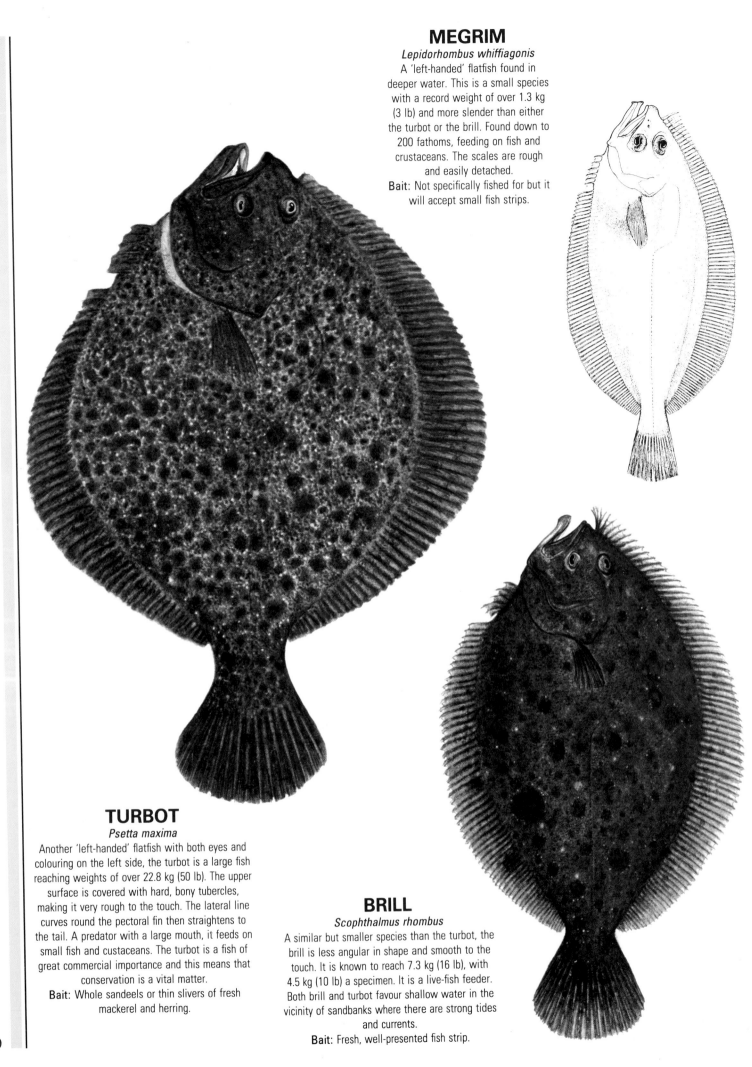

MEGRIM
Lepidorhombus whiffiagonis
A 'left-handed' flatfish found in deeper water. This is a small species with a record weight of over 1.3 kg (3 lb) and more slender than either the turbot or the brill. Found down to 200 fathoms, feeding on fish and crustaceans. The scales are rough and easily detached.
Bait: Not specifically fished for but it will accept small fish strips.

TURBOT
Psetta maxima
Another 'left-handed' flatfish with both eyes and colouring on the left side, the turbot is a large fish reaching weights of over 22.8 kg (50 lb). The upper surface is covered with hard, bony tubercles, making it very rough to the touch. The lateral line curves round the pectoral fin then straightens to the tail. A predator with a large mouth, it feeds on small fish and custaceans. The turbot is a fish of great commercial importance and this means that conservation is a vital matter.
Bait: Whole sandeels or thin slivers of fresh mackerel and herring.

BRILL
Scophthalmus rhombus
A similar but smaller species than the turbot, the brill is less angular in shape and smooth to the touch. It is known to reach 7.3 kg (16 lb), with 4.5 kg (10 lb) a specimen. It is a live-fish feeder. Both brill and turbot favour shallow water in the vicinity of sandbanks where there are strong tides and currents.
Bait: Fresh, well-presented fish strip.

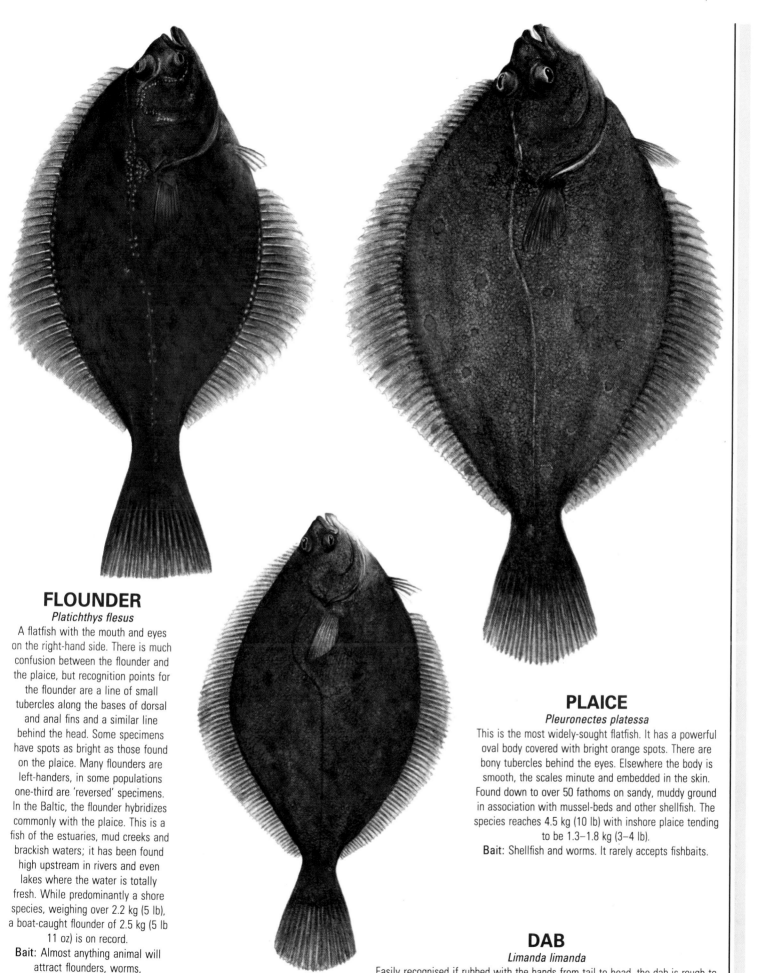

FLOUNDER
Platichthys flesus

A flatfish with the mouth and eyes on the right-hand side. There is much confusion between the flounder and the plaice, but recognition points for the flounder are a line of small tubercles along the bases of dorsal and anal fins and a similar line behind the head. Some specimens have spots as bright as those found on the plaice. Many flounders are left-handers, in some populations one-third are 'reversed' specimens. In the Baltic, the flounder hybridizes commonly with the plaice. This is a fish of the estuaries, mud creeks and brackish waters; it has been found high upstream in rivers and even lakes where the water is totally fresh. While predominantly a shore species, weighing over 2.2 kg (5 lb), a boat-caught flounder of 2.5 kg (5 lb 11 oz) is on record.

Bait: Almost anything animal will attract flounders, worms, crustaceans, molluscs, fish strip.

PLAICE
Pleuronectes platessa

This is the most widely-sought flatfish. It has a powerful oval body covered with bright orange spots. There are bony tubercles behind the eyes. Elsewhere the body is smooth, the scales minute and embedded in the skin. Found down to over 50 fathoms on sandy, muddy ground in association with mussel-beds and other shellfish. The species reaches 4.5 kg (10 lb) with inshore plaice tending to be 1.3–1.8 kg (3–4 lb).

Bait: Shellfish and worms. It rarely accepts fishbaits.

DAB
Limanda limanda

Easily recognised if rubbed with the hands from tail to head, the dab is rough to the touch because the scales are ctenoid (spiny) on the upper surface. It is a small flatfish, usually no more than 'sandwich'-sized, but it can reach a weight of nearly 1.3 kg (3 lb). Found from inshore down to 50 fathoms.

Bait: Small worms and shellfish.

HALIBUT
Hippoglossus hippoglossus
The largest and thickest of all flatfishes, the lateral line curves sharply over the pectoral fin of this right-handed fish. Most halibut caught in British waters come from rocky ground and areas which have a strong tidal race, the Pentland Firth, Orkneys and the West of Ireland all yielding specimens. Found at depths down to over 1000 fathoms, it is not common, but more anglers are travelling to halibut grounds and finding them, the top rod-and-line weight so far being a 106 kg (234 lb) halibut from Scottish waters. Commercial fishing in the North Atlantic, mostly on long-lines, has brought fish up to 456 kg (1000 lb) to the market.

Bait: Fish, either whole or as large lashes.

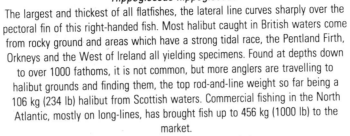

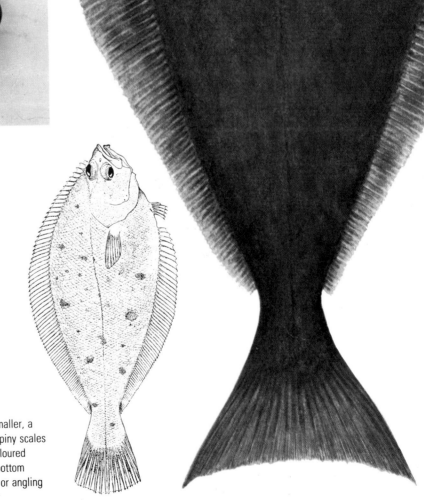

THE GREENLAND HALIBUT
Reinhardtius hippoglossoides
Is similar to the halibut but exhibits considerable colour variation. The dorsal side is dark greenish-black, ventrally a silvery-green sheen. Found in far north of the British Isles, essentially a Northern Atlantic species. Has a more pronounced lower jaw with sharp teeth.

Bait: As for halibut.

LONG ROUGH DAB
Hippoglossoides platessoides
This flatfish is rather similar to the halibut but much smaller, a specimen being no more than 142 g (5 oz). It has rough, spiny scales and the lateral line is almost straight. A brownish-coloured deepwater fish of the Northern waters, it feeds on bottom invertebrates and small fish and has no real commercial or angling importance.

WITCH

Glyptocephalus cynoglossus

A small-bodied fish, thin and elongated the witch has large eyes and usually stays down to about 300 fathoms, feeding on invertebrates and small fish so is not really an anglers' species. It is brownish grey with a straight lateral line. Strangely, a shore-caught witch of nearly 0.5 kg (1 lb 2 oz) is recorded.

LEMON SOLE

Microstomus kitt

A smallish tasty flatfish with a slimy, brown, marbled surface and small head. The name is a market term. It is found down to 100 fathoms where it feeds on small invertebrates. A specimen of .96 kg (2 lb 2 oz) is on record.

DOVER SOLE

Solea vulgaris

The dorsal fin begins on the blunt and sharply rounded snout of this fish. The eyed side of this true sole is brown, with large blotched markings on the body and along the junction of the fins. This nocturnal-feeding flattie is a highly prized table-fish and much sought by commercial netsmen.

Bait: Small marine worms, shellfish.

coasters are not suitable for some of the larger models of reels and can work loose under the strain imposed by large fish. Be sure that your reel is attached securely, otherwise you will suffer the catastrophe of a life-time, with the line and reel in one hand and the rod in the other.

The only other consideration when buying a shore rod is its casting rating: rods are usually marked 113 to 170 g (4 to 6 oz) or 170 to 226 g (6 to 8 oz) and this refers to the range of the weight of sinker the blank is capable of casting. If you are likely to fish in strong tides your choice might be the heavier weights, while for surf fishing, where the rod may be held, the lesser or an even lighter blank may be required. There is no such thing as a general-purpose rod and many proficient shore anglers may use several rods for their sea fishing, including a light spinning rod or a coarse fishing model for mackerel and mullet.

There are two main types of reel for shore angling, the fixed-spool and the multiplier. Many excellent models of both kinds are available and the quality of reels has greatly improved in recent years, especially among the foreign manufacturers.

For the complete novice the fixed-spool is the easier of the two reels to master and with it, straight from the wrapping, he can reach a distance of anything between 45.7 and 91.4 m (50 and 100 yards) without tangles. Over the past few years, changes in the design of the fixed-spool have given the sea angler models specifically made for shore fishing, not just large versions of the freshwater kinds. Gears are more robust and many reels now feature a more streamlined shape, coned spool and better salt-water resistance, as well as bale-arms that don't snap shut during the inertia of the cast and drags that can be tightened down and do not slip during casting. Fixed-spool reels are most suitable for shore fishing, although they are not always chosen by the proficient angler.

If you choose a fixed-spool reel, this is what to look for, or to avoid: An efficient drag setting that can be tightened down hard so that the spool will not slip during the cast; stern-drag reels are ideal; watch for reels with large bale arms and handles that might cause the bale to snap shut during the cast. (Some models have the bale arm wire cut off close to the line roller by their owners.) Go for a reel where the line roller actually revolves, it cuts down on wear; look for a shaped or coned spool that holds the amount of line you require for your fishing; do not choose a reel which holds lots of line under the impression that more line means it will cast farther. As a general rule, a reel which holds between 228.6 and 320 m (250 and 350 yards) of 6.8 kg (15 lb) b.s. line is suitable for shore fishing. Among the fixed-spool's drawbacks are that it is generally considered cumbersome and awkward to use and is not capable of handling heavy weights or big fish.

On the other hand, the multiplier is a treat to use and while the novice can get into the most dreadful tangle and birds'-nests if the spool is allowed to overrun, once mastered it is very much the reel for the job. This is no doubt the reason why the multiplier is the most popular reel on the beach where the more proficient anglers gather. Multiplier refinements such as magnetic brakes, high-speed

143

Alan Yates' reel and the controlling thumb position. His reel is used at the base of the casting rod, controlled by the thumb of the left hand.

retrieves, corrosion-resistance and lightweight carbon re-inforced plastic side plates, ball races and large handles are now a standard feature of modern reels and at last some of the manufacturers are making reels without that top bar reinforcing which restricts the thumb from grip-ping the spool during the cast.

Originally, the multipliers used in the UK followed a spinning multiplier design and were not intended for out-and-out distance casting with 113 and 170 g (4 and 6 oz) leads. Reels are now being produced for the UK market and aimed at its method of fishing: no top bar to restrict grip, one-piece frames which do not distort the way the old ones did, and easy-to-get-at spools for quick replace-ment and lubrication. Some reels still include level-lines which lay the line evenly on the spool during the retrieve; in my opinion they are not needed and novices would be advised to learn to lay the line evenly on the spool by guiding it with their thumb without drastically cutting casting distance, as the level-line does. If the level-line is really needed, buy a model with one which can be disen-gaged during the cast.

Both types of reel will cast very long distances and both have their followers. Whichever reel you choose, it is important that you load it with the correct size and amount of line for the fishing it is intended to do. Reel size and line diameter are linked, especially from the casting point of view, with line diameter crucial to spool size for maximum distance.

There are very many different multipliers available, but two basic sizes are most often used for shore fishing. For long-distance casting on a clear, sandy beach, a small multiplier (Abu-Garcia 6000 size) which holds up to 300 m (328 yards) of 6.8 kg (15 lb) (0.35 mm dia) b.s. line is usually the choice. For rough ground where there are rocks or snags, a bigger size (Abu-Garcia 7000) is the choice, having a line capacity of 200 m (219 yards) of

11.4 kg (25 lb) (0.55 mm dia) b.s. Equipped with both of these types of reel the angler can cope with any shore situation. In the case of the fixed-spool, two spools loaded with different breaking strains serve a similar purpose.

LINES

Line breaking strain and diameter affect the casting ability of line in relation to the reel type and size with which it is used. In general, 6.8 kg (15 lb) (0.35 mm dia) b.s. lines are preferred for used in conjunction with the small distance-casting reels, while 13.6 kg (30 lb) (0.60 mm) is the normal choice for short-range fishing over snags or in weed with the larger models. Lighter or heavier lines are used but the breaking strains I have given will suit a majority of reel types and sizes. Because neither of the breaking strains above will withstand the force needed to cast up to 170 g (6 oz) of lead, a short length of stronger line is used as a casting-shock leader. In most cases, 27.2 kg (60 lb) b.s. is adequate, with twice the length of the rod being sufficient. Shock-leader size can be gauged by multiplying the weight of the lead in ounces by ten. A 142 g (5 oz) lead, then, requires a minimum of 22.8 kg (50 lb) (0.70 mm) b.s. leader. The most efficient way to join the main line to the leader is by the knot in Fig. 2.

Most reels have a recommended line capacity and this decreases as the line diameter rises, so it is a case of the more line the reel holds the farther it can be cast; in fact the reverse is often the case. All reels, fixed-spools or multi-pliers, have an optimum amount and size of line that gives maximum casting distance. Overload or underfill the reel with line that is too heavy or too light and you risk casting problems, the worst of which is the multiplier's much-dreaded birds' nest. Such overruns are the product of the reel spool throwing out too much line in relation to the speed of the lead as it flies through the air. By loading a spool correctly, the amount of line the spool releases is in proportion to the speed of the lead. Good advice for the novice casting with a multiplier is to underfill the spool. On the other hand, the fixed-spool reel is very inefficient if underfilled, because the line hits the lip of the spool and lead-speed is rapidly lost. Wide-coned spools are far superior for distance casting with fixed-spools.

Modern lines come in many makes and colours with bright oranges and yellow taking over from sombre blues and greys. Colour may be unimportant, especially when fished in the average pea-soup sea, although an advantage of bright-coloured lines is that they are easily seen by the human eye, a factor which can be useful. You can tell where your line is when cast alongside rocks or pier piles, and lost line is easily seen and can be collected before it traps unwary birds or other animals.

There are two basic types of monofilament available. The cheaper lines are softer and usually not so strong per diameter as the more expensive lines. On the other hand, these may be stronger, but because of their manufacturing process, the smaller diameter per breaking strain often results in brittle line that fluffs up on the reel spool. I will leave anglers to choose their own brand of line as most of

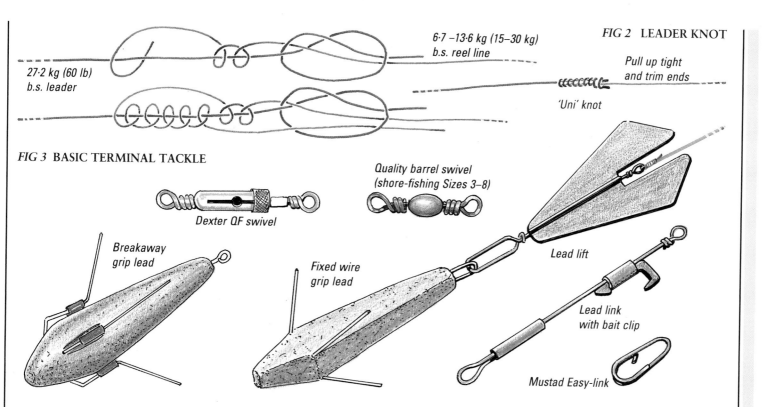

FIG 2   LEADER KNOT

6·7 –13·6 kg (15–30 kg)
b.s. reel line

27·2 kg (60 lb)
b.s. leader

Pull up tight
and trim ends

'Uni' knot

FIG 3 BASIC TERMINAL TACKLE

Dexter QF swivel

Quality barrel swivel
(shore-fishing Sizes 3–8)

Breakaway
grip lead

Fixed wire
grip lead

Lead lift

Lead link
with bait clip

Mustad Easy-link

TERMINAL TACKLE

Fish are creatures of instinct, they do not 'think' and although their sight is often acute they may not interpret what they see the way human beings do. Caught and often killed by the angler, sea fish have few chances to develop the coarse fishes' timidity that comes from being caught and returned to the water. Therefore tackle for sea fishing does not need to be refined, it is a mistake to go too light as this can affect bait presentation as well as creating tangles in rigs. The single general rule governing sea fishing terminal tackle is that it be kept as simple as possible. This includes hooks and the construction of terminal rigs themselves – leave the complicated set-ups to armchair anglers and base your terminal tackle on logic, not fancy. (Figs 2, 3)

LEADS

Leads fulfil two main functions, they must be heavy enough to tow baited hooks out to sea when cast and, secondly, they must stay put on the seabed under the pressure of tide and wind. A majority of shore anglers find the breakaway grip lead ideal for most of their shore fishing, especially the new model introduced in 1989. When strong tides are met, fixed wire grip-leads are required, in slack tides a plain lead will often suffice. I am a fan of the breakaway lead even in tideless conditions, because a lead which grips the seabed offers resistance against a biting fish, which will then hook itself rather than just towing the lead about. Breakaways and fixed-wire grip leads are used in tidal conditions to keep the bait and tackle in position. In many cases a fish taking the bait will not show a positive bite on the rod tip, and at the same time it is difficult to set the hook by striking when fishing at very long range. A grip-lead offers a bolt-rig set-up and while some sea anglers may feel that to strike gives them a bigger part to play in catching fish, with the bolt-rig the fish hook themselves.

It is not the lead that is pushed along by the tide, but the line and its corresponding diameter and the distance the tackle is cast both relate to the type of grip-lead required. Fine lines offer less resistance to tide, so in very strong tide a lighter line allows the angler to use a lighter grip-lead. In strong tides, heavier leads require heavier and more efficient fixed wire grip-leads. The angler must estimate the lead and line required on a given venue for best results. Fixed grip-leads are more difficult to retrieve because they continue to grip the seabed on the way in, while breakaways snap open and can be recovered easily. But when only a fixed lead will hold bottom its retrieve can be made easier by the addition of a lead-lift, a plastic vane which has the effect of planing the lead up off the seabed. It is also particularly effective when being worked over rough ground too.

The weights used for shore fishing range from 57 to 226 g (2 to 8 oz), although 142 g (5 oz) offers the best casting results for most anglers, and variations of weight are often used to suit individual requirements or weather conditions. For instance, a 113 g (4 oz) lead will match a lighter rod and also be more suitable for a younger angler. On the other hand, 170 or 226 g (6 or 8 oz) will drag baits through the wind when cast into the teeth of a gale and stay put when it hits bottom. The most popular patterns relate to their aerodynamic shape, with bombs the most popular in distance casting, while shapes such as cones, diamonds and torpedoes are used to combat tide. (Fig. 3)

145

HOOKS

The thousands of hook patterns available include many models designed for a given situation, species or bait. Hooks are produced in a variety of metals with various finishes and shapes. All this can confuse the beginner, who usually ends up buying a pattern because he likes the look of it. An additional problem is that dealers often carry the hook patterns which are the best sellers, but they are not always ideal in every locality.

There are two golden rules to observe when selecting hooks for shore fishing. First, base your choice on the bait you intend to use and the fish you seek. Those shiny, stainless steel hooks with the bait-holding barbs on the shank are not very good, and catch more anglers than they do fish. Worms and flatfish need long-shank hooks and there are many similar obvious pairings. Secondly, strength is most important although a hook which will bend rather than snap can be used to advantage. Flatfish often swallow the hook, so a long-shank hook which will bend can be removed easily and is useful for returning small flatties. Hooks which bend are also useful when fishing over rocks, kelp or rough ground as they can be pulled out of snags and save on time and fishing tackle. Obviously, the bigger species demand larger, stronger hooks, but it is possible to land large fish from the shore on relatively small hooks, with a 4/0 as a maximum for all but shore tope or conger.

Generally, a 2/0 will suffice for cod, bass and most of the other bigger fish. Modern, chemically sharpened and carbon steel hooks offer a strength and sharpness far superior to those of the past and this gives the shore angler the added advantage of being able to handle big fish on the smallest hooks. Sizes, too, can confuse because they vary between manufacturers, although most stay with the basic size range. Those for sea fishing range from 6 up to 6/0. The average shore-caught fish weighs about 0.45 kg (1 lb), so a Size 1 hook will be enough for most situations. By using a strong model such as the Mustad Viking, Kamasan Aberdeen and so on, the angler has a safeguard should a heavier fish take his bait.

Finally, before leaving the subject of hooks, we must discuss barbs. It has become popular in game and coarse fishing circles to use barbless hooks and in many cases they work very well. But the use of such hooks in many sea angling situations is impracticable because of the distances and circumstances in which fish are caught. In fact it is worth considering the use of larger barbs for conger, pollack, bass and mullet.

SWIVELS AND LINKS

In view of the dangers of breakage, the importance of links and swivels in terminal tackle cannot be over-stressed. It is essential to use nothing but quality links and swivels of sufficient breaking strain, for instance never use a 27.2 kg (60 lb) b.s. leader and then include 13.6 kg (30 lb) b.s. links in the trace, and a link of some kind must be used between the lead and the rig. Knots tied directly to the wire loop on leads soon get frayed on the retrieve by stones or barnacles. There are many low-quality, cheap links and swivels on the market, and many of the Taiwan imports are sub-standard, with Berkley and Mustad being the most reliable brands. For quick and easy change of terminal rigs the Dexter QF swivel is ideal, while the Mustad easy-links allow easy fitting and removal of leads.

BOOMS

Booms have always been popular among shore anglers, and the wire French and Yarmouth booms still have a place in the tackle box. The new breed of booms, however, are made in plastic, with the match-stick type a clear favourite with pier and estuary anglers after flatfish and codling. Other booms, which the angler can make at home, are produced from wire, pen refills or cotton buds. Do not discount the value of booms, they are sometimes a very effective way of fishing.

TERMINAL RIGS

The key to a successful terminal rig is its simplicity, a point I have stressed before. If a rig returns tangled after every cast it still may catch fish, but it will not be as effective as a rig which does not tangle. On land, a rig hanging free from the rod tip will not react the same way under water. One basic error that most anglers make is to construct hook snoods from too light line, and I never drop below 9 kg (20 lb) for hook snoods because small fish spinning in the tide can cause line damage, and 11.4 kg (25 lb) snoods stand off from the body of the trace and rarely tangle. It is also a mistake to make snoods too long, all that is necessary is to keep them short enough not to tangle with each other. When making hook snoods and traces, a good tip is to straighten the line with a small length of rubber inner-tube. It also has the effect of taking the shine off the line but this is less important.

My basic terminal rig is constructed by trapping small swivels on the main body of the trace with small beads and telephone wire or shrink-tube (Fig. 4). This way, snoods can be moved up or down the rig, providing alternatives to a basic monofilament paternoster. By lengthening the bottom snood and moving it close to the lead, I am able to fish two-up, one-down. Alternatively, rather than change rigs, I can remove hook snoods on a three-hook rig and fish with just one or two hooks if conditions demand it. Dimensions are important to avoid the rig tangling and I have included those most suitable on the diagram.

There are other rigs used by shore anglers, with the flowing trace a clear favourite among novices, mainly because of its easy construction, but this rig is not as efficient as a nylon paternoster. Other rigs worth consideration include the Wishbone (Fig. 5) which is most suitable for distance casting. It allows the angler to cast two small baits which are clipped close behind the lead, making them more streamlined by keeping the baited hook pinned to the trace body during the cast. The theory is that these clips release the hook on contact with the sea.

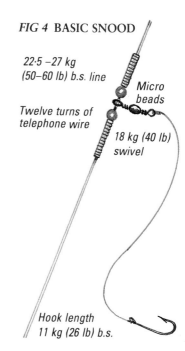

Many shorefishing anglers have altered their casting action. The pendulum cast gives longer distances and allows a smoother line delivery, resulting in fewer backlashes. Longer rods, coupled with the pendulum casting style and a low reel position, increase the arc of rod travel, considerably slowing up the speed of motion throughout the cast, which eradicates the jerky movements associated with short, stunted casting actions.

Fig 4 Adjustable snoods are invaluable and save a lot of time-wasting. *Fig 5* This nearly tangle-free rig aids distance casting. *Fig 6* The adjustable tandem hook rig holds baits of different length.

FIG 4 BASIC SNOOD

22·5 –27 kg (50–60 lb) b.s. line

Micro beads

Twelve turns of telephone wire

18 kg (40 lb) swivel

Hook length 11 kg (26 lb) b.s.

FIG 5 WISHBONE RIG

Construct bait-clip from 1 mm (0·04 in) twin domestic lighting cable

Swivel

Basic snood

Bait clip

Swivel

Swivel

25·4 cm (10 in) line

Link

FIG 6 PENNELL RIG

Adjustable plastic sleeve on top hook gives different baits a firm hold

Ragworm or lugworm

Plastic sleeve

They are most useful in keeping delicate baits whole during powerful pendulum casts and undoubtedly add to distance casting. However, they are not the last word in shore angling and in many situations actually restrict the angler's catch.

A major drawback of bait-clips is that they force the bait up the hook snood if a stop-knot is not included, this has the effect of placing the bait away from the hook. The Pennell rig (Fig. 6) is often the choice of the shore angler who is using a large bait for fish having big mouths, such as cod or bass. The rig entails two hooks on a single snood, with one hook at each end of the bait. With a bait of six lugworm, there is a hook at whichever end of the bait the fish takes. This Pennell rig is the most effective terminal rig to beat slack line bites, which are notoriously difficult to strike at.

In the past the storage of terminal rigs was a problem, now custom-made trace wallets are available which come in book form with the rigs stored in clear, sealable plastic bags inside the container.

WINTER COD FISHING

The cod is the most prolific of the British sea fishes and in spite of enormous commercial and angling pressure the species survives, its saturation spawning being the key to the cod stocks which remain. A single cod produces millions of ova and while the survival rate is known to be low, there are years when a good percentage of the fry live. Total survival of all cod ova would fill the seas in some eight years!

Over-fishing of certain other species in recent years may have helped the cod to withstand pressures from commercial fishing. Mackerel and herring predate on cod fry, but stocks of these predators have been severely hit and so more cod spawn reaches bottom-living age and size from the tiny surface-egg stage. Most species seem to thrive in ten-yearly cycles and the cod is no exception, producing spectacular numbers of codling in its 'big' year.

For the shore-based angler cod come within range through the autumn and winter, with a few exceptions including some lochs and deep-water venues in the West and North of Scotland, and Ireland, but most of Britain's cod fishing is done on the North East, East and South East coasts of England, and there mainly from Kent and East Anglian venues.

There is overlapping among the cod populations of the North Sea, English Channel and Atlantic, which makes it easy to understand why the Straits of Dover should be such a cod-anglers' Mecca. Where these seas meet, the funnelling effect of the tides in this area sees a great deal of cod activity during their migrations, but there are also localised stocks there.

From late September the cod move inshore, picking up summer sandeels which are moving away from the off-shore sandbanks. The winter mainstay of the cod are whiting and other small fish, with codling (usually those

147

under 2.7 kg (6 lb)) foraging in storm-lashed seas for crab and shellfish. Worms are the angler's most succesful bait for the species. In late winter, sprat shoals lure the cod away from the shoreline and by February most of the big specimens have vanished to spawn in deepwater.

The average size of cod caught inshore varies from year to year, the large stocks of fish from prolific seasons declining while a few individuals grow very big. This means that the angler will catch reasonable first, second or third-year fish, with fourth-year double-figure cod being difficult to find. The stocks fluctuate from season to season, but most years produce a few 9 kg (20 lb) fish, with those of 13.6 kg (30 lb) being rarer and more likely to be taken by the boat angler.

Most anglers hope for double-figure specimens but as with most fishing in natural habitats the size of the fish obviously cannot be decided by the fisherman. The big-bait-for-big-fish theory does not work in cod fishing because a mere 0.9 kg (2 lb) codling has a mouth capable of taking a large bait, while a large specimen fish might accept the smallest hookbait.

Perhaps the only way exclusively to fish for big cod is to use a live whiting, although this is only practicable in certain conditions. The method includes fishing a double-hook rig with a small hook and a similarly small worm (Diag. E). The theory is that a small whiting will hook itself on the worm and then a large cod will take the whiting. This works, but it requires patience. Many times have I retrieved a livebait after some three hours only to find that I have been fishing with a 1.3 kg (3 lb) cod as livebait after it took the original livebait! (Fig. 7)

Saturation fishing is the way to catch big cod, and this means catching more cod than the other anglers. It is simple arithmetic: the more cod you catch, the more are your chances of taking the biggest. There is a theory that the foulest weather offers the best fishing conditions and likelihood of catching cod.

No matter where the fishing is, cod are attracted by food thrown up by a storm. Sandbanks lashed by a gale release many edible things into the inshore surf, so if you meet these conditions while on the beach you should be in for a good day's fishing. Failing a gale, darkness offers the shore-based angler the best chance of catching cod. But all successful cod-fishing needs planning and there is a lot of truth in the statement that a third of all anglers catch all the cod.

A major fault of the average angler is his haste to get a bait into the water. He takes the first beach near the car, nearest the sea, and spends the night fishless. It is no accident that most easy-access beaches are crowded and popular, their reputation gained solely through the numbers of anglers fishing them. Pick a secluded beach which might involve a mile walk and you may well have all the cod to yourself. Fishing crowded beaches successfully requires the angler to have an edge over the others as well as the fish, either that or fishing is no more than a lottery. Better bait or the skill to cast greater distances are advantages, but find a beach to yourself if you possess neither. Another fault in novices is that they fish clear beaches rather than over rocks, but some lost tackle is a small price to pay for a terrific fishing session.

Tidal movement is very relevant to the successful cod angler, but the only generalisation is that the strongest tides bring the best catches, with spring tides offering the biggest likelihood of success. The most productive tide time varies from venue to venue, which means that there is no substitute for local knowledge. When the local peak tide times are known, the angler can fish these for short periods rather than fishing marathon all-night sessions, although many anglers rather like them.

The successful cod angler, too, will keep aware of how local venues are fishing and be ready to go to one at a moment's notice. Planned two months in advance, trips to the beach might occasionally be successful, but a session linked with a reliable catch report is much more likely to bring good fish. Cod seem to visit an area over several tides, take the available food and move on. Success, therefore, is a matter of following the local shoals or use a knowledge of catch reports to intercept them. Of course, one can just fish a venue regularly and sooner or later you will be fishing there when the cod arrive.

I prefer the instant-fishing approach and have built-up a diary of contacts for information about venues in the winter. Keeping such a diary and recording catches is a good idea, unless you have a photographic memory. You will find regular cycles of cod activity and also that with many venues their most productive fishing periods are repeated for generations of cod. My well-stocked bait

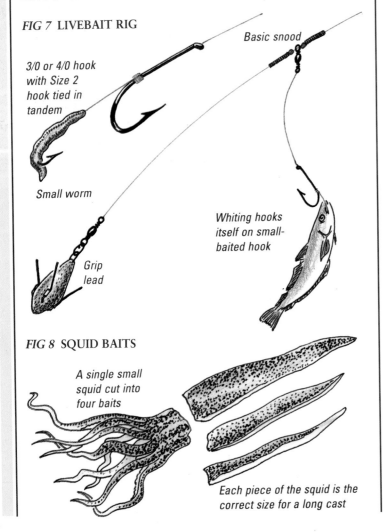

FIG 7 LIVEBAIT RIG

3/0 or 4/0 hook with Size 2 hook tied in tandem

Basic snood

Small worm

Grip lead

Whiting hooks itself on small-baited hook

FIG 8 SQUID BAITS

A single small squid cut into four baits

Each piece of the squid is the correct size for a long cast

fridge and freezer mean that I can get away at a moment's notice. As with all fishing, there is no substitute for the best bait and without doubt the freshest lugworms or peeler crabs are the top bait for cod.

Frozen squid can be used to add bulk to lugworm baits and frozen peeler crab works well for codling, but nothing beats three big, juicy yellowtail lugworms fished on a 3/0 Pennell rig, one of the hooks carrying half a peeler crab. Used as a tipping agent, snake-white lugworms are deadly for codling but do not attract the bigger specimens. When fishing with a large lugworm, the addition of a white ragworm to the hook-point-end of the bait often induces the codling to take the hook-end of the bait into their mouth, which naturally helps to ensure that the fish is hooked. (Fig. 8)

Once on the beach, there are several factors to be considered when selecting the pitch. If it is a crowded beach, fishing uptide of a novice or a group of anglers can mean that the tide will push your line downtide where it can be cast across and even pulled in. Spending all day or all night untangling crossed lines will not catch cod nor will it contribute towards goodwill, so try walking along the beach and away from the crowd. Most beaches have their hot-spots, with most of them close to car-parks and such, but cod usually work the length of most beaches. Weed can create problems, with large rafts of it clinging to lines and making fishing difficult, so when you see piles of weed on the high-tide line avoid the stretch.

Once you have selected your place, set up camp. On a cold, windy and wet beach, an angling umbrella is worth its weight in gold, and a dry, warm angler is an alert angler. The umbrella provides welcome shelter when the elements are really unpleasant.

Most cod anglers prefer to use two rods, one fishing at long range and one closer in, but if sport starts to become hectic it might pay to concentrate on the rod that is catching fish. Rods are placed on rod-rests, the monopod rod-holder being preferred on surf beaches because it enables the rod tip to be kept high, away from surf and weed. The rest does, however, promote a stiff neck if the angler sits too close and has to stare upwards for long periods. In a wind, a tripod rest offers most stability for the rod, with the tip placed low to make watching it easier. There are rod-rests with both the above facilities.

Casting into a blustery wind or a tide-swept sea invariably means that tackle will be moved. Tide and weed on the line will drag it downtide and in the worst conditions both line and rig can be buried under the surf and beach gravel. Angle the cast slightly uptide and when the lead grips place the rod-tip as high as possible, for the less line there is in the water the less there is to trap weed. By anchoring slightly uptide, weed catching the line will be driven inshore up to the rod-tip and once a bow is allowed to develop in the line that weed will drag the tackle downtide. Leader-knots are notorious weed-catchers, but knotless leader joints are possible, using Chinese cuff-grip fly-leaders to join leader and reel line.

Once the baited tackle is anchored the angler must wait, but remember that the main attraction of any bait is

A

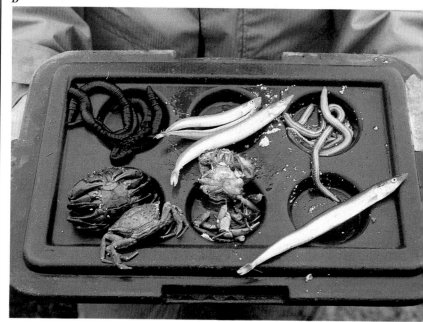

B

A Simplicity on the beach: a rod and reel, tackle box, tripod rod rest and the bait bucket or tray all to hand.

B The baits for a bass, ray and flounder fishing day: lugworm, peeler crabs, snake whites and frozen sandeels.

its scent, which decreases the longer the bait is left in the sea. Some 20 minutes is long enough to fish any bait at any time. Retrieve it after that, remove all the old bait and rebait the hook. This very important in all aspects of shore fishing; just bulking-up a washed-out bait with a fresh worm is not good enough.

During a venue's peak fishing time, the matchman's double-patting technique saves on baiting-up time. Between casts, rebait a spare rig, unclip the washed-out baited rig and slip-on the fresh one. The added bonus of this system is that small unwanted fish can be unhooked at leisure and more carefully rather than in one's haste to recast the tackle.

Cod bites come in all kinds, a full-blooded run with the rod tip pulled over dramatically usually results in a hooked fish, while the same bite in reverse with a bow of slack line indicates that you have missed it. But never be too keen to strike, for cod have very large mouths and can eject a bait as quickly as they can take it. They are intent in eating the offering and in most cases, given time and the angler's patience, they will do so.

Hook size has an influence on the hooking of cod and there is no doubt that a smaller, lighter and sharper hook is more efficient than a large heavy one. A hook such as a 1 or 1/0 will be taken deeper into the cod's mouth more quickly and will penetrate on touch, but a big hook, say a 6/0, is not so effective. However, once hooked on a big hook the fish has less chance at getting free; but small hooks will hook more fish. This is especially relevant since the introduction of the very strong and efficient chemically etched carbon-steel hooks.

I prefer off-set hooks to the extent that I put a small off-set in all the hooks I use, it has the effect of giving them another hooking dimension, and is important when the size of the cod's mouth is considered.

Having hooked the cod, the next problem is to land it. In a flat calm, one just reels the fish in. Cod from 0.9 to 4.5 kg (2 to 10 lb) pull well in short bursts but are not big fighters. Specimens over 4.5 kg (10 lb) use their weight and perform best in tide and swell. Landing a double-figure fish in a gale is not easy and a gaff is essential. The trick is to use the swell – bring the fish in with it, pulling only when the fish is moving towards you on the swell. The undertow has tremendous power and if you try to pull

a fish through it your line or the hook-hold will be broken.

Hold the fish in the backwash and wait for the swell to come towards you, then the fish can be gaffed or gilled out when its belly touches bottom. Never touch the rod tip or line when the fish is on because this stops the cushioning effect of the rod. Remember also that the more line between fish and rod-tip the greater the line-stretch and therefore the greater the degree of safety. Especially when fishing over rough ground, this means that is more advisable to stay at the top of the beach, or even move backwards, rather than go down to the fish.

SPRING FISHING FOR FLOUNDERS AND THORNBACK RAYS

For the shore angler, spring is one of the most exciting times. After several months of the late winter doldrums, when the cold sea contains nothing but immature whiting, dabs and flounders inshore, many anglers put their tackle away until the next winter. But as the warmth of spring seeps in in late April, with the same flourish as it does on land, a fresh set of angling experiences are here to be enjoyed. The key to much of the best early spring fishing is the common shore crab as it begins its rush to moult and breed. In May on some coasts the mass moult of the cock crabs results in huge carnage as the fish move inshore to feast on the extremely vulnerable soft-shelled crabs. For the angler it is a time when bait is plentiful and winter supplies of frozen peeler can be replenished.

A

A The late Leslie Moncrieff, father of modern beachfishing, with a cod catch from Dungeness. The fish, taken in the 1960s, came from the 'Dustbin', a noted cod hole off the nuclear power station.
B Late evening on a beach in Co. Kerry. The 1989 Diawa Pairs match is fought out on the strand at Smerwick Harbour. Tilley lamps cast patches of piercing light around each angler's pitch, enabling fast tackle changes to be made and easy baiting up of the paternoster rigs.

B

In its haste to find a safe place in which to shed its shell, the common shore crab flocks to the highest reaches of the tideline in the shallow estuaries, from where it can be collected among the mud and weed, groynes and warm-water pools between May and early June. Once the cock crabs have shed their old shells and the new ones have hardened, the hen crabs start to peel with the result that the period of peeler availability is prolonged through the summer. On some South West coasts peelers can be collected from estuaries where the Gulf Stream influences water temperature.

The fish which arrive round the British coastline at this time of the year are led by the common or silver eel, a species which is now in evidence where it once was a rarity. The eel, which can tolerate a much higher degree of pollution, has replaced shoreline species which have declined in numbers due to the deterioration of their habitat, a sad fact now much of the coast is bounded by industry and large populations.

With the eels come bass and flounders and in some areas, Ireland's south-east coast especially, thornback rays, stingrays and smoothhounds come within reach of the shore angler. All these species move inshore in search of the peeling shore crab and become so preoccupied with this food source that they will eat little else.

There are few thrills in catching eels and flounders but the pressure on other species in some areas is such that these two species are all there is for the angler. But they provide sport for thousands of anglers who are not fortunate enough to have thornbacks and smoothhounds within easy angling distance. Both these fish take peeler crab, probably the sea angler's most versatile bait alongside the sandeel.

Using peeler as a bait is not simple, it is not dug up and mounted on the hook. The crabs are collected in various stages of shedding their shells but are only right as a bait when they are just about to moult. At this time their internal organs are also soft and the yellow body fluids they contain have no equal in attracting fish. Collecting and storing crabs so that they can be used at this peak period is the key to their successful use. Peelers that are about to shed their shell can be used or the process halted by placing them alive in the fridge. In this way a ready supply of bait is assured.

Mounting peeler crab on the hook is not easy, the usual method being to remove the crab's soft shell (correctly called the carapace), wrap the body with elastic cotton then put it on the hook. But this makes for trouble when eel fishing because their small teeth become caught in the cotton, which puts them off. My preferred method is to peel the crab and cut it in half, make sure that every trace of shell and gills is removed, then using a short-shank hook thread the point in and out through the leg sockets. If this is carried out correctly there is no need to use the elastic cotton. (Fig. 9)

For bigger peeler baits for cod, bass or smoothhounds a whole peeled crab can be fished on a 2/0 or 3/0 short-shank hook, with the bait secured with a few turns of the light Knit-in elastic, available from most haberdashers.

C

C Mike Prichard with a plump flounder that snatched a bait intended for bass; from clean water it made a fine meal.

FIG 9 TWO METHODS OF BAITING WITH PEELER CRAB

Half crab with a short-shank hook threaded through leg sockets

Whole crab with the hook secured by elastic thread

Avoid using peeler crab unpeeled, it may catch wrasse or a few smoothhounds, but the bait is far more effective with all the shell removed.

Concerning the gills and associated organs, I remove these when fishing for the smaller species such as eels and flounders. Shed crab carapaces always contain the old gills and these are not eaten by fish or crabs, their removal gives a total soft bait with nothing to mask the efficiency of the hook-point.

SILVER EELS

The common silver eel is not every angler's favourite catch, many viewing its tangling rigs and covering them

CONGER EEL
Conger conger

The conger eel appears to spawn in an area which stretches from the Sargasso Sea across the Atlantic to Gibraltar in water 1000–1500 fathoms deep, the actual spawning taking place in mid-water. The leptocephali are similar to those of the European freshwater eel, *Anguilla anguilla*, although they are larger for each growth stage. The conger eel grows to much greater sizes than its freshwater counterpart, fish of over 45 kg (100 lb) have been caught on rod and line in British waters and there is now an established charterboat organisation based on fishing the many wrecks from two world wars. Conger favour deepwater reefs, wrecks and broken ground from which they can ambush the lesser species they feed on.

Bait: Whole strips of fish, particularly mackerel presented on a wire trace.

with slime as something they can do without! If you do fish for eels, always have plenty of old rags and a sealable container, for eels can wriggle out of plastic bags and suchlike. Relatively strong hook-snoods of about 16 kg (35 lb) b.s. are best because they are less likely to tangle. Holding on to an eel is a major problem, especially one of the boot-lace size, and the best method is trapping it between the forefingers. (Fig. 10)

The top bait for eels in the sea is a whole small peeler crab about 3.8 cm (1½ in) across. Estuary anglers often catch eels and flounders together when using peeler bait, with the flatfish preferring the biggest, juiciest half-peeler you can get on the hook. King ragworm, lugworm, harbour ragworm and boiled shrimps are also successful baits for flounders, but peeler reigns supreme for the really big fish, particularly in Ireland. The flounder is one of the most widespread British sea species, often coming very close to the waterline and is the ideal fish for the novice or junior angler.

Spring's bigger fish are the bass, thornback ray, smoothhound and, in some areas, the stingray. In spring, bass and smoothhound fall almost exclusively to peeler baits; the thornbacks take worm and fishbaits, while the stingray prefers ragworm.

A calm, clear sea is usually the best condition for catching smoothhound and stingray and round the British Isles the smoothhound has hot-spots off Sowley and Park Shores in the Solent, the stingray having a regular haunt at St Osythe, on the Essex coast. In Ireland, Morriscastle Beach, near Wexford, has long been known as a noted smoothhound and ray venue.

SMOOTHHOUNDS

The smoothhound has a reputation as being a dogged fighter and indeed its initial run has a surprising power, so when you strike into a big one it pays to have the reel drag on. Their shark-like shape and size, up to 9 kg (20 lb), adds to their attraction, but there is some confusion between the smoothhound and the starry smoothhound, the latter having star-shaped blotches over its back. There

EEL LARVAE

Stage 1
0.6 cm (¼ in), newly hatched

Stage 2
2.5 cm (1 in), two months old

Stage 3
4.5 cm (1¾ in), eight months old

Stage 4
7.6 cm (3 in), about one and a half years

Stage 5
7 cm (2¾ in), two and a half years

Stage 6
6.4 cm (2½ in), about three years old

Stage 4 was at one time thought to be a separate species, *Leptocephalus brevirostris*

Stages 4–6 show a gradual reduction in width and a slight reduction in length as the larva becomes an elver

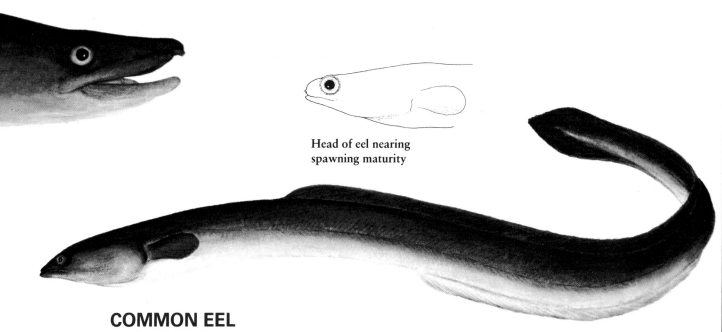

Head of eel nearing
spawning maturity

COMMON EEL
Anguilla anguilla

One of a large number of world-wide species of which two come from the North Atlantic, the European eel, *A. anguilla*, and the American eel, *A. rostrata*. The common eel lives in freshwater where it grows from the elver stage until returning to the sea as a spawning eel. Eels from Britain migrate to the sea about September, changing from yellow to the silver stage, with a noticeable increase in the size of the eyes. Migrating eels have never been caught outside coastal waters so little is known of migratory spawning routes. The species' mode of reproduction was learned by tracing the minute but developing larvae from a point of origin in the Sargasso Sea. Here, tiny larvae were found, but no eggs. Though 3000 fathoms deep, the immediate sea locale produces eel larvae at depths of 50–150 fathoms during March. Drifting on the warm currents, the leaf-shaped leptocephali are moved towards Europe and North Africa by the North Atlantic Drift. Four years after leaving the Sargasso Sea they arrive in huge numbers as elvers wherever freshwater enters the sea. The yellowish coloration develops after they enter freshwater.

Bait: Dead fish and bunches of worms. Small eels will take grub baits intended for other species.

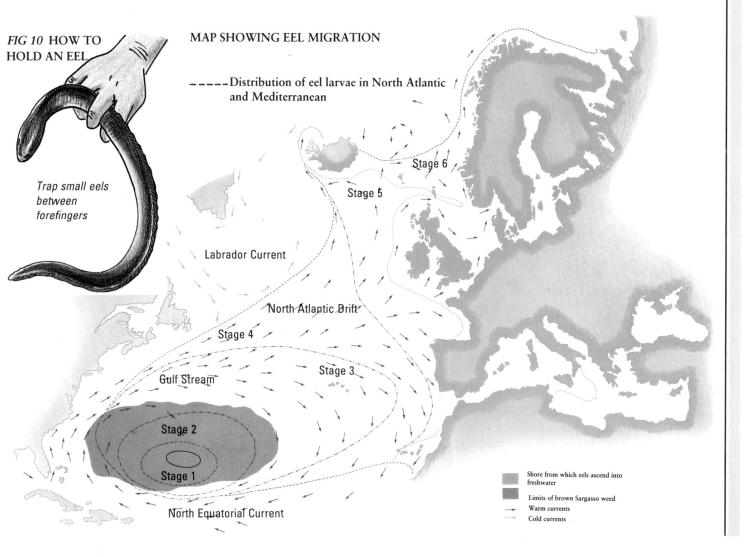

FIG 10 **HOW TO HOLD AN EEL**

Trap small eels between forefingers

MAP SHOWING EEL MIGRATION

– – – – Distribution of eel larvae in North Atlantic and Mediterranean

Stage 6

Stage 5

Labrador Current

North Atlantic Drift

Stage 4

Stage 3

Gulf Stream

Stage 2

Stage 1

North Equatorial Current

Shore from which eels ascend into freshwater

Limits of brown Sargasso weed

Warm currents

Cold currents

should be no confusion between them and the larger tope because while the tope has shark-like teeth the smooth-hounds have the flat, grinding teeth similar to those of the ray family.

THORNBACK RAYS

Thornback rays are far less spectacular fighters than the smoothhounds, even though their initial bite can sometimes pull the rod from its rest. In most cases all the angler sees is a small tap on the rod tip as they gently take the bait, but he should not strike too soon. Their fight has been described as equalling that of a wet plastic bag, but when first hooked their kiting use of the tide can at least provide the angler with some excitement.

There are a large number of ray species, with the identification of the thornback being easy because of the thorny spines protruding from the ray's back and on the female the underbody also. Beware of the thornback's strong jaws when removing the hook, it does not have pointed teeth but the jaw muscles are very powerful and can crush the unwary finger.

STINGRAYS

When fishing for stingray there are obvious dangers and accidents happen because they are hooked by chance by anglers fishing for bass, flounders or eels. The danger lies in the whip-like tail which carries a barbed venomous spine halfway along it. A wound from this is serious enough to bring your fishing to a halt for several days although the poison is not fatal. It has been the practice for trawlermen to cut the sting off before returning the fish to the sea but this is interfering with the fish's protective weapon against predators. If the stingray needs to be weighed, a better way to treat the fish with consideration is to wrap the spine with tape, but remember to remove it before putting the fish back. Stingrays are a squat species, very heavy for their size and capable of several powerful surges when first hooked.

BASS

Spring bass tend to be small, shoaling fish, but in some areas larger specimens come inshore in search of peeler crab. A single whole peeler fished at short range will help to keep eels and flounders off a bait intended for bass. The larger edible or velvet-backed swimming crabs in their peeler state are ideal for bass in the spring. Another favourite bait at this time of the year is a large edible crab which has already shed its shell and is in the 'crispy' state. Mount one of these on a large hook and it will be ignored by all but the bigger bass.

SUMMER BASS AND HARBOUR MULLET

There was a time when a fillet of kipper tied on the hook with bright red wool was the only bait you needed in order to catch bass from Kent shores. Then, bass teemed over

BASS
Dicentrarchus labrax

A beach-anglers' species with a clearly defined distribution, the bass is rarely found north of the Solway Firth, west coast of Scotland or Filey Brigg on England's east coast. In Ireland, with a few notable exceptions, bass are found

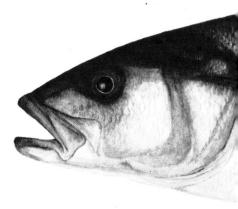

round the whole coastline. This is a dark-blue-backed fish, with brilliant, hard silvery scales along the flanks. There is a spiny first dorsal fin, spines on each gill-cover and in front of the anal fin. There are two distinct behaviour patterns which depend on the age and size of the individual fish. As school bass, up to 0.45–1.14 kg (1–2½ lb), they shoal up and chase brit and other small fry in the littoral waters; from 1.3–2.7 kg (3–6 lb) the fish move within a fixed coastal area feeding on marine worms, crustaceans and small fish species. Nearing 4.5 kg (10 lb) plus bass tend to become solitary, frequenting the deepwater reefs and moving into estuaries and harbours. Bass are not solely a summer species, they can be taken off the south-western shore every month of the year and at places with power-station warm-water outflows such as Dungeness, Kent, they can be hooked in the coldest weather. The bass can reach over 9 kg (20 lb) but 4.5 kg (10 lb) is a good fish.
Bait: Lugworm, ragworm, squid strip, fishbaits, artificial lures.

rocks and surf and to catch ten fish over 2.2 kg (5 lb) in one session was not unknown. Today, the bass shoals teem no more and the commercial and angling pressure from monofilament gill-nets and the highly efficient Redgill lure threaten the species with extinction. Even Ireland, a mecca for bass in the 1950s and 60s, has woken up to the bass's demise with the situation so bad that the fish has been taken off the species list by the Irish Tourist Board when advertising County Kerry's shore angling.

Efforts to save the bass are being made throughout the UK and Ireland with the introduction of nursery areas, bans on gill-nets and increases in the bass minimum takeable size. Anglers can play their part too by returning bass alive or imposing a personal catch limit, and indeed many organisations have banned bass from competitions and excluded them from specimen events.

Having been raised on bass fishing I spent my early angling years oblivious to many other species, which are in any case a rather mundane lot. Without doubt, the sleek, silver bass with more than a hint of a game species is the most prized of our saltwater species. Many anglers spend a lifetime fishing and never catch a bass, while the greatest novice has landed the biggest of specimens at his first attempt. The reasons for this lie in the bass's habit of swimming very close to the shoreline within even the beginner's casting range. This is a fish of the surf, dashing in and out of the backwash to pick up food dislodged by

An Atlantic surf strand, facing into the western blasts of autumn and winter gales. The breakers begin to form a couple of hundred yards out, then roll into the sand in regular lines. Theory has it that bass may lurk behind the third breaker.

the gentlest swell. On many venues a 91 m (100 yard) cast will put your bait well beyond the bass, with the Irish strands typical of this scenario. A bait lobbed into the third breaker is where you are most likely to encounter bass from the strand, while the joint between beach stones, rocks and sand is the hot-spot from most other British beaches.

When they are under 0.9 kg (2 lb) bass swim in large shoals and are easy to catch in certain areas, where they are known as school-bass. They are so prolific in the Hampshire Solent that they are considered a pest. Unfortunately the bass takes a long time to grow and a fish of 4.5 kg (10 lb) can be as old as 20 years. It takes about six years for a bass to reach breeding size and in that period the fish has to run the gauntlet of hook and net. Commercial fisherman seek the plate-size bass which are preferred by restaurants, which might be good for their profits but is bad news for the fish stocks. In recent years it has been recognised that fish in the 2.7 to 3.6 kg (6 to 8 lb) range are becoming rare, which will be reflected in future stocks, or lack of them.

It has been said that very big bass, those over 4.5 kg (10 lb) are solitary, but after a lifetime of fishing for them I know this to be incorrect. Bass are shoaling fish and they stay in year-classes, each shoal growing smaller as the fish are caught or die. Sooner or later the shoal may be less than six bass, giving the impression that the big ones are solitary. In areas where angling and commercial pressures are not so strong the shoals of large bass are evident. Under 4.5 kg (10 lb) the bass feed on brit and sandeel in the surf, but very large fish tend to be scavengers.

For the angler who seeks really large bass, the best bait is a mackerel head to which the entrails are still attached, or a whole calamari (squid, which can be bought frozen) fished somewhere with a big-bass reputation. Dover is such a place, holding the bass shore record at 8.7 kg (19 lb). Mackerel anglers, who gut and head their fish after each day's session drop a steady stream of fish offal from the local pier and the big bass feed well on it from June until October.

Bass are noted for being territorial, visiting the same reef or sandbank annually to patrol that area day after day. This means that the angler who finds the ambush point can catch bass each year at the known time. A rock gully funnelling inshore from a reef has bass swimming inshore at night in under 0.6 m (2 ft) of water in search of peeler crabs, worms, small fish and so on. The angler need do no more than drop his bait into the gully and wait for the fish to arrive. Such fishing is exciting as well as dangerous, with the hazards of slippery rocks, deep water and an incoming tide not to be forgotten. Catching bass like this, on a short line, also poses problems and it is wise to have the reel clutch set and a reasonable breaking strain line for these tactics. Sometimes an offshore wind whips up a surf and the bass appear from nowhere while the surf is pushing inshore, then vanish at high water or when the wind drops.

There are very few hard and fast rules governing the baits used for bass because their preference for certain

A

A Fishing out onto open sand from a rocky shore. Alan's companion climbs below to bring up a hooked ray.
B A small-eyed ray from Tralee Bay. There are many fine fish caught in this area.
C Just occasionally bass will swim behind the angler as he wades the surf to make his cast. The fish find food in the water that scours the flat beach.

food differs locally. Baits that are successful in one place are totally useless a short distance away. As an example, lugworm catches bass from the sandy Irish strands and the Sussex beaches, but this bait does not work for the Kent shores. Peeler crab is perhaps the universal bass bait, especially from rocky areas, with mackerel good for the bigger bass of late summer and autumn. (Fig. 11)

Bass feed at all states of the tide, with the early flood the optimum time at many venues. The fish is the first to comb the intertidal reaches where the crabs have shuffled into position under the cover of darkness. The known peeler holes are searched with the main target being a jelly-soft peeler which has just shed its shell. Crabs can only shed their shells with the support of water and are completely vulnerable and immobile at this time. If they have survived the 24 hours and their new shell has hardened their immunity returns.

As bait, the edible and velvet-backed crabs are very good, but they are not as easy to keep alive in their peeling state as the shore crab and must be kept in refrigerated water which is oxygenated. A fist-sized edible crab softly mounted on a 4/0 short-shank hook is the deadliest of baits for bass between 2.7 and 4.5 kg (6 and 10 lb). Terminal rigs for bass should be simple one-hook paternosters with the running kind (Fig. 12) preferred by some anglers but they are not essential.

MULLET

Among the most widespread of the world's fishes, the mullets are somewhat similar in appearance to bass but they are a totally different species, three being found round the British coast, the thick-lipped grey, *Chelon labrosus*, being the largest. The other two are the smaller, thin-lipped, *Liza ramada*, and the golden grey mullet, *L. aurata*, both of which are found in river estuaries and areas of salt-marsh, at times entering freshwater.

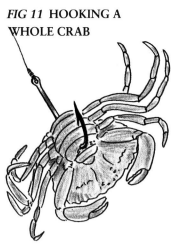

FIG 11 HOOKING A WHOLE CRAB

B

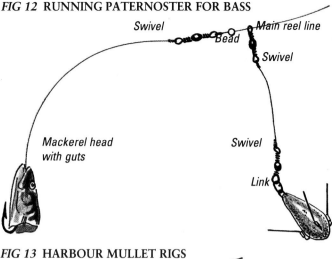

FIG 12 RUNNING PATERNOSTER FOR BASS

Swivel
Bead
Main reel line
Swivel
Mackerel head with guts
Swivel
Link

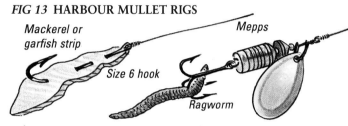

FIG 13 HARBOUR MULLET RIGS

Mackerel or garfish strip
Mepps
Size 6 hook
Ragworm

FIG 13A HOOKING GARFISH STRIP

Fold bait with skin inside
Not too much skin showing
Pass hook through several times

C

For the British sea angler the mullets are different from most other species in that they are rarely caught on standard sea-angling tackle and baits, the reason being that they feed on an otherwise unexploitable food source. Their poor diet includes algae, small molluscs and crustaceans sifted from the weed and mud, and the fishes' preference for harbours and estuaries has led them to eat man's waste with bread a clear favourite.

Mullet have the reputation of being difficult to catch, but this relates more to the difficulty of getting them to feed rather than inducing them into taking a baited hook. On occasion, feeding mullet can be easy to catch and the smaller thin-lipped and golden greys have been described as 'Kamikasi' fish along the South Coast of England because of their suicidal tendencies when anglers come on a feeding shoal. The larger thick-lipped mullet is not easily fooled, but groundbaiting techniques can induce them to go on feeding, especially if the offering is the same as the hookbait.

One way to attract mullet shoals is to fill an onion-bag with mashed bread and dangle it below the surface, where it releases a trail of bread particles in the tide. From rock marks a mixture of boiled fish and bread thrown in at intervals will often bring them towards the hookbait.

Tackle for mullet needs to be light and lines of 3.6 kg (8 lb) b.s. fished on a small spinning or coarse rod are ideal and one essential item of equipment is a landing-net, or a drop-net for use on piers or harbour walls. From these places, the most effective method is to fish a small piece of bread, flake or paste, on a Size 6 hook directly below the rod tip. A quivertip fitted to the rod tip aids bite detection while the addition of a small bullet will get the bread down and combat tidal flow. Bites come as a series of taps or, when the fish are feeding well, as a run with the bait after a definite bite or a slackening of the line.

At other times a float can be used to fish the bait just below the surface, with a small waggler float taking 3 SG shot being sufficient. Mackerel and garfish strip less the skin work well in Ireland. (Figs 13, 13A) Bread in all forms is versatile when added to crab flesh, kipper, sardine, and so on, adding to its attractiveness. Bread hookbait should be softened by holding it over the steam from a kettle. Small harbour-ragworm sometimes catch thick-lipped mullet, and they also work when used in conjunction with a small Mepps spinner for the thin-lipped species. When bringing a hooked mullet to the net, make sure to avoid retrieving the fish through the groundbaited area, the disturbance will put any other fish down.

AUTUMN: ROCK FISHING FOR CONGER, WRASSE AND DOGFISH

Without doubt, autumn is the most productive season for the shore-based sea angler. Following a warm June, July and August, those calm, settled 'Indian summer' days of early autumn see an overlap of summer and winter fish species. Mullet, bass, eels, dogfish, sole and even mackerel are some of the many species which stay until the days

THICK-LIPPED GREY MULLET
Chelon labrosus

This fish has two dorsal fins, the first with four sharp spines; the second has soft rays. The upper lip is swollen and prominent, the 'throat slit' is narrower than the other species. In the sea's upper layers, mullet are plankton feeders, so hookbait is a problem. In the West Country, fishermen entice the mullet inshore with a mixture of pilchard oil, mashed fish scraps and bread. Conditioned to it, they can be caught on small fish pieces and bread on small hooks.

At Dungarvan, Ireland, mullet are taken on a hookbait of cheesepaste to simulate the curds discharged into the harbour from a creamery. The species reaches weights to 4.5 kg (10 lb) or more, but a mullet of 1.3 kg (3 lb) is a specimen.

Bait: Minute fish pieces, breadpaste, flake, small ragworm, sea slater, maggots.

shorten and the temperature drops, then they retreat to their winter warm-water haunts. Before they leave they mix with the arrivals such as cod and whiting. At no other time can the shore angler encounter such a spread of species and have the chance of big specimens.

Summer and winter species are migrating round the coasts, many free from the constraints of breeding, feeding heavily for the journey ahead. Most notable of the October 'biggies' are the conger and bass, while a few turbot, anglerfish, rays and so on come close to the shore during their migrations. With such an increase in fish activity during autumn, particularly the arrival of the first cod inshore, sea anglers are out in force, the numbers fishing increasing ten-fold as reports of the first cod are published. The flat, sandy beaches become crowded, so now the most experienced anglers turn to rock fishing.

The mention of rocks and snags sends many a sea angler scuttling from a venue and while miles of sandy beaches are thronged with thousands of anglers there are hundreds of miles of rock and cliff venues going relatively unfished.

The vogue for casting distance with its associated light tackle shares the blame for many anglers never experiencing the excitement of landing a big fish from the rocks. Many are content to catch small dabs, flounders and pouting just as long as they can be seen to cast over 92 m (100 yards) and in many extreme cases casting has taken over with ego forbidding any kind of fishing other than that which includes casting a lead towards the horizon. But rocks offer few threats to the well-equipped angler

with the correct technique, and a few lost leads are a small price to pay for some excellent fishing and the possibility of some very big fish.

For fishing from rocks, the most basic item of equipment is a strong pair of boots – 'wellies' are most definitely out – and the kind of boots used for rock climbing are ideal as they provide ankle support. Modern trainers are suitable although some makes are not compatible with wet rocks, which can be treacherous.

Of the tackle necessary, a well-loaded reel with a fast retrieve is essential, for 13.6 kg (30 lb) b.s. line loaded to the rim of a big 5:1 retrieve multiplier comes back at the rate of a metre (a yard) per turn of the handle, and the addition of a lead lift to the sinker ensures that the tackle is retrieved unhindered. A simple one-hook rig supplies all that is needed for terminal tackle, if more than one hook is used the chances of snags in rock or kelp while having a fish on the top hook and then the lower one becoming lodged are increased. Rods should be substantial, not too soft, and with a blank suitable for 170 g (6 oz) casting.

When rock fishing, the basic technique for retrieval of tackle involves picking the rod up from the rest and winding in in one movement, the sharp lift brings the lead off the bottom and the fast retrieve keeps it moving with the lead-lift helping the tackle to plane to the surface as quickly as possible. The secret is not to pause, if you do you will be snagged. And once the cast has been made, leave it where it comes to rest, if the rod is picked up or the line reeled in the hook or lead will lodge in something. A soft-wire grip-lead can be used to stop the sinker falling

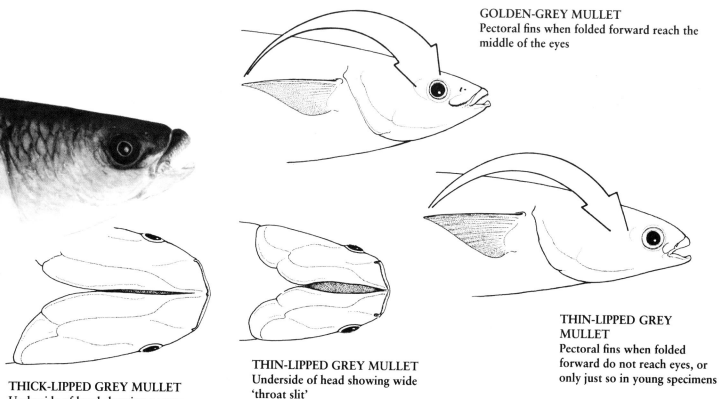

GOLDEN-GREY MULLET
Pectoral fins when folded forward reach the middle of the eyes

THIN-LIPPED GREY MULLET
Pectoral fins when folded forward do not reach eyes, or only just so in young specimens

THICK-LIPPED GREY MULLET
Underside of head showing narrow 'throat slit'

THIN-LIPPED GREY MULLET
Underside of head showing wide 'throat slit'

THIN-LIPPED GREY MULLET
Liza ramada
A fish that grows larger than the thick-lipped species, reaching over 6.4 kg (14 lb). It has a thin top lip and much broader throat slit. The pelvic fins are almost as long as the pectorals. There is a dark blotch at the base of the pectoral fin. It is bred in enclosures in some countries. All three true mullets are in evidence during late spring to early autumn months. They migrate northwards almost into the Arctic Circle.
Bait: As for the thick-lipped species.

GOLDEN-GREY MULLET
Liza aurata
This mullet is a smaller fish than the other two species and much rarer in the seas round the British Isles. A specimen caught from the shore in the Channel Isles weighed just over 1.2 kg (2 lb 11 oz). The body of the golden-grey mullet has a golden sheen covering the head and foreparts, but this is not a reliable identification feature on immature specimens. There is a golden patch on the gill-covers.
Bait: As for the thick-lipped mullet.

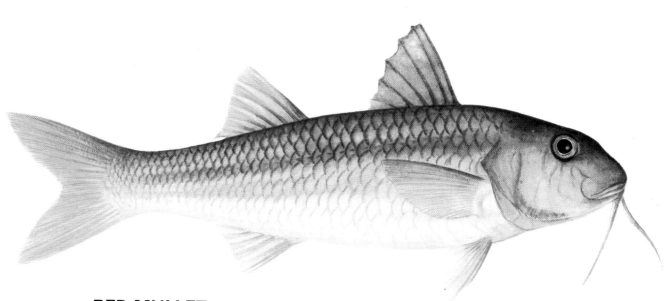

RED MULLET
Mullus surmuletus
Known also as the striped red mullet, this species is an occasional visitor to the west and southern shores of the British Isles. Unlike the true mullets, this is a bottom-dwelling species favouring ground which has a mixture of rocks and sand. Two lengthy barbules protruding from the lower jaw are used to detect edible life in the sand. It is known to reach weights of over 1.6 kg (3 lb 10 oz) but a fish of 0.9 kg (2 lb) is a specimen.
Bait: Marine worms and crustaceans.

159

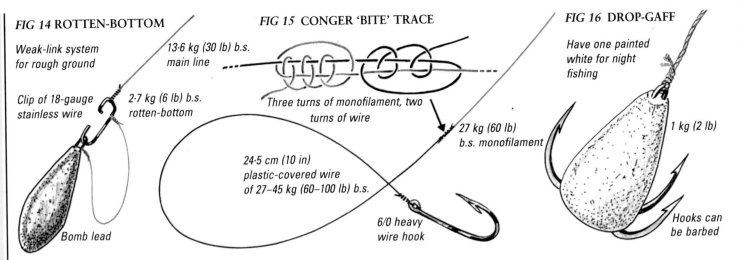

FIG 14 ROTTEN-BOTTOM

Weak-link system
for rough ground

Clip of 18-gauge
stainless wire

13·6 kg (30 lb) b.s.
main line

2·7 kg (6 lb) b.s.
rotten-bottom

Bomb lead

FIG 15 CONGER 'BITE' TRACE

Three turns of monofilament, two
turns of wire

24·5 cm (10 in)
plastic-covered wire
of 27–45 kg (60–100 lb) b.s.

27 kg (60 lb)
b.s. monofilament

6/0 heavy
wire hook

FIG 16 DROP-GAFF

Have one painted
white for night
fishing

1 kg (2 lb)

Hooks can
be barbed

into and lodging in a crevice, and a simple weak-line system, a 'rotten bottom' (Fig. 14), can help over particularly rough ground.

By using line as heavy as 13.6 kg (30 lb) b.s. straight through reel and rig it is a simple matter to tie another rig on when one is lost. When rigs are pulled free breakages in the line occur at knots and the first joint of the trace is where it usually happens. A leader is not required for rock fishing because distance is rarely important and is proportional to the chances of snagging, so the casting strain on the line is minimal. Tackle loss is inevitable at times and the angler must go prepared, with several ready-tied rigs.

There is one advantage in rock fishing: the risk of snagging while bringing a fish other than conger or wrasse is slight, because it tries to keep in open water and takes the terminal tackle away from snags.

CONGER

The conger is probably the biggest species the shore angler is likely to find. This eel is basically nocturnal in shore-fishing terms, but in daylight they can be caught in coloured water or where it is very deep. For this species the best conditions are a flat calm moonlight night during a spring tide, it is the time when conger are most likely to leave their holes to attack pouting, preferring fish flesh to everything else.

Small conger, called 'straps', sometimes can be caught on worm or crab baits but over 2.2 kg (5 lb) they are mostly caught on whole fish or fillets. When a conger takes one of these baits it picks it up and positions it before swallowing, the result being a series of tugs on the rod tip or, if the reel's ratchet is on, a series of clicks. Once the bait is in place inside the eel's mouth the fish moves away. The angler, then, is able to time the strike. If done too soon, the bait may be pulled from the conger's jaws, too late and the bait may have been swallowed and when the eel is landed it will have to be killed to recover the hook.

My method of striking when conger fishing is to pick the rod up immediately a bite is signalled, then I put the reel in free-spool and let the fish take line. After three pulls I strike twice. The strike might be affected by the mark and I strike early when fishing over the roughest ground or from pier walls known to have conger holes in them.

The strength of a 13.6 kg (30 lb) conger is formidable and while the species cannot be considered as fighters in the big-game sense of dashing about and making great runs, their sheer strength is incredible. Playing a conger is like trying to control a large, active dog on a lead; they can back-pedal quickly and if a very big one gets its tail lodged in rock or thick weed or retreats back into its crevice the angler has little chance of pulling it out again. So never give a conger line once it has been hooked. For this reason the tackle must be strong and include a plastic-covered wire or heavy monofilament trace at least to within 25.4 cm (10 in) from the hook, for its teeth can quickly chew through 13.6 kg (30 lb) b.s. nylon. (Fig. 15) Hooks for conger fishing should relate to the size of bait being used, standard being half a side of mackerel on a 6/0 heavy wire pattern.

An essential item of tackle for the conger angler is a gaff, it is impossible to land a big conger without one. I once hooked what was no doubt a 9 kg (20 lb) eel on a steep shelving beach, but did not have a gaff. Somehow I managed to pull the conger ashore and to the top of the ridge of the beach, then it slipped the hook and wriggled over the ridge, down the beach and my two companions and myself just could not hold the eel as it slithered between legs and arms. I was not welcome at home when I arrived back with my clothes smeared with conger slime – and no conger! The best gaffs for conger have a fixed head, if the fish is hooked at head or tail it can spin and the gaff head may become unscrewed.

When it comes to gaffing the conger, if you are fishing from rocks and before one is hooked, plan the forthcoming operation in advance. Work out your route down the rocks or somewhere safe to stand when you are ready. Gaff the conger in the middle or the vent and lift it clear of the sea in one movement. Two gaffs might be needed for conger over 9 kg (20 lb). Barbed gaffs have their uses, as do drop-gaffs in cliff or pier fishing. (Fig. 16)

Congers have a fearsome set of teeth and powerful jaws, but they will not attack the angler – unless fingers are put inside the mouth to remove the hook, then there is a good chance of losing or having lacerated fingers. Once landed, a conger is best put in a sealed sack and parked well up the tide line and away from the sea. Out of water, conger remain active for hours.

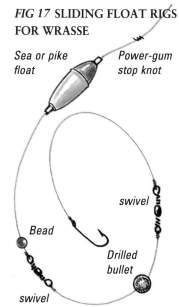

FIG 17 SLIDING FLOAT RIGS FOR WRASSE

Sea or pike float

Power-gum stop knot

swivel

Bead

Drilled bullet

swivel

Ballan wrasse are such beautiful and constant fish, always there off the rocky coastline and always on feed. But unless played out from shallow water and handled carefully they have little chance of survival.

WRASSE

Only one of the wrasse species, the ballan, *Labrus bergylta*, found in the sea round the British Isles is significant as an angling species, and it reaches a weight of some 3.6 kg (8 lb), although there are four others all considerably smaller. As shoal fish, the wrasses are strikingly coloured in deep reds, greens and yellows with seasonal and gender variations to further confuse the angler. All the species inhabit very rocky coastlines where they feed on crabs and shellfish prised from the rocks with their powerful teeth (seen on page 122).

These fish are obliging rather than sporting and once the angler has taken several from a rock mark their appeal soon wanes. Float or light ledger tactics will catch these fish which on seizing the bait dart back among the rocks, often costing the angler his terminal tackle. Rock marks within easy access quickly lose their wrasse shoals which are resident for all but the coldest months and in many areas in the South West and Ireland anglers regularly return their wrasse alive. The species will survive if unhooked and returned gently, but this can be impossible when the angler is fishing from a high vantage point.

For the angler seeking big wrasse, any rock mark which is difficult to reach, especially in Southern Ireland, will hold them. The bait simply needs to be lowered straight down into the deep water, casting is not necessary. Keep hold of the rod and when the bite comes strike and retrieve as quickly as possible before the fish tows the rig into rocks and weed.

A light sliding float outfit makes wrasse fishing more enjoyable and can be very efficient from really rocky marks. The species will accept most of the usual baits except fish or squid, with small wrasse liking ragworm.

Shore crabs work well, with a small whole hardback ideal for big ballan wrasse. Mount the crab on the hook by passing it through the shell once. (Fig. 17)

As in any rock fishing, tackle for wrasse should be kept simple. A one-hook trace, soft-wire hooks such as the 3/0 Mustad Viking 79515 and 79510 are ideal as these will bend out of snags when used in conjunction with 11.4 kg (25 lb) b.s. line. This saves the need to be continually making-up fresh rigs as the hook can just as easily be bent straight again or replaced. Beware of the hook-point bending over or breaking off.

Wrasse are not considered to be good eating and because of the ease with which they can be caught in some areas many anglers do not fish for them.

DOGFISHES

The dogfishes are one of the most wide-spread of all fish species caught round Britain and Ireland. Sometimes they will be the only species for the angler to cast to, turning up in clear water and bright sunshine when other species are long gone to deep water. In some areas off Scotland, dogfish reach plague proportions and are despised by many anglers after bigger species. The dogfishes were once prolific off the shores of the South and East of England but pollution and commercial pressures have stopped all that. Ireland, too, is feeling the pinch with trammel nets harvesting dogfish for pet-food and fertilizer, and so another species is being threatened. Anglers who moan about dogfish being a pest may one day miss this very obliging species, which should not be taken for granted.

Two species of dogfish are caught from the shore, with the lesser-spotted by far the most common, usually about

0.9 kg (2 lb), and there is a mystery as to why when caught all these fish are adult specimens, it being rare to hook an immature one. The larger bull huss, with specimens reaching 6.8 kg (15 lb) from the shore, inhabits many of the most rocky or weedy coasts of Ireland, Wales and the Isle of Man but is not so widespread as the lesser species. Both dogfishes prefer areas where they can scavenge for almost anything edible, with fresh dead fish, worms and crabs among their regular diet.

Dogfish offer an angling challenge not because they rip line off in long runs but because they can be difficult to hook. In no way sporting fish, the species lack fight and come up rolled in a ball with their eyes shut. But they can provide bites on days when nothing else is moving off-shore; match anglers like them because they can be caught in good numbers and the novice finds them useful for practising on.

A large fillet of mackerel hookbait tossed into the kelp will soon be found by a dogfish, which will pick it up, chew it, nudge it, everything but eat it, but if left long enough eventually the fish will hook itself. An early strike usually means a lost fish.

My dogfish angling is done during the summer in Irish contests, and an average of two fish every three bites is good fishing, one out of three being par. Some of the top dogfish experts come from the Isle of Man where this is the main species caught from the shore. These anglers have perfected 'doggy bashing', using 7–10 cm (3–4 in) frozen sandeels as bait on a Size 3/0 long-shank hook, a deadly combination, but the hook must not puncture the sand-eel's body.

SPINNING

The majority of shore fishing round the coasts of Britain and Ireland involves ledgering on the seabed, but there are several species which can be caught using lures and spinners. This technique is the most popular and widespread fishing style throughout the world and the imported and home tackle trade reflects this influence, particularly in reel design.

Unfortunately, our coloured and turbulent sea is generally unsuitable for spinning and lure fishing from the shore, so the style is largely ignored by British sea anglers, for the technique does have its limitations in our waters. On the rare occasion when conditions are ideal, spinning can be done in the South West, Ireland, West Coast of Scotland and the Isle of Man all offering suitable venues in summer and autumn.

MACKEREL

The mackerel is the most obvious species to be caught on lures or spinners and huge shoals of them come inshore in

Dogfish can be the mainstay of shore match angling but even these lowly creatures are under threat from commercial fishing. Matchmen have devised specialized tactics for the species, for they add considerable weight to the bag and are not too difficult to hook. Alan Yates doesn't swing the fish in, he goes forward to meet it.

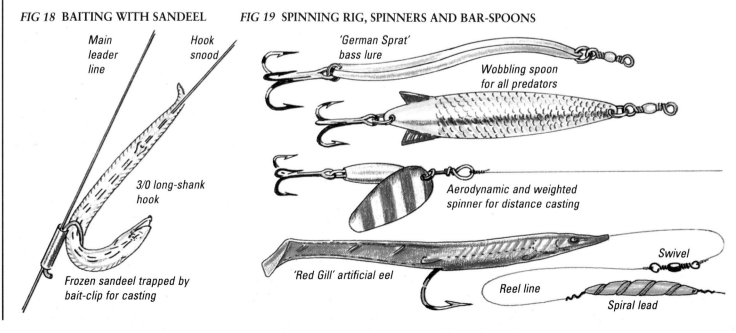

FIG 18 BAITING WITH SANDEEL

Main leader line

Hook snood

3/0 long-shank hook

Frozen sandeel trapped by bait-clip for casting

FIG 19 SPINNING RIG, SPINNERS AND BAR-SPOONS

'German Sprat' bass lure

Wobbling spoon for all predators

Aerodynamic and weighted spinner for distance casting

'Red Gill' artificial eel

Swivel

Reel line

Spiral lead

SEA ANGLING FROM THE SHORE

SANDEEL
Ammodytidae

There are three genera with five species in this group of fishes, three found in British waters. All the species are very similar, being elongated, with the lower jaw protruding beyond the edge of the upper. They are shoalfish, found in moderate groups and up to some thousands of individuals. Small ones sometimes remain on wet sand-flats after the fall of the tide, where they bury themselves. Large specimens move out with the tide, feeding on fish fry and minute animal life. As a very important bait for bass anglers especially, the sandeel is gathered in fine-mesh nets.

Bait: Strings of small, lightly dressed feathers; tiny fish strips.

summer, seizing everything they can. Anglers use coloured-feather lures, with modern fluorescent materials being used to make glittering mackerel feathers and lures. Fished sink-and-draw in strings of up to six, feathering can account for large numbers of mackerel either for bait or for the table. The purist prefers to use a light spinning outfit and single feather, lure or spinner and enjoys great sport.

HORSE MACKEREL

Horse mackerel, or scad, can be caught with similar tackle but this species is totally inedible being full of small bones and is not sought.

POLLACK

The pollack is perhaps the most obliging species which can be caught on lures from the shore. Spinning is for the roving angler and pleasure is greatest when the angler is mobile and not loaded down by too much tackle. Wandering along the shoreline, the angler can cast and explore all the close-in sea within reach, each cast likely to have a response. A 10 cm (4 in) Redgill or Delta lure fished on a 1.2 or 1.8 m (4 to 6 ft) flowing trace on a light spinning rod can provide excellent sport as fish up to 2.7 kg (6 lb) take the lure and dive for the kelp fronds. (Fig. 18)

My preference is for the green Redgills, but the blue and natural-coloured ones are also effective from Irish rock marks, Kerry and Clare both providing plenty of pollack action.

An even more deadly method is spinning a whole, dead sandeel, casting and retrieving as close to the kelp as you can get. The pollack dart up from the depths, seize the bait and dive back into the kelp at tremendous speed and nothing short of bullying the fish can bring it out from the weed. Of course, tackle is often lost but that is the price of great sport. Pollack are a delicate species so land them with a net and handle them with wet hands if you are going to return them alive. (Fig. 19)

Bass can also be caught on spinners or Redgills, but the scope for shore spinning is limited by sea colour and conditions and water clarity is paramount for this species, as is a minimum of lead close to the lure.

With a light lead, casting distance is restricted, making fishing from rocky points the angler's best bet, although distance is not important. What is, is the distance over which the lure is retrieved along the side of a rocky outcrop. All channels, crevices, clear patches should be explored thoroughly with the spinner.

A powerful and pollution-free Atlantic surf born far out in mid-ocean.

BOB CARNILL

FLY FISHING FOR TROUT

Since the mid-1960s boom in stillwater trout fishing there has been a steady and continuous increase right up to the present day, making it now the most popular branch of the game-fishing scene. The tackle trade has responded by producing rods far superior to any other material hitherto known. Carbon fibre, Boron and Kevlar have almost completely replaced built-cane and fibre glass. Not only have rods improved but so too have the rod rings (eyes, guides, and so on), reels, fly-lines and to some degree, even the angler's clothing.

CHOOSING TACKLE

RODS: To match one's tackle to a particular style of fishing is still sound advice though it is not as important as it used to be. Today's tackle is far more versatile if chosen wisely and a particular rod and line can be used to perform a wide range of duties. Not only have modern rods improved dramatically with regard to their lightness/power ratio, but they also offer the angler the action which will suit him best – as opposed to suiting the style in which he chooses to fish. A newcomer cannot be expected to know what his or her preferred 'action' will be, only experience will provide the answer.

For general fishing, a 3 m (10 ft) rod will take a lot of beating. However, for the matchman or a dyed-in-the-wool 'over-the-front' (loch-style) enthusiast, 3.2 m (10 ft 6 in), 3.3 m (11 ft), or even 3.5 m (11 ft 6 in) will be more acceptable. Such a rod allows the flies, particularly the bob-fly, to be dibbled in the surface at greater distances from the boat. In addition, true loch-style fishing does not

A

A Bob Carnill plies his trade on Lough Conn, a rugged, yet peaceful West of Ireland water.
B A wild brown trout grabbed at the fly and tore off upwind under the boat, coming perilously close to the drogue used to lessen the speed of the drift. *C* A slightly more relaxed Carnill plays the fish toward the dinghy.
D First of the fat-fleshed Lough Conn brown trout comes to the waiting net.

165

These illustrations show the gradual changes that are met in the trout family coloration, starting at the top with a sea trout from the sea, passing through to the illustration at the bottom showing a typical trout in breeding colour.

The head of an old
or 'cannibal' male trout

BROWN AND SEA TROUT
Salmo trutta

Like the salmon, trout are spawned in freshwater and live in brackish water. Some trout enter totally saline water, when they become known as sea trout. Brown and sea trout markings vary enormously, conditioned by their environment. At the parr stage, trout have vivid black and red spots, with a distinctive dark barring on the flanks. The adults retain this coloration, the bars disappearing in the smolt stage. Sea trout pass through a smolt stage when their parr colours change to a silvery livery. As adults, they exhibit black, cross-shaped spots. Trout are strongly territorial. As large fish they tend to be more solitary. Males and females undergo a marked change in coloration as the time for spawning nears. At the time of the coldest weather trout will move to gravel stretches in the smallest of feeder-streams where the males attempt to pair with several females. Depending on size, a female trout will yield up to 1,000 eggs. Trout can tolerate a high pH (alkalinity/acidity) range in water, making easy their introduction to a wide variety of waters both natural and man-made.

Bait: Live fish, natural and artificial insects, spinning lures, worms and crustaceans.

Trout parr

call for long distance casting so with a long rod the single roll-cast used to deliver just two or three rod-lengths of line can be made with one fluid movement as the flies are lifted from the water.

REELS: The 'receptacle to the hold the line' adage is neither true nor false, it depends on how one fishes. If the angler prefers to play a trout 'off-the-reel', then it becomes more than that. On the other hand, if an angler wishes to hand-line his fish the reel becomes a receptacle for storing line.

BACKING LINE: This is a narrow-diameter line spliced to the end of the much shorter fly line which allows a trout to run for distances far greater than a fly-line would otherwise allow. For all my trout fishing, I use a 8.9 cm

(3½ in) diameter reel with a wide drum. Depending on the diameter of the backing, I can load between 45.7 and 91.4 m (50 and 100 yards) of backing, plus the fly line. Never stint on backing because you could lose the trout of a life-time.

Heavy monofilaments used as shooting, running and backing line for shooting-heads are more prone to 'memory' coils than fly lines. These usually require a good stretch prior to fishing although 10 cm (4 in) diameter, wide-hub fly reels help tremendously in lessening or even eradicating the problem and are widely used nowadays by shooting-head and lead-core enthusiasts.

FLY LINES: The choice in fly lines is enormous, not only in profile, but in colour, density, and to some degree, length. Serious stillwater anglers will often have at least five different lines enabling them to fish efficiently at almost any depth. Taking lines in their natural order of sinking rate, they are a floating line; an intermediate or 'neutral', both of which actually are very slow sinkers; a slow-sinking; a fast-sinking; and possibly a lead core or lead-impregnated line, the latter being the fastest of the fast sinkers. A sink-tip may also be carried though these are not nearly as popular as they were a few years ago.

PROFILE: 'Profile' is the overall 'shape' – or taper – of a fly line. Once you have become familiar with the different profiles, you will immediately relate the profile name to its expected performance.

LEADERS: A leader is the length of monofilament which is attached to the fly line, to which in turn is attached the fly or lure. Leaders may carry more than just one fly on the point position by way of adding one or more droppers at various distances along the leader. A traditional cast will usually have three flies: the point fly, a middle dropper and a bob-fly (top dropper). In Scotland some anglers fish teams of four flies.

The leader is tapered so that the power flow will be continuous from the rod through the fly line and eventually through the leader. This not only offers the best possible presentation of the fly but also helps to prevent tangles in the leader. I have found that a 0.9 kg (2 lb) b.s. differential between the joined lengths of a leader to be quite acceptable. This step-down does not make knotting

Carefully applied finger pressure on the exposed rim of the reel brings the fight to a conclusion. Small fish are played on the line. This lightweight reel, the Leeda LC 100, with spare spools, makes changing lines easy.

RAINBOW TROUT
Salmo gairdneri

A species brought to the British Isles from the North Western States of the US. It thrives in stillwaters and has become the standard fish for man-assisted trout breeding both for sale as food and replacement stocks on fisheries. Anatomically, the fish resembles the brown trout in all but coloration. There is a vivid band of mauve-purple scales along the flanks roughly following the contours of the lateral line, and there are numerous black spots and blotches on the sides and back, extending to the caudal fin. The rainbow is not a successful spawning fish in our waters, indeed, most of the stocks in lakes and reservoirs will have been bred and introduced into them by fishery managements. There is some evidence to suggest that there are strains of rainbows that exist as naturally breeding populations in a few trout streams but it is not known if they will be viable over many generations. The rainbow is a useful addition to the angler's species; it seems more resilient to pollution and doubtful water conditions. It is a free-rising fish and with age does not become as predatory and bottom-living as the brown trout. Depending on the type of water, the rainbow is capable of growing to large weights, bigger than the brown and certainly faster. Fish of over 9 kg (20 lb) are known, and 4.5 kg (10 lb) is a specimen, but trout farms can rear them to double this weight before release into a fishery.

Bait: Natural and artificial flies, spinning lures, worms.

difficult, or too similar in diameter and strength.

Many brands of knotless tapered leader are now widely available, which can be spliced to the end of the fly line. There is a wide range of lengths, butt and tippet diameters to suit almost every requirement. Having attached the knotless leader to the fly line, the angler can fish a point fly, or he can 'tailor' the leader by cropping back into the steep part of the taper and then custom-build his leader by adding a different tippet strength, length, and/or droppers.

There are weather or water conditions where a level leader may be called for, particularly when lure fishing, and if one uses the wind to advantage, even long, level leaders can be used to good effect.

BUTT SECTIONS: These are short lengths of heavy nylon needle-knotted to the end of the fly line to which the leader is attached. Attachment to the leader can be by interlocking loops or a blood-knot. The butt section is a permanent fixture, replaced when it becomes damaged or too short to be of particular use. There is no set length for a butt section. The breaking strain of the butt section may also vary, some thick monofilament has been used, but this makes the step down into the leader material far too great, serving no practical purpose. I use 4.5 kg (10 lb) b.s. for my butt sections which is just 1.1 kg (2½ lb) greater than the 3.4 kg (7½ lb) b.s. first section of the leader; this gives a fluid power-flow with neat joining or knotting, whether using interlocking loops or a blood knot.

SHOCK ABSORBER: The Power Gum shock-absorber habit is becoming popular, especially among the ever-increasing band of stillwater dry and semi-dry fly enthusiasts. Because of the tiny flies often employed, coupled with a growing awareness that very fine tippets bring better results, the shock absorber will soon be an essential part of many an angler's rig.

Power Gum is an elastic monofil which stretches almost twice its length under maximum pressure, at which

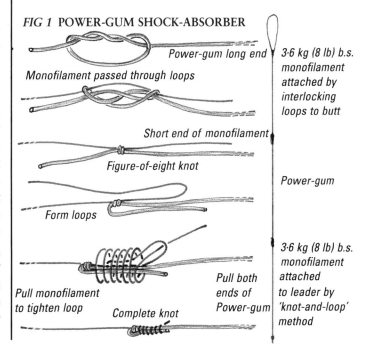

FIG 1 POWER-GUM SHOCK-ABSORBER

Power-gum long end

Monofilament passed through loops

Short end of monofilament

Figure-of-eight knot

Form loops

Pull monofilament to tighten loop

Complete knot

Pull both ends of Power-gum

3·6 kg (8 lb) b.s. monofilament attached by interlocking loops to butt

Power-gum

3·6 kg (8 lb) b.s. monofilament attached to leader by 'knot-and-loop' method

point it has a b.s. of approximately 4.5 kg (10 lb), depending on the brand. A Power Gum shock-absorber is usually inserted between the butt section and the leader. (Fig. 1, p. 169)

THE FISHING BAG: When bank fishing I use a large, stout canvas bag that keeps out the rain and has plenty of storage space in the main inner compartment; it has another large pouch to the rear and two generous pockets on the front.

THE LANDING NET: I prefer a net that will be serviceable whether one is fishing from the bank or the boat. My net has quite a large, bow-shaped, rigid frame supporting a deep net. It has a collapsible head with a carrying clip making it ideal for fishing on-the-rove. The extending handle is suitable both for boat fishing or steep banks.

THE DROGUE: This is an underwater parachute used to slow down the speed of a drifting boat while maintaining a given position in relation to the wind/waves and is essential. (Fig. 2)

THE G-CLAMP: A G-clamp may be used in connection with both the drogue and the anchor. On the drift, or at anchor, most boats yaw, due perhaps to hull design and/or the effect of wind, waves or current. Yawing may occasionally be used to good effect, but it usually spoils a day's fishing. When this happens, reposition the anchor point of the drogue or anchor rope. The best way to do this is to attach a G-clamp to the side of the boat and take the rope around it. By moving the clamp, one can quickly have the boat lying true.

A suitable alternative to the G-clamp is a length of rope fastened at the bow and stern of your boat. Draw it tight, fastening the drogue or anchor rope with a tight sliding knot. This system allows the 'anchor point' to be repositioned by sliding the knot to the required position.

THE ANCHOR: Anchors are becoming increasingly popular as an essential part of every boat fisherman's tackle. Apart from being a necessity at times, an anchor also forms part of one's safety equipment. In the event of motor failure and/or extreme weather conditions, your anchor could save the boat from being blown onto a dam wall or mid-water sandbank.

Make sure that your anchor is substantial, and will hold a heavy boat with two anglers in high winds and waves. Choose something with either three large grappling prongs or broad, articulating flukes. But no anchor will work without the addition of at least 1.8 m (6 ft) of substantial chain (more if you can afford it for those larger waters). The chain's job is to pull the prongs flukes downwards, forcing them to gain a purchase in the lake bed.

Do not fix the chain to the anchor directly to the ring at the top of the shaft. If there is a ring at the fluke-end of the shaft the chain should be attached there, using a D-link. Then tie it to the ring at the top of the shaft with a piece of string that can be broken by a pull from one man. If there is no ring at the fluke-end have one welded on. This method of attachment is called a breakaway rig and it will save you many anchors over the years should the anchor become wedged on the bottom. It works by hauling on the rope until the string breaks, which reverses the lift to the rear of the anchor – and up it comes. (Fig. 3)

ANCHOR ROPE: When buying anchor rope, purchase as much as you can afford – between 30.5 and 45.7 m (100 and 150 ft) allowing you to anchor in the deepest of our larger reservoirs. It is also an advantage to purchase synthetic rope, which does not rot.

THE STILLWATER SEASON

Trout can be caught on the fly on a fairly regular basis without one having the slightest interest in entomology; but not to observe and be curious about the trout's life is to deny oneself the very essence of what makes fly fishing so special.

MID-MARCH TO MID-APRIL

My observations are based on the Midlands area; therefore certain regional adjustments may be needed with regard to weather variations and its subsequent effect on plant and insect life to the north and south of this central point. In most areas the trout fishing season begins around

FIG 2 THE DROGUE

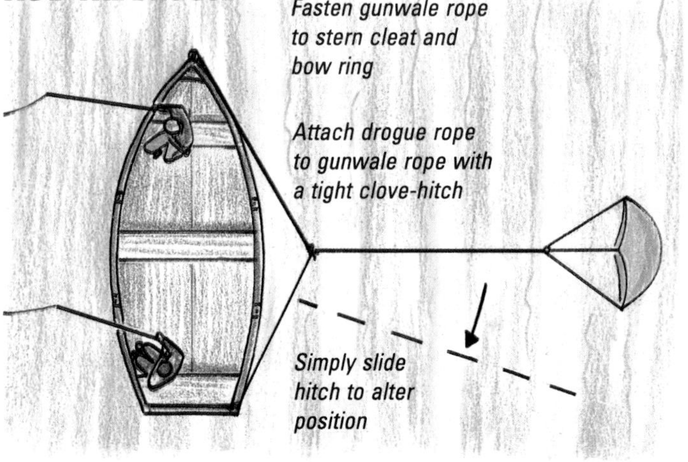

Fasten gunwale rope to stern cleat and bow ring

Attach drogue rope to gunwale rope with a tight clove-hitch

Simply slide hitch to alter position

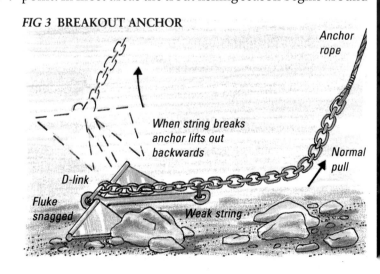

FIG 3 BREAKOUT ANCHOR

Anchor rope

When string breaks anchor lifts out backwards

Normal pull

D-link

Fluke snagged

Weak string

Bob Carnill's fly box. Every fly has been tied by him during the long winter months. Among these flies are many highly successful innovative patterns which he has designed and tied himself. Total conviction that a particular fly will work seems for some strange reason often to communicate itself to the feeding trout, with the result that an unexpected and 'bonus' fish comes to the net.

the middle of March. There is very little fly life in evidence and even less surface activity, but below the surface life will be stirring. Coupled with a gradual warming of the water, both insect life and the trout will become increasingly more active.

For most of March and into April the trout feed close to the lake-bottom, usually in and just beyond the deep margins. At this time, their diet will include bottom-dwelling invertebrates such as corixae, caddis larvae, shrimp, snails, chironomid (buzzer) larvae, water-beetles and their larvae, alder larvae, and occasionally daphnia.

Fish fry are occasionally found in the stomach of an early-season trout, but not in the quantities usually associated with the fry-bashing sprees of late summer and autumn. In addition, a few small, dark adult chironomids may be seen on or near the water, but the trout will usually ignore them and stay close to the bottom.

EARLY SEASON TECHNIQUES

Whether we fish from the bank or from a boat, the location and techniques may be very similar. In either case, our most productive areas will be found in deep water, fairly close to the bank. In the early season avoid fishing over shallow, stone-bottomed areas, or at the mouth, or general vicinity of streams or land drains. Such areas are the haunt of gravid, out-of-condition, black cock rainbows, easy to catch but not a worthy quarry.

When fishing from the bank during this period, I prefer

to have the wind coming over my back, it is much warmer and more comfortable and also crucial to the success of my favoured approach. The first thing I look for is deep marginal water within comfortable casting range where I expect to find concentrations of over-wintered, silver hen rainbows and perhaps the odd, large brown trout.

My rig would be the 3 m (10 ft) carbon rod matched to a WF#8 floating line. Leader length is 5.5 to 7.6 m (18 to 25 ft) with one or two droppers, the first spaced between 0.9 and 1.2 m (3 and 4 ft) from the point, and the top dropper at a similar distance.

My choice of flies for a two-dropper leader would be: for the point position one of the following: Pheasant Tail Nymph, Size 8, 10 or 12 long shank (L/S), Cased Caddis Size 10 to 14 L/S; Alder Larva 8 or 10 L/S, Worm Fly, tandem 2 × 10 or 8 standard shank, William's Size 8, 10 and 12 (standard shank) or a Shrimp 12 Yorkshire Sedge Hook.

For the first dropper: Black and Peacock Spider, Zulu, Mallard and Claret or Corixa. All are usually leaded for deep fishing in early spring – some very heavily. However, any pattern used on the dropper position ought to be smaller and lighter than its counterpart on the point.

When a top dropper is used, the following will be found useful: Mallard and Claret 12 and 14, Black Pennell 12 and 14, Black Spider 12 and 14, Buzzer pupa 12 and 14 (in black, brown or dark green). If there is any sun about try a small Silver Butcher.

A back-wind is not chosen just to aid casting. If one had

171

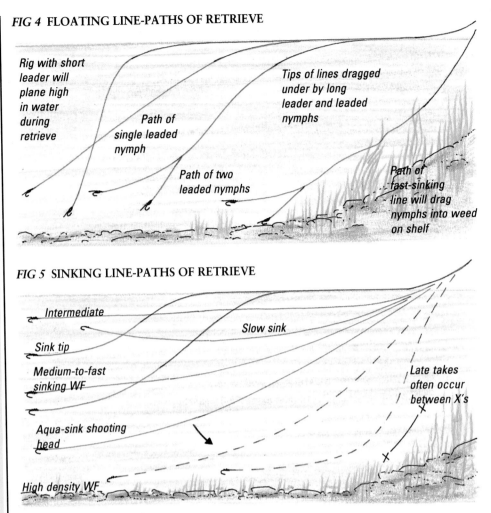

FIG 4 FLOATING LINE-PATHS OF RETRIEVE

Rig with short leader will plane high in water during retrieve

Path of single leaded nymph

Tips of lines dragged under by long leader and leaded nymphs

Path of two leaded nymphs

Path of fast-sinking line will drag nymphs into weed on shelf

FIG 5 SINKING LINE-PATHS OF RETRIEVE

Intermediate

Slow sink

Sink tip

Medium-to-fast sinking WF

Late takes often occur between X's

Aqua-sink shooting head

High density WF

A

chosen to fish across the wind in some other location, it would soon be discovered that before the nymphs could sink to their effective fishing depth the line would be hanging in the bankside where it would not be fishing at all. With a square-on back-wind a fly line will lay straight out in front of the fishing position for as long as it takes for the nymphs to arrive near the lake bed.

The retrieve is something to experiment with. Sometimes a figure-of-eight may attract the trout, or short draws on the line prove to be the most effective. Avoid a fast retrieve when fishing floating lines and long leaders, all it achieves is to make the leader plane increasingly higher in the water the longer the retrieve goes on, thus making the flies fish far too high above the trout.

Takes are never vicious. The shallow angle between the long leader and the fly line acts as a cushion and one experiences a 'going-heavy' on the line which must be responded to immediately. Better to strike at weed than chance missing an offer! (Fig. 4)

Why do I not use a sinking line and a shorter leader to achieve the same or similar effect? Slow retrieval means sinking lines go on sinking throughout the retrieve and before the retrieve is completed the line is dragging through remnant weed and other debris on the marginal shelf. A floating line will fish the flies cleanly and effectively right back to the bank-side. (Fig. 5)

However, for lure fishing from the same location, then I choose a sinking line suitable for the depth of water in front of me The difference is that having made the cast

and allowed the line to sink to the desired depth, the faster rate of retrieve usually associated with lure fishing would not let a sinking line sink farther; instead it would tend to plane at a given depth.

BOAT FISHING IN MARCH/APRIL

Open water is not usually productive during the cold-water period. Whenever I take a boat out in the early spring, it is only used as a portable casting platform and I usually head for known deep-water marks close to the downwind shore, anchoring the boat no more than 45.7 m (50 yards) from the bank. The same tactics described for bank fishing can be used to good effect when fishing at anchor, and provided that there are no bank fishermen on the chosen stretch, the boat may be taken ever closer to the shore, and along it, in search of a likely fish-holding spot. If the sport to the deep-sunk nymph proves non-productive, I try the deep-fished lure. My standard rig for this kind of fishing is the usual 3 m (10 ft) carbon rod to which is matched a fast-sinking shooting-head.

Leaders need not be very long when fished on high-density lines; 3 to 4.6 m (10 to 15 ft) is adequate. Taper can be done away with, a straight-through length of 3.4 kg (7½ lb) is quite sufficient and will be delivered straight and tangle-free if the velocity of the shooting-head is utilised correctly. When fishing the Dog Nobbler, I use one lure; this ensures that its action is not restricted. However, when I choose to fish marabou or hair wing

B

lures, I usually mount two, about 1.2 m (4 ft) apart.

MID-APRIL TO MAY

Given a normal spring, mid-April to May brings a vast improvement in the fishing prospects. Lengthening days and the stronger sunlight quickly bring the water to life. We now expect to see the first of the 'proper' buzzer rises. In warm, settled weather, columns of these midges may be seen dancing above hedgerows, hot-surfaced tarmac and ash-pad roads.

Buzzers are the most important food form where lake trout are concerned. The larvae are often physically disturbed from their lake-bed tubes and eaten in great numbers. After pupation, on their way to the surface, they are preyed upon even more avidly. For those which have survived the rigours of the ascent and hatching, their eventual end will probably be in the stomach of a trout, having been taken during or after egg-laying.

Not all rises during this period are to the buzzer. A warm, settled day will get lots of small, shell-back terrestrial beetles on the wing, many of which fall onto the water where they are eagerly sought by the trout.

TACKLING EARLY SEASON RISERS

THE BANK ROD: Casting to rising trout is considered to be the cream of the stillwater fly-fisher's sport. However, rises encountered during the early season period are most likely to come from small, isolated groups of trout.

At this time of year surface activity is not likely to get underway much before mid-morning – though it could be as late as mid-day to mid-afternoon depending on the weather. I set up two rods; one will carry floating line and deep nymphing rig; the other, a similar line (WF#8 F) but with a 4.6 to 5.5 m (15 to 18 ft) leader which is tapered 3.4, 2.5, 1.52 kg (7½, 5½, 3½ lb) if the trout do not run too large at the water being fished; or a 3.4, 2.5, 2.5 kg (7½, 5½, 5½ lb) if larger specimens are common.

The artificials mounted on the deep rig will be a combination of those already outlined; for the other rod, buzzer patterns would be my first choice. On the top dropper (bob-fly) I mount one of my Adult Buzzer (wet-fly) imitations; either a Blae and Black or a Black Duck Fly – this will fish just beneath the surface. On the middle dropper and point position, a buzzer pupa imitation. A Poly-rib Buzzer Pupa (own pattern) would be first choice, but at this point of the season the trout will take almost any buzzer imitation. Colour and size are important, Size 14 and 12 black, dark olive/green, claret and brown are among the most effective colours. I usually mount a Size 12 on the point, and a 14 on the dropper. (See seasonal chart for recommended A/B choice – Fig. 6, p. 174)

The most favourable weather condition to encourage an early season rise is a light, south-westerly breeze which is both warm and humid. A touch of sun, peeking through broken cloud, will certainly help. Given these conditions I try to find a bank where the wavelets are lapping at an oblique angle, carrying pupae and hatching flies from deep, open water to within easy casting distance – and bringing with them a fair following of feeding trout.

Trout moving to ascending and hatching buzzers are renowned for travelling straight up-wind. It is therefore advisable to place one's imitations upwind of target fish, allowing the leader to sink momentarily just below the surface before commencing a slow figure-of-eight retrieve.

A final word regarding selection, or re-selection of the artificial fly; it cannot be over-stressed just how important and helpful an early examination of the stomach contents of a freshly caught trout can be.

If a fish contains a predominance of terrestrial shell-back beetles, it may pay to swap the buzzer imitations for small, dark-coloured, hackled flies, such as a Size 14 or 12 Zulu, Black and Peacock Spider or a standard Black Spider. Such a cast of flies should be fished extremely slowly just below the surface in the general vicinity of surface activity.

It may also pay to try a small 'semi-dry' fly fished static in the surface film, so that it mimics a small beetle trapped by the surface tension. A Size 14 Zulu, a Bibio, or a Brown Palmer, is an ideal pattern for this approach; being small, therefore light in weight, their palmered body hackles allow them to float in the surface film without the aid of a floatant which could make them stand too proud.

Boat fishing during the mid-April to May period is quite unpredictable; it may be like the preceding period if the weather is unkind; or, given conducive conditions, one may be fishing to buzzer rises either at anchor or even on the drift. The most productive areas will be the same as described for the bank rod, though they could be a little farther out on open water and a boat drifted or anchored in such a spot during a buzzer rise will offer the chance of good sport. Resist the temptation to take the boat closer in to where bank sport is seen, observe etiquette and do not approach within 45.7 m (50 yards).

MAY: THE MONTH OF PLENTY

Buzzer hatches are prolific and varied, and the trout's appetite insatiable. Given the right conditions, the fish may rise all day. Without doubt, although buzzers are the most important food form during May and June there are many insect species appearing throughout the month. Perhaps the most important of the new arrivals is the lake olive dun; an up-winged fly. Lake olives may hatch the whole season through; but the largest hatches usually occur in May and June, and at the 'back-end' from about the third week in August, through to the end of September. Both the bank and boat fisherman can take full advantage of a rise to the lake olive.

A well-balanced rig usually has a nymph imitation on the point (occasionally lightly weighted), a winged fly on the middle dropper to represent a casualty of the hatch or a drowned adult and a 'hatching' imitation on the top dropper. Useful artificials include: for the point – a Pheasant Tail Nymph, a Border Angler's Nymph or the Grey Goose Nymph all dressed in Sizes 14 and 12 – some lightly weighted. For a drowned adult imitation on the middle dropper, a winged-wet Greenwell's Glory and its yellow-tagged variation will take some beating, but I experience good sport with my winged-wet Gold-ribbed Lake Olive. For the top dropper (bob-fly) position I use the winged-wet White Tailed Gold Ribbed Hare's Ear. This fishes well at almost any time and it is a superb hatching lake olive imitator. I use the standard darkish fur for early season, getting progressively lighter as the season progresses.

Trout feeding on ascending olive nymphs and the freshly hatched duns tend to quarter the water as they feed and although one casts ahead of a moving trout, the fish will not always cross the path of the leader. During the early part of a rise, cast in the general vicinity of moving fish, allow the artificials to drop-in and then commence a fairly steady figure-of-eight retrieve in the hope that a patrolling trout will come across the offerings.

If the rise intensifies I fish a full team of three winged imitations, casting them centrally over the boil of a rise, retrieving instantly by quickly hand-lining a short length of line at a time. In a frenzied feeding mood, trout take a fly savagely. This technique is particularly effective when one follows the wind-blown duns out over open water, fishing from a broad-side drifting boat.

Sometimes the trout feed steadily and confidently on the freshly hatched dun on the surface. A prime area for this activity is usually fairly shallow, becalmed water of an upwind shore. The rise form associated with this is an

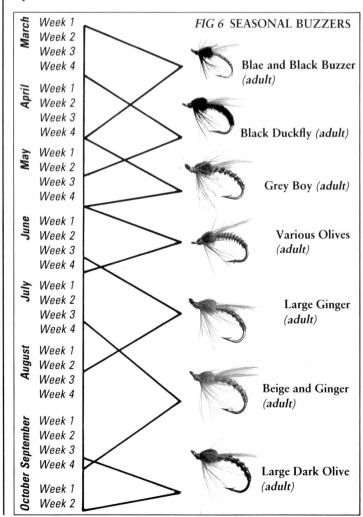

FIG 6 SEASONAL BUZZERS

March Week 1	
Week 2	Blae and Black Buzzer (adult)
Week 3	
Week 4	
April Week 1	
Week 2	Black Duckfly (adult)
Week 3	
Week 4	
May Week 1	
Week 2	Grey Boy (adult)
Week 3	
Week 4	
June Week 1	
Week 2	Various Olives (adult)
Week 3	
Week 4	
July Week 1	
Week 2	Large Ginger (adult)
Week 3	
Week 4	
August Week 1	
Week 2	Beige and Ginger (adult)
Week 3	
Week 4	
September Week 1	
Week 2	
Week 3	
Week 4	Large Dark Olive (adult)
October Week 1	
Week 2	

unmistakable, unhurried rise where just the neb of the trout breaks the surface.

Here, I usually cast a single dry-fly fished on a very fine, degreased tippet. On some days the best results come from casting to individual risers, on others the fly is best left undisturbed in an area of trout activity. In either case, when the trout takes the fly one must allow enough time for the fish to turn down before attempting to set the hook. An instant response usually results in a pricked fish, or no resistance at all on the line.

Not all surface activity in May will be due to aquatic flies, nymphs or pupae. There are two highly important terrestrial flies of which trout are very fond. The hawthorn fly can induce good rises when blown onto the water in large numbers. An appropriate dry-fly imitation is usually the best way of tackling such a rise, though I have often had good sport fishing a sunk imitation quite slowly just under the surface. In the absence of a suitable imitation, try a Size 12 Mallard and Claret, Connemara Black or Black and Peacock Spider.

Another important terrestrial, which appears about mid-May, is the tiny black gnat. Both the black gnat and hawthorn fly have a tendency to swarm in vast numbers in warm weather. The black gnat seems to be attracted to water and dances in columns low over the water, just a short way out over the margins. Trout become preoccupied with black gnats when large numbers are blown onto the water. Both the wet and dry-fly approaches are successful. A simple hackled pattern dressed on a Size 16

or 14 for both methods usually works. However, I have a special winged wet pattern I turn to when the trout are well and truly 'on' the black gnat.

The end of May and first half of June see the appearance of the mayfly. Trout take time to get used to the adult fly, perhaps intimidated by its large size. During this period the ascending nymphs are heavily preyed upon. So as soon as mayfly duns appear anglers should be searching the water with a suitably sized Mayfly Nymph or, as I prefer, a similar-sized Pheasant Tail Nymph. Recommended hook sizes for mayfly nymph imitations are Size 8 and 10 L/S – 2, 3 and 4X L/Ss are useful. (Fig. 7)

Once the trout have accepted the freshly hatched duns and spent spinners, good sport can be assured for a week or two. Casting an imitation dun or spinner into the path of a cruising trout and then watching it sucked down, can be heart-pounding. In all dry fly fishing, give the trout time to turn down before attempting to set the hook.

JUNE: THE WATER WARMS

Perhaps the most significant change in June is the water temperature and the effect this has on the trout's feeding pattern. As the water temperature rises, day-time activity becomes less intense, giving way to excellent early morning and late evening rises. There are also three new, significant food forms to interest the fish, two fitting in with the evening feeding pattern – the caenis and the sedge. The other important species is the damsel fly nymph, which fills the usually quiet mid-day niche.

The first half of June must not be ignored, it can provide the best buzzer fishing of the season. Points of land overlooking bays are the real hot-spots. Most buzzer hatches in June are usually widespread and given a ripple excellent sport can be had from a drifting boat. However, established water currents, created by waves being pushed around a point of land, often hold large numbers of feeding trout and should not be ignored. (Figs 8, 9, 10, p. 176)

If the wind speed reaches 16 kph (10 mph) or more, wind-lanes will form out on open water if the fishery is large enough. These can be highly productive areas, yet not all lanes will be used by trout, and the angler must search for the most productive drifts.

A

B

FIG 7 **CAPTAIN HAMILTON NYMPH HOOKS**
Medium-length hooks for large nymph patterns

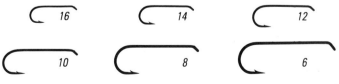

A A medium olive male dun. A very important fly as far as the trout fisherman is concerned. Extends throughout the season from April to October. A fly eagerly taken by trout and grayling alike.   **B** An artificial medium olive fly, tied by John Goddard.

By the middle of the month caenis and the sedge are well established, fitting perfectly into the summer feeding-pattern of the trout. Few anglers welcome the arrival of the caenis, the fisherman's curse, because of the frustratingly difficult rises they create. But the best caenis hatches occur during perfect summer fishing conditions, and they bring the trout to the top and in a feeding mood.

I do not worry over trout feeding on a soup of duns and spent spinners; on the contrary, I begin to fish in the late afternoon with a cast of Caenis Nymphs (own pattern), prospecting in and around sheltered and somewhat weeded bays. I fish the Nymphs until the surface of the lake is littered with the natural, creamy-coloured, freshly hatched duns and the trout are feeding madly. Then, rather than trying to get a trout to accept my dry imitation from among millions of naturals, I set up two rods to deal with the last two 'acts' of a typical summer evening's performance.

I mount sedge imitations on the first rod, usually a sedge pupa imitation on the point and first dropper, with a winged wet sedge, Invicta or Silver Knicker on the top dropper. On the other rod I fish buzzer imitations, usually two Size 10 black or dark claret buzzer pupa on the point and first dropper positions and a 10 Large Ginger Adult

FIG 8 BANKSIDE HOT-SPOTS

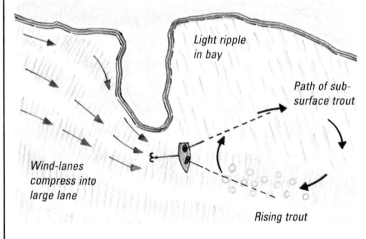

Figs 8, 9, 10 Rods 1, 2, 3, 8, 9, 12, 13 occupy the hot-spots and can cover rising fish with ease. Rods 4, 5, 6, 7, 10, 11 will have great difficulty – or even find it impossible – to do likewise. Pre-season visits can supply information about prevailing winds, the nature of the bottom and its contours, the various depths, the position of feeder streams or natural springs – all can be assessed and remembered when the time comes to cast a fly.

FIG 9 HOT-SPOTS ROUND A SHARP POINT OF LAND

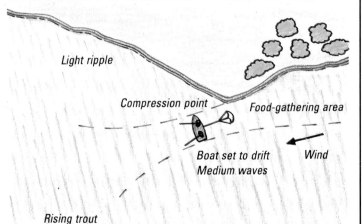

FIG 10 HOT-SPOTS ROUND A SMALL BULGE OF LAND

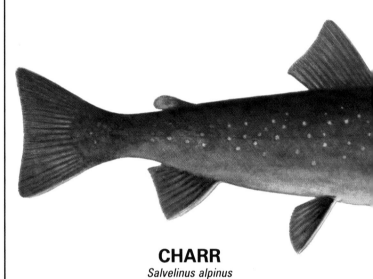

CHARR
Salvelinus alpinus
A minutely scaled member of the salmon family found in a few waters of the British Isles, where the charr population can be considered as land-locked, these are migratory fish that were stranded in a number of locations after the last Ice Age. Charr are found in some parts of Scotland, the north-west of England, Wales and Ireland. They inhabit deep, cold glacial lakes where the lack of rich feeding prevents them from growing to sizes attained in other parts of Northern Europe where the species is often sea-dwelling for part of the year, returning to freshwater to spawn. Resembling the trout in shape, there is a white fringing to the pectoral, ventral and anal fins. In the winter a vivid red breeding colour appears on the fins and belly. A charr of 0.9 kg (2 lb) is a specimen.
Bait: Artificial flies and small spinners.

The stomach content of a pot-bellied trout taken on Lough Conn produced hundreds of minute charr fry.

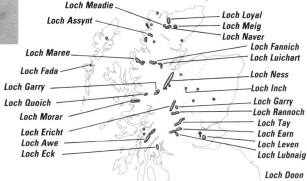

MAP SHOWING DISTRIBUTION OF CHARR, *SALVELINUS ALPINUS*, IN THE BRITISH ISLES, BOTH EXTINCT AND EXTANT

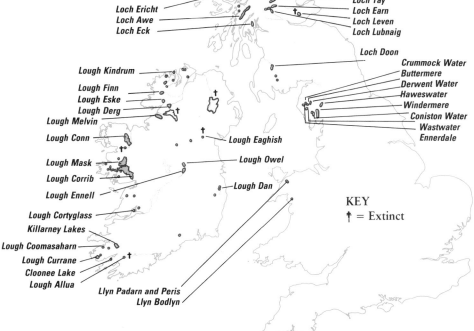

Loch Girlsta

Loch Hellyal

Loch Meadie
Loch Assynt
Loch Loyal
Loch Meig
Loch Naver
Loch Fannich
Loch Luichart
Loch Maree
Loch Fada
Loch Ness
Loch Garry
Loch Inch
Loch Quoich
Loch Garry
Loch Morar
Loch Rannoch
Loch Tay
Loch Ericht
Loch Earn
Loch Awe
Loch Leven
Loch Eck
Loch Lubnaig

Loch Doon
Crummock Water
Buttermere
Derwent Water
Lough Kindrum
Haweswater
Lough Finn
Windermere
Lough Eske
Coniston Water
Lough Derg
Wastwater
Lough Melvin
Ennerdale
Lough Conn
Lough Eaghish
Lough Mask
Lough Owel
Lough Corrib
Lough Ennell
Lough Dan
Lough Cortyglass
Killarney Lakes
Lough Coomasaharn
Lough Currane
Cloonee Lake
Lough Allua
Llyn Padarn and Peris
Llyn Bodlyn

KEY
† = Extinct

NORTH AMERICAN BROOK TROUT
Salvelinus fontinalis

This species was introduced into British freshwaters from the eastern States of the US in 1884, at about the same time as the rainbow trout was brought to Europe. Another introduction was made from the Continent, in 1869. The brook trout is not a trout but a charr and is sometimes called the speckled trout or speckled charr. The species does not seem to have survived the initial introductions, although there are a few fisheries that have more recently established a thriving population of this fine fighting game fish. A specimen of 2.65 kg (5 lb 13½ oz) is recorded.

Bait: Artificial lures and worms.

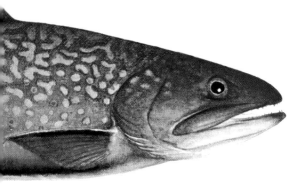

buzzer on the top. In this way I am prepared in anticipation of the switch.

On a text-book evening, while the trout are still gorging on caenis, a steady stream of mature sedge flies will trickle out over the water. Often, a new hatch of sedge flies commences at the same time. The first switch of the evening is made as soon as there is enough sedge activity to divert the trout's attention away from the caenis.

The trout's rise to the sedge in its various forms may last into the dark, providing fast and exciting sport. But, as suddenly as it started, it can cease. The sedge-suggesting patterns which have proved so successful are ignored, even though rising fish can be seen and heard all around. The third and final switch has now taken place and it is time to pick up the other rod, already rigged for a buzzer rise.

The trout are still feeding on large buzzers when most anglers are leaving the water. Now, anglers can fish by sound for rising trout, or by instinct if they can. Or they can position themselves facing the western sky-line so that the rise forms are silhouetted.

Not all anglers can fish at the prime times, many find themselves at the water-side in the worst period, mid-

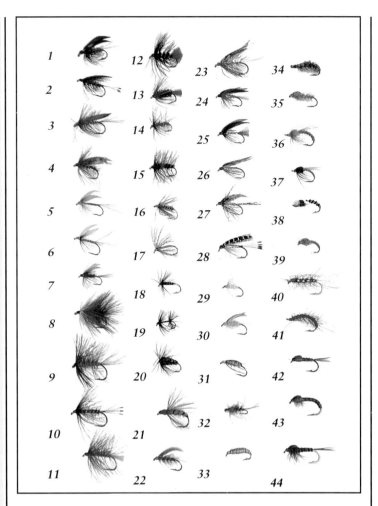

TROUT WET FLIES, NYMPHS AND BUZZERS

1	Watson's Fancy	24 Kingfisher Butcher
2	Mallard and Claret	25 Silver Butcher
3	Wickham's Fancy	26 Silver Knicker
4	Green Peter	27 Silver March Brown
5	Ginger Quill *(winged wet)*	28 Teal Blue and Silver
6	Greenwell's Glory	29 Wingless Cameo Lady
7	Iron Blue Dun	30 Cameo Lady
8	Loch Ordie	31 Corixa
9	Golden Olive Bumble	32 Gold-Ribbed Hare's Ear
10	Claret Pennell	*(original)*
11	Wingless Wickham's	33 Killer Bug *(Sawyer)*
	(amber tag)	
12	Zulu	34 Red Spot Shrimp
13	Red Tag	*(N. Patterson)*
14	Grenadier	35 White-Tailed Gold-Ribbed
15	Bibio	Hare's Ear Nymph
16	Waterhen Bloa	36 Large Ginger AB
17	Partridge and Orange	37 Black Duckfly Adult Buzzer
18	Black Spider	38 Poly-Rib Buzzer Pupa
19	Knotted Midge	39 Olive Buzzer Pupa
20	Black and Peacock Spider	40 Shipman's Buzzer
21	Drone Fly *(T. Saville*	41 Seal's Fur Bloodworm
	winged wet)	42 Hot-Spot Pheasant Tail
22	White-tailed Gold-Ribbed	Nymph
	Hare's Ear *(winged wet)*	43 Cove Nymph
23	Silver Invicta	44 Pheasant Tail Nymph

Wet flies, nymphs and buzzers tied by Bob Carnill

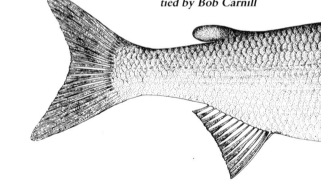

morning to mid-afternoon. Yet, given favourable conditions, there is a very good chance that fair numbers of damsel fly nymphs will be migrating shorewards to hatch (transform, being a better term) affording the chance of some unique sport.

These sightings tell the angler to fish a single damsel fly nymph imitation through the marginal waters. Whenever I fish the artificial in a situation like this I use one on the point of a very long leader, say 4.6 to 6 m (15 to 20 ft), depending upon conditions. In a calm or near calm, the leader is lengthened, and in a reasonable ripple or light wave it may be shortened. The most productive retrieve is a long, steady draw on the line, keeping the nymph just beneath the surface, where the trout will be.

JULY: THE PATTERN IS ESTABLISHED

Fishing can be easy, it can be difficult, it can be frustrating or even heart-breaking, it all depends on the weather and the adaptability of the angler. One thing is certain, the summer feeding-pattern is well established, with early morning and late evening providing the bulk of our sport. The trout's menu is much the same as it was in June, with sedges and buzzers rating high on the list. Daphnia have been available all season; it is now that trout tend to feed on them seriously.

Another form of food which tends to keep the daytime period alive are the millions of coarse-fish fry. Most hatched out around the first week in June, but it is only now that trout take them really seriously. Fry-bashing

VENDACE AND POLLAN
Coregonus albula

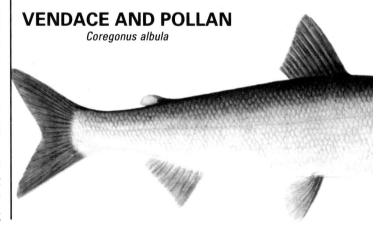

POWAN, SCHELLY AND GWYNIAD
Coregonus lavaretus

THE COREGONIDS OR WHITEFISH

Fishes of the Salmonidae: *Coregonus lavaretus* (powan, schelly and gwyniad); *C. albula* (vendace and pollan); *C. oxyrinchus* (houting), but Unesco (1984) recognises only the vendace, *C. albula*, and houting, *C. lavaretus*. All six fish have similar characteristics, like a herring with small scales but possessing an adipose fin. With the exception of the vendace they have pointed snouts with protruding upper jaws. They share a feeding behaviour on plankton and small animal-life feeders and inhabit stillwaters, mostly in the north and west of the British Isles. In Europe the coregonids live in rivers and lakes, with some migratory species. In Eastern Europe the houting is partially sea-dwelling.

trout are notoriously difficult. Having had every lure offered them the trout become conditioned to it and more subtle methods are required to take these easily accessible trout. Fishing a floating-fry imitation is one method that is extremely popular nowadays, though this approach peaks during August and September.

The technique is simple enough. Locate an area of activity. If fry-bashing is taking place there will be agitated fry in the surface film. The shoal swims away from the predator by fanning out on the surface, and showers of tiny fry leap from the water as a trout closes in, then a slashing attack leaves many injured and struggling on the surface.

The floating-fry was designed with these casualties in mind. After an attack, the trout will return to feed on dead and dying fry as they float in the waves. Rise forms, as trout take fry from the surface, are reminiscent of a nymphing fish.

Most floating-fry patterns these days use a white expanded foam of some kind or another to form the fish-like shape and provide the necessary buoyancy. It is advisable to match the size of the artificial fry against that of the natural fish.

Fishing the floating-fry is not unlike fishing a dry fly. It is cast out into an area of activity, allowed to float unrestricted on the ripple or wave or simply left static in a flat calm. Once the floating-fry is taken, setting the hook should be delayed just long enough for the fish to turn

HOUTING
Coregonus oxyrinchus

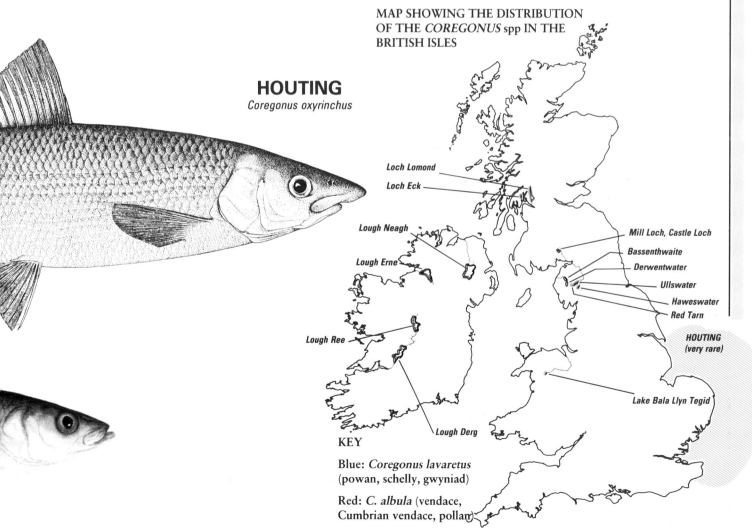

MAP SHOWING THE DISTRIBUTION OF THE *COREGONUS* spp IN THE BRITISH ISLES

Loch Lomond
Loch Eck
Lough Neagh
Lough Erne
Lough Ree
Lough Derg
Mill Loch, Castle Loch
Bassenthwaite
Derwentwater
Ullswater
Haweswater
Red Tarn
HOUTING (very rare)
Lake Bala Llyn Tegid

KEY

Blue: *Coregonus lavaretus* (powan, schelly, gwyniad)

Red: *C. albula* (vendace, Cumbrian vendace, pollan)

down and properly close its mouth. Most anglers will use just the one fry on the point, but I often use two. The second lure is on a 10 cm (4 in) dropper, about 1.2 m (4 ft) from the point. Sometimes a twitched fry will prove more attractive to the trout than one fished static. As with all trout fishing, experimentation is a must.

MID-JULY TO MID-AUGUST: THE DIFFICULT PERIOD

These are the dog-days when the trout are fat and summer-fed, and water temperature is at its highest. Early morning and evening are the most productive periods of the day. Sometimes the dog-days get a reprieve when a high wind stirs, cools and oxygenates the surface layer of water, which can make it very attractive to the trout, even during mid-day heat.

During a good blow, one of the most exciting methods is to fish the wake-lure over the front of a drifting boat. Since the late 1960s, the Muddler Minnow has become synonymous with this style of fishing. Its highly buoyant spun deer hair head makes it ideal but many variations have been tied on the basic theme. In some cases, cork and hard foam have replaced the traditional spun deer's hair. One thing that cannot be changed is the principle that makes this type of lure so attractive to the trout.

Most wake lures are what might be called water-movers, they do not skim lightly over the water, the rear-end sits within it while a broad head ploughs a furrow of disturbance in the surface. One may fish a wake-lure as a single lure on the point, or as part of a team. For team work, the wake-lure is fished either on the point with two dropper flies above or, more popularly, on the top dropper, with the two droppers fishing behind. The latter combination is somewhat out of balance so far as casting is concerned, but of the two it is generally recognised as being the most effective.

The theory is that any disturbance made by the wake-lure homes the trout on to the trailing nymphs or flies and it works, for it is common to see a trout appear from nowhere to chase the lure for quite a distance before turning down and taking one of the trailing artificials. There are days, however, when all the attention and takes come to the wake-lure.

AUGUST: THE SPORT CONTINUES TO IMPROVE

August starts right in the middle of the dog-days. Whereas the sport went from excellent to difficult in July, it can now be expected gradually to improve. Sedge flies, large buzzers, daphnia and fry still form the basis of the trout's food but from the middle of the month through much of September there is a swing to corixae feeding where this species proliferates. Large numbers of chironomid (buzzer) larvae may also be found in trout stomachs. Several species of larvae may be present in the autopsies but the red variety, bloodworm, appears to be most favoured by the trout.

The appearance of bloodworm and other larvae during

A TROUT DRY FLIES

1 Tup's Indispensible
2 Pale Watery Dun
3 Gravel Bed
4 Brown Palmer
5 Wonder-Wing Alder
6 G & H Deer Hair Sedge
7 Red Sedge (Walker)
8 Little Red Sedge (Skues)
9 Winged Black Gnat
10 Hackled Black Gnat
11 Knotted Midge
12 Winged Rough Olive
13 Ginger Quill
14 Orange Spinner
15 Grey Duster (parachute hackle)
16 Grey Duster

Flies to be fished in surface film:

17 Amber Spinner (T. Clegg)
18 Ginger Spinner
19 Terrestrial Beetle (Carnill)

B RESERVOIR NYMPHS AND STREAMERS

1 Blue and Silver Terror
2 Brailsford's Green Nymph
3 Cased Caddis (Carnill)
4 Wormfly
5 Damsel Nymph (Carnill)
6 Montana Nymph
7 Wadham's Floating Fry
8 Baby Doll
9 Sweeney Todd
10 Goldie
11 Muddler Minnow (original)
12 Breathalyser
13 Leprechaun
14 Appetiser
15 White Marabou
16 Zonker
17 Black Dog Nobbler
18 Vulture
19 Hanningfield Lure

warm, settled conditions appears to be directly linked with the gas-inflated mats of algae which regularly break away from the lake bed and float up to the surface. During August the floating fry really comes into its own. It can be a day-saver and regularly produces some of the heaviest bags of trout to be recorded for the whole season. The best sport from corixae-feeding trout is usually to be found in the areas of heavy fry-feeding activity.

For many years, trout stomach contents have proved that during August there is a marked preference for the immature, larval corixae. Many are taken from the surface where they rest briefly after shedding their outer skin in order to grow-on. Trout taking these tiny corixae often do so with head-and-tail rise, which suggests that they are feeding on nymphs or pupae.

My favourite way of tackling trout feeding in this manner is to position myself so that I can cast across the ripple, upwind of a feeding area. Mounted on my leader will be a trio of Size 16 buff-beige hackled flies, a smaller version of my Cameo Lady minus the wing. When wet, these patterns look remarkably similar to the translucent natural insect. The leader is usually given a light smear of Muscilin grease, though the short droppers and 5 cm (2 in) or so of the point are de-greased to ensure that the artificials work just below the surface. One final touch is to squeeze the flies below the surface of the water so as to soak them thoroughly.

Once the cast has been delivered upwind of a feeding area, the flies must be allowed to drift freely round and over the hot-spot. The slightest retrieve of the line will make the flies skate and ruin everything. A take will register as a pulling tight on the line, which only requires leaning into to set the hook. Should a take not occur, wait until the team of flies has floated clear of the hot-spot, before lifting off to re-cast upwind and letting it come round again.

The majority of corixa patterns are intended to imitate the adult insect and they do it admirably. Some are weighted to allow for deep fishing, while others will be

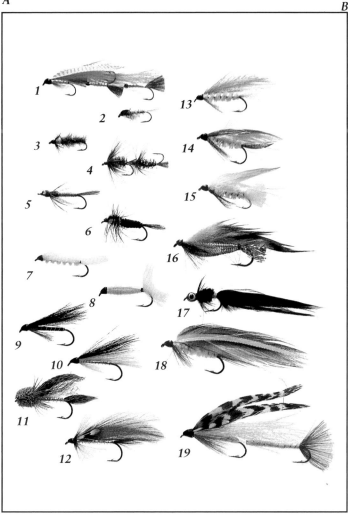

lightly dressed, ideal for shallow water and prospecting around weed beds.

What do I use when imitating the adult corixa? My Cameo Lady is not a cure-all during the corixae feeding period, but the winged-wet Cameo Lady is my first choice when the trout are eagerly feeding on adults of this species. It has little in common with the adult corixa, but the trout accept it, particularly when the artificial is retrieved quite quickly.

Fishing over-the-front from a drifting boat can be excellent during this month provided, as for July fishing, there is a good wind. With a good wave, bushy flies such as the Soldier Palmer and all its variants are ideal for top-dropper work; with straggly bodied seal's (or substitute) fur patterns on the point and middle dropper. Suitable patterns include the Grenadier, Shredge and the drowned Drone Fly.

August is also a good time for searching deep, open water for the daphnia-feeding rainbows and gaudy lures usually bring the best results. In August, however, one may be confronted with a pea-souper of an algal boom, making the need for bigger, even more gaudy lures that much more important.

The golden dun midge is the most important buzzer species for the month with the main hatches occurring during middle to late evening. Huge hatches of this fly frequently coincide with very settled conditions which often produces the dreaded flat calm few anglers can cope with. On evenings such as this the lake may be a mass of various rise forms. There could be trout slashing at sedges and/or egg-laying buzzers, others slurping and sucking down spent flies while other fish head and tail as they cleave the struggling pupae from the surface film.

The angler's fly line and leader are his main enemy when coping with a flat calm. Both stand out on the surface of the water and have trout-scaring properties. The use of an intermediate fly line can do the trick when using both imitative patterns and lures, which become increasingly effective the darker the evening, particularly for those larger-than-average brown trout which 'lift' in the water with the onset of darkness.

By the end of the month the quality of the fishing improves. The weather and water temperature are more conducive to good sport with the return of the black gnat and the lake olive. Both may appear in vast numbers, steadily increasing as September progresses. A few daddy-long-legs appear at the end of August.

SEPTEMBER: TIME TO STOKE UP

This is the most favoured month for the fly fisher. The 'over-seasoned' trout are in absolute prime condition and their appetites voracious, giving the impression that they sense the onset of winter and are stoking-up for harder months ahead.

This is the time when every trout-fisher can employ his or her most favoured method, wet-fly, dry-fly, nymph or lure. In the mellow days of this month, trout may be on the move from sun-up to sunset. Throughout September, the trout will be fry feeding or taking even larger coarse fish. Sedge flies are still in evidence, still forming an important part of the diet, as do corixae, lake olives, black gnat and that giant terrestrial the daddy-long-legs.

Fry-feeding trout may be moving at first light or before, often very close into the margins, and another bonus is that the same trout which became conditioned to lures earlier in the season now seem to throw caution to the wind and will often attack them quite viciously.

From about mid-morning to mid-afternoon lake olives and black gnats can be expected and these are rarely ignored by the trout. The techniques described for these species for the May/June period will still apply and should produce excellent results.

Given anything like a stiff breeze to a good blow, some of the daddy-long-legs which hatched the previous evening will be blown out on to open water. As with the mayfly, it takes a little time in the early days of their emergence for the trout to get used to and accept this larger-than-normal fly. Nevertheless, once the trout have got the taste of the daddy good sport may be experienced from both the bank and the boat.

Out on the boats, and on the right day, the dapped daddy can produce fascinating and extremely exciting sport. Depending on the fishery rules, both the artificial or the live daddy may be used. For this fishing, a longer-than-average rod is a must, upwards of 3.6 m (12 ft) being the norm, but enthusiasts of the dap will usually use rods nearer to 5.1 m (17 ft). The principle behind dapping is to allow the wind to carry the fly aloft, well in advance of a broad-side drifting boat, then by lowering the rod the fly is allowed to settle lightly on to the surface without any part of the leader coming into contact with the water. The fly is then deftly bobbled along on the surface, punctuated by occasional pauses.

In order to use the strength of the wind and be able to control the artificial perfectly, a special line, often referred to as a blow-line, is necessary. Instead of floss silk, modern technology has given us an ever-increasing range of synthetic flosses. For moderate wind strengths, about 2.7 m (9 ft) of floss is usually sufficient, but should be considerably shorter in high winds.

The reel-end of the dapping floss is usually attached to a generous supply of about 3.6 kg (8 lb) b.s. monofilament and for the leader, a length of 2.2 to 2.7 kg (5 to 6 lb) b.s. mono. Whichever method of attachment is adopted it is vital that the uppermost knot passes easily through the top eyes of the rod. Leader length is a debatable subject; some fishermen will advocate one as short as 1.2 m (4 ft), whereas others will go for 1.8 or 2.0 m (6 or 7 ft). It is how a particular rig is performing in a given wind strength that matters, if one feels the need to lengthen or shorten a leader in order for it to be more controllable, then so be it.

For much of September evening fishing can be excellent, with sedges and buzzers often being taken simultaneously by the trout and all the early season methods are still good. Often it makes good sense to have two rods set up in advance, one carrying sedge-suggesting patterns and buzzers imitations on the other.

During a good season, excellent sport may continue right through to the month's end. However, from about the middle of the month and through into October, on some stillwater fisheries shoals of trout are beginning to take up residence in certain parts of the lake, usually within casting distance from the bank. This shoaling behaviour affects both trout species but it is more noticeable among the brown trout.

The favoured gathering grounds of brown trout are in fairly shallow water, over a hard, stony bottom. Shoals are evident by the restless leaping of the fish, rather than by rising in the recognised manner. Most of the trout are males in breeding colours and they have not gathered to feed. They may lack appetite, but they have plenty of aggression and a medium-to-slow retrieve of a lure through their territory will be chased or attacked.

OCTOBER: THE WEATHER FACTOR

The right weather conditions are always a key factor to successful trout fishing, though October seems to be more finely balanced in this respect than most. Good sport can almost be guaranteed should mild weather extend into October. On the other hand, bitter north-east winds are to be expected and they can kill the sport. The season usually closes as the end of the month approaches, regardless of local rules which, in some areas, permit fishing for rainbows to continue throughout the winter. The close season for brown trout is variable throughout the different regions. It may be closed as from the 1st of October in one, or as late as the 30th in another. Nevertheless, tactics for brown trout remain the same as for the latter part of September.

Brown and rainbow trout are the two most common species stocked in our lakes. Of the two, the rainbow is the most desirable quarry as we reach the last week or so of October. Most rainbow trout reach spawning condition later than the brown trout and therefore retain their condition considerably longer. Many fisheries have now introduced Triploids (genetically engineered asexual trout) and similar all-female rainbows to their waters. This has a beneficial effect on the quality of the back-end winter fishing where it is encouraged and the early part of the following season. Triploids being asexual retain their condition throughout because the reproductive organs are undeveloped and the all-female stock fish either shed their ova or re-absorb it, and by so doing, they too quickly regain condition.

Given a normal October the stomach contents of trout will reveal an ever-decreasing amount of food with each passing week. In the early part of the month, fish fry and fingerlings will still be eaten, and so too will snails. During the more settled milder days, there may be rises to buzzers and the last of the sedges, the latter emerging in the early afternoon sunshine and not the evening, when the air-temperature usually drops very low, very quickly.

There are exceptions to the rule. Not all seasons are the same so we must always be alert and prepared to take advantage of the unexpected. In most years I have stopped

A Fishing the wet fly across and downstream to a trout that had risen repeatedly, indicating its position, to take struggling, emergent flies on the streamy surface current.
B Fishing the dry fly upstream and across the River Suir in late afternoon. Flies hatched sporadically throughout the sunlit hours but emerged in thousands, to induce a feeding frenzy in the hungry trout as twilight came to the river.

A

trout fishing by the middle to last week in October, preferring only to follow the traditional trout season from spring through to autumn.

RIVER TROUTING

The seasonal behaviour of trout in running-water is very similar to that of lake trout: during the cold-water period of early spring they will be found close to the river bed, usually in the deeper and slower parts of the pools. Apart from their usual diet of bottom-dwelling invertebrates, spring-caught river trout are frequently found to contain bullheads, stone loaches and small grayling.

As the water warms in the spring sun, the trout move higher in the water and begin to feed greedily on ascending nymphs, hatching and freshly hatched flies. During this period fish quickly regain their former strength and condition, having been depleted by spawning and the winter which followed, and so they begin to occupy lies in the faster, shallow water. This will usually be at the head and the tail of the pools or close to the bank in the pool itself where the main current channels a steady supply of water-borne food to them.

Like the stillwaters, rivers also have their dog-days, although they usually arrive a little earlier in the season. From about the middle of June through to August, the day-time period can be very dour indeed. A fish or two may be found rising if one walks the banks in search of them. Evenings are now usually the most productive part of the day. In settled conditions an evening rise is to be expected and sport is brisk provided that the correct artificial fly is found in time.

Late August and all of September sees renewed daytime surface activity from the trout. This is due to several factors: (1) on many rivers, if not most, flies will be in an abundance, (2) the shortening days and cooler nights lower the water temperature and appear to re-vitalize trout, and (3) like their stillwater counterparts, river trout can sense the approach of winter and to survive the rigours of spawning and winter they must feed well.

Sport can be good to the end of the season if the weather is fine and water levels remain favourable. Where grayling occur they can provide excellent sport for the fly-fisher through the winter while the river is in good order.

B

THE RIVER TROUT'S DIET

The nymphs and larvae of aquatic flies form a very important part of the river trout's diet, with the up-winged or 'day-flies' being the most important. These are followed closely by the caddis flies, the stoneflies and alder flies.

Not all waters will have the above insect species. Some will be rich with aquatic insect life, while others will be poor. Where scarcity occurs naturally, terrestrial flies and beetles will take the place of aquatic food forms. In areas where this occurs, the trout are usually very free rising and feed less selectively. Among the many terrestrials which the trout will take are the black gnat, hawthorn fly, cow-dung fly, heather fly, various crane flies, soldier and sailor beetle, bees, flying ants, aphids, bracken clocks (beetles), caterpillars, and others. On many waters, too, freshwater shrimp (Gammarus) and water-snails will also form an important part of the trout's diet.

TACKLE: For the larger rivers, stillwater (reservoir/lake) rods, lines and terminal tackle will be perfectly suitable. For the smaller rivers, streams and becks, particularly those generously canopied by overhanging trees, a much shorter rod and a light line are not only more desirable, they are a necessity.

TACTICS: Many of the dry-flies, wet-flies and nymphs used for lake fishing will be equally useful on running-water, but their application is different. The flow which makes rivers so appealing and inviting is the beginner's greatest enemy before it becomes his friend. To present an artificial fly correctly so that it attracts trout, as opposed to putting them down, we must be able to recognise and understand the different kinds of current and make them work for us.

DRY-FLY FISHING

The classic dry-fly approach is to delicately cast the fly between 0.3 to 0.6 m (1 to 2 ft) upstream of a rising trout, without any portion of the nylon leader crossing the fish, and then collect the loose fly line with the free hand as it is carried back downstream on the current. The line may be collected in loops or by using the figure-of-eight method. Whichever is adopted, the speed at which the line is collected must match that of the current, but without disturbing the artificial. The angler must be in full control at all times and able to set the hook should the fly be taken.

Even on a glass-smooth glide it is rare for the current to run at one speed between the angler and his target fish. Trout are notorious for taking up feeding positions where the flow of the main current is altered. The usual reason for the fish choosing such a spot is because water-borne food is being channelled and carried quickly along on the swifter current created by the diversion.

Each rising fish must be approached on an individual basis and with an open mind for no two lies are exactly the same. The best results may come from carefully choosing an angle of approach which will allow a straight line and leader to be delivered. Where this is not possible or if the current is particularly tricky, then the 'snaky' (loose) line and leader approach may be the only solution.

The snaky-line not only comes in handy when fishing the up-stream dry-fly, but also when we need to fish across the current or even downstream. Turning one's back on the current and casting downstream may be considered unethical on some fisheries. However, for the majority of rivers where wet and dry-fly are the accepted methods, learning this technique can come in very useful in a situation where an up-stream or across-the-current approach is not possible.

To throw a snaky-line we must cast the fly in the usual way, but aimed to over-shoot the mark by about half a metre (1 or 2 ft) when fishing up or across the stream, or a metre (3 or 4 ft) when casting downstream. Then as the cast unfurls, instead of following through as normal, the rod is stopped rather higher. This has the effect of a shock absorber and a spring, i.e. it will stop the fly line while still quite high above the water, and the recoil of the rod will suddenly pull the fly line and leader backwards to fall lightly on to the water in a snaky formation. The recoil which creates the loose-line effect can be increased by pulling the rod tip back at the end of the cast, and then quickly lowering it. Any variation in the current between angler and trout will then work on straightening out the snaky line, thereby allowing the fly to float unhindered over the trout's position.

LEADERS: Presenting the dry-fly demands accurate and delicate casting. One of the surest ways of achieving this is to use a good-quality knotless tapered leader. Cast correctly, this type of leader will give a perfect turn-over and an accurate delivery, allowing the fly to alight gently. Knotless tapered leaders are expensive and not everyone would be prepared to buy a leader that costs approximately ten times as much as one made up by joining three short lengths of mono together. Sometimes I am caught without a knotless leader during a good wet-fly fishing spree, then the trout suddenly turn their attention to flies floating on the surface. When this happens I put a leader together myself. A taper of 3.4, 2.5 and 1.5 kg (7½, 5½ and 3½ lb) b.s. will be more than adequate. However, should the trout be preoccupied with really minute food forms, an additional short section of 0.7 or 0.9 kg (1½ or 2 lb) b.s. ensures that the artificial fly fishes correctly.

It cannot be over emphasized just how important tippet diameter is. Always err on the finer side rather than the heavy. If too heavy it will dominate the fly, preventing it from sitting correctly on the surface of the water; in addition it may also restrict the fly from following faithfully the small movements of the current.

Greasing the dry-fly leader has been a controversial issue for a very long time. For example, in a lively stickle at the head or neck of a pool it really doesn't matter. In this kind of water the fly passes very quickly over the trout and in any case leader-shadow, which is what we are trying to avoid, will be lost among all the other shadows thrown

A

B

A Verdant bankside growth and lush water plants create the perfect trout fishery. The streams draining surrounding hills ensure a plentiful, clean and continuous water flow to the Suir.

B Shallow margins on a limestone lake provide prolific weed growth. In these conditions one can expect huge numbers of invertebrate life. Wading is taboo and trout feed in very shallow water.

across the river bed by the action of the ruffled surface water. In this situation it usually pays to lightly grease-up so as to prevent a drowned leader from doing like-wise to the fly.

At the other extreme is a shallow, gin-clear chalk-stream glide over a light-coloured river bed where every speck floating on the surface throws down an exaggerated shadow. Here we would be advised to camouflage the leader's presence by encouraging it to sink just below the surface. This is achieved by rubbing the leader down with a proprietary sinking/de-greasing agent, a home-made concoction, or soft bankside mud.

DRY-FLY FLOATANTS

Perhaps the greatest step forward in modern floatants was the introduction of silicone-based products. The beauty of Permaflote and others is that we can give the artificials a quick soak, after which they dry out very fast indeed leaving them thoroughly water-proofed well in advance of being used.

There are times when the trout show a distinct preference for a fly floating in the surface film, as opposed to standing on it. The more conventional patterns specifically designed for this type of fishing are parachute flies and those dressed with a wide variety of spent wings. There is, however, an ever-increasing swing to straggly bodied flies of dubbed fur. For buoyancy, these patterns rely solely on the treated, picked-out body fur.

WET-FLY ON RIVERS

Wet-fly includes nymph fishing as well as the more traditional wet patterns, and like the dry-fly, wet-fly/nymph fishing can be practised up, across, and downstream. When fishing up or across the current many of the guide-lines given earlier for the dry-fly will apply with equal importance to both the wet-fly and nymph. Any pattern fished in this manner, albeit sunk below the surface, must be allowed to ride freely with the current, unhindered by drag of any kind.

In very clear water the artificial and the trout may be observed at all times, allowing us to fish and react accordingly. On less clear or broken water, the tip of the fly line or leader must be watched where it enters the water and there must be instant reaction on seeing the slightest dip, falter, or stopping of one of them, by tightening into what will probably be a take. Sometimes a sub-surface boil or a silver or golden flash will be seen as the trout turns down after taking the fly and the hook should be set immediately, otherwise the fish may be lost.

DOWNSTREAM WET-FLY AND NYMPH FISHING

Fishing the wet-fly or nymph down and across the current is perhaps the most under-rated and most criticized form of fly fishing. When fishing the down-stream fly or nymph, a trout may be indicating its position by rising, which makes things decidedly easier, or it may not. In the case of the latter, it may well be that trout are lying quite deep in the water and feeding on nymphs being carried along on the current. This may occur at any time throughout the season, but during the early days of spring it is often the norm. Whether we are presenting our fly just sub-surface to a riser or combing the depths with leaded nymphs in search of a feeding trout, the problem is to deafeat the speed of the river's flow and the various currents it creates, and maintain the depth at which we wish the fly/nymph to fish. If we fail in this respect the current will lift the leader and flies, and even heavily weighted nymphs, and make them skate unattractively across the surface.

Leader-lift and skating flies are two natural hazards which quickly become evident when we first start to learn the art of downstream wet-fly fishing. The power of the current constantly plays on the angle of the leader and tries to lift it to the surface. There are several ways of taming the current and making the flies fish at the correct depth. We could use a sinking line in any of a variety of densities, or a sink-tip, but I use neither. The former I dislike immensely in running water, the latter I prefer to do without. My preference is for a full floating line, flies and nymphs dressed to suit the occasion, and as much upstream mending of the line as is necessary in any given location.

For really deep fishing, mending the line and leaded nymphs go hand-in-hand and form a deadly combination which allows us to search the water very effectively in most currents. 'Mending' the line means throwing a loose

Four well-fleshed brown trout caught from the Castle Fishery on the River Suir, a noted Irish game-fishing water in County Waterford. The brown trout there share this beautiful river with a fine run of good-sized salmon.

upstream loop, or series of loops, in the fly line which momentarily prevents current drag on the foremost part of the line and leader, thus allowing the heavy nymphs to sink deep without restraint of any kind. The loose line which forms the mend(s), is held in a large loop below the reel. Having mended the line to our satisfaction, it is allowed to straighten with the pull of the current. This will make the nymphs suddenly spring to life and swim enticingly across the current, close to the river bed.

So far I have been referring to nymphs as opposed to 'the nymph'. The reason for this is that in heavy and/or quite deep water, it is advisable to use two leaded nymphs because their combined weight not only assists greatly in achieving the desired depth in the water, but their distribution offers a better profile.

Why do I prefer the floating line to a sinker? First, the sinking line vanishes from view and teaches us nothing so far as surface currents are concerned. In addition, trying to lift a lot of sunk line out of a current before each cast is made is hardly conducive to river trout fishing as I see it, and in no way can it compare with the sweet lift-off and fluent rhythm one experiences when using a floater. (Figs 11, 12, pp. 189, 191)

SOME AQUATIC FLIES AND THEIR IMITATIONS

ORDER: EPHEMEROPTERA

The March Brown (Hook Size 12): Period, March/April.
NYMPH: March Brown Nymph (Skues)***; March Brown Spider**; Partridge and Orange; also, a standard W/W March Brown with the wings and hackle trimmed back to short stubs makes an excellent nymph pattern.
WET-FLY: W/W March Brown; March Brown Spider; Silver March Brown***; Gold March Brown***.
DRY-FLY (Dun): March Brown (winged); March Brown (hackled).
SPINNER: Not important.
Large Spring Olive (Hook Size 14): Period, March/April and Sept.
NYMPH: Sawyers Pheasant Tail Nymph***; Hare's Ear Nymph**/***; Waterhen Bloa; Greenwell's Spider.
WET-FLY: Waterhen Bloa; W/W Rough Olive***; W/W Gold Ridded Hare's Ear; W/W Dark Greenwell's Glory.
DRY-FLY (Dun): Rough Olive; Dark Greenwell's Glory; Gold Ribbed Hare's Ear; Blue Dun; Blue Upright.
SPINNER: Pheasant Tail***; Red Quill***; Red Spinner***; Lunn's Particular***.
Small Dark Olive (Hook Size 16): Period, March to September.
NYMPH, WET-FLY, DRY-FLY AND SPINNER: As recommended for the Large Spring Olive but in smaller sizes.
Medium Olive (Hook Size 14 and 16): Period, April to October.
NYMPH: As recommended for the Large Spring Olive but in smaller sizes.
WET-FLY: W/W Olive Quill; W/W Olive Dun; W/W Rough Olive (dressed 'medium'); Light W/W Greenwell's Glory.
DRY-FLY (Dun): Olive Quill***; Olive Dun***; Olive Upright***; Greenwell's Glory; Gold Ribbed Hare's Ear.
SPINNER: As recommended for the Large Spring Olive.
Mayfly (Hook Size 8, 10 and 12): Period, Late May for about three weeks.
NYMPH: (Hook Size 12, 10 and 8 long shanks): Walker's Mayfly Nymph**/***; Large Pheasant Tail Nymph.
Dun and Spinner; there are many patterns to represent the dun, spinner, and the spent fly, sometimes referred to as 'Spent Gnat', listed below are just a sample.
DUNS: Green Champion; Brown Champion; Irish Mayfly; French

Partridge; Goulden Favourite; Fore and Aft; Stragglebug; and J. R. Harris's Greendrake.
SPENT PATTERNS: Moneymore; Spent Black Drake; Spent Drake; and Little Spent Gnat (Lunn).
All the above Mayfly patterns (excluding the nymphs) may be found in A. Courtney Williams 'A Dictionary of Trout Flies' ***.
Blue-winged Olive (Hook Size 14): Period, May to end of season.
NYMPH: Poult Bloa; B-W. O. Nymph (J. Veniard);
B-W. O. Nymph (Preben Torp Jacobsen)*.
WET-FLY: Poult Bloa; W/W Blue-winged Olive (Skues)***.
DRY-FLY (Dun): B-W. O. Dun (David Jacques)*; B-W. O. Dun (Jim Nice)*; B-W. O. Dun (Reg Righyni)*.
SPINNER: Sherry Spinner; Orange Quill; Orange Spinner; Pheasant Tail.
Iron Blue Dun (Hook Size 14 and 16): Period, April to end season.
NYMPH: Iron Blue Nymph (Thomas Clegg)*; Dark Watchet; Waterhen Bloa; Snipe and Purple.
WET-FLY (Dun): Waterhen Bloa; Dark Watchet; Snipe and Purple; W/W Blue Dun; W/W Iron Blue Dun; Hackled Iron Blue Dun.
DRY-FLY (Dun): Iron Blue Dun; Blue Dun; Adams.
SPINNER: Rusty Spinner; Houghton Ruby; Pheasant Tail.
Pale Watery (Hook Size 14, 16 and 18): Period, May/June to end season.
NYMPH: Grey Goose (Sawyer)**/***; Pale Watery Nymph (Sawyer)**; Tup's Indispensable***; Poult Bloa***.
DRY-FLY (Dun): Tup's Indispensable; Little Marryat***; Enigma**; Daily Dun**; Goddard's Last Hope**/***; Ginger Quill.
SPINNER: Pheasant Tail; Lunn's Particular.

ORDER: TRICHOPTERA

Depending on locality, this family of flies may be referred to either as sedge, or caddis flies. In appearance they are very similar to small moths both in flight and at rest. Quite surprisingly, in view of the fact that there are more than 190 species of sedge present in Britain and Ireland (rivers and stillwaters), the dry-fly enthusiast needs but a few imitations to see him quite successfully through the season. Three sets of patterns similarly dressed to represent the dark, medium, and light coloured naturals will cover most eventualities provided that they are dressed on hook sizes 14, 12, and occasionally a size 10. Any from the following groups can be highly recommended.
Dark Sedges: Hambrough's Sedge*** (Hook Size 14, 12, 10): Small Dark Sedge*** (H/S 14); Gilbey's Little Dark Sedge*** (Hook Size 14 and 12).
Medium Sedges: Cinnamon Sedge (various); Little Red Sedge (Skues)***; Little Brown Sedge (Taff Price)**; Large Brown Sedge (Walker)**; Wickham's Fancy; Caperer.
Light Sedges: Grey Sedge (J. Veniard)***; Silver Sedge (Taff Price)**.
In addition, any of the patterns listed under 'medium-sedges' may be dressed in pale, 'washed-out' colours to represent the insipid, freshly emerged fly of most species. I find the most effective dressing for any 'dry' adult sedge pattern is a palmered body hackle from shoulder to tail, a wing dressed low over the abdomen and well past the bend of the hook, and a slightly longer, very full-wound collar hackle in front of the wings.

ORDER: PLECOPTERA

Stoneflies are of great importance to fly-fishermen who have access to fast, boulder-strewn rivers which sport plenty of good, clean gravel. Northern Britain, Wales and the West Country are well endowed with this particular type of river and it was from those areas that many of our stonefly patterns evolved. The most important members of this Order, so far as the fly-fisher is concerned, are as follows:
February Red: (Hook Size 14): Period, (Two species) Feb/April and March/July.
WET-FLY: Partridge and Orange; Old Joan***; February Red (Roger Fogg)**; February Red (J. Veniard)**.

Early Brown: (Hook Size 14): Period, Feb/May.
WET-FLY: Winter Brown (Pritt)***; Light Woodcock (Pritt)***; Dark Woodcock (Pritt)***; Early Brown (R. Fogg)**.
DRY-FLY: Early Brown (R. Fogg)**.
Needle Fly: (Hook Size 14 and 16): Period, Feb/April.
WET-FLY: Dark Spanish Needle (Pritt)***; Light Spanish Needle (Pritt)***.
DRY-FLY: Needle Fly (J. Veniard)**.
Yellow Sally: (Hook Size 14 and 16): Period, April/August
WET-FLY: Yellow Sally (Pritt)**.
DRY-FLY: Yellow Sally (anon)**; Yellow Sally (Henry Wade)****; Yellow Sally (Taff Price)**.
Willow Fly: (Hook Size 14 and 12): Period, Aug/November
WET-FLY: Partridge and Orange; Brown Owl; Dark Spanish Needle; Light Spanish Needle.
DRY-FLY: Willow Fly (Taff Price)**; Willow Fly (W. H. Lawrie)**.
Spent female: Eric Taverner****; G. E. M. Skues***.

ORDER: MEGALOPTERA

Alder *(Sialis lutaria, S. fuliginosa).*
No list of river patterns would be complete without mentioning the alder, a largish fly, very similar to the sedge fly. It has two pairs of large wings which, when at rest, lie roof-like over the abdomen and extend well past its tip. Unlike the sedge, the wings of the alder are heavily veined and lack the covering of fine hairs.

Recommended patterns:
SPECIES: Period May/June.
Alder: (Hook Size 12 and 10).
Larvae: Alder Larva (C. F. Walker)**; Alder Larva (Bob Carnill)**/****. Alder Larva (Stewart Canham)****.
WET-FLY: Oughton Alder (Richard Walker)**; Canon Eagles Alder***; Adult Alder (Charles Kingsley)**/***/****.
DRY-FLY: Adult Alder (Charles Kingsley)**; Herefordshire Alder ***; Oughton Alder (Richard Walker)**; Adult Alder (David Jacques)**/****; Wonderwing Alder (Bob Carnill).
(The latter dressing is not to be found in any reference book); briefly, it is as follows:-
Hook: 10 and 12 standard shank.
Silk: Black.
Body: Bronze peacock herl, dressed slim.
Wings: Two dark body feathers from a grouse, dressed 'wonderwing-style', tied-in roof-like and low over the back to extend beyond the bend of the hook.
Hackle: Black or very dark brown cock, wound in front of wings.
This is the only fly I now use when the alder is on the water. It has proved exceptionally effective on my home water (Derbyshire River Derwent) for trout and grayling.

NOTE: W/W prefix indicates 'winged-wet' as in wet-fly.
* The Truth About Fluorescents (Thomas Clegg).
** The New Illustrated Dictionary of Trout Flies (John Roberts).
*** The Dictionary of Trout Flies (A. Courtney Williams).
**** Robson's Guide (Kenneth Robson).

A rainbow trout cruising in clear, shallow water takes remarkably little notice of the presence over its head of the photographer.

SEA TROUT

Like salmon, young sea trout migrate seawards as smolts from their native waters, and return one year later as herling, weighing up to 0.45 kg (1 lb), or two or more years later as sea trout, reaching 9 kg (20 lb) or even more. Unlike salmon, sea trout can be caught from a much wider range of aquatic habitats.

Salmon migrate far out into the ocean to feed, but sea trout hug the coastlines taking small fish and crustaceans. In some of the Irish loughs, Shetland voes and from some Hebridean storm beaches, they can be hooked on spinning gear or on the fly. Small Mepps, Devon Minnows or Toby spoons are very effective spinning lures. Even more exciting is a sand-eel imitation or Hugh Falkus's Sunk Lure, fished on a single-handed fly rod with a sinking line.

On their return to freshwater they pass through estuaries, in some of which they do not feed and are difficult to catch. In others, such as the Scottish Spey and Ythan, Cumbrian Leven or Irish Moy they do feed and are caught on natural sand-eel baits, or the same kinds of fly and spinner that are used in the sea.

SEA TROUT TACTICS

For most anglers, sea trout fishing means night fishing on wild rivers, or drift fishing in a boat on Scottish or Irish waters. Through one summer's night on a sea trout river several tactics must be employed, though too many anglers arrive at the river at dusk with just one rod and line and a box of similar small trout wet flies. As the light fails, sea trout might be caught using small flies such as a Williams' Favourite or Teal and Silver. But when darkness falls much larger flies such as the Medicine and Stinchair Stoat's Tail, dressed on Sizes 2–6 salmon hooks, are more often successful.

Early in the night, when the river is running clear and low, a floating line or sink-tip might be used. If the river is running high and clearing after a spate – when often the fish will be running in good numbers – a sinking line might be more appropriate. Later, after about midnight, it is invariably best to fish these large flies, together with even bigger tandem-hooked lures, slowly in the deeper pools on a fast-sinking line.

In the blackest night some fish might take a wake-lure, for example Falkus's cork Surface Lure or Greenhalgh's Night Muddler. These are fished on a floating line so that they drag across the surface, creating a wake. They ought to be in the armoury of every night sea-trout angler, for on some nights they will succeed where all others fail. Finally, as dawn breaks, the small trout wet flies might take a final sea trout before the sun puts the fish down. So at least two sets of tackle are needed.

GRAYLING
Thymallus thymallus

A sleek, beautifully coloured fish with a large dorsal fin, the grayling lives in clean rivers and streams that have a fairly fast-flowing current. It is a salmonid, but does not enjoy the brown trout's same protection in both seasonable and in reputation terms. Both species live together, the trout taking first place in the minds of anglers. But the grayling is not only a fighter, it makes good eating and brings an additional period of sport for the game fisherman after the trout is denied him. The grayling is not a large species, a fish of 1.8 kg (4 lb) is a good one. It spawns in the spring, about March to late April, so tends to be thought of as a coarse fish. The grayling puts up a good fight on artificial flies and is noted for the way in which it uses the large dorsal fin to cut across the stream in an effort to throw the hook.

Bait: Flies and trotted worms, grub baits as for coarse fish.

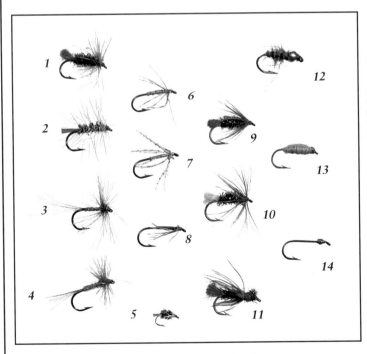

GRAYLING FLIES

Dry flies
1 Sturdy's Fancy
2 Grayling Witch
3 Greenwell's Glory
4 Kite's Imperial
5 Green Insect

Standard wet flies
6 Orange Partridge
7 Yellow Partridge
8 Snipe and Purple

Special wet flies
9 Red Tag
10 Treacle Parkin
11 Bradshaw's Fancy

Weighted Bugs
12 Hare's Ear Goldhead (Greenhalgh)
13 Killer Bug (Sawyer)
14 Bare-hook nymph (Kite)

Grayling flies tied by Malcolm Greenhalgh

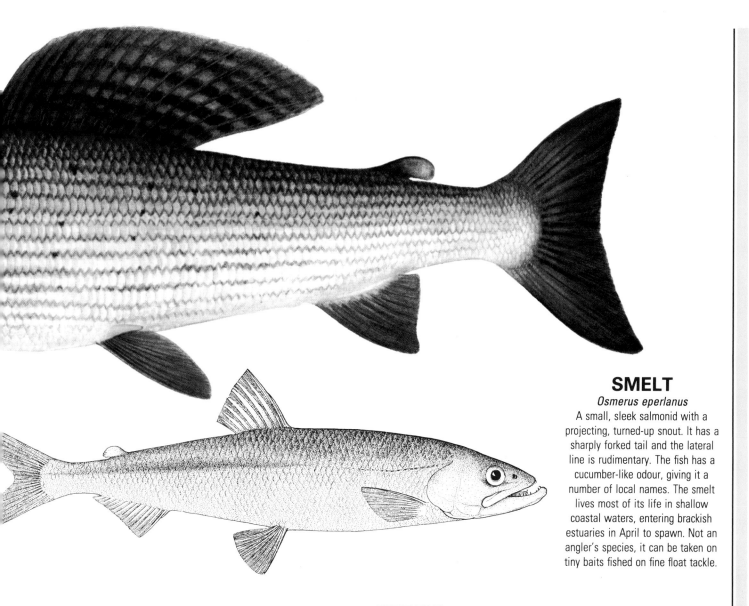

SMELT
Osmerus eperlanus
A small, sleek salmonid with a projecting, turned-up snout. It has a sharply forked tail and the lateral line is rudimentary. The fish has a cucumber-like odour, giving it a number of local names. The smelt lives most of its life in shallow coastal waters, entering brackish estuaries in April to spawn. Not an angler's species, it can be taken on tiny baits fished on fine float tackle.

DAPPING

Many sea trout are caught from the lakes of Ireland and Scotland by two contrasting methods. The first is by dapping, where a 4.8 m (16 ft) rod is necessary. The line is made of light floss silk and known as dapping, or blow-line. At the end of the monofilament leader a large bushy dapping fly is attached. The art in dapping is to keep the rod held high so that only the fly touches the water, bouncing from wave to wave in front of the drifting boat. When the fly is taken the rod is slowly lifted to hook the fish. Using the wind, dapping can place flies in areas difficult to reach by other means and strangely the pattern does not seem particularly important. The strike is important – it must never be fast and snatchy.

WET FLY

Although dapping can be successful, wet fly is far more popular. A wide range of two or three wet fly casts will work, including those that are commonly used for catching lake brown trout and salmon. However, where there are lots of sea trout and they are the sole intended quarry it is better to employ flies specially designed to catch them. As a point fly, few can rival the Goat's Toe. The bob fly must be heavily dressed so that it creates a wake as it is drawn through the water surface; the Grey Ghost, Blue Zulu or Claret Bumble are excellent in this respect. On some days only the point fly is taken, on others the bob fly.

Sea trout are exciting fish to catch, whether on maggot, worm, spinner or fly. But by far the best is at night, when a

FIG 11 FISHING FOR GRAYLING AT THE CORRECT DEPTH

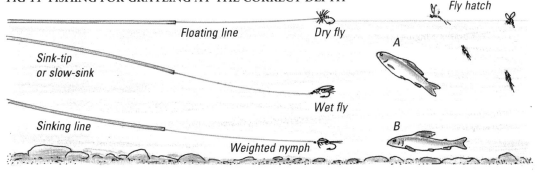

Floating line — Dry fly
Sink-tip or slow-sink
Wet fly
Sinking line
Weighted nymph
Fly hatch
A
B

Fig 11 (A) **When natural flies are rising to the surface to hatch, or resting on the surface, grayling will rise to take them and a range of dry flies fished on the surface and wet flies fished *below* the surface. (B) When there is no hatch then the grayling must be fished for *at their depth* with a suitably weighted fly.**

189

specimen takes the fly in the pitch dark, or on the vastness of a loch, when a leviathan reaches for the dap.

GRAYLING

A curious species of fish the grayling, with that small, fleshy adipose fin behind the dorsal placing it in the salmon and trout family. But it spawns in spring, has the same close season as the coarse species and may be weighed-in during coarse-fish matches. Further, on many trout and salmon waters the grayling has long been considered vermin because it is said erroneously to compete with the trout. Happily, this attitude is changing as an increasing number of game anglers come to appreciate this superb fish that permits the trout angler to continue the sport of fly fishing when the trout are out of season.

THE SEASON FOR GRAYLING

When the grayling season opens in mid-June the fish are usually still in poor condition following their spawning season. River trout fishing is still at its best then, so most serious grayling anglers do not seek them until late summer or early autumn, about mid-August. Then, right through to the opening of the next trout season in March the grayling provides exciting sport.

The grayling season can be divided into three periods. The first, which traditionally ends on November 5, is the period when there are large hatches of river insects and when dry-fly or traditional wet-fly fishing scores well. The second is through November and December when the water is cooling down and there are few hatches of fly at the water surface. Wet-fly or unleaded nymphs work well in this period.

The third period is from late December to the end of the season, when there is little insect activity in the water and the fish hug the riverbed and refuse to move even a short distance through the water to take a fly; then most anglers turn to trotting a maggot or tiny gilt-tail worm down the stream beneath a large float, but grayling can still be caught on fly on even the coldest of days provided the fly is weighted to get it to the depth that the fish are lying.

WHAT TO OFFER GRAYLING

Grayling are far less selective than trout when it comes to artificial flies. When they are feeding on a hatch of pale wateries, a Sturdy's Fancy or Grayling Witch is very successful, or during a hatch of blue-winged olives the artificial is Kite's Imperial or Greenwell's Glory, both on Size 14 or 16 hooks. Grayling are very partial to tiny midges and reed-smuts, which are often on the water in late summer. Then the same dry-fly patterns, or a Green Insect tied on very small hooks (down to Size 24) will take fish. Alternatively, wet flies might be tried, especially on the rivers of Northern England and Scotland; an excellent three-fly cast for grayling includes Orange Partridge (point fly), Yellow Partridge and Snipe and Purple (bob fly). In November and December fancy grayling wet flies are often more efficient than the insect-like patterns: flies such as the Red Tag, Treacle Parkin and Bradshaw's Fancy are particularly useful.

FISHING METHODS

With no insects on the water surface and the grayling not rising, no matter what time of year, one must assume that the fish are taking food drifting underwater in front of them. In the clear chalkstreams of Southern England and the limestone rivers of Derbyshire one can see grayling darting about to take shrimps, hog-lice and nymphs close to the riverbed. Here, use a leaded fly that will fish at the correct depth (X), a leaded shrimp, or Sawyer's Killer Bug (once called the Grayling Bug), or a Gold Head or even Kite's Bare Hook Nymph – a hook with several turns of gold wire behind the eye.

On Northern streams, fancy grayling flies are often used such as the Red Tag or Priest, with several strips of lead wire tied under the body. One of these is attached to the leader-point and cast upstream of a shoal of fish so that when it has drifted downstream to them it is at their depth, just off the bottom. If you can see the fish it is easy. Watching the fish intercept the fly, all one does is hook, play and land it. When the shoal cannot be seen one must watch the tip of the floating fly line. As a grayling seizes the fly the tip of the line might twitch, jerk downwards or merely stop. The fish has the fly in its mouth, so tighten immediately, for if you wait a split-second later the fish will spit the fly out.

A

A A typical winter grayling from the River Ribble. This fish's pear-shaped eyes, long and beautiful dorsal fin and underslung mouth are its distinctive features.

FIG 12 FLY LINES

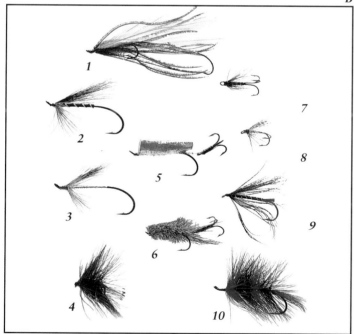

Floating fly line

Slow water

Sink-tip fly line

Faster water

Faster water

Sinking fly line

B

Fig 12 For sea trout, select a line density that will fish the fly properly. Slow waters may accept a floating line; in faster water a line more dense will be needed. The faster the flow, the denser the flyline needs to fish a sub-surface line at the correct depth. In very heavy currents, a very high-density, fast-sinker might be needed.

C A late July evening as night falls over the River Spey at Grantown and another sea trout session is about to begin.

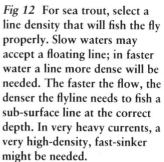

C

D

B SEATROUT FLIES

1 Falkus Sunk Lure
2 Stinchair Stoat's Tail
3 Medicine
4 Cock Robin *(dapping)*
5 Falkus Surface Lure *(cork)*
6 Greenhalgh Night Muddler
7 William's Favourite
8 Teal and Silver
9 Goat's Toe
10 Claret Bumble *(Rogan)*

Seatrout flies tied by Malcolm Greenhalgh, except the Claret Bumble tied by Rita Rogan of Ballyshannon.

D Four fine trout from a lake on the River Fergus system in Co. Clare. The larger fish is a sea trout.

CRAWFORD LITTLE

SALMON: AMAZING AND MARVELLOUS

Crawford Little on his home river, the Nith above Auldgirth. Many years ago this great Solway river was severely poached and had suffered neglect. Then riparian owners and anglers got to work and after much determination, a great deal of hard work and argument, the Nith was brought back to something like its past greatness. Will it ever yield a salmon the size of the fish Jock Wallace took in 181. reputed to have weighed 30.6 kg (67 lb) on the bank in the Bargarg area?

The life history of the salmon is a wild tale of amazing nature. No one who has seen silver-flanked salmon fling themselves again and again at a sheet of falling water as they strive to pass a waterfall, until they reach the point of exhaustion, can fail to stand in awe of the instinct that drives the fish to behave in this way. Truly, they are marvellous fish.

All salmon found in British waters are of the Atlantic kind. A group of salmon species are found in the Pacific Ocean and its rivers but there is only one true native salmon of the North Atlantic, *Salmo salar*, although a stray 0.681 kg (1 lb 8 oz 1 dr) Coho salmon, *Oncorhynchus kisutch*, is listed in the British (Rod Caught) Record Fish list, being caught off a Guernsey, Channel Islands, beach in 1977. The main Atlantic-salmon producing countries are the British Isles, Norway, Iceland and the Maritime Provinces of Canada, but their distribution is far greater. They can be found from Portugal up to the Arctic coast of Russia in the east, and most major European rivers once had mighty runs of Atlantic salmon at one time but in most cases they were destroyed by pollution. In the west the salmon ranges from the Connecticut River, USA, to Ungava Bay, northern Quebec, Canada.

Salmon are hatched from the egg in freshwater, where they spend their early years, passing through the gradually maturing stages of alevin, fry and parr, by then looking very much like small brown trout. And it is then that these young fish are transformed, assuming bright silver coats, and becoming known as smolts. They fall downstream to

SALMON
Salmo salar

From the moment the salmon is spawned in the redds to the time it grabs at the angler's fly it is under attack from the world's major predator – man. As a parr, it is taken by the tiny flies of the trout fisherman. But fed well, it becomes bright silver, is called a smolt, and begins the journey to the sea. There, it grows fast on shrimps and krill and then on small fish of the herring and other shoal species. Then comes sexual maturity and the desire to spawn. Nearly always, the salmon will return to its home river. Arriving in estuarine waters its body changes, allowing it to live in freshwater. On its oceanic feeding grounds the salmon was constantly harried by deepwater trawlers, but as it approaches inshore waters the danger becomes greater, for off-shore boats and estuary nets seek the returning fish. As the salmon ascends the river it has to pass netsmen and then rod-and-line anglers – and poachers. Its numbers have been so drastically reduced that man has to artificially breed salmon to maintain the stocks. Spawning takes place in the middle of winter and it will not feed, though the fish may have returned to the river in any month of the spawning year. Living on its accumulated fat, the fish changes its coloration to a nuptial dress before gathering on the gravels to produce the eggs and milt. Spawning is a rigorous occasion, and now as kelts few will succeed in returning to the sea.

Bait: Artificial flies, metal spinners, plugs, worms, prawns, trailed fish.

the estuary in shoals and then to the sea to disappear. The smolts have set off on an incredible journey to the Atlantic Ocean's rich feeding grounds close to Greenland.

They remain at sea, feeding and growing. Eventually, batches of salmon break away from those vast, maturing shoals, responding to the wild call of nature that draws them back to the river of their birth. It is on their return to the river to mate, spawn and give life to future generations that they may be caught on rod and line by the sportsman.

Salmon do not all return to the river at the same age. Some, called grilse, will have spent only one winter of feeding in the sea's rich larder. Because they have had limited time in which to grow they may only weigh 0.9 to 1.3 kg (2 to 3 lb) and will often be mistaken for sea trout. These fish may also be as heavy as 4 or 4.5 kg (9 or 10 lb), in which case they will be mistaken for the more mature salmon. The only certain way to tell the difference between a big grilse and a small salmon is by examining the scales under a microscope and counting the annual rings. Most anglers are just happy to have caught such a fine fighting fish and for the sake of convenience describe any salmon of less than 3.2 or 3.6 kg (7 or 8 lb) as a grilse.

A true salmon will have spent at least two winters at sea. Some will have spent three, four or more winters in salt water before returning. During this extended time of feeding they will have reached quite magnificent proportions, specimens of 9, 13.6 kg or more (20, 30 lb or more) – the stuff of the salmon fisherman's dreams and the angling press headlines.

SALMON RUNS

Somewhere, salmon and grilse will be returning to a salmon river on virtually every day of the year. This is not the same as saying that all rivers enjoy steady and prolonged returns of fish. On the majority of individual rivers we associate the bulk of returning salmon with certain times of the year, when we expect the heaviest runs of salmon from the sea to enter the river, the runs being described by the season of the year in which they occur. Here, the point becomes a little stretched because there are spring runs and springers from the opening of the season right through to May, and there is nothing spring-like about a January day on a northern river. Spring runs are followed by summer runs which, in September, make away for autumn runs bringing the population of salmon in the river to its eventual peak. Because such a high proportion of their fish return in the autumn months, on

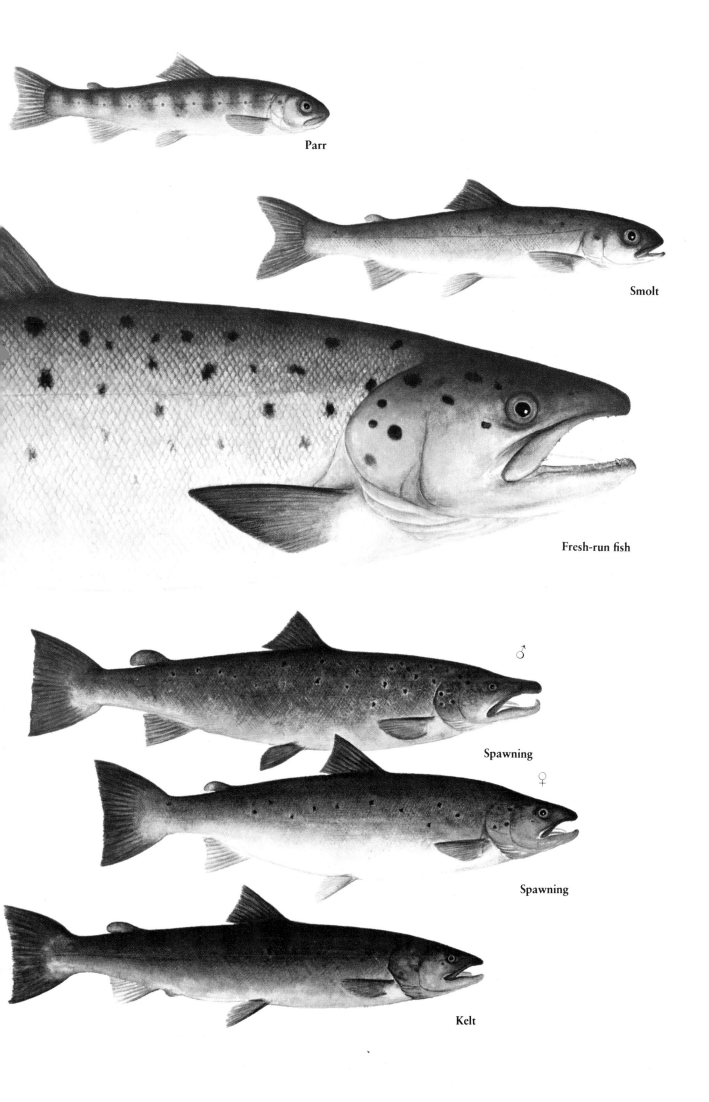

Parr

Smolt

Fresh-run fish

♂

Spawning

♀

Spawning

Kelt

Many river systems in Britain and Ireland are dominated by runs of small summer salmon known as grilse. This typical 2.7 kg (6 lb) fish is from Lough Conn on the River Moy system of Co. Mayo. Grilse have spent only one year feeding in the sea.

rivers such as the Tweed and the Nith the season is extended to the end of November.

All these are important points for the rod and line fisherman to recognise. If he is planning a trip to fish for salmon in the Solway rivers of South West Scotland he should be aware that they have only a trickle of fish in spring, a few more in summer and then in autumn the number of salmon returning soars, as do rod and line catches. On the other hand, on a river such as the Aberdeenshire Dee, the general pattern is for heavy runs in the spring, dwindling into summer and very few, if any, salmon returning in the autumn.

So, it becomes obvious why the chances on the Solway are limited until autumn because earlier in the year there are very few salmon in its rivers. On the Aberdeenshire Dee, however, the salmon must still be there in the autumn, having entered the river in spring and summer. So why not fish the Dee later in the year? The answer lies in the nature of the salmon's river life and behaviour and the presence of fish does not necessarily mean that they will show an interest in the fisherman's lure, and, more significantly, it does not mean that they will even be worth the catching. The reason for this is that the salmon stops feeding on its return to freshwater.

RIVER LIFE AND BEHAVIOUR

'Salmon do not feed in freshwater. They may go as far as to swallow worms, but they do not digest them. The scientists assure us that they do not even absorb the juices out of the worms. Nevertheless they do respond to the lures of the angler – artificial flies and spinning baits; metal spoons; and natural baits both fresh and preserved, including sprats and worms.'

Those are the words of the late Reg Righyni, writing in an earlier version of this encyclopedia. In those few well-chosen words that great and much-missed game fisherman summed up the magic, mystery and at times the frustration of salmon fishing.

Tens of thousands of words have been written in seeking an answer to why a salmon takes. It is one of the great mysteries of salmon fishing. It fills long hours with deep thoughts for armchair fishing theorists. But, at the end of the day, nobody can make anything more than broad and rather vague suggestions. And equally, for the practical fisherman theorising is not as important as discovering the when, where and what of the salmon's taking behaviour.

WHEN A SALMON TAKES

From that moment in coastal waters when a salmon stops feeding and enters the river, the fish has started on a long, downhill slope of gradual decline. Its stores of energy are being used up and there is nothing to replace them. *The salmon does not feed in freshwater.* Clever old Nature at work again! Imagine what would happen if thousands of mature salmon returning to a river were to feed. In no time at all a vast amount of food would be taken and mature fish would have no alternative but to prey on the young of their own species and thus destroy the future generations.

How does this affect the salmon's behaviour? Salmon return to the river with all the vigour of well-fed sea fish. Their hard pink flesh is encased in a coat of silver flanks and blue-black ebony back. They have stopped actively feeding to be sure, but they are still active and alert. It is not surprising that it is among fresh fish newly entered the river that the fisherman is most likely to find one that is likely to respond to his lure. Here, then, is the first indication as to when a salmon is likely to take: when it is fresh off the tide.

Having entered the river the salmon's physical decline is started but it is a gradual process, for a salmon can survive on its own fat and flesh for up to a year in freshwater. It is only the final, violent exertions of mating and spawning that finally sap the last of the salmon's energy reserves. Only about 5 per cent of salmon survive spawning, after which they are known as kelts and return to the sea.

After the first few weeks of the salmon's return to the river, while the fish is still very strong and active, it must settle down into a fairly comatose existence if it is to survive to spawning time. The fish will seek out some quiet, safe temporary lie in which to stay and seems to spend most of its time in a near-trance state. Unless there is some external factor to disturb the salmon and put it on the alert, its natural behaviour will be totally to ignore every offering that the angler might make to it. In spite of its inactivity, the salmon is slowly but steadily losing condition.

By the autumn, those fish that entered the river in spring and summer will be transformed. The silver and ebony sheen of their coat will have faded to a motley mixture of reds, purples and browns. The lower jaw of the cock fish will have developed an ugly, hook-shaped kype. Scottish ghillies will describe such a fish as an 'auld kipper in his tartan breeks'. The bellies of dark hen fish are heavy and distended with thousands of growing eggs, ripe for spawning. The sportsman does not wish for such a fish and the cook will see it as unfit for the table. If one is caught, it is far better to return it alive to the river with great care, for such fish hold future salmon generations and sport in their bellies.

But before their deterioration salmon are worth catching and keeping for months after their return. So what about this class of fish? As we have seen, after leaving the sea the fish will adopt a quiet existence and will generally ignore the fisherman's offering unless something happens to disturb it and put it on the alert. This disturbance must be of a positive nature. For example, rocks thrown into a pool full of salmon will certainly disturb them and, occasionally, it might cause one to take. But it is far more likely to put an end to any chances the fisherman might have had of catching one. This is a negative kind of disturbance. Another is where, perhaps due to low water, a large number of salmon are concentrated into one short section of water, and there is competition for resting places; the

fisherman sees disturbed fish lunging on the surface, jumping in an aimless way and again the salmon are not likely to take. These negative disturbances do little if anything to improve one's chances of taking a fish. What, then, is a positive disturbance?

We know that positive disturbance occurs through natural means and at those times when salmon are likely to run up-river. The nature of the salmon's progression from river-mouth to spawning redd must be understood, for it does not follow the steady progress of a well-planned cruise. The salmon's journey is one of stops and starts, with trots, sprints and rests, rather than a steady swim upstream.

Salmon enter a river and run up it on a rise in water level. Dark clouds gather over the hills, rain falls, filling the burns and streams that feed the main river. Salmon that are already in the river will respond to the start of the rise in water, alert and feeling the urge to be on the move. For a brief time, perhaps the first hour and small rise in water-level, the salmon are likely to respond to the angler's offering. But then the river is rising quickly; the force of the current becomes such that the fish are forced to find shelter out of the main streams. Then the spate passes, the water begins to clear and to fall.

At the height of the spate, water flowing off peat moorland will be black and carry a creamy-coloured froth. Rivers in spate flowing through richer, agricultural land can turn the colour of potter's clay. The froth clears on highland rivers and the colour of clay fades to strong

Playing a good salmon on Scotland's River Dee. Estimated to weigh 13.6 kg (30 lb), the fish was lost after a struggle of 45 minutes. The famed Dee, Britain's greatest salmon river, flows 145 km (90 miles) down to Braemar and has produced a fish of 25.5 kg (56 lb), taken from Ardoe Pool in 1886. The Dee's great attraction is its gin-clear, shallow runs.

tea in the lowlands. The full force of the flood is abated and soon salmon will be on the move. Peak running time occurs when the water has cleared and fallen to about a third of its full height. In other words, following a 1.8 m (6 ft) spate the fisherman's chances of catching salmon will be at their best when the water is showing 0.6 m (2 ft) on the gauge.

When the salmon are rushing through rapid water and leaping falls is a time of intense excitement on the river. It is in such conditions that they are most likely to be caught. Salmon show in purposeful, porpoise-like rolls as they swim up from the rough, broken water and into the pool tails. The angler sees them leap once more into the body of the pool, then up in the throat, alongside the mainstream, before they move on to the next pool and the next.

WHERE A SALMON TAKES

When salmon are running upstream following a full spate they are likely to be covering ground at a rate which may be as slow as 1.6 km (1 mile) in three hours. On other rivers they may be faster. So considering the far greater speed at which a fish the size of a salmon can travel, it is obvious that they are not continually on the move. They must be pausing and resting for about three-quarters of the time during which they are running upstream. It therefore is not difficult for the fisherman to predict where he should be fishing his lure. Consider the nature of a typical salmon river: deep pools alternate with shallower rapids of fast, broken water. Having shouldered its way up through these rapids, the salmon is likely to pause in the tail, the downstream end of the pool, to regain its strength. No wonder, therefore, that the tail of a pool is a favourite place to fish when salmon are on the move, for there the salmon may pause for a few brief moments, perhaps minutes. Swim an attractive lure in front of it and it is on!

Where else should the angler try for a pausing fish? It enjoys a fairly easy passage up through the body of the pool and then begins to feel the push of the streams that enter into the neck of the pool. It senses the rough water upstream and pauses to summon up its energy for the race ahead. Here are likely takers, these salmon that are pausing on the cheeks of the streams fanning out into the body of the pool.

WATER HEIGHT

At this stage the novice salmon-fisherman may ask when and where he should try for a salmon when there has not been a recent spate to bring in fresh fish off the tide and set those on the move which are already in the river. It might be suggested that having travelled a huge distance and spent hundreds of pounds on tackle, fishing rents and accommodation, the hopeful angler will just have to grin and bear it, but of course that is not the case. For the persevering angler, so long as there are salmon in the river there is always the chance of taking one. But it must be emphasised that water height and running and pausing

A

fish are what is needed to create good fishing prospects where salmon fishing is concerned.

There is no point in pretending that salmon fishing is easy for the holiday visitor. But then, one year, he arrives when the conditions are just right. Locals will be taking up their rods and laying aside their gardening tools and paint-brushes. The spate has cleared and the water is falling. The rich salmon harvest is about to be taken and having once encountered it there is no turning back.

Take the example of a river such as the Spey. In the early season the height of this river is dependent upon snow melt and, with fairly warm weather conditions on the Cairngorms after deep snow in winter, it will maintain water heights and fishing prospects throughout the spring. Then, once the snow is but a memory the height of the Spey and level of sport that it can produce become dependent on rainfall.

A long period of drought on any salmon river means that there will be few if any salmon entering the river off the tide. Those salmon that are already in the river will have settled in long-term lies rather than temporary resting places. The chances of finding a taking fish grow ever slimmer until rain and freshwater arrive to transform the river and fishing scene.

TIME OF DAY

As well as water height, the hour of the day affects the chances of an angler finding a taking fish. Even in a good

A A fine hen 'springer' of 11 kg (24 lb) from the River Tweed.

B A late summer evening on the River Spey near Abernethy Forest. Spey casting is essential to effectively cover such a wide and powerful river.

B

height of water there are times when salmon are most likely to take. This reflects their tendency to run at particular times. In the cold water and weather conditions encountered during the opening and closing months of the season, peak salmon activity occurs at about midday, so the angler fortunate enough to find himself fishing the Helmsdale in February or the Tweed in November should not waste time over a lengthy lunch. The last hour of light can also be productive.

Conversely, from May until the end of November, peak salmon activity occurs at dusk and dawn, so late to bed or early to rise become the maxims for summer salmon fishermen. Even when the water is low during a summer drought, fish will respond to the urge to be on the move by cruising up to the head of the pool to tarry for a while before returning to their resting places. This behaviour creates the best opportunity for catching summer salmon and grilse. In the summer it would be wise to swap the last or first few hours of the day for all the rest.

OUR OFFERING TO THE SALMON

It has already been stated that the salmon stops feeding on its return to freshwater. This might seem to create major problems. We know that there are salmon in the stretch that we intend to fish, the water height is at a nice 0.6 m (2 ft) after a 1.8 m (6 ft) spate, the time of day is best to improve our chances and we have established in which part of the pool we are most likely to find a taking fish. But

if the salmon is not feeding what manner of lure should we offer for its inspection? Well, as has also been stated, the experience of generations of anglers shows that salmon will respond to artificial flies and spinning baits, metal spoons and natural baits such as prawns and worms.

Salmon fishing, however, is undertaken within what is usually a clearly defined set of rules. Besides the law of the land, any proprietor of salmon fishings may introduce whatever rules he chooses. Associations have rules as to what lures or baits may be used, when and where. Often, this will mean that the spinning rod is acceptable only when the water is above a certain height, the worm may be used in a spate, and the prawn is banned entirely. It will be noted that there is little if any restriction on fishing the fly. Indeed, many rivers, particularly those in North East Scotland, have introduced a fly-only rule.

To some, this might be seen as little more than arrogant snobbery. Certainly on some rivers the fly-only rule would be a piece of nonsense. Generally, however, on most rivers the fisherman who concentrates on fishing the fly throughout the season will find that his catches do not suffer and he gains great pleasure from fly casting with ever-increasing effectiveness as his experience grows.

SALMON FLIES

We call them salmon flies but they bear little resemblance to any natural insect other than perhaps those gaudy butterflies found in the Amazon jungle. What we are

SALMON TUBE FLIES

Black and Yellow
(clear water)

Willie Gunn
(falling water)

Comet
(falling water)

Yellow and Orange
(coloured water)

SALMON FLIES

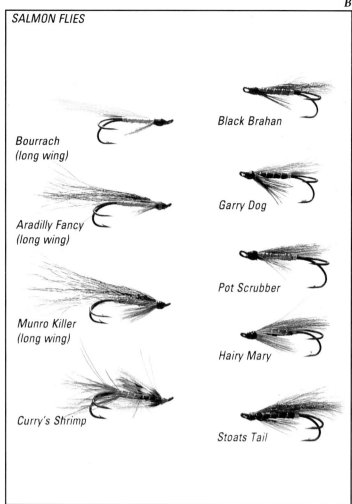

Bourrach
(long wing)

Aradilly Fancy
(long wing)

Munro Killer
(long wing)

Curry's Shrimp

Black Brahan

Garry Dog

Pot Scrubber

Hairy Mary

Stoats Tail

fishing at the ends of our fly lines are, in their larger sizes, representations of small fish and in their smaller sizes they could be said to imitate even smaller fish or crustaceans such as shrimp. We do not know what the salmon mistake them for, we can only assume that our salmon flies act as a stimulus, provoking a memory of their ocean-feeding days, that produces an instinctive, predatory response from the salmon.

What we do know, because experience has shown it to be so, is that in cold water salmon are most likely to respond to a larger fly fished deep; in warmer water they will respond best to a smaller fly fished quite close to the surface. We accept that their shift of interest occurs when the water temperature passes the figure of 10°C (50°F). While the water temperature remains below 10°C (50°F) we fish with flies that are 50 mm (2 in) or more in length and use sinking lines. When the water temperature is above 10°C (50°F) we fish with flies of 25.4 mm (1 in) or less and use a floating fly line. These are the broad, general rules of salmon fly fishing.

COLD-WATER FLIES

The salmon season opens at a time which, frankly, is mid-winter. The angler should not be fooled by any talk of 'spring' fishing and 'spring-run' salmon. Often, January and February are the hardest months of the year, even the early season river may be frozen over. The vastness of the sea is less readily affected than rivers by plunging air

A Salmon tube flies tied by Crawford Little.   *B* Salmon flies tied on double hooks by Simon Ashworth of Sowerby Bridge, Yorkshire.

Fig 1 An outstandingly strong hook, the traditional salmon irons. With a reasonably long, very sharp point. For all styles of the heavier type salmon flies. Used in deep or fast-flowing water. Very popular in the past but now superseded by trebles and doubles for the modern styles of dressing.

temperatures and salmon are not inclined to leave salt water if its temperature is higher than that of the river.

When these early-season fish arrive it will be found that they are fairly lethargic and prefer slow, deep-water lies out of the main push of the current. They do not seem prepared to move far in order to take the fly and experience shows that what flies they do take will normally be long ones.

It is only during the past quarter-century that the modern, articulated style of fly has been used on a wide scale. Prior to that time, big salmon flies for use in cold water were tied on single hooks in sizes best known to big-game fishermen. Now, single hooks are very much a thing of the past for salmon fishing. The commonest of the modern articulated patterns are tube flies. We describe them as 'articulated' because the hook is separate from the shank on which the pattern is tied, the same principle as an articulated lorry. The great advantage of this system is that once the fish takes and is hooked on the relatively small hook, leverage on the hold is minimised. In the case of the tube fly armed with a treble, the tube is free to slide up the leader in very much the same way as a Devon Minnow. In the days when big, single hooks were the only option for use in cold water an angler would think that he was doing exceptionally well if he eventually landed one out of every four or five salmon that came to his fly. Today, with tubes and trebles, we land far more salmon than we lose.

Thankfully, the choice of size of these long flies creates few problems. If a cold-water salmon is likely to take anything at all, it will probably take a 50 mm (2 in) tube armed with a Size 6 treble. Where variety can and should be introduced is in the material from which the tube is made. Brass, copper, aluminium and plastic tubes offer

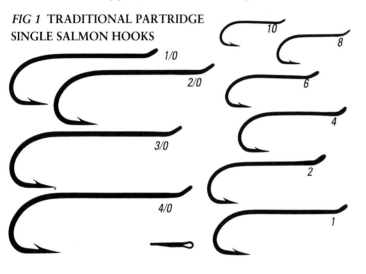

FIG 1 TRADITIONAL PARTRIDGE
SINGLE SALMON HOOKS

the full permutation of heavy, medium and light cold-water flies. (Fig. 1)

Why bother to carry tube flies in different weights? The reader will remember that cold-water salmon prefer deep-water lies and are not prepared to move far in order to accept the angler's offering. A light fly is fairly buoyant and while it will work well in quite gentle flows, it cannot produce the same action in deeper or streamier water where the line and fly must cut down through the water to swim close to the resting salmon.

What pattern of cold-water fly should be tried? If there is just one pattern that stands head and shoulders above the rest in tempting salmon during the opening and closing months of the season it is the Willie Gunn. This is an absolutely deadly fly and yet it is a very straightforward creation. Dress a black floss body on the tube, rib it with gold tinsel, tie on a wing of mixed black, orange and yellow bucktail or goat hair and there it is. Simple, but quite deadly to salmon.

The Willie Gunn is particularly well suited to fishing a falling and almost cleared water – conditions that have been described as almost ideal for fishing a taking salmon. For this period it is very good but there are alternatives for fishing in different conditions. While the water is still high and coloured, a bright fly with a gold or gold-ribbed black body and a mixed-hair wing of orange and yellow can prove very useful. The Garry Dog is another fly that works well in coloured water and toward the end of the season when autumn fish are entering the river. In its tube fly

form, the Garry has a silver ribbed black body with a few strands of red in an otherwise yellow hair wing.

At the other end of the scale in terms of water conditions, the early season river may be flowing clear and it is then that an all-black fly with its funereal garb of black wing and body relieved only by a silver tinsel rib can work to the best advantage.

WARM-WATER FLIES

When the water temperature of the river exceeds 10°C (50°F), experience shows that salmon are more active. They are now to be found in faster, streamier water and they are as a general rule most likely to show an interest in a fly of about 25.4 mm (1 in) or less in length.

Most authorities on salmon fishing have committed themselves to the belief that from mid-May until September in a normal season the size of salmon fly that we use in warm-water conditions is vitally important. It certainly seems that some salmon ignore, say, a fly tied on a Size 6 hook, but take one tied on a Size 8. The salmon's choice seems to depend on a number of factors: water temperature, its colour and height as well as the strength of the flow. From all that, it might seem that a riverside computer will be required to work out all the possible permutations, but thankfully this is not so. The river is likely to be cooler, higher and flowing powerfully all at the same time. In exactly the same way it will be warmer, lower and more gentle at the same time in summer drought conditions.

Bearing that in mind, we can discuss the size of flies used for warm-water salmon fishing. These generally range from Size 4 down to 10 tied on double or long-shanked treble salmon hooks. Make a start with a Size 4 when the water temperature is above 10°C (50°F) and the river is running high and with a touch of colour. Use the same fly also when the water has cleared but the river is running high in powerful flows such as the Spey. On smaller, more gentle rivers use a Size 6 at such times. As the water falls still further and is running clear a Size 6 would be a first choice on a big, powerful river while a Size 8 might be first choice on the gentler stream. Size 10 would be kept for those times when water levels fall under a summer sky. The application of a little common sense goes a long way in choosing the appropriate size of warm-water fly. The warmer, lower, clearer and more gentle the river that we are fishing the smaller our fly should be.

What patterns of flies should be carried? There are hundreds from which to choose. Nowadays, hair wings are favoured rather than feather. In the larger sizes, 4 and 6, the Munro Killer has gained the same reputation as being irresistible to salmon as the Willie Gunn has as a cold-water fly. Indeed, in terms of colour, black, orange, yellow and gold, the two patterns are very similar. In smaller sizes, 8, 10 and perhaps 12 for when a small river is really low and clear as well as warm, there are few patterns to beat the Stoat Tail and its Silver cousin. The Stoat has a silver-ribbed black body and a black hackle and wing. The Silver Stoat is identical except that its body is flat silver tinsel. Here, then, are three patterns, so let us keep things simple and suggest just three more: Blue Charm, Hairy Mary and a Shrimp Fly.

These six patterns in a range of sizes from 4 down to 10 can be regarded as a useful, basic set for warm-water use. Of course, there are many others and most rivers have a particular local favourite. It is always worth while visiting the local tackle shop to ask what fly, if any, has been doing well for other anglers, or what the proprietor would advise. Such shops can be a mine of information as to which fly to try, where and when and the cost of a few flies is a small price to pay for such an obviously short cut to success on an unfamiliar water.

Soon, the novice angler's fly box will be bulging. He will learn of the always-successful Such-and-Such and, very wisely, add a few to his collection and another and another. But, as with cold-water flies, he should start with a basic selection and concentrate on fishing them well rather than wasting too much time worrying whether a this or that fly might not prove that bit better. It is the fly in the water, not the one in your thoughts, that catches salmon – so long as it is fished well.

OTHER TACKLE

It might seem odd to have started with a discussion about salmon flies before mentioning other tackle, but there is logic in this. Our chances of success in tempting a salmon, or any fish come to that, depend heavily if not entirely on what we have on our hook. It is those few pence-worth of hook, floss, tinsel and fur that is the most important part of our tackle and we should work back from it in order to achieve a balanced outfit.

LEADERS

Leaders are a length of nylon monofilament which act as a link between the fly and the thick, heavy fly line. Normally we make them about 1.8 m (6 ft) long when fishing long flies in cold water and 3 m (10 ft) when fishing smaller flies in warm water.

Besides varying the length of the leader we should alter its thickness and weight to suit the fly that we are using. A large and heavy fly could crack-off when casting if light nylon is used. Tied to heavy nylon, on the other hand, a small fly will not fish well because its swimming action is destroyed. And so for those long, cold-water flies we use 6.8 to 9 kg (15 to 20 lb) nylon depending on whether we are using a plastic, aluminium or brass tube. The 6.8 kg (15 lb) nylon would also be suitable for a Size 4 warm-water fly, 5.5 kg (12 lb) for a No. 6, 4.5 kg (10 lb) for an 8, and 3.6 kg (8 lb) for a Size 10.

FLY LINES

There is very little weight in a salmon fly, even a relatively heavy brass tube fly is only a fraction of the weight of a metal spinner or ledger weight. But we need weight in order to work the fly-rod and be able to cast. In the case of fly fishing that weight is to be found in the fly line itself.

Modern fly lines can be considered as a plastic coating over a braided core with the weight of the line incorporated into the plastic.

Any line-manufacturer's catalogue will show that they have taken this concept of line much further. For a given weight of line, the angler is able to choose from a whole range including floaters, floaters with sinking tips, intermediates, slow sinkers, medium, fast, very fast, ultra-fast, express and even lead-cored lines. All that is very impressive but except in fairly exceptional circumstances the salmon fly-fisher is fully served by just two of these options. He will have a floater for fishing Size 4 down to Size 10 flies close to the surface in warm water, and a fast sinker for fishing his long flies deep in cold water conditions, the best known of this class being the Wetcel 2.

Other options to be considered are the line profile. Nowadays it is rare to find a level fly line. The weight-forward line tapers out from a relatively thin point into a section of heavy line that is about 9 m (10 yards) long behind which is thin running line. The idea is rather like casting with a lead weight. The line is drawn in until the heavy section is just outside the rod tip. The cast is made and the heavy front section flies out, carrying the thin running line with it. The double taper, by comparison, is a much simpler affair with tapers from fine points at either end leading into a long and thicker central section. This might seem a disadvantage. There is certainly not the same potential for shooting line in the cast. And yet most experienced modern salmon fishermen choose the double taper. This is because they rely heavily on the Spey rather than the overhead cast with a fly rod. Casting techniques will be dealt with later in this section of the book. For now, it has to be accepted that the double taper line will be the correct choice.

We have looked at the weight of the line but have not yet said what it should be. Line weights are defined by the AFTM system. This gives a number for a given line weight; the higher the number the heavier the line. Those lines that are normally available range between AFTM 3 and 12. What weight of line should the angler choose?

A big salmon fly is a bulky, wind-resistant object to cast and therefore we need a heavy line in order to be able to cast it effectively. Lines in the range of AFTM 10 to 12 prove ideal for presenting cold-water flies. Smaller, warm-water flies are less of a problem and can be cast with ease on line of AFTM 8–10.

But the matter cannot be left there because, as is about to be demonstrated, rods are matched by their power to a certain weight of line. Thus, a powerful rod would be best suited to an AFTM 12 line and a far gentler, softer model to an AFTM 8. If we wish to fish with perfectly balanced tackle regardless of fly size, then we have to invest in perhaps three rods: AFTM 8, 10, and 12. With the cost of modern salmon rods, that represents a very serious capital investment. One rod is quite expensive enough for most of us, and therefore we should seek a compromise. This will be found in a rod and line rated at AFTM 10. There may be times when we would prefer just that little bit more power when fishing with long brass tube flies, or a shade

A A well-matched graphite rod, reel and line from an economy range, offering the salmon angler an inexpensive start to outfitting himself for the challenges he will face in this exciting sport.

B A contented young angler with a fresh-run fish from Lough Currane, Co. Kerry. Salmon have only 1.6 k (1 mile) to travel before reaching the lough as it is connected to the sea by a very short river, including the famous Butler's Pool.

more delicacy when a size 10 double in low, clear water, but the AFTM is as near to being the ideal solution as can be found for the one-rod salmon fly fisherman, and thus he will choose AFTM 10 in floating and sinking lines.

THE FLY ROD

Much of what has aready been said in the context of lines applies equally to the choice of rod. We have already seen that it should be a model rated at AFTM 10. That only leaves questions as to length and material.

Dealing first with the question of material, virtually all modern salmon fly rods are made of carbon fibre. You can save a bit of money by searching out a fibre-glass model, but it will not perform as well. Also, carbon fibre is by far the lightest rod-building material; at the present time, if you wish to achieve true potential in salmon fly-fishing, there is no alternative to the carbon rod.

That leaves us with the question of length. There is a strong tradition on British rivers toward double-handed rods. Some traditions should be put out with the rubbish, but not this one. Longer, double-handed rods make casting a long line far easier and improve our control of the line and thus how the fly is fishing. Looking at the two extremes, gentle rods of 3.9 and 4.2 m (13 and 14 ft) loaded with AFTM 8 lines are ideal for presenting the smaller class of flies, while big and powerful 4.8 and 5.1 m (16 and 17 ft) rods are unmatched for presenting the largest flies in heavy conditions. But unless we wish to give

family and bank manager a hard time, we will again be looking for a compromise. This we find in a 4.6 m (15 ft) model – the general-purpose weapon that meets virtually all our needs for most of the time.

THE REEL

Very little need be said about the salmon reel. It should be a single-action centre-pin with a diameter of about 10 cm (4 in) in order to accommodate the fly line and about 91 m (100 yards) of backing. This backing may be monofilament nylon of 11.4–13.6 kg (25–30 lb) b.s., attached to the fly line with a needle knot. We all dream about catching a big, powerful salmon that runs us down to our last piece of backing before finally giving us the fight! An exposed rim and variable check are great advantages in playing a fish. Anything else should be viewed with a suspicion and perhaps as nothing more than gimmickry.

WADERS AND ACCESSORIES

Waders are a necessity on all but the smallest of rivers in order to cover the water effectively. Thigh waders may be suitable at times but anything they can do is more easily achieved by chest waders, and on large rivers these can make all the difference between success and failure. When you are wading a river with a powerful current or one with which you are not familiar a wading stick is invaluable, acting as a third leg and perhaps saving you from a ducking. Take an ordinary staff, weight it at the bottom with about 0.45 kg (1 lb) of lead and attach a lanyard at the top. An unweighted staff will float and catch in your line but when it is weighted only the top sticks out of the water, instantly to hand if you lose your footing. Any angler who is a poor swimmer should also purchase one of the buoyancy suits specifically designed for fishermen.

Blunt-nosed or folding scissors are very useful for cutting leaders and trimming knots. Polarised glasses reduce glare on the bright days and help avoid headaches. They also protect the eyes from a wayward hook should a bad or mistimed cast be made. A spool of insulating tape is vital for taping joints of carbon-fibre rods, something that must be done if you intend to use the Spey cast. Otherwise the joints become twisted, work loose, the tip section flies off and may well break in the process.

CASTING

Having purchased a 4.6 m (15 ft) fly rod rated AFTM 10 and both floating and sinking lines to match, plus all the other paraphernalia of the sport, all that remains is to learn how to use it in something approaching its and the angler's potential. It is impossible to learn casting and fishing with a fly rod in a few hours, and it would be silly to pretend that casting can be learned by studying diagrams and descriptions in a book or on video. The actual motions of the various casts are fairly simple and straightforward but it is the timing of the casting that baffles most people and this can be learnt only on the riverbank in company with a competent instructor.

Most anglers come to salmon fishing after previous experience with trout. For salmon, they may need to do little more than change the pattern and size of the flies they are using, sticking with conventional downstream wet-fly fishing and overhead casting. Such anglers will certainly catch salmon and particularly in summer when neither the size of fly, nature of the river, nor size of fish are likely to be too powerful or heavy. However, over a season or more they will have problems if they stick to trout tackle and technique.

Spey casting and long rods are best for the majority of experienced salmon anglers. Once the single and double Spey casts have been learned there is no looking back. Like riding a bicycle, after some initial help it all starts to come naturally. Casting 27.4 m (30 yards) of fly line and any size of fly for maximum effect using the minimum of effort with a 4.6 m (15 ft) rod is just one of the advantages and pleasure of the Spey casts: they make the overhead cast virtually redundant.

The only other cast besides the Spey that needs to be learnt is the roll cast and this is required only when fishing a sinking line. The roll is the most simple of all casts, simply raise the rod to the vertical, then punch it down, rolling up a loop of line and lifting the sunk portion on to the surface from where the Spey cast can be started. To try to Spey cast or overhead come to that, when the line is deeply sunk is to overload the rod and court disaster. You must start off with that initial roll cast.

A

B

FISHING A POOL

Experience shows that most salmon are tempted by a fly that swims over them quite slowly. Salmon flies do not generally need to be fished fast. The slowest moving fly of all is one that is hanging at the end of a straight line directly below the angler. We describe a fly thus as being 'on the dangle'. It is not moving laterally across the stream but because it is relatively light it will respond to the vagaries of the current, hovering, rising and falling as its hair-wing works in a lifelike fashion.

In order to cover all those fish that are lying out farther from the bank than be covered by the dangling fly, the fly must be cast out at an angle to the stream and fished across. Cast the fly too square and the river's central current catches the line and swims the fly across too quickly. Cast straight down the stream and although the fly will swim attractively on the dangle the water is not being covered properly. In these circumstances the usual solution is to cast downstream at an angle of about 45 deg to the flow. (Fig. 2)

Line and fly swim slowly across the river like a pendulum. A salmon may have followed the fly across without taking. When the fly comes on to the dangle, draw in a few yards of line. This causes the fly to accelerate forward in the water, and the previously uncommitted salmon may grab the fly as it speeds away. That arc of water has now been covered. Take one or two paces downstream and cast again. By casting at the same angle with the same

A, B Crawford Little, Spey casting on the River Nith.
C Line is retrieved as the fly swings 'on the dangle'.
D The rod is bent, the line tight and the gillie waits with sunk net. Salmon fishing on Ireland's Burrishoole Fishery.

FIG 2 COVERING THE WATER AND 'MENDING' THE CAST

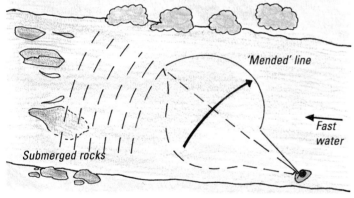

Fig 2 Never make a hopeful cast to where a salmon might be. Plan your approach.

Fig 3 Hold your salmon by this grip. Any other and the fish will slip from your grasp.

FIG 3 TAILING BY HAND

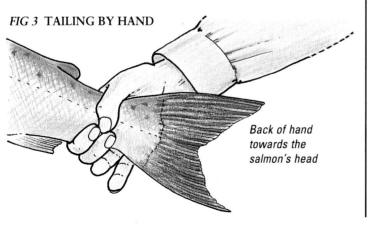

length of line, the water is covered systematically by taking a good pace between casts.

You may be asking which parts of the river should be covered. You will understand that salmon rivers are generally divided into pools and runs. The runs are shallow, streamier sections of water between the pools. It is the pools themselves which yield the majority of salmon. Now, we said earlier that the tails and necks of the pools are particularly good following a spate when fish are running. Equally, there are some pools that fish well in high water but others that only fish well when the river is low.

Without local advice the angler does best to fish each pool from top to tail, taking a pace or two between casts and persevering just so long as there is sufficient current to swim the fly. Some gentle handlining to aid the fly across slower sections can be a great help when required to maintain life in the fly.

This, then, is the basis of salmon fishing with the fly. It does not matter whether we are fishing a long fly on a sinking line in cold water or a much smaller fly close to the surface of warm water with a floating line. Start up at the top of the pool. Repeat the casts with a yard or two more line each time until you have got as long a length of line as you can comfortably handle, making your casts at an angle of 45 deg. When the fly has swum around on to the dangle, draw in a few yards of line by hand, then take one or two paces downstream and cast again. Over and over, down the pool, a pace with each cast until that wonderful moment arrives when you feel your line pulling tight and then realise that you are attached to one of the gamest fighting fish in river or sea.

GRASSING THE SALMON

It is one of those little niceties of salmon fishing that the fish is 'grassed' rather than landed whether the fish is brought ashore on to shingle, rock or anything else.

There are a number of ways of getting a salmon ashore. First, there are what might be described as the mechanical methods involving a gaff, tailer or a net. Nowadays it is rare to see a gaff in action because nearly all salmon anglers believe that sticking a metal hook into a salmon's side is a singularly cruel and ignoble end for a noble fish. Mechanical tailers have also fallen out of fashion. These consist of the noose to be drawn up round the wrist of the fish, just above the tail. Last of the mechanical means of grassing a salmon is a net. It must be big, more than 0.5 m (20 in) in diameter.

If we decide against the mechanics what are we left with? It has been said that the Almighty in His wisdom gave us two hands, one to hold the rod and the other to wind the reel-handle or to pick up an exhausted fish from the water. Experience brings confidence in this matter, but it really is a simple task to wade in quietly alongside the fish, reach down and close the hand tight around the wrist of the tail, then carry it ashore.

Another very useful alternative is to beach the fish, but this does require a fairly gentle, shelving shore. A pebble or sandy bay is ideal. With the played-out fish on a fairly short line, hold the line to the rod handle and walk the fish ashore like a dog on a lead. When the salmon's head comes out of the water it will give a few last, feeble kicks. Walking backwards steadily, the angler uses these kicks to get the fish father out of the water. With the salmon now stranded, the angler walks down to it, picks it up and carries it away from the water's edge.

THE FINAL SCENE

Just before you administer the *coup de grace* take a quick look at the fish you have just grassed. It is to be hoped that it is a fresh, shining bar of silver, blue and ebony, but it might not be and there are some fish that should be returned to the river.

In the opening months of the salmon season, fish that have spawned in the previous season will still be in the river. They are known as kelts. It is illegal to kill them and they must be returned. A well-mended kelt may fool the novice into thinking that it is a fresh fish, but things to look for are a thin body with the back and belly almost parallel, an apparently over-sized head in relation to its body size, a 'tinny' sort of silver sheen and the presence of freshwater maggots in the gills. If in doubt, you are advised to return any suspect fish.

Another class of fish that should be returned, this time in the closing months of the season, is the salmon close to spawning. These are instantly recognisable, their silver

coats have turned to the rusty colours of the rainbow, their bellies are a greyish, yellow white rather than pearl and heavily distended with ripe spawn or milt. Now, the law does not say that you should return such fish but we should be sportsmen rather than slaughterers and I for one see no excuse for killing the heavily pregnant female of any animal species. Besides that, the flesh of a gravid fish is, like that of the kelt, not worth the eating. Far better to take a little pride and satisfaction in returning coloured salmon with the knowledge that you have done something to ensure more salmon for the future.

Take some care when returning live salmon to the water. Cause the minimum of injury when removing the hook and waste no time in getting the fish back into the water. In fact, far better not to remove the salmon from the water at all, but carry out the operation in shallow water with one hand grasping the wrist of its tail. Lay your rod down and get to work. With the hook free, do not let the fish go, but hold it with its head facing into the current and hold on to the fish until it regains strength and swims away to freedom. (Fig. 3, p. 205)

Now let us put all that to one side and assume that we have caught a real beauty of a fresh-run fish. We do not know whether fish suffer on being taken out of water but lest they do the fish should be struck firmly on the back on the head as soon as possible. And this is where you may find that sticks and stones of suitable proportions are like policemen, never there when wanted. This is why you should carry a priest, so named because it administers the

A Crawford Little fishing downstream and across on the River Nith, a prolific and rewarding salmon river. Following conservation measures the Nith is recovering much of its former glories.

B Fishing for salmon on the Cumbrian Eden. *C* A fine cockfish taken from the Dee while spinning. *D* Action and vibration are vital in a lure, then come colour combinations and flash patterns to trigger attack response. New generation Kilty lures designed by Finbarr McSweeney fulfil the criteria *l to r*: the 'Sonic' has a slow wobbling action; 'J3' takes almost any predator; '15' a lure for distance casting, and the Flying 'C', an upstream casting lure for salmon.

C

The 'Sonic'

J3

K15

Flying 'C'

B   *D*

last rites. Your priest can be an old chair-leg, my priest is a length of brass rod inside an alkathene pipe and about 25 cm (10 in) long. I do not buy those expensive ones from tackle shops because I lose them.

Weigh and photograph your salmon, then gut it and throw the entrails back into the river. This is not an ancient, bloodthirsty ritual, it aids the flesh to remain as fresh as possible. If you want a nice, whole fish to lay out on a silver platter back at the hotel, at least remove the gills, which are the first part of a fish to deteriorate. Place the fish in a cool spot. If you are fishing a private beat there may be a stone or a marble slab in the fishing hut. And use some common sense, do not place the fish in the closed boot of your car on a hot summer's day.

SPINNING FOR SALMON – WHEN TO SPIN

Once experienced anglers realise that there is more to fishing than catching fish, many find little enjoyment or satisfaction in any method other than fly. But at times spinning becomes a logical alternative.

First, safety. Handling a large, heavy tube fly on a fast-sinking line is a challenge. In a gale it can become dangerous unless the fisherman has mastered the technique of roll and Spey casting.

Secondly, depth of water. The fly is ideally suited to searching out water down to a depth of about 1.8 m (6 ft), or slightly more, but salmon can be found in deeper water. Here, one must fish really deep to be in with a chance on

some stretches. The spinner achieves this most effectively.

Thirdly, casting range. On a big river, a hefty proportion of the salmon in a pool may be lying beyond the range of a normal fly cast, or even a long one. A spinning rod will double that range.

Fourthly, overgrown bushes and trees, with fishing reduced to a few casts here and there. In cold water a large lure can be used and in summer a tiny spinner can be usefully employed. To attempt to use a fly rod in such circumstances could become time-wasting and frustrating.

Finally, the spinner may be used only where and when it is allowed. Entire rivers or stretches of them are subject to a fly-only rule. On others, the spinner is allowable only when the water is above a certain height.

SPINNING RODS, REELS AND LINES

Glass and carbon-fibres have produced long but light spinning rods. A sensitive 2.4 m (8 ft) model may be right for flicking out a tiny summer lure, and one of 2.7 m (9 ft) will suffice on a medium-sized river. My longest and most powerful rod is 3.6 m (12 ft) of carbon-fibre. It will hurl a lure out, control the spinner with ease and play a big salmon to the shore with the maximum efficiency.

The choice of reel comes down to a fixed-spool or a multiplier, the former the easiest to master and generally cheaper. However, once the multiplier has been mastered it will be recognised as an excellent casting, fishing and salmon-fighting reel. Fixed-spools are at their best when fishing fairly light lines, while the multiplier proves its worth with heavier lines.

So, the fisherman equipped with a 2.4 m (8 ft) rod, medium-sized fixed-spool reel and 4–4.5 kg (9–10 lb) b.s. line, plus 3 or 3.33 m (10 or 11 ft) rod fitted with a multiplier and 6.8–8 kg (15–18 lb) b.s. nylon, may consider himself ready for any British salmon, and perhaps for some of the considerably larger fish to be found in Norway or Alaska.

SPINNING RIGS

As in most fresh and saltwater situations, the best advice on rigs is 'Keep it simple'. Attach a swivel to the end of the line, then tie about 0.6 m (2 ft) of nylon to the opposite eye of the swivel to make a leader. Ball-bearing swivels are expensive but extremely efficient and avoid line twist.

Two lures have emerged as the outstanding salmon catchers: the Devon Minnow and the Toby spoon. My preference is to fish the Toby in streamier, fairly fast water and reserve the Devon for gentler flows. Devons are available in basic types separated by weight. Wooden and plastic Devons are generally lightweights. Plastic models with heavy, metal inserts are heavyweights along with the metal ones. The lightweights will need some weight to be added to the trace in order to cast effectively. Now that lead substitutes are available in many forms, the best alternative is an anti-kink style weight, attached to but above the swivel.

In cold waters, stay with Devons ranging in size from 50–76 mm (2–3 in). The colour range is enormous and one should heed the advice of the local tackle shop, but thousands of salmon have fallen to brown and gold! In warm water, where and when spinning is allowed, try a small, sombre Devon or a Mepps spoon.

SPINNING

On the river, spin in the same way as you fished the fly. Cast the spinner out at about 45 degrees downstream. Do not turn the reel handle until the spinner is on the dangle. A few turns to tempt a following fish, then reel up quickly; take a pace downstream and make another cast, searching the water systematically. If the lure is scraping and catching the bottom, exchange it for a lighter one.

You will have set the slipping clutch on your reel so that a fish can take line. To recover line when a fish is being played requires a pumping action. Playing a fish has been summed up this way: 'When it pulls, let it go; when it stops, then you pull!' This may sound fairly basic, but, how it works!

There is perhaps some temptation to hurl a spinner out as far as possible but being able to cast a Devon Minnow a huge distance does not automatically confer on the angler the badge of the expert. Distance and catching salmon are not the same thing, for spinning demands the same understanding of the fish as that required by the angler who prefers the artificial fly.

In some circles, spinning for salmon was considered not the done thing, not respectable. There are anglers who still feel this way, but in all fishing there is but one simple objective, that of inducing a fish to take a bait, fly or lure fished on the end of the line. To this end, spinning is but one of the choices open to the person on the bank.

Spinning in the autumn in Scotland. The River Nith has a late closing date, because of its autumn-running fish. There is hardly any spring run.

Knots for the Fisherman

Many knots are used in fishing, but these are the basic ones which will preserve the breaking strain of nylon and Terylene materials. All these knots are simple and have proved to be effective.

BLOOD LOOP
Used to form a snood or dropper for hook attachment. The loop may be any length and is cut close to the hook to make the hook link.

Always lubricate nylon well before pulling tight

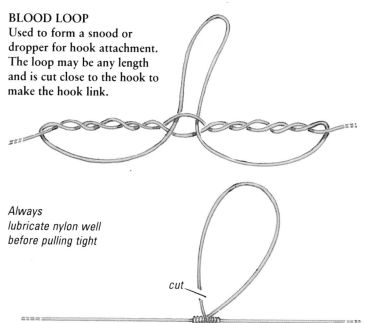

cut

TUCKED HALF-BLOOD KNOT
For attaching booms, hooks, lures or swivels to nylon monofilament line.

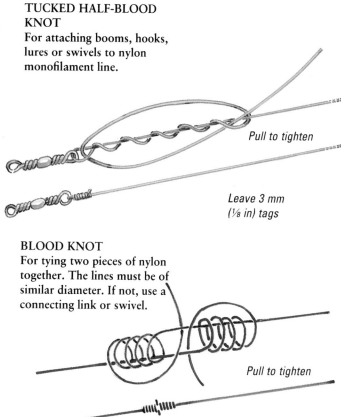

Pull to tighten

Leave 3 mm (⅛ in) tags

BLOOD KNOT
For tying two pieces of nylon together. The lines must be of similar diameter. If not, use a connecting link or swivel.

Pull to tighten

Glossary of Fishing Terms

ABSTRACTION Every riparian owner of a watercourse has the right to abstract from it water for his own domestic use including watering livestock. Water can be abstracted for other purposes *providing it does not injure the rights of other riparian owners.* It is alleged that severe abuses of certain rights has led to the deterioration of many rivers.

ADIPOSE FIN A fleshy appendage between dorsal and caudal fin on members of the salmon family.

AFTM Association of Fishing Tackle Makers.

ALASTICUM Single-strand, stiffish wire used to form short traces. Withstands the cutting action of sharp teeth and resists rust.

ANGLERS' COOPERATIVE ASSOCIATION By far the most active body representing anglers and their fight against pollution. Founded in 1947, the ACA has a long history of success against public bodies responsible for allowing a deterioration of water quality.

ANTENNA A float that has most of the body supporting weight and bait below the surface of the water. The fine tip is relatively unaffected by strong breezes.

ANTI-INERTIA A stiffening-up of the bale arm release mechanism to prevent the bale closing in mid-cast.

ANTI-KINK A lead or plastic vane used in spinning. It is designed with a keel to prevent line twist while retrieving and sometimes adds weight.

BACKING Braided or monofilament line attached to a fly line to extend the amount of line that a strong fish can pull off the reel spool.

BAG The number of fish forming an angler's catch.

BALE ARM A hinged metal arm that picks up the reel line on the retrieve and distributes it round the spool of a fixed-spool reel (which see).

BARBULE A fleshy appendage found on the head or round the jaws of fishes, often in pairs or fours, and used as sensory organs.

BEAT A length of water and bankside allocated to one or more game anglers.

BELLY A curve in a fly or other fishing line caused by a current moving the line downstream faster than the fly or bait, resulting in drag.

BITE Indication from a fish, either visual or tactile, that a bait or lure has or is being taken by a fish.

BLADDERWRACK A brown seaweed, *Fucus vesiculosus*, with wavy-edge fronds and a number of swollen air-bladders along the central rib of each frond or branch.

BLANCHED MAGGOTS Maggots which have been put into heated water. This stretches them so that they cannot wriggle down into the mud and silt and makes them ideal for loose feed.

BLANK A hollow-glass, carbon or kevlar fibre tube from which a finished angling rod can be made.

BLOODWORMS Not true worms but the larvae of midges found in the mud and detritus of small ponds.

BLOW A fly 'blows' a suitable food-source for its maggots when it deposits its eggs there.

BLOW-LINE A light fly line by which a natural or artificial fly is dapped (see DAPPING) on the water's surface to catch feeding fish. The technique relies on a breeze to carry line and lure out.

BOB FLY In a team of artificial flies, that nearest the fly line. The bob fly is intended to 'bob' or dance attractively on the surface.

BOMB An aerodynamically shaped casting weight.

BOOM A metal, plastic or nylon accessory designed to make hook droppers stand away from the reel line. Also a device intended to slide freely on a line.

BRAIDED LINE Man-made line that instead of being used as a monofilament is braided into a multi-strand line. It retains its suppleness but the breaking strain is multiplied by the number of given-strength strands.

BREAD FLAKE Bread bait pinched out from the soft inside texture of a new loaf.

BREAD PUNCH A cutting tube used to form small pellets of bread of equal shape and size.

BREAKING STRAIN (BS) The pull in kilos or pounds at which a fishing line will break in the dry state.

BUNG A thick-bodied, onion-shaped float, usually used for pike fishing or to support a heavy bait.

BUTT INDICATOR A form of bite indicator located near the butt section of a fishing rod. Used in ledgering (which see).

BUZZER Angler's name for any *Chironomid* fly, midge and gnat that hovers close to the surface of the water.

CARBON-FIBRE Introduced from the US and originally used in the manufacture of light spinning rods, carbon-fibre is now used for all kinds of equipment including rodblanks and reel casings.

CASTER The chrysalis stage of the maggot, and a useful hookbait and addition to groundbaits.

CASTING The act of propelling the hooked bait or fly out to where the fish are assumed to be. Propulsion is gained from the power inherent in the flexibility of the rod.

CENTRE-PIN REEL A revolving-drum reel having a fixed spindle with a 1:1 gear ratio. The handle is fixed to the side of the drum.

CHARTER-BOAT A boat, usually skippered by a professional, which can be hired by individuals or clubs for a period of fishing. Strict safety and insurance conditions are laid down for this work.

CHECKING THE FLOAT Halting the passage of a float down-stream to ensure that the baited hook-link precedes the float.

CHUM Small pieces of chopped fish fed into the water to attract predatory species.

CLOUD-BAIT Particles of fine groundbait intended to slowly sink down through the water, producing a cloud of edible, attractive, but not filling items to bring fish into the swim.

CLUTCH A mechanism whereby the reel drum can be put in or taken out of gear to revolve freely. Also a slipping system of washers which allows powerful fish to pull line off the reel before the breaking strain of the line is reached.

COCKTAIL A mixture of two or more different baits on the same hook.

CONSERVATION The consideration shown by all sections of the sport for the well-being and preservation of fish stocks, the maintenance and proper upkeep of fisheries and the future of the sport.

CONTROLLER A form of float used to provide sufficient weight to cast an ultra-light bait without resort to additional weights.

CRIMPING, CRIMP A method of securing accessories to wire lines by using a special tool to squeeze metal ferrules round the wire line.

CUDDY A collapsible hood or shelter in the forward section of a small boat; sometimes also called a dodger.

DAN BUOY A floating marker, usually a buoy topped by a flag, placed at the end of a long-line or drifting net.

DAPPING The art of presenting a natural or artificial lure by skilfully presenting the bait through bankside obstacles. Also using a BLOW-LINE (which see) to float a natural or artificial fly out on the breeze.

DEAD BAITING Using a dead fish as bait for a scavenging or predatory species.

DEVON A wooden or metal spinning lure that revolves round a wire mount carrying a treble hook. Plastic vanes are fitted to impart spin.

DINGHY A small boat of wood or glass-fibre, used for inshore or enclosed-

OVERHAND KNOT
Forms a loop in a hook snood, dropper or fly cast.

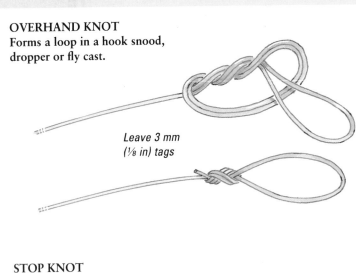

Leave 3 mm
(⅛ in) tags

WHIPPING KNOT
For tying spade-and or eyed hooks to nylon links or droppers.

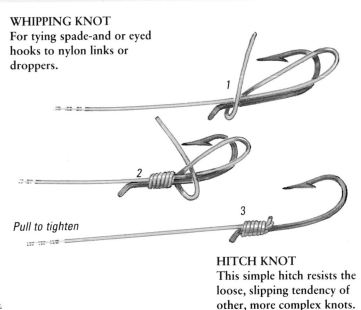

Pull to tighten

STOP KNOT
Allows a carerful correction of float-fishing depth as it slides freely along reel line.

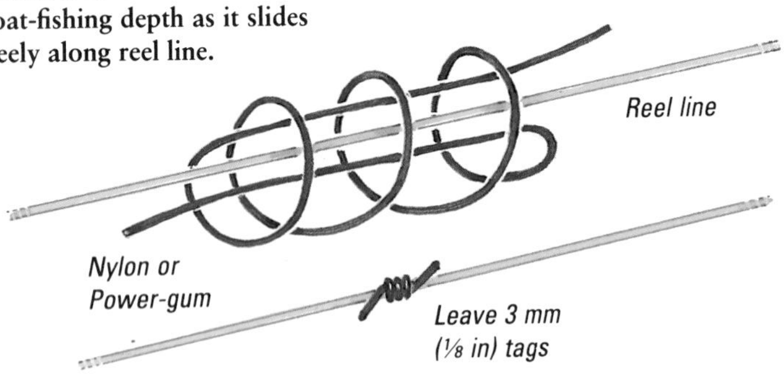

Reel line

Nylon or Power-gum

Leave 3 mm
(⅛ in) tags

HITCH KNOT
This simple hitch resists the loose, slipping tendency of other, more complex knots.

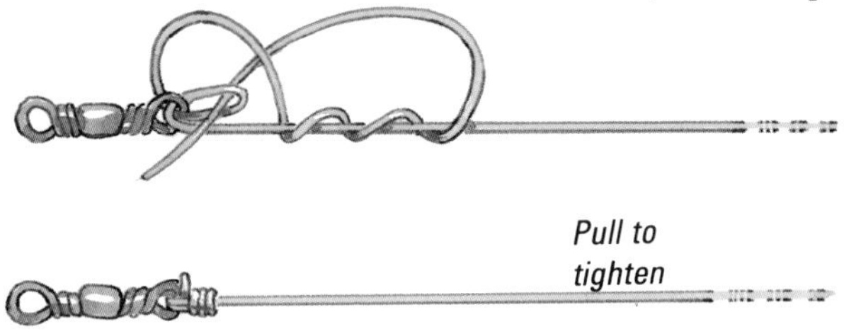

Pull to tighten

---

water fishing.

DODGER See CUDDY.

DORSAL Strictly 'top-side', but used to identify fins sited on the top of a fish's body.

DOUBLE TAPER A fly line which has a swollen middle section, tapering at each end.

DOUGH BOBBIN A simple method of bite detection made by squeezing a piece of bread-paste on to the line. Its weight registers the pull of a biting fish.

DRAG Unnatural movement of a fishing line caused by the line and lure travelling at different speeds. Also the slipping clutch found on most multipliers and fixed-spool reels.

DRAINS Man-made canal-like waterways which drain huge areas of agricultural land, mostly in the Fens and East Anglia.

DRESSINGS Combinations of different materials – fur, feather, silk, tinsel and so on – that are used in fly-tying.

DROPPER A hook-link of nylon or wire attached to the reel line. Also the nearest artificial to the rod of a string of wet flies.

DRUM On a fishing reel, usually a fixed-spool (which see), the spool round which line is wound.

DRY FLY An artificial fly so tied that it floats on the surface of the water.

DT4F This describes a Double Taper Size 4 Floating line.

DUN The emergent fly after it leaves its nymphal case.

ECHO-SOUNDER An electronic device that transmits a signal to the seabed from where it rebounds and is picked up as a returned, delayed, signal. The time interval taken for the return of the signal is an indication of the depth below the boat.

ELASTICATED THREAD Used by dressmakers to gather pleats and so on, but in fishing it is perfect for tying a soft bait to a hook so that it can be presented correctly.

FALSE CASTING In fly-fishing, a method of casting a fishing line back and forth several times to remove water from the artificial and line so that they float.

FATHOM A nautical term for 1.8 m (6 ft), and as such is used to indicate depths on sea charts.

FIXED-SPOOL REEL A fishing reel on which a rotating bale arm (which see) wraps the line round a spool set at right-angles to the axis of the rod. The spool itself does not turn to recover line, although it can be allowed to revolve to provide a slipping-drag facility.

FLASHERS Spoon blades or metal strips used to attract predatory fish species by their movement and flash in the water. Usually used in conjunction with natural baits.

FLATFISH True flatfish begin life as normal, upright fish, but soon after birth one eye migrates over the head to join the other and the fish spends the rest of its life on one side. Plaice, turbot, flounders and so on are flatfish. Skates and rays are round fishes.

FLOATANTS Once grease but now usually silicone-based aerosol sprays applied to fly-lines and artificial flies to ensure that they float on the surface of the water.

FLOAT FISHING A fishing style which employs a float of buoyant material to suspend bait and weight at the required depth. The float also registers the bite of a taking fish.

FLY A loose term describing most lures presented on a fly line and rod. These artificials may simulate flies, fish or invertebrates.

FLYING GAFF A sea-angling gaff used for very large, powerful fish. When the gaff is pulled home the handle comes away, leaving the gaff on a stout chain and length of high b.s. rope which can be attached to the boat.

FLY LINE A line which has weight so that it sinks, or has buoyant materials coated on the line so that it floats.

FLY SPOON A tiny metal lure that can be cast using a fly rod and fly line.

FODDER-FISH Species of small shoaling fish which form much of the food of the predatory species.

FORWARD TAPER A fly line that tapers in one direction only, toward the fly.

FREELINING A fishing style that dispenses

with any form of float or weight to carry the bait out to the fish.

FRY Very young, immature fish of most species.

GAFF A metal hook fixed to a shaft and used to impale a fish and lift it from the water. A barbarous fishing accessory that is rapidly going out of use in these conservation-minded times.

GEAR RATIO This is the difference between one turn of the reel handle and the number of turns produced on the reel spool or drum. It is given in figures such as 1:35.

GORGE FISHING Once common but now illegal, gorge fishing uses a method of allowing a fish to take the baited hook down into its stomach, ensuring the fish's death.

GOZZER A maggot produced by a fly *Calliphora eryphrocephala* and a favourite for home-breeding. The fly blows (see BLOW) in the dark, producing a large, white, succulent grub ideal as a warm-weather bait.

GRAPNEL An instrument resembling a huge treble hook, used to anchor a boat over rocky ground. Unlike a true anchor the prongs are designed to straighten-out under pull.

GRILSE A small salmon, generally thought to have spent only a single year feeding at sea.

GRIP LEAD A sea-angling lead with grip wires or protrusions that tend to hold in sand, mud and shingle during strong tidal conditions.

GROUND BAITING Feeding a predetermined area of water with cereal or hookbait to attract and hold fish near to the angler's baited hook.

HACKLE POINTS Two stiff hackles from a cockerel cape, used to represent wings.

HATCH The time when the nymphal form of some water-living fly rises to the surface and hatches to emerge as a fully-winged insect. At such times it produces a frantic feeding frenzy among the trout.

HOLT The place where a pike lies up after feeding. A resting place.

HOOK LENGTH The length of nylon to

which hooks are whipped. The hooks are whipped commercially to various lengths which are looped for quick attachment to the reel line.

HOT SPOT One kind of hot-spot is that place where two or more fish-patrol paths cross. Here, at regular times, fish are present and the thinking angler will watch and note these times for future reference.

IGFA International Game Fish Association, based at Fort Lauderdale, Florida, US. The IGFA publishes lists of world record fish, at least those notified to it.

JARDINE TACKLE See SNAP-TACKLE.

KELP A loose term to describe a number of strong, lengthy thong-like seaweeds that have holdfasts (root systems) permanently covered by water.

KELT A salmon in its weakened state after spawning. Many kelts die in their attempt to return to the sea. It is illegal to take fish in this condition.

KNOTLESS TAPERED LEADERS A one-piece nylon cast in which there is a continuous taper from butt to point.

KYPE At spawning time the males of salmonids develop a hooked protuberance of the lower jaw, large enough for it at times to prevent closure of the jaws.

LARVA A grub that has hatched from the eggs of an insect and which is mobile. This is the stage before the pupa, or chrysalis.

LASH, OR LASK A thick slice of flesh cut from the flank of a dead baitfish, usually from head to tail in the shape of a fish.

LATERAL LINE The line of connected cells running along the flanks of fish which sense vibration, water-borne sounds and pressure changes. It is part of the fish's nervous system.

LAYBACK STYLE A method of shore casting devised by the late Leslie Moncrieff.

LAYING ON A float-fishing technique where the bait is fished hard on the bottom. Some weight is also lying on the bottom, with the float virtually tight-lined.

LEADER A length of nylon line preceding

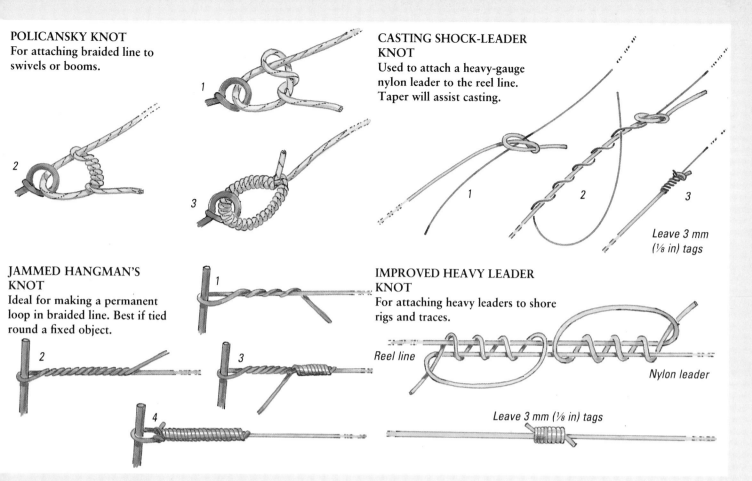

POLICANSKY KNOT
For attaching braided line to swivels or booms.

CASTING SHOCK-LEADER KNOT
Used to attach a heavy-gauge nylon leader to the reel line. Taper will assist casting.

Leave 3 mm (⅛ in) tags

JAMMED HANGMAN'S KNOT
Ideal for making a permanent loop in braided line. Best if tied round a fixed object.

IMPROVED HEAVY LEADER KNOT
For attaching heavy leaders to shore rigs and traces.

Reel line

Nylon leader

Leave 3 mm (⅛ in) tags

the main line. It can be of lesser or greater breaking strain.

LEADER KNOT A knot for joining a shore-fisher's reel line to the shock leader that will pass easily through the rod rings.

LEADS Various forms of weight used to assist casting or to sink baits and floats. (See LEAD SHOT REGULATION)

LEAD SHOT REGULATION From 1 January 1987 the import, sale and use in angling of lead shot between No. 8 shot (0.06 g) and 28.35 g (1 oz) was banned by HM Government. The legislation was to reduce the alleged deaths of mute swans through ingestion of anglers' lead shot. Lead used in swim-feeders (which see), self-cocking floats, lead-core lines and weighted lines was not affected.

LEAD SUBSTITUTES Substances devised by the manufacturing industry which act as substitutes for the lead shot which is now illegal between certain size parameters (see LEAD SHOT REGULATION).

LEDGERING (LEGERING) Fishing with the bait held on the bottom by a weight and usually without a float. Ledgering with a float is called float ledgering.

LIE A known resting place of fish.

LINE-BITE A false indication of a bite brought about by the body of a fish striking or rubbing against the line or some part of the terminal tackle.

LINK An accessory used to join various items of tackle together or to lines.

LINK SWIVEL A useful swivel for quick attachment of traces and casts.

LOADED (WEIGHTED) FLOAT A float carrying an in-built weight to assist casting. It also overcomes some of the float's natural buoyancy.

LOCK SHOT Split-shot placed either side of the float to fix its position relative to the depth of fishing. See also LEAD SHOT REGULATION.

LUGWORM A soft-bodied sea worm found in sand and mud. It is a standard bait for sea anglers.

LURE Any artificial bait, spinner, plug, pirk or fly.

MAGGOT The larval form of the fly of any Diptera species.

MAGGOT-DROPPER A case that is filled with maggots, dropped into the swim and capable of being opened by the angler to release the offering accurately into position to entice fish near the hook-bait.

MARK An area or plotted navigational position marked on a skipper's chart which is known to hold fish.

MENDING THE LINE A means of avoiding drag and sinking an artificial fly down in the water. It is accomplished by throwing a loop of line upstream.

MULTIPLYING REEL (MULTIPLIER) A drum reel that is geared to rotate for more times than the handle is turned.

NYMPH A larva of the *Ephemeridae* group of flies or an angler's artificial representation of the same.

OPERCULAR BONES The group of several bones that form the gill-case or cover which protect the delicate gill filaments of fish.

OVER-RUN A bunch of intertwined nylon on the drum of a multiplying or centre-pin reel caused by inefficient casting and/or poor line control.

PASTE Hookbait made by soaking bread, squeezing out the water and kneading it into a stiff dough.

PATERNOSTER A form of terminal tackle having the weight at the bottom and fished with a tight line to the rod. Booms are used to suspend hook links and baits.

PATTERN A fixed, often traditional design of materials and positioning of parts that form an artificial fly.

PECTORALS Paired fins behind the gill-case (see OPERCULAR BONES).

PEELER OR SOFTIE (CRAB) Stages in the growth of crabs, which when mature shed their shells in an annual moult. Anglers use them in the softie stage before the new shell has hardened, and in the peeler form when the shell can easily be removed from the body.

PEG A numbered position drawn by a match-fisherman which allots him a limited stretch of bank of a contest venue.

PELAGIC Life that inhabits the surface and upper layers of water.

PELVICS Paired fins situated low down on the fish's body, usually behind the pectoral fins (which see) and sometimes called the ventrals.

PENNELL TACKLE A two-hook rig with the hooks placed in tandem.

PICK-UP The bale arm (which see) of a fixed-spool reel.

PINKIE The maggot, or grub, of the greenbottle fly, of the Dipteran flies.

PIRK An artificial, metal bait having sufficient weight so that it acts as a sinker and a fish lure.

PITCH A place from which an angler fishes, in front of which is the swim (which see).

PLANKTON (ZOO- AND PHYTO-) Minute animal and vegetable life, free-floating and moving, found in salt and freshwater.

PLUGS Artificial lures, usually of wood or plastic, intended to simulate the movements of fish and other aquatic creatures.

PLUMB-BOB, PLUMBING By use of a weighted plumb-bob the depth of water anywhere in front of the angler can be assessed. The weight is attached to the hook and lowered down, the float's position on the line can then be adjusted so that the bait is suspended at the required depth.

POINT The finely tapered end section of a fly cast, or the fly at the tip of the team. Also sharp end of the hook.

POLLUTION The greatest threat to angling and must be fought at all levels.

PRICKED When the point of the hook is pulled lightly into a fish so that the contact is felt but momentarily, the fish avoiding being properly hooked. The fish has been 'pricked'.

PUT-AND-TAKE WATER A fishery where trout are placed into the water for anglers to catch, the fish having been reared to a certain size elsewhere.

QUILL MINNOW An old-timer's light artificial bait for use when spinning for trout in fast, streamy water.

QUIVERTIP A sensitive rod-tip bite indicator that visibly trembles when a fish takes the baited hook.

RATCHET A checking device that prevents line running too freely off the reel and gives an audible warning of a pull on the bait.

RAYS A group of cartilagenous fishes comprising the skates and rays. Not true flatfishes they are flattened when seen from above and have the pectoral fins elongated into 'wings'.

REDGILL Probably the most well-known, attractive and also efficient fish lure of its kind. It is made from soft plastic to simulate and represent the movements of a swimming sandeel.

RIG A number of tackle items joined by a length of nylon. Some rigs tend to be complex, but the simple ones are usually more efficient and less prone to tangling while on their way down to the seabed.

RIM CONTROL An exposed rim on a fly-reel drum which allows an angler to control line running out to a hooked fish by applying light finger-pressure.

RINGS Circular guides, whipped or sleeved on to a rod blank that spread the stress of playing a fish along the entire length of the rod, and which also allow free passage of line on and off the reel while casting or playing a fish.

RISE The surface indication of the presence of a fish, usually indicated by a series of widening rings or the dimpling of the surface.

ROACH POLE A multi-sectioned, very long fishing rod to the end of which is fixed a short length of line and hook length. A reel is not used, and a fish retrieved and unhooked by unshipping pole-sections until the hook length is to hand.

ROD REST Usually made of metal, rod rests support fishing rods at angles suited to the style of fishing being practised, such as ledgering. For beach anglers, they will hold the rod vertical to keep the line running out above the waves breaking inshore.

ROLL CAST A method of fly-casting in

211

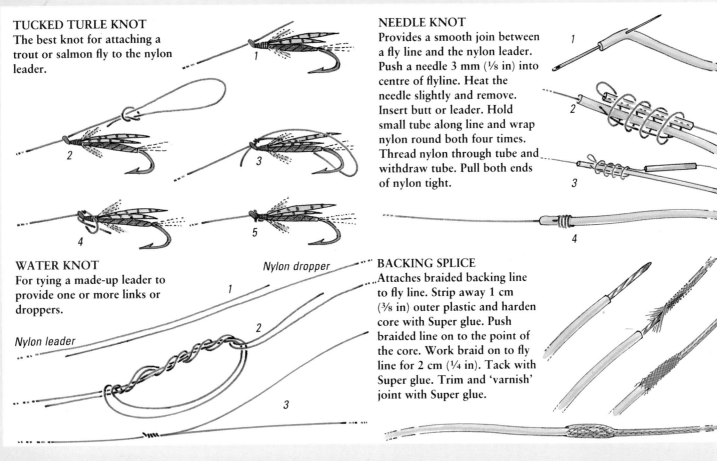

TUCKED TURLE KNOT

The best knot for attaching a trout or salmon fly to the nylon leader.

NEEDLE KNOT

Provides a smooth join between a fly line and the nylon leader. Push a needle 3 mm (⅛ in) into centre of flyline. Heat the needle slightly and remove. Insert butt or leader. Hold small tube along line and wrap nylon round both four times. Thread nylon through tube and withdraw tube. Pull both ends of nylon tight.

WATER KNOT

For tying a made-up leader to provide one or more links or droppers.

Nylon dropper

Nylon leader

BACKING SPLICE

Attaches braided backing line to fly line. Strip away 1 cm (⅜ in) outer plastic and harden core with Super glue. Push braided line on to the point of the core. Work braid on to fly line for 2 cm (¼ in). Tack with Super glue. Trim and 'varnish' joint with Super glue.

---

places where there is no room for a back-cast.

RUBBY DUBBY An unpleasant mixture of fish offal and oil, mixed sometimes with bran, that is mashed up and shovelled into sacks to be hung over the gunwale. There they are pounded against the side so that the contents ooze steadily out to form a predator-attracting slick which runs down-tide, drawing fish, usually sharks, to the baited hook suspended in the stream.

SANDBAR A barrier of sand and silt swept down an estuary by the ebbing tide and deposited where the current loses its power as it is met by the incoming tide. A sand-bar forms a hazard to deep-keeled boats but is often a good place to find fish.

SANDFAST A lead weight, shaped like an upside-down pyramid, that pulls into sand and soft ground, holding a bait there securely.

SEA WRACK A general term for the brown and red seaweeds. It is often applied to all weed thrown up on to the shore during a storm.

SEDGES Waterside plants; insects belonging to the Order Trichoptera.

SHOCK LEADER Nylon that is stronger than the reel line, and is intended to absorb the shock of casting.

SHOT LOAD The amount of weight that a float will carry before sinking below the surface.

SINKING LINE A fly line with built-in weight that sinks below the surface.

SKIMMER (BREAM) Small freshwater fish which when hooked come skimming back across the surface on their flat-sided bodies.

SLIDER FLOAT A float that allows an angler to fish at a greater depth than the length of the rod. The float is held by a stop knot (which see) that can be any distance from the hook, yet will pass easily through the rod rings when line is being retrieved.

SMUTTING Surface-feeding trout that are taking minute flies, midges and other small insects.

SNAP-TACKLE Two treble hooks joined by

a wire trace on which a live or dead fish is mounted when fishing for pike.

SNOOD A short piece of nylon attached to a hook and then looped so that it can be joined to split links or link swivels to form a rig.

SPECIMEN A good-sized fish when compared with the average size of the species found in the water.

SPIGOT A modern method of joining two sections of hollow-glass rods, replacing the ferrules of the cane and split-cane rods.

SPINNERS A general term for metal artificial lures although the description should apply only to those that spin round the axis of the lure rather than wobble through the water.

SPIRAL A form of lead or weight with a spiral of grooves round which the line is wrapped. The positioning of the weight along the trace can then be adjusted.

SPLIT CANE Top quality rods were once produced by glueing together usually six lengths of best bamboo to form a hexagon. Strength and the traditional 'sweet' action were the hallmark of these fine rods.

SPOONS Metal fishing lures that wobble or move erratically but do not spin (see SPINNERS).

SQUATT The maggot or grub of the common housefly (*Diptera*).

STOP BEAD A bead placed between a slider float (which see) and stop knot (which see), or between a running boom and swivel (which see) to prevent jamming of the knots.

STOP KNOT A knot used to stop or fix the depth of a slider float (which see).

STRAND An Irish term for a beach.

STREAMER FLIES Large artificial flies tied generally to represent small fish.

STRET PEGGING Float-fishing down-stream in stages. The bait is allowed to settle and fish for a short period. If bites do not come the float is lifted and the bait allowed to move farther down-river in a series of static fishing movements until the float is too far away for a strike to be made.

STRIKE The sharp movement of the rod-tip

that sets the hook firmly in the fish's jaw.

STRIPPING LINE A term that describes two operations: (1) pulling a fly line off the reel by hand, and (2) playing in a fish by pulling line back through the rod-rings by hand rather than retrieving it by reeling in.

SWG Standard wire gauge.

SWIM An area in a coarse-fishing situation known to hold fish.

SWIM-BLADDER Found in most bony fishes. More correctly the gas-bladder, it is filled with air to allow the fish to adjust its buoyancy at different depths to compensate for varying pressures.

SWIM-FEEDER A container attached to the terminal tackle from which maggots or other forms of feed can trickle in close proximity to the hookbait.

SWINGTIP A swinging, hanging arm, through which the line runs, that is lifted by the pull of a biting fish. It is screwed into the rod-tip.

SWIVEL A metal device for joining lines and preventing line twist from being transmitted back along the line by the actions of a spinning lure.

TACKLE An embracing term that describes all of an angler's fishing gear; also just the hook end of the terminal tackle.

TAKES Bites from fish, either successful or missed. Usually applied to game fishing.

TAKING SHORT A bite from a fish where the bait or lure is only nipped at the extreme end, missing the hook.

TAPER The amount of decrease in diameter of a rod from butt to tip.

TARES A species of pea used to feed pigeons, but also used as a hook- and groundbait by coarse anglers.

TEAM OF FLIES Three wet flies fished on a game-fisherman's cast.

TEASER A bait presented to predatory fish in a lifelike way to induce them to strike at a hookbait.

TERMINAL TACKLE The trace, rig or combination of parts that form the business end of the angler's gear. The hook, swivels, and so on nearest the hook.

TEST CURVE The amount of pull on a line

that will put a curve into a rod so that the tip and butt section are at right-angles. Often used as a way of expressing the line strength (in kilos or pounds) that a rod can accommodate.

TILLEY LAMP A paraffin-pressure lamp that emits a strong light. Used by anglers when night fishing, mostly those beach fishing.

TINSEL Thin-strand metal foil wound round the body of an artificial fly to give flash or to break up its outline.

TRACE A length of nylon or wire used to form any rig or terminal tackle.

TRAIL The hook length between the ledger weight and hook-bait.

TREBLE HOOK Three hooks joined together on to a common eye, mostly used on spinning lures, tube flies and pirks.

TROLLED BAIT A bait, or lure, that is towed behind a boat at a speed slow enough to attract predatory fish.

TROTTED A lure or bait that is allowed to run downstream at the speed of the current.

TUBE FLIES Salmon and trout flies where the dressing is applied to a tube made of plastic, aluminium or brass, depending on the weight of lure needed. The line or cast runs through the tube to a treble hook.

WARP A cable-laid steel rope often used to anchor a large boat.

WET FLY An artificial fly intended to fish below the surface in the manner of a small fish. The hackles are tied to sweep backwards.

WINGS The slip of joined fibres, taken from the wing feather of various birds to form the wing of an artificial fly; also the 'wings' of skates and rays.

WORM CASTS The spirals of sand forced up out of the wet beach by the passage of a marine worm through that medium and of the sand itself through the worm, which feeds on microorganisms living there.

WRIST The section of a fish's body just before the tail (or caudal) fin.

ZOOMER An antenna-type float with an in-built weight to give long and accurate casting.

Index

Italic = illustration
IFC, IBC = inside front cover, inside back cover

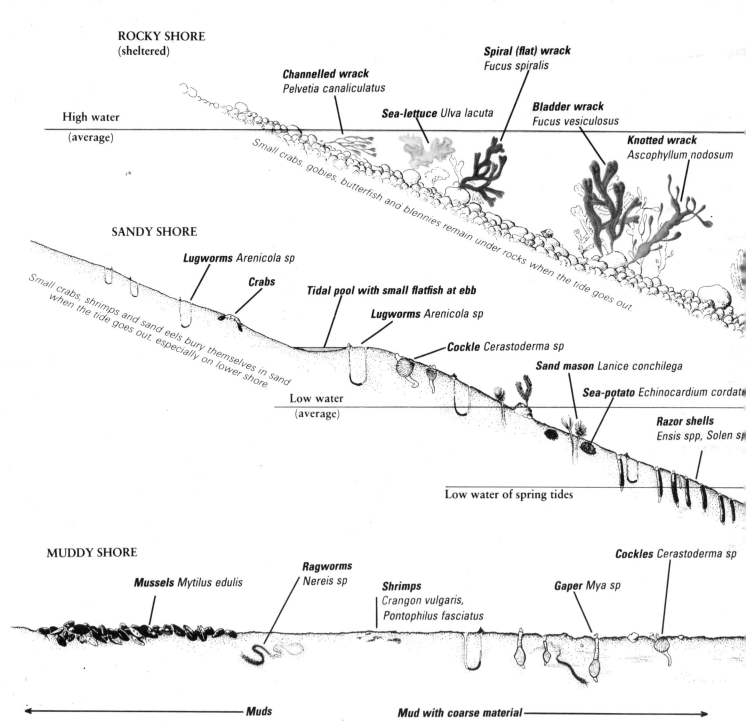

ROCKY SHORE
(sheltered)

Channelled wrack
Pelvetia canaliculatus

Spiral (flat) wrack
Fucus spiralis

Sea-lettuce Ulva lacuta

Bladder wrack
Fucus vesiculosus

Knotted wrack
Ascophyllum nodosum

High water
(average)

Small crabs, gobies, butterfish and blennies remain under rocks when the tide goes out.

SANDY SHORE

Lugworms Arenicola sp

Crabs

Tidal pool with small flatfish at ebb

Lugworms Arenicola sp

Cockle Cerastoderma sp

Sand mason Lanice conchilega

Sea-potato Echinocardium cordat..

Small crabs, shrimps and sand eels bury themselves in sand when the tide goes out, especially on lower shore.

Low water
(average)

Razor shells
Ensis spp, Solen sp..

Low water of spring tides

MUDDY SHORE

Cockles Cerastoderma sp

Mussels Mytilus edulis

Ragworms
Nereis sp

Shrimps
Crangon vulgaris,
Pontophilus fasciatus

Gaper Mya sp

◄───────── **Muds** ─────────► ◄──── **Mud with coarse material** ────►

The British coastline can be broadly divided into four main types. There are the exposed rocky shores, steep shingle and sandy shores and, finally, muddy, gently shelving shorelines. Here again the plant growth and aquatic life along the shore and rocks varies from zone to zone. This shoreline chart will assist the reader to identify the kind of life to be expected round the various shorelines and at different water depths.

To use this chart, select the shoreline which you are about to explore. For the exposed and rocky areas and for the typical sandy shore, high and low-water readings, the low waterline of spring tides and open water conditions off the coast are given. .

For example, one can see from the chart which species of water life are left behind on the rocky shore by the retreating tide. One can also see the pools left on the shore at low water. Here, special species of flora and fauna flourish because of the perpetually sheltered conditions. Muddy shorelines are dealt with separately because the flora and fauna are little affected by tidal action.